NARRATIVE F

NEW DIRECTIONS

ESSAYS IN APPRECIATION OF W. EDSON RICHMOND

NARRATIVE FOLKSONG

NEW DIRECTIONS

ESSAYS IN APPRECIATION OF W. EDSON RICHMOND

EDITED BY CAROL L. EDWARDS AND KATHLEEN E. B. MANLEY
WITH A FOREWORD BY BRUCE A. ROSENBERG

Printed by Westview Press
Boulder, Colorado, 1985

LIBRARY OF CONGRESS CATALOGING-IN-PUBLICATION DATA
Main entry under title:
Narrative folksong, new directions.
   1. Ballads—History and criticism—Addresses,
essays, lectures. 2. Richmond, W. Edson (Winthrop
Edson), 1916-   —Addresses, essays, lectures.
I. Edwards, Carol L.   II. Manley, Kathleen E. B.
ML3545.N18 1985   784.4'9   85-20258
ISBN 0-961-5687-0-4

ACKNOWLEDGMENTS

We would like to acknowledge permission to reprint materials from the following institutions: Bókaútgáfa Menningarsjóðs, Reykjavík, Iceland; the British Library, London, England; The Houghton Library, Harvard University; Odense University Press, Odense, Denmark; Rosenkilde and Bagger, Copenhagen, Denmark; Stofnun Árna Magnússonar, Reykjavík, Iceland.

CONTENTS

Foreword

Nashua is an austere red brick city in the solitudes of Southern New Hampshire, no longer the thriving mill town of its nineteenth-century past. Its population has dwindled, and the region is more desolate than before. Only the long and fierce winters remain constant, and the prevalent belief that good fences make good neighbors. It was here in 1916 that Winthrop Edson Richmond was born. No wonder that as an adult he would be smitten by Norway and by its sparsely-peopled vastnesses, its protracted and bone-chilling winters, its tight-lipped inhabitants. From that winter society he came, inwardly warm, painstakingly precise--yet forgiving--and helpfully critical.

When did his love affair with Scandinavia begin? Perhaps on his first visit to Oslo in 1953, on a Fulbright to the Norsk folkeminnesamling, where he would return every few years. He has been a Fulbright Professor at the Universities of Helsinki and Abo, a Ford Foundation grantee for research in Scandinavia (in 1963), Visiting Research Professor (again in Oslo) in 1976. It was a love affair for both parties: in 1977 Edson was elected to the Norwegian Academy of Sciences and Letters.

This is not an unsociable man, this former President of the Society of Fellows of the American Folklore Society, this lover of quiet, remote places. And while he does not crave the company of crowds, neither does he shun them. Edson Richmond feels comfortable in the long winter nights of Norway: "you get used to the dark, and besides, the moon throws enough light to get by." He brings novels to meetings of the American Folklore Society to keep him company after the professional meetings have gone to bed. He was also comfortable on the Board of Governors of the American Folklore Society.

He must think of the extended nights of Scandinavia as opportunities to reflect, to contemplate the ballads which have been at the center of his professional life, to organize his spirit. It is too easy to think of a consulting editor of Types of the Scandinavian Medieval Ballad sitting in a book-lined study, a small lamp fending off the dark; but that is not the image of the man his students and colleagues have; with Edson, one also thinks of the vigorous life, of skiing and of racing sloops.

ix

The influence of Edson Richmond is felt in Europe and America in several ways. As a member of Indiana University's selection committee for Fulbright grantees to Scandinavia, he continues the bonds between Old World and New that he has himself helped to forge. On the University of Chicago Folklore Prize Committee he helps establish canons of excellence in folklore scholarship. And he has assisted in setting the directions American folklore scholarship has taken with his service on the editorial boards of Hoosier Folklore, Midwest Folklore, the Journal of American Folklore, the Journal of the Folklore Institute, Indiana Names, and the Chaucer Review.

And his scholarship has left its individual mark. With a little imagination--perhaps too much--one sees Edson waiting, in silent patience, until some commonplace, vulgar error has become too popular, and then rising to smite it down. Or holding his peace while some misconception runs its course, bestirring himself to shatter widely held faiths when they have clouded our understanding too long.

"A New Look at the Wheel" is that kind of essay: Edson examines several cardinal, basic assumptions about the ballad and finds them lacking. The ballad is defined as a kind of song; Edson points out that slightly more than half of them (in the Child canon) have never been in oral circulation. Kittredge had claimed that ballads were first formed during the Middle Ages; Richmond replies, sixty years later when the ideas have become gospel, that no ballads were recorded that early, and that Middle English did not accommodate itself to stanzaic narrative folksongs. A ballad is a song, no? Not necessarily; Edson supplies evidence that many ballads existed in oral tradition without musical accompaniment. Ballads are characterized by refrains. Again, no. More than two-thirds of the English language ballad types lack refrains, and it does not seem likely, therefore, that refrains were used to bring an audience into communal participation as either dancers or singers. Oral transmission entropies the narrative component of many ballads, often reducing them to non sequiturs.

Nearly all definitions of folklore rely on the idea of oral transmission, and many on the unceasing change that process entails. In two related articles--"The Textual Transmission of Folklore" and "Some Effects of Scribal and Typographical Error on Oral Tradition" (reprinted in The Critics and the Ballad)--Edson argues that human memory is by no means the only cause of folklore variation. "A tremendous amount of variation in oral literature may be explained in terms of the attempts which tellers of tales, singers of songs, and . . . editors and collectors of

folkloristic materials have made . . . to explain what they
have heard in terms of what they know." Some informants,
additionally, have tried to memorize their lore; for them
performance is not re-creation but an attempt at
replication.

When James Jones' article arguing for the oral-
composition of the ballads first appeared, it was
immediately refuted by Albert Friedman (both essays were
published in the same issue of Journal of American
Folklore). The situation was ideal for Edson to publish his
study of "Den utrue egtemann: A Norwegian Ballad and
Formulaic Composition." A lot of Edson's professional
lifestyle is encapsulated in this essay. Perhaps most
characteristic was his stepping into a controversy about
theory as unofficial moderator, and without rancor or
acerbity declaring where the truth lay. Not unexpectedly
the data used came from the corpus of Norwegian folksong,
though it reveals a reflective intimacy with the entire
range of Scandinavian ballads as well as with the Child
collection. This essay also shows Edson's concern for
historical perspective--he is as well a medievalist--as do
his articles on "Paris og Helen i Trejeborg" and "Romantic-
Nationalism and Ballad Scholarship," significantly subtitled
"A Lesson for Today from Norway's Past."

A comforting depth and perspective permeates his work,
encompassing onomastics, dialectology, medieval and
comparative literature, and linguistics. In Edson's thought
there is no important distinction between these disciplines;
they are artificial obstacles, there is only a truth (or a
body of them) to reflect upon and then to reveal, and that
truth is not bounded by such labels as folkloric truth,
literary truth, onomastic truth. It is fitting, however, to
publish a book in the one field his most important work has
illuminated: the folk ballad. More than a score of
outstanding scholars on this subject, all friends and
admirers of Edson Richmond, have collaborated to create a
volume presenting the most recent and, international,
thought. As Edson has inspired hundreds of students at
Indiana University since his first days there in 1945, so it
is fitting that this book inform and inspire thousands more.
It is the most appreciative gift the international community
of scholars can present to a colleague who would certainly
be represented in these pages were he not their recipient;
appropriately, it also honors an admired teacher.

B.A.R.

Introduction

In addition to further advancing important developments in traditional ballad scholarship, this book sets forth the exciting and valuable new directions such scholarship has taken over the past few years. To this end, we've balanced the collection between case studies of individual ballads and critical examinations of specific theoretical issues. In attempting to be as inclusive as possible, we offer studies of traditional British, Scottish, and Irish ballads, the British ballad in America and native American ballads, as well as Finnish, Bulgarian, German, Icelandic, Scandinavian, and Spanish medieval and traditional ballads. Within those areas, articles concern the sub-genres of traditional, sentimental, blues, and broadside ballads, and such related forms as the Schwank, rímur, and romancero.

As its title indicates, one of the book's implicit new directions is redefining the ballad as "narrative folksong." D.K. Wilgus suggested this redefinition in 1973, in an article that distinguishes between types of traditional narrative songs.[1] Wilgus includes the traditional, vulgar, blues, and sentimental ballads under this more inclusive term. He also considers peripheral types such as the obituary song, the catalogue, and the panegyric. As standards for determining narrative song, Wilgus suggests the amount of action contained in such a song and the song's traditional status. The most controversial inclusion is the lyric song, which critics have always opposed to the ballad in genre studies. In recognition of that point, several pieces in this collection discuss the fine line between lyric and narrative songs. Traditional approaches to the ballad have included ballad origins, collection and classification, transmission, and variation. That most of these approaches deal either with collecting and its accompanying apparatus, or with the ballad's history, shows, as Roger deV. Renwick points out, how seldom folksong scholars have analyzed the ballad's meaning within its cultural context. As scholars began to break out of these necessary but ultimately limiting paradigms, they naturally turned to current narrative theory, applying functionalism, contextualism, structuralism, performance theory, and semiotics to narrative folk song.

Beginning with the essential topics of ballad origin and development, the first group of articles re-examines accepted conclusions to those problems. Tracing the history of the Icelandic ballad about Saint Olaf, Vésteinn Ólason shows its relation to the religious lyric and to the <u>rimur</u>, metrical romances based on the prose sagas. Ólason carefully defines and describes these genres, contrasting each one to its immediate precursor. In showing how this song about Saint Olaf changes from a meditational song that substitutes for a prayer, to a religious and heroic encomium, then to a narrative song concerned with romance and domesticity, Ólason examines the cultural background that accounts for this shifting focus. In effect, he "analyzes the dialectic between the official and the private in terms of social class." Iørn Piø argues that the flower of chivalric Danish ballads, <u>Ebbe Skammelsøn</u>, actually originated in the sixteenth century as a broadside. As well as showing that the ballad is poignant, finely ironic, and chilling in its direct, impersonal portrayal of family tragedy, Piø distinguishes between the various threads of tradition: elite, folk, and popular. Ultimately, he concludes that this ballad is no older than the sixteenth-century broadside tradition.

The section that follows deals with problems of classifying ballads either through an examination of previously unclassified material or by using new theoretical approaches. Tristram Potter Coffin classifies the love lyric with its "floating stanzas." These lyrics have an identifiable emotional core, which, along with the fixed stanza, offers a classificatory tool. In including the inconstant stanzas in his system, he expands it so that the lyrics are classified by both thematic and textual similarities. Applying onomastics to ballads, W. F. H. Nicolaisen shows how place names create a mental ballad map, providing plausible space and spatial relationships. Ultimately, he notes, the locatory force of these place names becomes as persuasive as the best known names of actual cities or rivers.

Next, scholars survey the history of folksong scholarship, or of genre development and its accompanying changing critical attitudes. In a survey of Finnish narrative folksong, Anneli Asplund traces the development of new genres from the time of the Kanteletar, examining transitional songs, the ballad, broadsides, and the changing songs. In so doing, she shows how the meter changes from Kalevala meter to the new meter of the ballad. At the same time, she explains and comments on changing critical attitudes toward these genres. She concludes by suggesting the influence of traditional composition on certain popular songs derived from folk music. In a state-of-the-art survey, Samuel Armistead reviews ballad style and scholarship. He first describes the Hispanic ballad's characteristics, uncovering its traditionality as well as

its breadth as a genre. Next, he establishes its strikingly
original form, placing it in its diachronic and synchronic
context. Establishing the scholarship's beginnings in
Menéndez Pidal, he then draws on those early approaches to
set up a pattern of divergent critical evolution.

Scholars have long studied the re-creation of narrative
song, disagreeing about means of transmission and allowable
variation. Otto Holzapfel examines a traditional ballad
which is moving toward the lyric mode, while Flemming G.
Andersen and Thomas Pettitt begin with a printed broadside
which gradually takes on traditional characteristics. In a
definitive study for narrative folksong, Andersen and
Pettitt reveal the process by which a ballad is created. In
seeking the genesis and evolution of "balladic narrative
style," they illustrate how a broadside, passing into oral
tradition, takes on characteristics of the ballad. They are
able to do this because of the contemporaneity of their
material: they possess the original broadside, with
contemporary variants, and oral versions collected 70-90
years later, in which the printed song now has clearly
become closer to the ballad of tradition. Holzapfel
analyzes the specifics of type through which the essence of
the "balladic" is to be understood, beginning with a
consideration of the folk ballad's "epic-formulaic style."
He then considers the amount of variation allowable before
the ballad becomes a lyric.

Suzanne Petersen surveys the Institutio Menéndez
Pidal's computer-based research project on the oral Hispanic
ballad tradition. The project intends to make available the
entire corpus of romances in the four Hispanic languages
from the fifteenth century to the present. It also intends
to define the structure and style of this particular type of
narrative folksong. The material recorded in the computer,
in effect, presents a song type comparable to those of the
Tale Type Index. The song type model takes into account
variation within episodes, and, further, indicates which of
the listed variants include which particular motifs. The
material also includes information on syllabic and stanzaic
patterns and on region of origin.

The next group of articles examines narrative folksong
within its cultural context. Through analysis of the
classic ballad Barbara Allen, Christine Cartwright considers
the "dynamics of crisis in Anglo-American culture." She
shows that this ballad of romantic love opposes love and
death (rather than love and hate, or life and death). The
ballad shows a cultural preoccupation with something
potentially deadly: a wound "from which one may not
recover." Barbara Allen deals with the psychology of such
cultural concerns as experiencing strong emotions, forgiving

unfaithful lovers, and desiring to die because of romantic rejection. Cartwright shows how the ballad's red, green, and gold colors and the rose and briar love knot provide cultural continuity between romantic and sacred narratives and between romantic traditions and the ballad. Rainer Wehse considers whether, as is commonly thought, the <u>Schwank</u> and other humorous broadside songs deal with social criticism. He distinguishes between genuine social criticism, which he finds involves a direct critical evaluation, and merely neutral representations of reality, or such representations with a moral added. Olav Bø analyzes the love triangle in <u>Margjit and Targjei Risvollo</u>, arguing that the lover is a supernatural being. In a culture which would condemn a woman who took a lover while engaged to another, the sympathetic response of the fiance and maid suggest that the being can only come from another world. Bø offers textual and linguistic evidence for this analysis. Because of its concern with the supernatural, its relation to Norwegian beliefs and customs, and its farming community setting, the ballad no doubt originated in a Norwegian rural community.

In the section that follows, scholars look at ballad performers, applying performance theory to the singers' repertoires and styles. James Porter applies performance theory to his study of Belle Stewart, a member of the famed Scots family of Travellers. At the outset he establishes the paradox for traditional performers: their impulse both to preserve and invert the norms of their tradition. That impulse derives from the performer's ambivalence about that tradition, and about her own identity in relation to it. As a means of expressing such ambivalence, parody and satire provide escape valves for the singer from the constraints of tradition--what we might call its psychological limitations. The impulse to satirize that tradition stems, of course, from the same impulse that creates narrative folksong. The singer simply views such creation ironically, desiring instead to mock or parody tradition. But the parody of necessity builds on that tradition and thus provides a "socially sanctioned mediator" between the community's conservative forces and the singer's own impulse toward innovation. Klaus and Juliana Roth study a Bulgarian professional street singer's repertoire, tracing the origins of his songs in chapbooks and broadsides. As "one of the last active performers of urban market-place singing in Bulgaria," Nikolov composed most of his original work in a brief period shortly before the Second World War. In their study, the Roths place Nikolov at the diachronic periphery of the street singing tradition. Mary Ellen Brown uncovers the history of a traditional street singer of Jacobite times: Charles Leslie, alias "Musle mou'd Charlie." In a model of historical reconstruction, Brown places Leslie in the context of his time, examines his Jacobite sympathies, and creates a corpus for him. At the same time, she examines the influence of print and literacy on the ballad tradition. Leslie's songs, she argues, can be considered transitional texts. As Brown herself says, such biographical material gives life and resonance to a body of texts.

In their application of structural and semiotic theory to narrative folksong, the next two articles offer new ways to find meaning in these songs and to place that meaning in its cultural context. Drawing on Vladimir Propp's oppositions of abstract tale roles and concrete characters, David Buchan uses this structural system to isolate three basic patterns for the Wit-combat ballads. In these songs the tale roles of Poser and Matcher remain stable, while individual characters vary. In his analysis, Buchan identifies an underlying structural stability, dependent on these tale roles, which unifies these narrative songs. By revealing oppositions which exist on two levels, the structural and the textual, Buchan is able to identify cultural patterns. The genre's concerns are "woman and her adversarial relations with men" (group B) and with "unmortals" (group A). Roger deV. Renwick calls for scholars to carry out in-depth analyses of meaning in folk songs. For such studies, he presents a paradigm derived from structuralism and semiotics. Taking as his texts several of Joe Scott's songs, he sets up an interrelated series of oppositions: material, temporal, and systemic. By examining motifs in these ballads derived from nature and culture, Renwick shows how Scott endows his songs with his personal view of the world, revealing, at the same time, his growing disaffection with society. Renwick convincingly presents a systematic approach to ballad episodes and motifs, one which reveals the paradigms of meaning that inform narrative folksong.

In a definitive study, D. K. Wilgus and Eleanor R. Long consider the blues ballad's relation to narrative folksong. Originally considered part of the lyric or blues tradition, the blues ballad actually shows characteristics of narrative folksong. And Wilgus and Long describe the "way of singing a story" peculiar to the blues ballad as "elliptical, allusive, organic." They then trace this sub-genre's history, showing the antiquity of the "blues ballad idea," its persistence in Irish narrative song, and its flowering in the South after the Civil War. Its stressed rather than syllabic verse shows its derivation from Early Irish and Anglo-Saxon traditions. In fact, it pre-dates the blues, which are modeled on blues ballad strophic and harmonic patterns. Wilgus and Long also reexamine their earlier definition of the "ballad idea," testing accepted definitions of the ballad against it.

Any book of this nature owes much to the advice, encouragement, and help of others. We would like to thank Samuel G. Armistead, Mary Ellen Brown, Judith McCulloh, Patrick K. Ford, Wayland D. Hand, Eleanor R. Long, Robert Orosz, James Porter, Nina Smith, Asbjørn Volstad, Donald Ward, and D. K. Wilgus, with special thanks to Professors Hand and Ward for their generosity, and to Professor Porter for his patient and helpful advice. Irene Chow deserves special thanks for her excellent typing of the manuscript. We also would like to apologize to the many people we were unable to include as contributors. Thus we beg the indulgence of W. Edson Richmond's many appreciative colleagues and students.

Richmond himself deserves such admiration. As graduate students at Indiana University, we took his ballad and medieval romance courses, finding both introductions to the kind of precise research so rare these days. In his numerous articles, too, W. Edson Richmond upholds what must be seen as his own exacting standards of scholarship. As Bruce Rosenberg makes clear in the Foreword, Richmond wrote ground-breaking articles, not just in ballad scholarship, but also in onomastics and in medieval literature. And he always wrote gracefully. His piece in Folklore and Folklife on "Narrative Folk Poetry" remains the most coherent introduction to the ballad available. Indeed, his discussion therein of the ballad, arising as it does out of the centrality of his research to ballad scholarship, anticipates the "narrative folksong" of this book's title. As a scholar, Richmond respects his material; as a teacher, he illuminates it. He is a man who inspires the praise of Rosenberg's Forward and the admiration and affection of all the contributors.

Los Angeles   C.L.E.
Greeley   K.E.B.M.

January 14, 1983

[1]D.K. Wilgus, "The Future of American Folksong Scholarship," Southern Folklore Quarterly, 37 (1973), 315-329.

TABULA GRATULATORIA

Flemming G. Andersen
Odense University
Denmark

Samuel G. Armistead
University of California, Davis

Anneli Asplund
Finnish Literature Society
Helsinki

Jon Hnefill Aðalsteinsson
University of Iceland
Háskóli Íslands

Mac E. Barrick
Shippensburg University
Pennsylvania

Richard Bauman
Beverly J. Stoeltje
University of Texas
Austin

Roy Berkeley
Historian
Shaftsbury, Vermont

Inger and Olav Bø
University of Oslo
Norway

Mary Ellen Brown
Indiana University
Bloomington

Jan Harold Brunvand
University of Utah
Salt Lake City

David Buchan
Memorial University of Newfoundland
St. John's
Canada

Mary Burgan
English Department
Indiana University
Bloomington

Christine A. Cartwright
Memorial University of
   Newfoundland
St. John's
Canada

Richard L. Castner
State University of New York
Brockport

Tristram Potter Coffin
University of Pennsylvania
Philadelphia

Norm Cohen
Westchester, California

Alfred David
Indiana University
Bloomington

Theodore T. Daniels
Philadelphia, Pennsylvania

Eva Danielson
Svenskt visarkiv
Stockholm

Dansk Folkemindesamling
Copenhagen

Deutsches Volksliedarchiv
Freiburg

G. Ronald Dobler
Morehead State University
Kentucky

Herbert J. Dunavent
Sacramento, California

Drake Memorial Library
State University of New York
Brockport

Carol L. Edwards
University of California,
    Los Angeles

Hallfreður Örn Eiríksson
Stofnun Árna Magnússonar á
    Íslandi
Reykjavík, Iceland

Etno-folkloristisk   institutt
Bergen, Norway

J. Manuel Espinosa
Glen Echo, Maryland

Robert N. Fanelli
Doris Devine Fanelli
Independence National
    Historical Park
Ardsley, Pennsylvania

The Folklore Institute
Indiana University
Bloomington

Edith Fowke
York University
Toronto, Canada

Albert B. Friedman
Claremont   Graduate School
Claremont, California

R. D. Fulk
Indiana University
Bloomington

Kenneth S. Goldstein
University of Pennsylvania
Philadelphia

Herbert Halpert
Memorial University of
    Newfoundland
St. John's
Canada

Wayland D. Hand
University of California,
    Los Angeles

Jeanne Harrah-Conforth
Bruce Harrah-Conforth
Indiana University
Bloomington

Michael Heisley
Santa Monica, California

Joseph C. Hickerson
Library of Congress
Washington, D. C.

Theodore C. Humphrey
California State   Polytechnic
    University
Pomona

Linda T. Humphrey
Citrus College
Citrus, California

Jeffrey F. Huntsman
Indiana University
Bloomington

Hiroko Ikeda
University of Hawaii at Manoa
Manoa

Institut für Deutsche und
    vergleichende Volkskunde
Munich

Edward D. Ives
University of Maine
Orono, Maine

Bruce Jackson
State University of New York
    at Buffalo

Gladys M. Johnson
Southeast Delco School Distric
Pennsylvania

Herbert Johnson
Calais, Vermont

John William Johnson
Indiana University
Bloomington

Bengt R. Jonsson
Svenskt visarkiv
Stockholm

Michael Owen Jones
University of California
Los Angeles

Eugene Kintgen
Indiana University
Bloomington

Bengt af Klintberg
Stockholm

Deborah Kodish
Philadelphia, Pennsylvania

Jens Henrik Koudal
Dansk Folkemindesamlung
Copenhagen

Ben Kroup
NYSOPRHP
Waterford, New York

Reimund Kvideland
Etno-folkloristisk institutt
Bergen, Norway

Carl Lindahl
University of Houston
Houston, Texas

John Lindow
University of California,
  Berkeley

Eleanor R. Long
University of California,
  Los Angeles

Peter B. Lowry
University of Pennsylvania
Philadelphia

Judith McCulloh
University of Illinois Press
Champaign, Illinois

Beatrice Kane McLaine
University of Alabama
Tuscaloosa

W. K. McNeil
The Ozark Folk Center
Arkansas

Pricilla Osouski Manwaring
Bloomington, Indiana

Kathleen E. B. Manley
University of Northern Colorado,
  Greeley

Stephen A. Mitchell
Harvard University
Cambridge, Massachusetts

W. F. H. Nicolaisen
State University of New York,
  Binghamton

John Niles
University of California,
  Berkeley

Mortan Nolsøe
The Faroese Academy
Faroe Islands

Holger Olaf Nygard
Duke University
Durham, North Carolina

Vesteinn Ólason
University of Iceland
Reykjavík

Kansallis Osake-Pankki
Finland

Suzanne Petersen
University of Washington
Seattle

Thomas Pettitt
Odense University
Denmark

Iørn Piø
Copenhagen

James Porter
University of California,
    Los Angeles

Roger deV. Renwick
University of Texas at Austin

Warren E. Roberts
Indiana University
Bloomington

Bruce A. Rosenberg
Brown University
Providence, Rhode Island

Neil V. Rosenberg
Memorial University of
    Newfoundland
St. John's
Canada

Klaus Roth
Juliana Roth
Universität München
West Germany

Jón Samsonarson
Stofnun Árna Magnussonar á
    Íslandi
Reykjavík, Iceland

Harold Scheub
Madison, Wisconsin

Anthony Seeger
Indiana University
Bloomington

Hugh Shields
Trinity College
Dublin

Carol Silverman
University of Oregon
Eugene

Catherine A. Shoupe
St. Mary's College
Notre Dame, Indiana

Tuula Stark
Hermosa Beach, California

Shirley L. Steiner
University of California,
    Los Angeles

Svenskt visarkiv
Stockholm

Barre and Miiko Toelken
Utah State University
Logan

Stefaan Top
Seminaire voor Volkskunde
Leuven, Belgium

Paul L. Tyler
Indiana University
Bloomington

D. K. Wilgus
University of California,
    Los Angeles

Donald J. Ward
University of California,
    Los Angeles

Karen Weidel
Oaklyn, New Jersey

William H. Wiatt
Indiana University
Bloomington

Rainer Wehse
Enzyklopadie des Märchens
Göttingen, West Germany

Otto Holzapfel
Deutsches Volkliedarchiv
Freiburg

ORIGINS AND DEVELOPMENT

ÓLÁFS VÍSUR

1. Ólafur kóngur Haraldsson
   hann gefi oss sigur og tíma
   so að eg hafi djörfung til
   um aðferð hans að ríma.

2. Ólafur kóngur Haraldsson
   hann reið um þykkvan skóg:
   hann sá litið spor í leir,
   slík eru minnin stór.

3. Svaraði hann Finnur Árnason,
   var honum á því þokki:
   "Fallegur mundi sá lítill fótur
   væri hann í skarlats sokki."

4. "Heyrðu það, Finnur Árnason,
   hvað eg segi þér:
   áður en sól til viðar rennur
   meyna fáðu mer."

5. Þeir sáu fram á fögrum skógi
   eina mey so fríða,
   þeir buðu henni á stofn að stíga
   og so með sér ríða.

6. En so svaraði kóngurinn,
   hann dvaldist þar um stund:
   "Hvert er heiti þitt, fagra fljóð,
   sem komið er á minn fund?"

7. "Álfheiður heiti eg, göfugur herra,
   síst mun virðing þrjóta.
   Nú er eg komin á yðar fund
   og þar mun eg giftu af hljóta."

8. "Farðu heim til drottningar
   og þjóna þú henni með sóma,
   þá muntu í mínu ríki
   njóta sigurs og blóma."

9. "Heyrðu það nú, dýra drottning,
   trúa máttu mér:
   Ólafur kóngur Haraldsson,
   hann skipaði mér hjá þér."

10. Drottning braust frá göfugum herra,
    varð henni að því mein
    því hún varð um vintrarnátt
    að byggja sængina ein.

11. Það var einn so snemma myrgin,
    sólin skein í tíma,
    drottning sendi Álfheiði
    að leita saxa sinna.

12. Álfheiður sig til svefnskemmu gekk,
    þessi brúðurin svinna.
    Kóngurinn spurði það einkafljóð:
    "Hvað vildir þú finna?"

13. En því svaraði Ólafur kóngur,
    hann fréttir vífið teita,
    hún lét sér það orð af munni verða,
    hún kvaðst sér sonar leita.

14. En so svaraði kóngurinn,
    að því gefur hann gætur:
    "Stígðu upp í sæng til mín
    og þvoðu vel þína fætur."

15. Það var rett með fullu tungli
    og miðju sjávar flóði,
    byrjaður var á drottinsdag
    Magnús kóngurinn góði.

16. Með fullu tungli og flóði að sjá,
    tel eg af góðs manns æði,
    tiggi byrjaði tiginn son
    fyrir utan angur og mæði.

17. En so svöruðu kóngsins menn,
    so er á bókum ort,
    fyrri hafði hann bætt þá synd
    en hann hafði hana gjört.

18. Álfheiði dreymdi fyrsta draum
    og var sá lengst í loti
    að henni þótti á sinni ævi
    Noreg öll á floti.

19. Álfheiði dreymdi annan draum,
    sté hún á kirkjugólf,
    að henni þótti á sinni hendi
    kveikjast ljósin tólf.

20. Álfheiði dreymdi þriðja draum,
    get eg hún giftu fangi,
    að henni þótti hinn fagri geisli
    fljúga sér úr fangi.

21. Álfheiður hugsar um sinn hag
    af alls öngum þjósti,
    finnur hún það með sjálfri sér
    að hún hafði barn fyrir brjósti.

22. Drottning bauð við hennar draumum
    tólf sín bestu bú,
    gifta hana lendum manni,
    neitaði hun því þó.

23. En því svaraði kóngurinn:
    "Vant er um að velja,
    þú skalt aldrei þína drauma
    rétt með verði selja."

24. En því svaraði kóngurinn
    áður hann reið til hófa:
    "Eigðu sjálf og unntu vel
    og njóttu draumsins góða."

25. Álfheiður fangar þunga sótt,
    sú gekk helst af magni,
    konurnar sögðu körlum til
    að lítið væri að barni.

26. En so svaraði hann Sighvatur skáld,
    so er á bókum ritað:
    "Hvort viljið heldur skíra barn
    eða fyrir svörum sitja?"

27. En so svöruðu kóngsins menn,
    prýddir vel til dáða:
    "Þennan bjóðum vér kostinn þér,
    vær látum þig sjálfan ráða."

28. Sighvatur gekk þar inn í höll
    sem kóngurinn sat yfir borðum:
    "Skylt væri mér inna til
    eitt . . . tal með orðum."

29. En so svaraði kóngurinn:
    "Legg eg við so ríkt:
    hvör gaf þér, Sighvatur, orðlof til
    að skíra barnið mitt?"

30. "Því lét eg hann Magnús heita,
    gjöra skal á því grein:
    eg vissa ekki æðra nafn
    veraldarkóngs í heim."

31. En so svaraði kóngurinn,
    hann hélt á borða ljóma:
    "Þú skalt alla þína ævi
    /honum/ Magnúsi þjóna."

32. Jesús Kristus Maríuson
    leysti oss frá nauðum,
    þar næst hjálpi hann allri þjóð,
    bæði lífs og dauðum.

     May King Ólafur give us courage to make a rhyme about
his deeds. King Ólafur rides through a forest and sees a
footprint. Finnur Árnason says that this small foot would
look pretty in a scarlet stocking, and the king tells him to
find the maiden before sunset. They bring a beautiful maiden
who says that her name is Álfheiður and that their meeting
is going to bring her luck. The king tells her to go and
serve the queen and foretells that she shall enjoy "victory
and flower." The queen leaves the noble lord and has to
sleep alone. Early one morning, the queen sends Álfheiður to
search for her scissors. She comes to the king's chamber and
tells him that she is looking for a son. The king asks her
to wash her feet and step into his bed, and King Magnus is
conceived on a Sunday. It is written in books that the
king's men said that he had atoned for this sin before it
was committed. Álfheiður has three dreams: the whole of
Norway is covered with water (floating); she steps into a
church and sees twelve lights being lit in her hand; she
dreams that a beautiful ray is shining from her bosom. After
this, Álfheiður realizes that she is pregnant. The queen
offers to buy her dreams with twelve good farms and marry
her to a gentleman, but she refuses. The king says that she
should keep her dreams and enjoy them. Álfheiður bears a
child which women consider to be sickly, and the poet
Sighvatur asks whether the courtiers want to christen the
child or answer to the king. They leave the choice to him.
Sighvatur goes before the king who asks him who has given
him leave to christen the king's child. Sighvatur answers
that he gave the name Magnus to the child, because this is
the noblest name for a king that he knows. The king answers
that Sighvatur shall serve Magnus as long as he lives. Jesus
Christ has redeemed us; may he help all people, living and
dead.

Vésteinn Ólason, ed. Sagnadansar. Reykjavík, 1979, pp. 298-
301.

VÉSTEINN ÓLASON

SAINT OLAF IN LATE MEDIEVAL ICELANDIC POETRY

Olaf Haraldsson, King of Norway (1015-1030), later called Saint Olaf, is a prominent figure in Icelandic literature. During his lifetime, court poets composed numerous works about him in intricate skaldic metres, singing his praises and relating his deeds. Although most skaldic poetry sounds extremely formalistic and impersonal to the modern ear, there are exceptions. Many of Sighvatr Þórðarson's stanzas about Olaf, for instance, express personal sentiments such as friendship and admiration.[1]

The skaldic poetry in which Olaf figures as a saint was, naturally, composed later. A magnificent example is Geisli, a drápa written in the years 1152-53 by Einar Skúlason (born c. 1090), and recited officially in the cathedral at Nidaros (Trondheim). Einar deals with Olaf's life and with his death, which is here likened for the first time to the Passion of Christ; several miracles are also recounted. The drápa glorifies Olaf as the holy and eternal king of Norway.[2]

Among the stories of kings written by Icelanders in the twelfth and thirteenth centuries, sagas concerning Olaf hold a central place. That written by Snorri--composed originally as a separate work, but later incorporated into Heimskringla--is universally agreed to be an outstanding masterpiece of saga writing;[3] and it has inspired even contemporary classics of story-telling, such as Halldór Laxness' Gerpla. In the latter work Olaf is, however, portrayed in an altogether different light than in Heimskringla.[4]

The Icelandic literature of the late Middle Ages does not enjoy the high reputation of the older poetry and sagas, being neither as original, nor as appealing to modern tastes. Nonetheless, during the fourteenth and fifteenth centuries the native literary heritage was cherished and, indeed, saved from oblivion by copyists, while new literary forms were adopted or created through foreign influence. All of the significant developments were, however, in the field of verse, while prose deteriorated.

The most important poetic innovations of this time were: (1) religious songs in rhymed meters (though the composition of religious verse in skaldic meters also continued); (2) <u>rímur</u>: metrical romances drawing upon prose sagas (mostly legendary) for their subject matter; and (3) ballads of Scandinavian origin in couplet or quatrain ballad measure. Although ballads have not, it is true, been preserved in any medieval Icelandic manuscript, comparative studies reveal that the genre must have been present in Iceland at least as early as the fifteenth century.[5]

It so happens that both the oldest <u>ríma</u> and the oldest Icelandic ballad ("oldest" here meaning "preserved in the oldest manuscript") deal with King Olaf; these are <u>Ólafs ríma Haraldssonar</u> in a manuscript from <u>circa</u> 1390 and the ballad <u>Óláfs vísur</u>, recorded in a manuscript from the early seventeenth century, now lost, and preserved only in a copy from the early eighteenth century.[6] There are four preserved religious lyrics about Olaf, <u>Óláfs vísur I-IV</u>, probably all composed in the fifteenth or early sixteenth century.[7]

The traditional ballad has often been studied as a separate genre; but one can only appreciate its special functions in medieval society by contrasting it with other medieval genres. It seems to me that late medieval poetry about Saint Olaf offers an opportunity to make a contribution in this direction. All the texts in question are based upon the same prose sources: What was it in these sources that interested the poets? How do they handle their themes? (For practical reasons, I shall deal with only one of the religious lyrics about Olaf, <u>Óláfs vísur IV</u>.[8])

<u>Óláfs vísur IV</u> has been attributed to a certain Gunni Hallsson, nicknamed "Hólaskáld," who lived in the vicinity of Hólar in Northern Iceland <u>circa</u> 1455-1545. The oldest manuscripts containing the poem have been dated around 1500; and even if the attribution to Gunni Hallsson is incorrect, there is no reason to date <u>Óláfs vísur IV</u> farther back than the late fifteenth century.[9]

The poem consists of thirteen rather long stanzas in a meter which is most accurately described as a canzone with ten lines in each stanza rhymed <u>aabaabcccb</u> and with internal rhyme and alliteration according to traditional Icelandic rules. The first stanza (with alliteration and rhymes here underlined) will serve as an example:

> <u>H</u>erra kong Óláf, <u>hj</u>álpari Noregs <u>l</u>anda,
> þig kom til <u>handa</u> með <u>h</u>elgum <u>anda</u>
> eilíf náð fyrir Iesúm Krist.
> <u>H</u>eiðurinn þinn mun um <u>h</u>eiminn norður st<u>anda</u>;
> þú <u>k</u>omt oss báði úr <u>kv</u>ölum og v<u>anda</u>,
> <u>k</u>enndir trú með <u>k</u>rafti og <u>l</u>ist.

Musteri klén þú vígðir væn,
villa brotin og miskunn sén.
þú fékkt þar lén af guði í gén,
herradæmi og himnavist.

Lord King Olaf, helper of the lands of Norway,
To you came with the Holy Ghost
Eternal Grace through Jesus Christ.
Your renown will remain in the northern parts
    of the world;
You saved us from anguish and trouble,
(You) taught the faith with force and art.
You consecrated temples fine and fair,
Heresy was shattered and mercy shown.
You were rewarded for this by God
With authority and a place in Heaven.

The poem's intricate metrical form, for which we have no direct parallel in medieval poetry, contrasts with its simple language and style.[10] The language is typical of the period and, on the whole, purely Icelandic, although some Scandinavian influences may be detected. The syntax is simple, and there are no rhetorical tropes or specially poetic words.

The poem praises Olaf for his missionary activities and for his firm and just rule, and describes how this led to the rising of the people and the king's death as a martyr. The solar eclipse at Olaf's death is mentioned, and this reminds the poet of the Saviour on the Cross. In the middle section of the poem several miracles are recounted: a light burns over the place where his body rests; a blind man who spread Olaf's blood over his eyes gets his sight; and, later, Olaf comes to the help of people who appeal to him in moments of difficulty.[11] At the end of the poem, Olaf is again praised, and the end of the last stanza is a prayer urging him to lead us to the Saviour's knee.

Every stanza of the poem is addressed directly to Olaf with the opening words: Herra kong Olaf, while there is very little narration and no dialogue inside the text. Speaking in a lyrical mode, the poet thus evokes a direct confrontation with his subject.

The lyric has a distinctly religious emphasis: Olaf's good qualities as a ruler are mentioned, but the poet is primarily concerned with his martyrdom and his miracles. Appropriately, the poem ends with a prayer.

Although Ólafs ríma Haraldssonar acquires a religious flavor towards its close and ends with an address and prayer to Olaf, it has an entirely different character. Here we find a narrator who (except in the last stanza) speaks of Olaf in the third person, introduces a great many other characters, relates particular events at length, and creates scenes with dialogue.

This _ríma_ is in the so-called _ferskeytt_ meter-- quatrains with 4+3 stressed syllables in each half, rhymed _abab_, and with regular alliteration--which is the most common stanza form of the genre, and which appears here fully developed.[12] Again, we can use the opening stanza as illustration:

> Ólafr kongr örr ok fríðr
> átti Noregi at ráða;
> gramr var æ við bragna blíðr,
> borinn til sigrs ok náða.[13]

> King Olaf, generous and handsome
> Ruled over Norway;
> The king was always gentle with people,
> /He was/ born to victory and grace.

Rímur have inherited important features of the diction of skaldic poetry, but these features are not as prominent in Ólafs ríma as in many younger rímur. The most peculiar features of skaldic style are the unnatural order of words and sentences--at first sight everything seems to be permitted--and the wealth of substantives, including kennings and the so-called _heiti_. The kenning is "a periphrasis consisting of two or more substantive members, which takes the place of a noun,"[14] while the _heiti_ is a poetic noun not used in prose. In rímur the order of words and sentences is almost always simple and straightforward, and in Ólafs ríma it comes close to that of the spoken language. The number of kennings is relatively low, and those we find are very simple and entirely traditional; there are four kennings denoting battle, one for "sword," one for "man" (or "soldier"), one for "breast," and one denoting "wolf." Characteristically, they all appear in passages describing fighting. Only one of them, _fálu hestr_ ("the horse of a giantess," i.e., "wolf") contains a mythological allusion.

Heiti are much more frequent than kennings, but those that occur are well known and would have been immediately understood by a fourteenth-century audience. There are fifteen _heiti_ denoting "king," and a few for "soldier," "battle," and "sword."

Although the skaldic diction is sparingly used, its presence connects the _ríma_ with the tradition of Norse battle-poetry. There is, on the other hand, surprisingly little influence from the specifically Christian kenning style that developed in the religious poetry of the tenth to the fourteenth century. The only examples we find are _drottinn himna hallar_ (lord of the heavenly mansion) and _himna gramr_ (king of heavens). Contrasting with the style of the rest of the poem is the image _Krists et bjarta blóm_ ("the bright flower of Christ," namely, Olaf), which appears near the end of the poem.

In _Ólafs ríma_ the poet begins by praising Olaf in general terms, and then enumerating his most important achievements: he christianized five countries (this is usually attributed to Olaf Tryggvason in Icelandic sources), punished robbing and stealing, forbade heathendom, made strict laws, and punished traitors with death. After this introduction the main narrative begins. The uprising against the king is described and its leaders enumerated. Then the king's gathering of forces is recounted and his most eminent followers are mentioned. Special attention is given to persons who joined Olaf shortly before the Battle of Stiklarstaoir, whom he received on the condition that they were baptized. Then, certain events that took place just before the battle--both in Olaf's camp and that of his adversaries--are described. It is emphasized that Olaf gave money for the souls of enemies that were going to be killed in the battle. A central part of the poem depicts the battle itself, climaxing with the king's death. After that the eclipse of the sun is mentioned and the final battle described. We are then told about miracles surrounding the king's dead body, about his burial, miracles at the grave, and the translation of the body. The final stanzas describe Olaf's glory: he is now at God's right side in Heaven; in the last stanza the poet begs Olaf to be his spokesman before the King of all Nations.

The narrative of _Ólafs ríma_ is swift and lively, and the subject matter is well-arranged. The Battle of Stiklarstaðir and Olaf's death occupy the most space, but the poet emphasizes moments where Olaf appears as a religious hero rather than a military one. The dramatized incidents all have a religious core; miracles are mentioned but not narrated in detail.

Although the poem is in a relatively popular style, it is obviously a literary creation. The poet never departs from the narrative content of _Heimskringla_ (except in the above-mentioned remark on the Christianization of five countries); but he uses the saga text for his own purposes,

picking what he wants from it and emphasizing only such
details as serve his main purpose, which is quite different
from that of Snorri.[15] Snorri is intent on relating the
events of Olaf's life with accuracy and apparent objectivity
without mixing his own person into the text, and he is more
interested in politics than religion. Einar Gilsson does
nothing to hide his subjective attitude: his interest lies
in the religious lesson the story teaches and the
glorification of the saint. Nevertheless, the richness of
his narrative material, his method of dramatizing the
climaxes of the narrative, and his interest in the
historical event, make the character of his poem very unlike
the religious lyric of Gunni Hallsson.

On the other hand, his narrative technique is
fundamentally different from that of the ballad. He
introduces, for example, many characters who have no
narrative function, and presents a longer and more
complicated chain of events than would any ballad poet.

These two examples must suffice to indicate the
literary scene into which the ballad enters in the late
Middle Ages. From the evidence of later sources we can
assume that it was well-received and must have fulfilled
needs different from those fulfilled by preexisting poetry.
Its functions ought then to be explicable in terms of the
features that distinguish it from the most closely related
genres, rímur and religious lyrics.

An obvious difference lies in the oral nature of the
ballad. But this difference should not be over-emphasized.
Although rímur and religious lyrics were literary
compositions, they were certainly aimed at--and well
received by--the general, unlettered public, and were, like
ballads, communicated in song. On the other hand, Icelandic
ballads with claims to be medieval--as for instance Óláfs
vísur--show traces of literary style and may be based on
written sources.

The ballad Óláfs vísur is composed in thirty-two
regular ballad quatrains without refrains.[16] It begins with
an indirect, third person address to the protagonist who is
asked to bestow good fortune on the poet so that he may
venture to rhyme about the king's deeds. Then the story
starts in medias res by telling how King Olaf, riding
through a forest, sees the footprints of a woman whom he
orders his men to summon before him. She comes and predicts
that their meeting will bring her luck. The king sends her
to serve the queen and, in due course, takes her into his
bed and begets a child with her. The young woman has dreams
foretelling the glory of her future son but refuses to

describe these dreams to the queen. When the boy is born, he
is sickly, and, the king being temporarily unavailable, the
court poet Sighvatr decides that the child shall be baptized
Magnus. When the king learns this, he is angry; but is soon
appeased, and orders Sighvatr to serve Magnus as long as he
lives. The ballad ends with a prayer to Jesus Christ.[17]

The addresses to King Olaf and to Christ at the
beginning and end of the ballad are a feature unlike the
ballad, obviously influenced by religious lyrics and even by
the ending of Ólafs ríma. There are also some authorial
intrusions in the narrative and occasional traces of ríma
style which clearly show familiarity with that genre.
However, these non-balladic features are only superficial,
as a close inspection of the poem reveals.

The subject matter is taken from Snorri's saga. There
we find all the characters as well as the main incidents:
King Olaf had an illegitimate son with his concubine
Álfhildr (Álfheiður in the ballad); the son was born sickly
and immediately after his birth baptized Magnus on the
advice of Sighvatr, who afterwards succeeded in satisfying
the king about the reasons for this act; after an interim
rule of Olaf's enemies, Magnus succeeded him as king with
Sighvatr as one of his closest advisors.

It is only the last part of this story which is
dramatized in Heimskringla, but the first part, which deals
with the king's affair with Álfheiður, is here amplified
with ballad-themes and dramatized in a balladic manner. The
finding of the footprints may have a fairy tale character,
but the triangle that is established, as well as the dreams,
are themes which are likely to have been borrowed from other
ballads.[18]

The style of the ballad is quite simple, while the
story advances through scenes which are linked only loosely,
or not at all. Dialogue appears in 50% of the stanzas,
whereas in Ólafs ríma only 14% of the stanzas contain
dialogue. None of the stanzas of the poem are found in other
ballads, but the language is formulaic to some extent,
especially in the introductions to direct speech. There is
one instance of incremental repetition (stanzas 23-24).

Although Olaf's reputation as king and saint
undoubtedly made him an interesting figure for the ballad
poet and his audience, neither saintliness nor royalty is
the focus of interest in the ballad. Instead, we are here,
as in most ballads, drawn into the sphere of domesticity and
intimacy. We first meet the king riding in the forest,
apparently for his pleasure. At home, the bed, not the

throne, is the scene of the most important action. And even when seen in his official capacity, he is deciding about matters which concern his erotic passion for the young girl he has discovered in the forest and his relationship to his illegitimate son. His relationship to his son is certainly a matter of importance for the realm, since it concerns the passing on of kingship and even the king's luck (gæfa) to the next generation, but the matter is interpreted in terms of personal and emotional relationships.

The religious attitude of the poem is ambiguous, if not directly heretical. The sin of begetting an illegitimate child--and on a Sunday at that!--is said to have been atoned for before it was committed. (That the poet may have had some qualms about this statement can be seen by his referring to the authority of books on this point: "so er á bókum ort.") The chain of events is to a great degree seen as governed by fate and luck, rather than by providence. However, the moral leniency seen in the ballad has many parallels in medieval literature, and the picture of Olaf as a man with ordinary human foibles and difficulties surely struck a more sympathetic chord with ordinary folk than did the idealized pictures drawn in the ríma and the religious lyric.

Ólafs vísur shows that the Icelandic medieval ballad had many points of contact with other literary genres. Yet it appears to have fulfilled needs fundamentally different from those satisfied by more respectable poetry about saints and kings. These were, in particular, the needs to dramatize in poetic form emotional conflicts arising among ordinary people in the intimate sphere of life: in the relations between lovers, between husband and wife, and between father and son.[19]

It is impossible to decide the age of Ólafs vísur with any certainty. We can be fairly sure that it was composed before the Reformation of the Icelandic church in the mid-sixteenth century, but it can hardly be very old since it is relatively well preserved and shows signs of influence from other ballads. It may be about the same age as Ólafs vísur IV by Gunni Hallsson, or possibly somewhat older.

The author of Ólafs ríma Haraldssonar, Einar Gilsson, was for a short period lögmaðr (law-man), which was one of the highest secular posts in the country in his time.[20] Gunni Hallsson was an ordinary farmer; but he was befriended by the bishops of Hólar and spent the last years of his long life in their household, and it is most likely that he earned their favors with his poetry. In light of these facts, it does not seem far-fetched to suppose that the poetry written by these men reflected ideals of the ruling powers in Iceland, secular as well as spiritual: the glorification of the Holy and Eternal King of Norway (and consequently Iceland at this time) and willingness to put one's affairs in the hands of him and the Lord. The simple language and style of this poetry made it understandable and appealing to the general public, and thus an efficient vehicle for propagation of official ideology. This does not mean, of course, that the poems were composed with the manipulation of the public in mind. It is much more likely that the poets were simply expressing a sincerely felt admiration for their protagonist.

We do not know anything about the person who composed the ballad _Ólafs vísur_, but he or she was obviously more interested in Olaf as an ordinary human being than as a king or a saint. The ballad seems to testify to the fact that although the common people may have accepted (more or less uncritically) poetry embodying ruling class ideals, it left some of their needs unmet. So they created their own poetry, working out and mediating compelling conflicts in their daily lives.

Although I have analyzed the dialectic between the official and the private in terms of social class, I do not mean to imply that people were divided by class in their poetic tastes. The ballad does not express a conscious opposition to the official picture of Saint Olaf, and it has undoubtedly pleased people of all classes, although the clergy may have frowned upon its moral attitudes.[21] In any case, the difference in status between ballads, on the one hand, and _rímur_ and religious songs, on the other, clearly appears in the fact that medieval ballads were not written down until decades or even centuries after their composition, when humanism and a new nationalism had begun to influence the official ideology.[22]

It appears clearly from the sagas about kings, as well as the skaldic poetry, that King Olaf was a figure of immense ideological importance in Norway and Iceland in the high Middle Ages. The poems studied in this article reveal that his importance did not diminish in the following centuries.

NOTES

[1]Den norsk-islandske skjaldedigtning (Copenhagen: Rosenkilde og Bagger, 1973), I:A 223-75, esp. 272-73.

[2]Skjaldedigtning, I:A, 459-73.

[3]For the saga published separately, see Saga Ólafs konungs hins helga, ed. Oscar Albert Johnsen and Jón Helgason (Oslo: Jacob Dybwad, 1941). Heimskringla exists in many editions, see, e.g., Íslenzk fornrit, 26-28, ed. Bjarni Aðalbjarnarson (Reykjavík: Hið íslenzka fornritafélag, 1941-1951).

[4]Halldór Laxness, Gerpla (Reykjavík: Helgafell, 1952); The Happy Warriors, tr. Katherine John (London: Methuen, 1958).

[5]See Vésteinn Ólason, The Traditional Ballads of Iceland (Reykjavík: Stofnun Árna Magnússonar, 1982).

[6]Ólafs ríma Haraldssonar in Rímnasafn, ed. Finnur Jónsson, (Copenhagen: Samfund til udgivelse af gammel nordisk litteratur, 1905-1912), 1 ff. Ólafs vísur in Íslenzk fornkvæði, ed. Jón Helgason (Editiones Arnamagnæanæ, B, 13, Copenhagen: Munksgaard, 1963), IV, 11 ff.

[7]Íslenzk miðaldakvæði (ÍM), ed. Jón Helgason (Copenhagen: Munksgaard, 1938), II, 433 ff.

[8]ÍM, II, 455-59.

[9]See Kvæðasafn eptir íslenzka menn frá miðöldum og síðari oldum, ed. Jón Þorkelsson (Reykjavík: Hið íslenzka bókmenntafélag, 1922-1927), I, 221; further, ÍM, II, 444-55.

[10]Various forms of the canzone appearing in late Medieval Icelandic poetry are described in H. Schottmann, Die isländische Mariendichtung (München: Fink, 1973), pp. 499-503.

[11]All these miracles appear in Saga Ólafs konungs (see note 3), pp. 588, 591, 633-38, 650-54.

[12]For discussion of this stanza form, see Vésteinn Ólason, "Nýmæli í íslenskum bókmenntum á miðöld," Skirnir, 150 (1976), 72-74, and The Traditional Ballads of Iceland, pp. 57-58, 65-68.

[13]Rímnasafn, I, 1.

[14]Roberta Frank, Old Norse Court Poetry, Islandica, No. 42 (Ithaca and London: Cornell University Press, 1978), p. 42.

[15]The narrative matter of the first 19 stanzas is scattered throughout the saga; stanzas 20-26 are based on Chs. 157 and 200 (all chapter numbers in this note refer to Saga Óláfs konungs); the description of the battle and Olaf's death summarize Chs. 201-27, while stanzas 58-62 are based on Chs. 236, 238, and 244.

[16]The meters of Icelandic ballads are described in Sagnadansar, ed. Vésteinn Ólason (Reykjavík: Bókaútgáfa Menningarsjóðs, 1979), pp. 33-40. Most ballads found in Iceland have a refrain, but seven examples in quatrains, all of which seem to have been composed in Iceland, are without refrain.

[17]For more detailed information about this ballad and its sources, see The Traditional Ballads of Iceland, pp. 292-98.

[18]See, e.g., The Types of the Scandinavian Medieval Ballad (Stockholm and Oslo: Svenskt visarkiv and Universitetsforlaget, 1978), D 207, D 232, D 397.

[19]Although Óláfs vísur may be classified as a historical ballad, it follows from the analysis that it (like most Icelandic ballads) can equally be called a family ballad. The emphasis on family life seems to be a general phenomenon in European balladry, as stated by one of Europe's foremost folklorists: ". . . auch in die Lieder der anderen Grossgruppen spielen Familienbeziehungen immer und immer wieder hinein, die Träger der Volksballade scheinen von dem Komplex Familie geradezu besessen zu sein. . . ." Max Lüthi, "Familienballade," in Handbuch des Volksliedes, ed. Rolf Brednich, Lutz Röhrig, Wolfgang Suppan, I (München: Fink, 1973), 89. It is noteworthy that the Icelanders, who had an abundance of heroic literature of their own, seem to

have cared nothing for the heroic ballads of their neighbours in Norway and the Faroes; the ballads they imported were almost exclusively family ballads.

[20]See Björn K. Þórólfsson, Rímur fyrir 1600, Safn Fræðafjelagsins, 9 (Copenhagen: Hio Íslenska fræoafjelag, 1934), pp. 298-99.

[21]See Kvæðasafn fra miðöldum, I, 221.

[22]The social and ideological conditions that led to the collection of Icelandic ballads are briefly discussed in Sagnadansar, pp. 21-22.

University of Iceland
Reykjavík

EBBE SKAMMELSEN

Sofia Sandberg's Manuscript, _circa_ 1622*

1. Skammel he lives up here in Thy,
   Merry and well to do:
   He has five sons so proud and strong,
   Two them came to woe.
   --And thus roams Ebbe Skammelsen
       on many stormy trails.

2. Three of them died long ago.
   The other two were left;
   Verily, I tell you,
   They were brave and deft.

3. Ebbe was the younger,
   He rode far and wide;
   Proud Adeluds, the lovely maid,
   He asked to be his bride.

4. Proud Adeluds, the lovely maid,
   He asked her for her troth;
   Then he took her home to his mother,
   And then he rode abroad.

5. Ebbe serves in the house of the king
   And acts with honor there;
   Peter, his brother, stays at home
   And courts the maid he has dear.

6. There was Peter Skammelsen
   He dressed in velvet all,
   Looking for proud Adeluds
   He went into the hall.

7. "Here I find you, proud Adeluds,
   Give me your troth and grace;
   I shall honor and love you
   All my living days."

8. "Be silent, Peter Skammelsen,
   Don't talk this way to me;
   I'm betrothed to your brother,
   This shall never be."

9. Answered Peter Skammelsen,
   Richly in velvet dressed:
   "Ebbe serves in the house of the king,
   To him you are just a jest."

10. Then said Ebbe's mother,
    For him she didn't care:
    "You take Peter Skammelsen,
    Ebbe is false, I swear.

11. Ebbe serves in the house of the king
    And acts with honor there;
    A maiden in the house of the queen
    He yearns for and holds dear.

12. Better you take my older son,
    With castles golden-red,
    Than wait for Ebbe Skammelsen,
    He loves another maid."

13. "Harken, Peter Skammelsen,
    You take another wife;
    No other man shall bind me
    While Ebbe is still alive."

14. Answered her Ebbe's mother,
    Her voice had an honest ring:
    "I'll tell you the truth, proud Adeluds,
    Ebbe he died last spring."

15. Then proud Adeluds stood up,
    The delightful rose,
    And she gave Peter Skammelsen
    Her silken hand in troth.

16. They prepared for the wedding
    And bought both wine and brew;
    Ebbe served in the house of the king,
    So little about it he knew.

17. Ebbe awoke at midnight
    And told what he had dreamt;
    His companion lay awake
    Thinking of what it meant.

18. "I thought I saw my stone house
    In flames and all alight;
    There burned my brother Peter
    Together with my bride."

19. "You thought you saw your stone house
    In flames and all alight:
    That is because your brother
    Betrothed your lovely bride."

20. Then arose young Ebbe
    And tied the sword at his side,
    Then he asked for furlough,
    As homeward he would ride.

21. There was Ebbe Skammelsen
    He rode a furious race,
    Three days he used to ride the road
    That erst took thirty days.

22. There was Ebbe Skammelsen
    He rode so fast away,
    He came to his father's house
    On the first wedding day.

23. There was Ebbe Skammelsen
    Rode into his father's yard;
    There he saw a little page,
    Dressed in a mantle smart.

24. "Harken to me, my little page,
    And answer me my query:
    Who are all these people here
    Who're gathered and make merry?"

25. "All these people that you see
    Who are gathered here,
    Came as Peter, your brother
    Weds the maid you have dear."

26. Entered then his sisters two
    And welcomed with joy their brother;
    They were gladder to see him again
    Than both his father and mother.

27. To one he gave a diadem,
    The other a golden band,
    Both he had bought for his lovely bride,
    Brought from a foreign land.

28. To one he gave a golden band,
    The other a gold ring so wide:
    Both he had brought from a foreign land,
    Brought for his lovely bride.

29. Ebbe he turned his steed around,
    He wanted to ride away;
    But his mother took hold of the reins,
    Demanding that he should stay.

30. Doggedly she held on to the reins,
    Demanding that he should stay;
    Now she rues so deeply
    She stopped him from riding away.

31. His mother offered him cushion and chair
    And place at the table to dine;
    His father asked him to go around
    And pour the golden wine.

32. Ebbe poured wine for Adeluds,
    She shone like a golden sprite;
    And he became so sorrowful
    Whenever he looked at the bride.

33. There was Ebbe Skammelsen
    He poured as time went on;
    Then he asked his father for leave
    To rest himself and sit down.

34. There he sat for a little while,
    Until his mother said
    That it might be the best for him,
    If he would go to bed.

35. Ebbe Skammelsen arose
    With Adeluds on his arm;
    Verily, I tell you,
    His heart felt hurt and harm.

36. Ebbe Skammelsen he asked,
    Out on the balcony:
    "Do you remember, Adeluds,
    You pledged me loyalty?"

37. "All the troth I got from God,
    I gave to Peter, your brother;
    I promise, all my living days
    To care for you as a mother."

38. "I wooed you not for my mother,
    I asked you to be my wife;
    Now shall Peter Skammelsen
    Pay for it with his life.

39. Harken to me, proud Adeluds,
    Together let's go away;
    Then I will kill my brother
    And suffer for you this dismay."

40. "If you take your brother's life,
    You'll lose me, too, for sure;
    And you shall grieve yourself to death
    Like a wild bird on the moor."

41. There was Ebbe Skammelsen
    He drew his sword from his side,
    Turned to lady Adeluds
    And killed his brother's bride.

42. Under his scarlet mantle
    He hid the bloody sword;
    Then he went and stood before
    His brother in the hall.

43. "Peter, my brother, get to your feet
    And hie yourself to the bride;
    Too long she's sitting in her bed
    Longing for you at her side."

44. "Harken, Ebbe Skammelsen,
    Do not spoil for a fight;
    I promise, brother dear, that you
    May sleep with my bride tonight."

45. There was Ebbe Skammelsen
    The sword from his side he drew;
    There was his brother Peter's head
    He servered with a blow.

46. He wounded his father grievously,
     His mother lost a hand;
     And thus roams Ebbe Skammelsen
     On many wild trails in the land.
     --And thus roams Ebbe Skammelsen
         on many stormy trails.

Erik Dal, ed. Danish Ballads and Folksongs. Trns. Henry
Meyer. Copenhagen: Rosenkilde and Bagger, 1967. Tune
collected in 1809 in Stenderup by C. Plesner and reprinted
from Danmarks Gamle Folkeviser. Ed. Thorkild Knudsen, Svend
Nielsen, et al. Copenhagen: Akademisk Forlag, 1935-59, XI,
278.

*For the ballad in the original Danish, see the several
versions in Piø's article /Eds./.

EBBE SKAMMELSØN (DgF 354):
A Sixteenth-Century Broadside Ballad

Characterizing this ballad as "the most superb our medieval poetry has to show," as "one of the most beautiful poems of the Middle Ages," Axel Olrik asserts that as a work of art, Ebbe Skammelsøn "expresses the highest achievement of the Danish Middle Ages."[1] In Danmarks gamle folkeviser, Olrik classifies it with the many chivalric ballads; in fact, as Erik Dal notes, it "is generally recognized as the primary ballad of chivalry."[2] Olrik expresses his basic attitude toward the chivalric ballads in some lectures at the University of Copenhagen in 1905-1906:

> Danish ballads about the life of chivalry must have been created by poets who lived among, or were members of, the nobility of the Middle Ages, that is, the upper class. And in the sixteenth century they still thrived vigorously among the nobility. But, in the nineteenth century, when a Jutland smallholder's wife out on the heath sang them for her young children, they had slid down into the lower class.[3]

Even more than Svend Grundtvig, Olrik was convinced that all extant sixteenth- and seventh-century ballad manuscripts are manuscripts form the nobility, and consequently, that they comprise an elite tradition. According to Olrik, folk songs are court poetry that later became commoners' or peasants' songs. And this opinion still prevails.

During a 1976 symposium arranged by the Centre for the Study of Vernacular Literature in the Middle Ages at the University of Odense, I questioned this opinion.[4] And since then, as a visiting researcher at the Medieval Center, I have struggled with the growing suspicion that the last 150 years of ballad research have built upon an incorrect reading of the old ballad manuscripts. Oddly enough, no one has ever carried out a critical source study of the total ballad tradition in these manuscripts.[5] This I have now tried to do. My material includes the entire ballad corpus, not only from the manuscripts, but also from additional sources.

As a result, I have formed an opinion fundamentally different from those of Grundtvig and Olrik, whose opinions no one has ever questioned. The ballad as a genre--and I mean precisely this direct and highly visual manner of narrating in song, characteristic of the old ballads--was created in the marketplace during the medieval period. After the invention of printing, the broadside authors and their producers took over the major market, selling ballads and songs to people who loved to sing about bygone days, preferably in the old style, the style, Otto Holzapfel calls characteristically "balladic."[6]

But let me present my theory. In it, my suppositions about the market-place and broadside traditions are inextricably connected with my hypothesis. I suggest a bipartite division of the texts of the oldest ballad manuscripts into folk (in the sense of peasants or townspeople), and noble traditions. In other words, by applying new methods to my sources, I will attempt the following:

> 1. To separate out the folk tradition already written down in the sixteenth and seventeenth centuries. This folk tradition consists of old ballads (before 1500), and new ballads in the old style (broadside ballads after 1500). Version D of Ebbe Skammelsøn is an example of a "new" ballad from the beginning of the sixteenth century, which was written down from oral tradition at the end of that century. Version Ca of that ballad is an example of a text copied from the broadside tradition by noblewomen in the beginning of the seventeenth century, and thus later than the text presupposed by the D-version.

> 2. To prove that the ballads among the nobility in these centuries partly consist of (more or less) adapted folk tradition, and partly of songs they have composed themselves for their evenings of song and dance at the manors. Versions A and B of Ebbe Skammelsøn are examples from a sixteenth-century nobleman (A) and noblewoman (B) who have adapted the broadside tradition which the D-redactor must have known. In the same way, a broadside composer has later adapted the ballad (Ca). Consequently, Ebbe Skammelsøn was not written by a nobleman or noblewoman.

> 3. To prove that from about 1500 to 1800 new ballads in the old style have been composed

by broadside authors, and have appeared in print, and that this broadside tradition is an important part of the folk tradition known since the sixteenth century. Ebbe Skammelsøn, in fact, originated as a broadside ballad in the beginning of the sixteenth century.

The following analysis should be understood with these points in mind. At the same time I emphasize that my characterization of the Ebbe Skammelsøn ballad variants also builds on the rigorous analysis I have made of my sources. In carrying out my project, I first analyzed these sources, and then each ballad. I emphasize my methodology particularly in this context, where I offer neither my sources, nor the entire results of my research, but instead, analyze only a single ballad in a simplified version.

Through my analysis, I will try to prove the following:

1. That D, which was written down, from folk tradition, by one of Anders Sørensen Vedel's scribes, in the 1570's or 1580's, is an orally transmitted version of a "new" ballad that originated in a broadside at the beginning of the century.

2. That A, which was written down by a friend of the young nobleman Jens Bille at the end of the 1550's, is an adaptation of the broadside tradition which the folk singer (D) also knew.

3. That B, circa 1580, which exists in the collection of an educated noblewoman interested in the ballad, Margrethe Lange, also is an adaptation of the D-tradition.

4. That Ca, which exists in an anonymous noblewoman's ballad collection, from about 1622, is a copy of a broadside version which is later than the one presupposed by the D-tradition.

During my analysis, I will compare D and the A, B, and Ca variants with a common, reconstructed version, which contains only stanzas found in at least two of these four variants. (Only two stanzas, 9 and 11, are found in only one variant, A, as I note during my analysis). I have created the common version as a tool which will make it easier to show clearly how A, B, Ca, and D compare to each other. Fundamentally, I understand the stanzas which the variants hold in common as belonging to the oldest tradition that we can accept with reasonable certainty from the existant sources.[7] These sources are, in my opinion, the ballad narrative as it was created in a broadside about 1500. In general, I regard the stanzas which only appear in one of the versions, as later additions by the <u>folksinger</u> (D), the <u>nobleman</u> (A), and the <u>noblewoman</u> (B), who all sang or recorded the ballad before 1590, and by the <u>broadside composer</u> (Ca), who presumably adapted the ballad after 1590 from an earlier copy. The analysis, then, will uncover the original ballad narrative stanza by stanza (not, of course, the original text). Despite its importance in getting closer to the unknown composer of the original ballad, the common version--I repeat--is simply an analytic tool. I do not intend it as and alternative to Olrik's reconstruction (see p. 52).

INTRODUCTION

1. <u>Skammel han bor sig nør i Thy</u>
   <u>han er både rig og kåd</u>
   <u>så høviske haver han sønner fem</u>
   <u>de to gåes verden imod</u>
   <u>Fordi træder Ebbe Skammelsøn så mange sti vild.</u>

   D1, A 1, B 1, Ca 1

/Skammel lives up north in Thy, / Wealthy and content. / He has five sons so courteous; / Fate turned on two of them. / And thus roams Ebbe Skammelsen on many stormy trails._/

In his version, the folksinger adds an extra stanza which says that the deceitful brother should have been a priest (D2). As found in humorous ballads and tales, a popular opinion held that priests were lechers who seduced honest men's wives.

In her version, the noblewoman weakens the introduction by adding two stanzas for emphasis. Beginning with the formula, "This I will say, to tell the truth," the stanzas stress that one of the brothers had a hard fate (B1 and 3). Adding a new stanza which offers unimportant information about the five brothers, the broadside's composer reveals that three of them are dead, while two others are "brave nobles" (Ca 2).

FIRST SCENE: Ebbe becomes Betrothed to Adelus

2. Det var Ebbe Skammelsøn
   han rider op under ø
   og fæster han sig stolten Adelus
   hun var så væn en mø.

D 3, B 4, C 3

/There was Ebbe Skammelsen: / He rode to distant lands. /And he plighted proud Adelus: / She was so fair a maid./

The folksinger then adds a stanza the meaning of which is clear enough, but which doesn't rhyme. Evidently the stanza has been created from an oral version of the ballad, because in including it, the singer shifts too soon to two later stanzas which he then partially repeats:

D4. "Hil sidde I stolten Adelus   see 6:1
    I gemme vel eders tro   see 6:2
    alt men jeg tjener i kongens gård   see 3:1
    alt både for guld og ære."   see 3:2

/"Here you sit, proud Adelus / You treasure well your troth; / I mean to serve at the king's court, / Both for gold and honor."/

Also aware of stanza 2, the noblewoman adds a stanza whose origin appears to have been the same failure of memory as that of the folksinger, above (D 4). She tries to cover up her error with a desperate rhyme, rhyming "honor" with "honor" (B 5). The broadside's composer adds a new stanza which says of Adelus that "she was a lily /liljevand/" whom Ebbe brought to his mother before he went abroad (Ca 4).

SECOND SCENE: Peter tempts Adelus

3. Ebbe han tjener i kongens gård
   alt både for hæder og ære
   og hjemme er hans broder
   han lokker hans hjertenskære.

D 5, B 6, Ca 5

/Ebbe serves at the king's court, / Both for glory and honor, / And at home is his brother, / Who entices his beloved./

4. Ebbe han tjener i kongens gård
   både for guld og fæ
   og Peder hans broder lader bygge et skib
   han rejser op sejle-træ.

         D 6, A 2, B 7

/Ebbe, he serves at the king's court, / Both for gold and kine, / While Peter, his brother, builds a ship / And raises up the mast._/

Allowing Peter himself to build the ship with which he sails to court Adelus, the folksinger says, "he raises the sail," which makes sense, though it doesn't rhyme.

* * *

5. Det var Peder hans broder
   han svøber sig hoved i skind
   og så går han i højeloft
   for stolte Adelus ind.

        D 7, A 3, B 8, Ca 6

/There was Peter, his brother-- / He wrapped his head in a cloak; / And so he went to the high chamber, / Went before proud Adelus._/

The folksinger sings of Peter: "And he wraps himself up in a cloak," imagining, perhaps, that he is putting on a fur coat. The predominant ballad formula, used by the noblewoman (who was obviously familiar with the tradition), "He wraps his head in a cloak" (han svøber sig hoved i skind) means that Peter intends no good. But apparently it means nothing to the folksinger. He prefers a metaphor from his own daily experience. The nobleman also begins the stanza with a formula: "In the middle of the yard, he cast his cloak over his shoulder" (da aksler han sin skind), which implies Peter's honest intent. Here, the young nobleman isn't completely familiar with this formula. The broadside's composer has watered down the formula to "dresses in scarlet robes," a pseudo-medieval archaism which contrasts with the folksinger's every-day motif for Peter, who dons a warm coat.[8]

* * *

6. "Hør I stolten Adelus
   I giver mig eders tro
   jeg vil eder elske og ære
   den stund jeg leve må."

        B 9, Ca 7

/"Listen to me, proud Adelus, / I offer you my troth. / I will love and honor you / Each hour I live."/

Since the folksinger clearly doesn't know this stanza, he condenses the whole conversation (see below, stanzas 10 and 12).

* * *

7.   "I tie kvær Peder Skammelsøn
    I siger ikke så
    jeg haver trolovet eders broder
    det ikke være må."

B 10, Ca 8

/"Be quiet, Peter Skammelsen; / Don't speak so to me. / I'm engaged to your brother; / This shall not happen."/

This stanza is rewritten by the noblewoman:

B 10. "Hvorlunde skulle jeg eder love
       med eder at bygge og bo
       spør det Ebbe eders broder
       jeg haver hannem givet min tro."

/"How shall I love you, / With you make my home? / Ask that of Ebbe, your brother. / To him I have given my troth."/

* * *

8.   "Her sidder I stolten Adelus
    I syer hr. Peder klæ'r
    Ebbe han tjener i kongens gård
    han spotter eder og hader."

A 4, Ca 9

/"Here you sit, proud Adelus; / You sew Lord Peter's robes. / Ebbe serves at the king's court, /And mocks you, hatefully./

Starting with this stanza, the broadside's composer adds a plot device totally out of keeping with the ballad's history: the mother has always regarded Ebbe as faithless and deceitful:

Ca 10. Det svarede Ebbes moder
       for hun var hannem ikke huld:
       "Lover I Peder Skammelsøn
       Ebbe han er svigefuld."

/Then said Ebbe's mother-- / For she was disloyal to
him: / "Do love Peter Skammelsen; / Ebbe is faithless
himself."7

> Ca 11. Ebbe han tjener i kongens gård
> både med tugt og ære
> den jomfru er i dronningens gård
> der han i hjertet haver kær.

/"Ebbe serves at the king's court, / With both chastity and
honor; / a maid-in-waiting to the queen / he cares for in
his heart."7

> Ca 12. Bedre må I love Peder min ældste søn
> med sin' borge så røde
> end I bi'er efter Ebbe Skammelsøn
> han lover en anden mø."

/"It's better to love my older son, / With his castles so
red, / Than to await Ebbe Skammelsen, / Who loves another
maid."7

> Ca 13. "Hør du Peder Skammelsøn
> love du dig en anden viv
> jeg vil aldrig nogen anden love
> den stund din broder er i liv'."

/"Listen, Peter Skammelsen-- / You take another wife; / I'll
not love any other / As long as your brother lives."7

* * *

> 9. Svared det stolten Adelus
> og svared hun for sig:
> "Han spotter ingen stolt jomfru
> end halve sige mig."
>
> A 5

/Then said proud Adelus, / And she answered to him: / "He
mocks no proud woman, / Much less does he mock me."7

This stanza is known only by the nobleman. Even so, it must
have belonged to the contemporary tradition upon which he
builds, since, in this stanza, as in stanza 11 (A7), the
conversation progresses in an elementary and logical
fashion. First, Peter lies about Ebbe's unfaithfulness
(st. 8). And, when Adelus doesn't believe him (9), he says
that Ebbe died "last year" (10). But, because he says it in
the same tone of voice as he used when lying about Ebbe's
unfaithfulness, she doesn't believe this lie either.

Expressed prosaically, her response implies, 'you must be in a worse state than I am, if you lie in the same shameless way about his death as you lied about his finding another.' Undoubtedly, we should understand these verses in this way. In any case, not until he says "so trustfully," that Ebbe died "in the autumn" (stanza 12), does Adelus become his betrothed (stanza 13).

* * *

10. Hør I stolten Adelus
    I giver mig eders tro
    det vil jeg for sandingen sige
    det Ebbe døde i fjor."

D 8, A 6, B 11

/̄"Listen, proud Adelus, / You plight me your troth; / This will I say, to tell the truth: / Ebbe died last year."_7

The folksinger reports that Ebbe died "yesterday," i går, his interpretation of "last year," i fjor.

* * *

11. Svared det stolten Adelus
    og svared hun for sig:
    "Halv mere skade får I deraf
    end jeg venter mig."

A 7

/̄Said then, proud Adelus, / And she answered to him, / "More harm will come of this, / Than even I expect."_7

That only the nobleman knows this stanza is explained above, under stanza 9.

* * *

12. Det var Peder hans broder
    han svared et ord så trøst:
    "Jeg siger eder sanden stolten Adelus
    Ebbe han døde i høst."

D 9, Ca 14

/There was Peter, his brother; / He answered so trustfully,
/ "I tell you the truth, proud Adelus, / Ebbe died in the
autumn."/

While the folksinger knows this stanza, he includes, in
line 2, "I giver eders tro trøst," "confidence," which
combines two lines he recalls: "I giver mig eders tro /you
give me your faith/" (D8, line 1 repeats st. 10, line 2),
and "han svared et ord med trøst /he answered in a confident
tone/" (Ca 14 line 2 repeats st. 12, line 2). While the
broadside writer also uses this stanza, here it is Ebbe's
mother who replies: "Hun svared et ord så trøst" (She
answered so trustfully).

* * *

13. Op stod stolten Adelus
så smal som en liljevand
så gav hun Peder Skammelsøn
sin tro med hviden hand.

B 12, Ca 15

/Then arose proud Adelus, / Slender as a lily, / Gave to
Peter Skammelsen / Her white hand in troth./

14. Drukke de det fæstensøl
og end den samme nat
brylluppet end før måneds dag
de råde det i-så brat.

A 9, Ca 16

/And on that very night / They drank the bride ale; / And
within the month, / Hastily, set the wedding day./

The broadside's composer rewrites the stanza:

Ca 16. De lod købe både mjød og vin
de rede til bryllup bedst
Ebbe han tjener i kongens gard
så lidet han deraf vidst'.

/They brought both mead and wine, / To ready the wedding
feast. / Ebbe serves at the king's court, / So knows little
of their plans./

THIRD SCENE: Ebbe's Dream

<u>15.</u> <u>Og det var Ebbe Skammelsøn</u>
<u>han vagned om midje-nat</u>
<u>og siger han sin næste svend</u>
<u>af sin drøm sa brat.</u>

D 10, A 10, B 13-14, Ca 17

/And there was Ebbe Skammelsen, / Awakened in the middle of
the night, / And he told the one next to him / Of his
unexpected dream.7

While the folksinger forgets the rhyme, he remembers the
meaning: "And tells his strong dream /drøm7/ to the one
lying next to him /næst7" (3-4).

The noblewoman, on the other hand, draws out the one
stanza into two:

B 13. Det var Ebbe Skammelsøn
han vågner af søvnen så brat
det vil jeg for sandingen sige
han drømte den samme nat.

/There was Ebbe Skammelsen, / Awakened from sleep suddenly.
7 This I'll say, to tell the truth, / He dreamed that same
night.7

B 14. Det var Ebbe Skammelsøn
han talte sin stærke drøm
vågen lå hans næste svend
han gav det vel igen.

/There was Ebbe Skammelsen, / He told his vivid dream. / His
companion lay awake, / And gave much thought to it.7

The broadside version is almost identical with stanza 14 of
the B version.

＊ ＊ ＊

<u>16.</u> <u>"Mig tykte min stene-stue</u>
<u>stod alt i brændend' lue</u>
<u>der brændte Peder min broder</u>
<u>og sa min skønne jomfrue."</u>

D 11, A 11, B 15, Ca 18

/"I thought my stone hall / Stood all in blazing flames; / There burned Peter, my brother, / And my fair virgin, too."/

Relying on the popular touch, the folksinger refers to the stone hall in the feminine gender: "she was in a blaze."

* * *

17. "Det I tykte din stene-stue
stod alt i brændend' lue
det bliver: Peder eders broder
drikker bryllup med jer stolte jomfrue."

D 12, A 12, B 16-17, Ca 19

/"You thought that your stone hall / Stood all in blazing flames / Because Peter, your elder brother, / Drinks wedding cup with your proud love."/

That lines one and three of the folksinger's version begin with og, "and," indicates an oral performance. Prior to this stanza, the noblewoman has added a stanza which forshadows the ballad's ending: the dream warns of the "drawn sword," cautioning that "there will be a tragic outcome" (B 16).

FOURTH SCENE: Ebbe's Homecoming

18. Det var Ebbe Skammelsøn
ganger for kongen at stand':
"Min here I giver mig orlov
alt til min faders lande."

D 13, A 13, B 18-19, Ca 20

/There was Ebbe Skammelsen, / He stood before the king: / "My lord, please grant me leave / To ride to my father's lands."/

In an added stanza with a human touch, the noblewoman's version explains that Ebbe will be missed by the king, who says, "therefore, hurry back to me again" (B 19). On the other hand, even though this is the stanza he rewrites, the broadside's author doesn't even let Ebbe ask the king for permission to leave:

Ca 20. Op stod Ebbe Skammelsøn
han bandt sig sværd ved side
så tog han sig orlov
hjem til sin fader at ride.

/Ebbe Skammelsen stood up, / His sword bound by his side; 7 So he took his leave, / Home to his father to ride.7

* * *

19. Det var Ebbe Skammelsøn
han bad sadle sin hest
det red han i dage to
som før var måneds frist.

D 14, B 20, C 21

/There was Ebbe Skammelsen, / He bade them saddle his horse, / Covered in two days the road / That before had taken a month.7

Using the more vivid variation of this formulaic stanza, the folksinger portrays an impatient and even furious Ebbe who "jumped to his horse" (2), and "rode almost more in two days, than in three months."

* * *

20. Det var Ebbe Skammelsøn
hån kom fra leding hjem
så stærke var de tidend'
der Ebbe går igen.

/There was Ebbe Skammelsen, / He came home from his travels, 7 So strong was the news / That Ebbe now heard.7

D 15, B 21

In the noblewoman's version, line 2 reads "came to his distant home."

FIFTH SCENE: Ebbe at the Castle's Entrance

21. Det var Ebbe Skammelsøn
han kom til borgeled
ude stod de smådrenge
og hviled sig derved.

D 16, B 22

/There was Ebbe Skammelsen, / He came to the castle's entrance; / There stood a small page, / And rested by the gate.7

22. "Hør I liden smådreng'
    alt hvad jeg spørger eder ad
    hvem bør disse karme til
    som stander her i dag?"

D 17, B 23

/"Listen, little page boy, / To what I ask you about. /Whose
carriages are these, / Which stand here today?"7

That line 4 of the folksinger's version says, "som stander
her," "who stand here," suggests that he may have spoken
rather than sung this verse, since he didn't remember it
very well. In a subsequent stanza the noblewoman allows the
small boy to answer: "It is the ladies . . . who live north
of the fjord. / They attend Peter Skammelsøn / Who drinks
the cup with his virgin bride."

SIXTH SCENE: Ebbe in the Courtyard

23. Det var Ebbe Skammelsøn
    han kom der ridend'i gård
    og ud stander hans moder
    hun var vel svøbt i mår.

D 18, A 14:1-2, B 25, Ca 22-23

/There was Ebbe Skammelsen, / He rode into the court; / And
there stood his mother, / All swathed in marten fur.7

Line 2 of the nobleman's version uses "in the town," instead
of "in the court" (see below, st. 24). While the noble-woman
knows this stanza, she first allows Ebbe to meet his
sisters, lines 3-4: "Then his two sisters came out. They
were dressed in marten" (B 25).

The broadside's composer creates two stanzas:

Ca 22. Det var Ebbe Skammelsøn
       han kom så vel i lag
       han kom til sin faders gård
       den første bryllupsdag.

/There was Ebbe Skammelsen, / He came at so fast a pace;
7 He came to his father's court / On the very first wedding
day.7

Ca 23. Det var Ebbe Skammelsøn
       han kom der ridend' i gård
       ude da stod den liden smådreng
       var klædt i kjortel blå.

/There was Ebbe Skammelsen, / He came riding into the court; / Out there stood a little page boy / Clad in a mantle of blue._7

* * *

24. "Hør I det min kære moder
alt hvad jeg spørger eder ad
hvem er disse mange folk
der er forsamlet idag?"

D 19, A 14:3-4, B 27, C 24

/"Listen to me, my dear mother, / And answer my question: / Who are all these people, / Who gather here today?"_7

Again, in line 4 the nobleman's version has "from town," and "in town" (see above, st. 23). Though the noblewoman is familiar with the stanza, she has Ebbe ask "my dear sisters two" (see above, st. 23). On the other hand, the broadside's composer, who also includes this stanza, has Ebbe ask his "small boy."

* * *

25. Hans moder hun svared
af angest og nød:
"Det er Peder din broder
drikker bryllup med din mø."

D 20, A 15, B 28, Ca 25

/His mother then answered him, / In distress and dread: / "It is your brother Peter, / Drinking the wedding cup with your love."_7

Since the folksinger knows this stanza, his version is one which the original singer himself might have written, despite stanza 26. At first his stanza seems simply a poetic metaphor. But it is, in fact, a realistic observation: "It has stayed bright a long time this evening." Besides adding poetic realism, the stanza functions to allow his mother to warn Ebbe not to stay, since she suspects that some tragedy will occur:

D 21. "Solen hun sidder så højt i aften
du ma vel heden ride
og bliver du her i denne nat
du gør os alle stor kvide."

/"The sun is so high this evening, / You can ride well over the health. / And you shouldn't stay here; / You'll cause much trouble for us."7

In the nobleman's version of stanza 25, "The little virgin/ all in her red dress," is the one who answers. But in the noblewoman's version, her two sisters answer, "out of much necessity." Since in his version Ebbe's page boy answers, the broadside's composer must have rewritten the stanza somewhat (see above, st. 24):

> Ca 25. "Det er os det møgle folk
> som er forsamlet her
> det volder Peder eders broder
> drikker bryllup med eders hjertenskær."

/"All these people you see / Gather here to celebrate, / Because Peter, your brother, / Drinks the wedding cup with your love."7

* * *

> 26. Ebbe han vender sin ganger omkring
> han ville af gården ride
> hand moder tog i tøjlen og holdt
> og bad hannem hjemme bide.

A 16, B 31, C 29

/Ebbe turned his horse around; / He would ride from the court. / His mother seized the bridle / And bade him stay at home.7

While the folksinger doesn't include this stanza, apparently influenced by it, in stanza 21 he also rhymes "ride," and "bide" (see above, st. 25). At this point the nobleman includes a stanza in which Ebbe says that it would be best for all parties if he rode away (A 17).

In the noblewoman's version, not until this stanza does the mother appear in the yard. But since by this time Ebbe has long spoken with his sisters, and since he has given them the gifts intended for Adelus, she adds a stanza as a prelude to stanza 26:

> B 30. Den ene søster bad hannem hjemme være
> den anden bad hannem hen ride:
> "Tøver du her i denne nat
> det bliver os alle til kvide."

/One of his sisters bade him stay, / The other bade him
ride: / "You should not delay; / To stay will cause much
woe."_7

Here the broadside includes a stanza in which the
mother simultaneously asks Ebbe to stay and mourns because
she can't allow him to stay. While this emotional moment is
understandable since a mother is speaking, it belongs in a
sentimental broadside rather than in an impersonally
narrated ballad:

> Ca 30. Hans moder holdt i tøjlen hårdt
> og bad hannem hjemme bi'e
> nu sørger hun så såre
> for hun lod ham ikke ride.

/His mother gripped the reins, / And bade him stay at
home;_/ Now she regrets so sorely, / That she didn't let him
ride._7

* * *

> 27. Ud kom Ebbes søstre to
> de favnet der deres broder komme
> han var dennem meget bedre kommen
> det både med glæde og fromme.

> D 22, B 26, Ca 26

/Out came Ebbe's two sisters, / Who rejoiced at his return;
7 They were so pleased at his coming, / Both showed delight
and joy._7

Again, in the folksong line 1 begins with the oral "og,"
"and." In her version, the noblewoman revises line 4 to
"home to our own country." The broadside's composer also
varies this stanza:

> Ca 26. Ud da gik hans søstre to
> de favnet deres broders komme
> han var dennem meget bedre kommen
> end enten sin fader eller moder.

/Out came Ebbe's two sisters / Who rejoiced at their
brother's return; / They were more _pleased at his
coming, / Than either his father or mother._7

In this stanza the broadside's author deliberately allows
the mother to speak evil of Ebbe.

* * *

28. Den ene gav han guldbrasen på bryste
    den anden guldringe på hand
    dem tjente han i kongens gård
    havde agtet sin liljevand.

                    D 23, A 18, B 29, Ca 27

/Gave to one a gold pin for her breast, / The other, a gold
ring for her hand; / While serving at the king's court, / He
bought them for his lily-white love./

Again, in this stanza, the folksinger begins a line, line 3,
with the oral "and."

SEVENTH SCENE: Ebbe in the Bridal Hall

29. Hans moder bød hannem hynde og stol
    bad hannem sidde til bænk
    hans fader fik hannem kande i hånd
    bad hannem gå at skaenk'.

                    D 24, A 19, B 32, Ca 31

/His mother offered him cushion and stool, / Bade him sit at
the bench; / His father took up the pitcher, / Asked him to
pour the wine./

In his version of this stanza, the folksinger is
uncertain about line 3, which he doesn't fully remember:
this line, which begins, "he got the pitcher," is thus
spoken rather than sung.

In addition, he opens the scene in the wedding room
with a formulaic stanza:

D 24. Det var Ebbe Skammelsøn
      han ind af døren tren
      og det var hans kære moder
      hun stander hannem op igen.

/There was Ebbe Skammelsen, / He came in through the
door; / And there was his mother dear-- / So as to receive
him, she stood./

In line 2, the nobleman stresses that Ebbe sits in "the
upper benches." The broadside version, on the other hand,
simply states that they "asked him to sit at the table and
bench," making the line too long with this variation.

                    * * *

30. Det var Ebbe Skammelsøn
    ham gange at skænke vin
    men hvergang han til bruden så
    da rinder hannem tåre på kind

D 26, A 20, B 33, Ca 32

/There was Ebbe Skammelsen, / He went to pour the
wine; / But at each filling of Adelus' cup, / The tears ran
down his face._7

Formulating this episode in a slightly different
fashion, the nobleman adds two stanzas of competent
narration about Ebbe's irritation because the women speak of
nothing but his grief. While these stanzas are well-
composed, unfortunately, they impede the ballad's dramatic
progression:

A 20. Skænkte han den brune mjød
       og så den klare vin
       hver tit han til bruden så
       da randt ham tår' på kind.

/He poured out the brown mead / And also the clear
wine, / But as often as he served the bride, / The tears ran
down his face._7

A 21. Mælte det de fruer
       alt på de øverste bænke:
       "Hvi mon Ebbe Skammelsøn
       så sørgendes gå at skænke?"

/Then a woman spoke, / All from the topmost bench: / "Why,
my Ebbe Skammelsen, do you / So sorrowfully pour the wine?"_7

A 22. "I æder og I drikker
       mjød og klaren vin
       at få I andet at tale
       end om sorrigen min."

/"You eat, and you drink / Mead and clear wine / That cause
you to speak freely, / Even about my sorrow."_7

By having Ebbe ask his father if he might be excused
from pouring the wine, the broadside's composer draws out
this episode. He further extends it by having the mother,
totally without feeling for the situation, advise Ebbe that
"he should go to bed." This line, might, of course, be
understood as advising Ebbe to accompany Adelus to the
bridal chamber:

Ca 32. Ebbe han skænkte for bruden vin
       hun skinned' alt som en guld
       hver en sinde han til bruden så
       da blev han sørgefuld.

/Ebbe, he poured wine for the bride, / She shone like
precious gold; / Each time he filled her cup, / He felt so
sorrowful./

Ca 33. Det var Ebbe Skammelsøn
       han skænked' alt så længe
       så bad hav sig lov af fader sin
       om han mått' gå til bænke.

/There was Ebbe Skammelsen, / He poured for so long a
time; / He asked his father for his leave, / So he might go
to his bench./

Ca 34. Der stod han en liden stund
       og ikke halve længe
       råde hans kære moder hannem
       at han ville gå til senge.

/There he stayed but a little while, / And there not half as
long / When his dear mother advised him / That he should go
to bed./

* * *

31. Det var silde om den aften
    der røgen faldt på
    det var da den unge brud
    hun skulle til sengen gå.

                              D 27, A 23, B 34

/It was late in the evening, / He fire had died
down; / There was the young bride / Who must go to her bed./

In this stanza, the folksinger doesn't recall lines 3 and 4
very well: he combines stanzas 31 and 32.

* * *

32. Ledte de den unge brud
    alt til sit brudehus
    da bad Ebbe sig lov dertil
    at bære for hender blus.

                       D 27, A 24, B 35, Ca 35

/They led the young bride / All to her bridal
chamber; / Then Ebbe asked her leave / To bear a light for
her./

In his version, the folksinger combines this stanza with
stanza 31.

The broadside variant, however, offers a totally
different stanza:

> Ca 35 Det var Ebbe Skammelsøn
> tog bruden under sin arm
> det vil jeg for sanden sige
> hans hjerte det var vel harmt.

/There was Ebbe Skammelsen, / He gave the bride his
arm; / This will I say, to tell the truth, / He was so
sorely angry./

EIGHTH SCENE: Ebbe and Adelus in the High Chamber's Balcony

> 33. Det var Ebbe Skammelsøn
> han kom på højeloftsbro:
> "Og mindes eder, stolten Adelus,
> I gav mig eders tro?"

> D 28, A 25, B 36, Ca 36

/There was Ebbe Skammelsen, / He came to the balcony
high: / "Do you remember, proud Adelus, / You pledged to me
your troth?"/

In lines 1 and 2 of his variant, the nobleman adds a courtly
touch: "He led the young bride along the high chamber's
balcony," and in line 4, a more literary phrase: "And hold
you that in mind?"

* * *

> 34. "Al den tro der Gud mig gav
> den giver jeg Peder eders broder
> all de dage jeg leve må
> da vil jeg være eder for moder."

> D 29, A 26, B 37, Ca 37

/"All the troth God gave me, / I gave to Peter, your
brother; / All the days of my life, / I will be to you as a
mother."/

The folksinger commits a serious error in line 4, which reads, "I will care for him /Peter7 as a mother."

* * *

35. Det svared Ebbe Skammelsøn
     både med tugt og ære:
     "Jeg lovet eder til min fæstemø
     ikke til min moder at være."

                              A 27, B 38, Ca 38

Then answered Ebbe Skammelsen, / In all chastity and honor: / "I pledged you for my true love, / Not to be my mother."7

In his variant, for line 2, the nobleman says, "A tear ran down his cheek," and in line 3, "I intended you to be my wife."

     The broadside balladeer also varies this stanza:

          Ca 38. "Jeg lovet eder ikke til min moder
                  jeg lovet eder til min viv
                  derfor skal Peder Skammelsøn
                  lade sit unge liv."

/"I pledged you not for my mother, / I pledged you as my wife. / Therefore shall Peter Skammelsen, / pay for this with his life."7.

                         * * *

36. "Hør du stolten Adelus
     du følger mig af land
     da vil jeg slå min broder ihjel
     og tåle for eder den vand'."

                              D 30, A 28, B 39, Ca 39

/"Listen to me, proud Adelus, / Follow me from this land. / I will slay my brother, / And bear for you this crime."7

37. "Slår du Peder din broder ihjel
     siden skal du mig miste
     så må du sørge dig selv ihjel
     som vilden fulge pa kviste."

                              D 31, A 29, B 40, Ca 40

/"If you kill your brother Peter, / You shall also lose me, / Then you'll die of sorrow, / Like a wild bird on a branch."7

Line 4 of the noblewoman's variant reads: "Like turtledoves on twigs."

* * *

38. Det var Ebbe Skammelsøn
og han sit sværd uddrog
det var jomfru Adelus
han alt i stykker hug.

D 32, A 30, B 43, Ca 41

/There was Ebbe Skammelsen, / And he has drawn his sword; / There was the maiden Adelus: / He cut her all to shreds.7

Clearly meaning surpasses form in lines 3 and 4 of the folksinger's version: "Then he cut the noble Adelus / into little bits" (alt i stykker små).

In a more fully developed episode, the noblewoman leads up to the killing slowly, to reveal even more detail:

B 41.   Det var Ebbe Skammelsøn
han vredes ved de ord
han blev i hans hu så mod
han svared dog ikke et ord.

/There was Ebbe Skammelsen, / He's angered by these words; / He remains fixed in his purpose, / Yet still says not a word.7

B 42.   Så fulgte de den unge brud
i det brudehus ind
det var Ebbe Skammelsøn
drog sværd under skarlagenskind.

/So he follows the young bride / Into the bridal chamber; / There was Ebbe Skammelsen, / Drawn sword under cloak so red.7

B 43.   Det var Ebbe Skammelsøn
han tøved' og ikke længe
så vog han den unge brud
alt for sin brudeseng'.

/There was Ebbe Skammelsen / He lingered not at all; / The young bride he slew / All by her bridal bed._7

> B 44. Han vog bruden for brudeseng
> det var så stor en harm
> det var den høje guldkron'
> hun i det røde svam.

/He slew her by her bridal bed-- / That was so heavy a cut, / That was her high gold crown: / She swam in her own red blood._7

NINTH SCENE: Ebbe and Peter

> <u>39.</u> <u>Så tog han det blodige sværd</u>
> <u>alt under sit skarlagenskind</u>
> <u>så går han i brudesal</u>
> <u>for Peder sin broder ind.</u>

D 33, A 31, B 45, Ca 42

/Then he took the bloody sword / All under his scarlet cloak, / Went then to the wedding hall, / For Peter, his brother, within._7

Terms for the scene of the slaying differ from variant to variant: the folksinger sets it in the "high loft" (the upper chamber), the nobleman, the "stone hall," the noblewoman, the "bridal hall," and the broadside's composer, the "hall." Line 1 of the broadside portrays a more grisly action: "Then he took the blood-stained head."

* * *

> <u>40.</u> <u>"Hør du Peder Skammelsøn</u>
> <u>du dvæler alt for længe</u>
> <u>bruden længes fast efter dig</u>
> <u>udi sin brudeseng."</u>

D 34, A 32, B 46, Ca 43

/"Listen, Peter Skammelsen, / You tarry all too long; / The bride steadfastly awaits you, / All in her bridal bed."_7

In presenting this scene in two stanzas rather than one, the nobleman creates, in his second stanza, a favorable picture of Peter, who sits in the stone hall, preoccupied with a game:

A 32. "Hør du Peder Skammelsøn
       og du tøver alt for længe
       det er alt en sejerstund
       sid'n bruden gik til senge."

/"Listen, Peter Skammelsen, / You linger all too long;
7It's been all of an hour / Since the bride has gone to bed."7

A 33. "Hør du Peder Skammelsøn
       du får far' alt med leg
       bruden sidder i brudeseng
       bi'er dig efter bleg."

/"Listen, Peter Skammelsen, / Stop playing your game; / The
bride sits in the bridal bed / Awaiting you, so pale."7

The broadside's composer reworks the stanza a bit:

Ca 43. "Du stat op Peder broder min
        skynd dig til brudeseng
        din unge brud haver så længe sidd't
        og lidt fast efter dig."

/"Stand up, Peter, my brother / get yourself to the bridal
bed; / Your young bride has sat so long, / And awaits you
steadfastly."7

* * *

41. Hør de Ebbe Skammelsøn
     du lad bortfare din harm
     jeg lader dig i denne nat
     at sove i brudens arm.

D 35, A 34, B 48, Ca 44

/"Listen, Ebbe Skammelsen, / Let your anger cool; / I'll
allow you--for tonight-- / In the bride's arms to sleep."7

Further, the noblewoman includes a few stanzas about
Peter, who is so terrified of Ebbe that he pleads for mercy
on his knees:

B 47. Det var Peder Skammelsøn
       han var i hjertet så ve
       sa vel kunn' han på Ebbe se
       at han var vorden vred.

/There was Peter Skammelsen / He felt terror in his
heart; / He saw only too well, / That Ebbe was filled with
rage./

B 48 is identical to 41

B 49. "Hør du det Ebbe Skammelsøn
        og kære broder min
        jeg vil give dig stolt Adelus
        dog hun er unge brud min."

/"Listen to this, Ebbe Skammelsen-- / And you're my brother
dear-- / I'll give you proud Adelus, / Who is my young bride
still."/

B 50. "Du stat op Peder Skammelsøn
        og gak til din mø
        første du kommer til din brudeseng
        den er med roser strø'd."

/"You stand up, Peter Skammelsen, / Go now to your
love; / First you'll come to the bridal bed / All with roses
strewn./

A version of this stanza used by the broadside's writer
may well have been the source for stanzas 47 and 49 of the
noblewoman's version. He creates a weak stanza:

Ca 44. "Hør du Ebbe Skammelsøn   same as B 49:1
         du gør dig ikke så vred   see B 47:4
         jeg lover dig kære broder min see B 49:2
         at sove selv hos unge brud din." see B 49:4

/"Listen, Ebbe Skammelsen, / Don't be so angry; / I promise,
my dear brother / That you'll sleep with my young bride."/

* * *

42. Det var Ebbe Skammelsøn
     og han sit sværd uddrog
     det var Peder hans broder
     han alt i stykker hug.

                        D 36, A 35, B 51, Ca 45

/There was Ebbe Skammelsen / And he has drawn his
sword; / Shere was Peter, his brother, / Ebbe cut him to
shreds./

The noblewoman reworks the stanza in a rather effective way:

B 51. Det var Peder Skammelsøn
        han over bordet løb
        det var Ebbe hans broder
        han kløv hannem hoved i skød.

/There was Peter Skammelsen, / The table he o'er
leapt; / There was Ebbe, his brother, / Struck Peter's head
in his lap._7

CONCLUSION

43. Hans Fader gjorde han ilde sår
hans moder miste en hand
fordi træder Ebbe Skammelsøn
så mange vild sti om land
Fordi træder Ebbe Skammelsøn så mange sti vild.

D 37, A 36, B 52, Ca 46

/His father was wounded sore, / His mother lost her
hand; / Thus roams Ebbe Skammelsen / On many wild trails on
land. / Thus roams Ebbe Skammelsen on many wild trails._7

The folksinger has a different version:

D 37. Det var stor ynk i brudehus
og end halvmere harm
Peder han miste sit unge liv
hans moder sin højre arm.

/There was great misery in the bridal chamber / And even
much more harm; / Peter has lost his young life, / His
mother, her right arm._7

The noblewoman's version of this episode recalls D 37,
above:

B 52. Der var ynk i brudehus
i salen der var stor harm
brud og brudgom de blev der død
Ebbes moder miste sin højre arm.

/There was misery in the bridal chamber, / in the hall there
was great harm; / bride and bridegroom were dead, / Ebbe's
mother lost her right arm._7

But thereafter she adds a marvelous scene which seems
lifted from the devotional literature she must have been so
deeply absorbed in when she wasn't studying the old ballads.
Here she adds the educated woman's common knowledge of
penance by iron in the middle ages:[9]

B 53. Ebbe han lod sig jerne-slå
både om fod og hand
siden trådt' han så mange vild sti
så vidt i fremmede land.

/Ebbe is in iron bands, / Fettered both hand and
foot, / Then he roams many wild trails, / Many wild trails
in foreign lands._7

> B 54. Det var Ebbe Skammelsøn
> gik over Peders grav
> alle var de jerne-bånd
> de sprang hannem selver af.

/There was Ebbe Skammelsen / Passing o'er Peter's
grave / When the bands of iron / Sprang off of their own
accord._7

> B 55. Det var Ebbe Skammelsøn
> han rakte op hænder sine:
> "Lovet være Gudfader i Himmerig
> forladt er synder mine."
> Fordi træder Ebbe Skammelsøn så mange sti vild.

/There was Ebbe Skammelsen; / he lifted up his
hands: / "Praise to the good Father in Heaven-- / gone is my
visage of sin." / Thus roams Ebbe Skammelsen on many wild
trails._7

Having compared the ballad variants, I would like to
discuss the relationship of the broadside Ca with the
Tragica variant, Ha, from Vedel's collection, and with a
variant from the more recent folk tradition, Hf. At his
death in 1616, Vedel left an uncompleted manuscript of a new
collection of ballads, which should have continued his well-
known 1591 edition. Among the ballads which he had started
to adapt was Ebbe Skammelsøn. In 1656, the noblewoman Mette
Gjøe published his manuscript under the title Tragica. While
she published it anonymously, and out of respect for the
grand old man of medieval balladry, she still has added
stanzas in places where she had found some missing. This
Ebbe Skammelsøn text has since been reprinted several times
by the broadside publishers in the seventeenth and
eighteenth centuries.

Axel Olrik discusses this variant's sources:

> The Tragica variant mainly is a
> compilation of versions B and C; in addition,
> Vedel knew E, in an older version than we now
> possess. Further, aside from an occasional
> line, he has written stanzas 6-7, 14, 23, and
> 70, himself. He also has had in hand the D
> variant, which he has started to correct, but
> which he has instead put aside since it is
> highly distorted.[10]

No doubt Olrik correctly says that Ha is a compilation of the B and C texts. This assumption also has been confirmed by Sophus Larsen, in his precise analysis of the _Ebbe_ variants.[11] But Vedel can't have composed the complete _Tragica_ text, because he didn't know the B variant from Margrethe Langes' collection. On the other hand, we can now prove that he has used Ca, referring, at the same time, to D, which was in his own ballad archives. Mette Gjøe, _Tragica_'s publisher, has added some stanzas from the B version of Margrethe Langes' collection, which Gjøe owned, and which, by the way, she is said to have used for her edition. Among other things, Vedel has borrowed the newly written scene from Ca, in which Ebbe's mother says that Adelus should marry Peter, because Ebbe is faithless or deceitful.

As mentioned before, Ca exists in a noblewoman's manuscript form 1622, namely the one which archivists call Sophia Sandberg's manuscript. My researches have shown that both this manuscript, and other noblewomen's manuscripts from the beginning of the seventeenth century, contain many copies of broadside ballads, which seemed old to them. They sometimes borrowed these broadsides from their servants or neighbors, returning them after having made a copy. No doubt Vedel had come across a copy of that variant of the ballad which we now know only from Sophia Sandberg's manuscript. For Vedel didn't keep these cheap prints. Strangely enough, his ballad archives contain not one single extant broadside print, even though in a few cases we can prove that he obviously has copied a broadside print available elsewhere.

At times it is impossible, solely from stylistic criteria, to determine whether an older ballad has been adapted by a noblewoman, or by a professional ballad writer. We can argue for the latter if we later find in the folk tradition the adaptation that has been made. If we do find it in oral circulation, this fact testifies to its having been made for the use of a more popular audience. Apparently, such is the case with Ca. In 1870 Ane Johanne Jensdatter from Gellerup in the Hammerum district of Jutland remembered some characteristic fragments of the Ebbe ballad (Hf).[12] Those portions she recalled tell that the faithful Adelus gives way to Peter only because Ebbe's mother has advised her to do so. Also, Adelus tells Ebbe that he shouldn't kill Peter, because by so doing he will be exiled, and thus will lose her.

Olrik writes that these fragments are the "only trace of the fact that the Ebbe ballad persists in oral tradition, partially independent of the broadside tradition"--in this case the _Tragica_ text. Olrik can prove that Hf, which he terms Ane Johanne Jensdatter's fragment, contains a few characteristic expressions and phrases from "the old written collections." To a certain extent Olrik's basic opinion suggests a _gesunkenes kulturgut_ approach. However, it appears that among those "old written collections," Ca shares a few features with Hf. In my opinion, this correspondence further testifies to Ca's having been published in a broadside, that is, for popular use.

The ballad itself, then, originated as a broadside in the early sixteenth century. It was composed at a time when, in the wake of common interest in past traditions, the ballad producers began writing ballads based upon ancient Danish local myths and upon events from Danish history. The Ebbe Skammelsøn tradition is from Jutland, and, judging from the sixteenth-century versions (A, B, D), it seems to have enjoyed special favor there. These three versions all show certain Jutlandish touches. As Erik Dal notes, Kristian Hald, in a unpublished paper on the Ebbe ballad, ties the ballad "to Jutland even more strongly than it previously has been connected." Further, Hald rejects "attempts to localize the ballad, as well as to find other chronological clues for it, other than those the genre itself offers as evidence."[13] Through a broadside, especially in the Ca variant, the ballad has been known in Sweden, where it appears in a ballad manuscript from the beginning of the 1620s.[14] In the nineteenth century, it appears in both Swedish and Norwegian folk tradition.

But which of the extant versions of Ebbe Skammelsøn do critics consider the best? Olrik, who dates the ballad at "the earliest, about 1263, the latest, about 1300," has tried to reconstruct its basic form. This reconstruction, which at essential points builds on A, has dominated research on the Ebbe ballad. In fact, many scholars have simply taken for granted that this version is the ballad about Ebbe Skammelsøn. Olrik prints this reconstruction both in DgF and in his selections for popular use.[15] Hakon Gruner-Nielsen[16] and Ernst Frandsen,[17] who do not intend to include reconstructions in their popular editions, choose A as the best text. And Jørgen Lorenzen does so also.[18] Even Erik Dal says, "...few will deny that the old version, A, ...is the best of the genuine versions. We have, however, after much deliberation, selected another version / Ca /, in order to show that the /ballad/, can be, and most often is, broader in its composition than it is usually seen, without its, for this reason, ceasing to be a masterpiece /within/ its genre."[19]

Though Ernst von der Recke's reconstruction hasn't added to scholarly knowledge, his opinion of the ballad variants is sound. He considers it "most likely, that the two old Danish manuscript versions, B and D,...have kept the plot lines purest." On the other hand, according to von der Recke, A shows an "impossible combination" of episodes, and C, while more consistent than A, "is most strongly of all characterized by unoriginality. Furthermore, it is only here we come across additional episodes and features. In B, on the other hand, the additions are mainly the all too familiar padding, which usually belongs to the period when they were written down."[20] This observation suggests that without realizing it, von der Recke perceives that the folksinger's version is the best, because he has maintained the plot in its purest form.

That Olrik uses the nobleman's adaptation in his reconstruction so frequently, and that several ballad scholars prefer A, is significant. Without realizing it, they who don't wish to reconstruct, use a reconstruction of the ballad. Something similar has happened to Dal, who, though completely unaware of it, uses Ca, a broadside writer's adaptation from the end of the sixteenth century. And it is a better choice than that of his predecessors, in so far as it is a version for popular use. If, however, we want to show in a popular edition that the ballads are folksongs, not ruins of poetry from the medieval period, which are worthless until reconstructed by scholars or nobility, we should, of course, choose D, the folksinger's version.

NOTES

In general, the reader is referred to Iørn Piø, <u>Nye veje til folkevisen: Studier i Danmarks gamle Folkeviser</u> (Copenhagen: Gyldendal, 1985). Since my view of the sources of Danish ballads differs significantly from the prevalent opinion, many of my assertions about <u>Ebbe Skammelsøn</u> can be fully understood only by consulting this book. In it I also explain why E, F, and G, which were all recorded, adapted, and copied by the nobility in the seventeenth century are not included in my analysis. Further, I explain the relationship between Ca and Cb, Cc, and Cd.

[1]Axel Olrik, <u>Danmarks gamle Folkeviser</u>, VI (1895-98; Rpt., Copenhagen: Universitets-Jubilæets Danske Samfund, 1967), pp. 197-252.

[2]Erik Dal, ed., <u>Danish Ballads and Folksongs</u>, trans. Henry H. Meyer (Copenhagen and New York: American-Scandinavian Foundation; Rosenkilde & Bagger, 1967), p. 273.

[3]Axel Olrik, <u>Nogle grundsætninger for sagnforskning</u> / Principles for Folklore Research /, ed. Hans Ellekilde, <u>Danmarks Folkeminder</u>, No. 23 (Copenhagen: Schønbergsske, 1921), p. 41.

[4]Iørn Piø, "On Reading Orally-performed Ballads: The Medieval Ballads of Denmark," in <u>Oral Tradition-Literary Tradition: A Symposium</u>, ed. Hans Bekker-Nielsen, et al. (Odense: Odense University Press, 1977), pp. 69-82.

[5]Iørn Piø, "Nyvurdering af den danske middelalderballade" /"A New Evaluation of the Danish Medieval Ballad"/, <u>Humaniora</u>, 4 (Copenhagen, 1981), pp. 119-23. Also see my "Walrabe, Werwolf und Wassermann: Mittelalterliche Überlieferung und romantisches Pastiche in skandinavischer Balladentradition," <u>DFS-Translations</u>, No. 3 (Copenhagen: Dansk Folkemindsamling, 1975), a revision and translation of my articles in <u>Danske Studier 1969</u> (DgF 33, 60) and <u>1970</u> (DgF 38). Also see my "Markeds- og folkeviser i skillingstryk" /"The Market- and Folksongs in Broadsides"/ in <u>Budskaber gennem det trykte ord</u>, Udsendt i anledning af 500-året for bogtrykkunstens indførelse i Danmark (Copenhagen: Dansk Typograf-Forbund, 1982), pp. 49-59, and "Folkeviseproducenten H. L. S. Winding fra Fyn," in <u>Hvad Fatter gjør</u>

... Boghistoriske, litterære og musikalske essays tilegnet Erik Dal (Herning: Poul Kristensen, 1982), pp. 362-70.

[6]Otto Holzapfel, Det balladeske: Fortællemaaden i den ældre episke folkevise / The Balladic: Narrative Style in the Early Epic Folk Songs / (Odense: Odense Universitetsforlag, 1980).

[7]Compare Olrik, Nogle grundsætninger, p. 117.

[8]Compare Holzapfel, Det balladeske, especially pp. 50-51, with additional references in his Studien zur Formelhaftigkeit der mittelalterchen dänischen Volkballade. Diss. (Frankfurt am Main: Universitat, 1969). Among other things, Holzapfel encourages a closer analysis of the variations in formulas and the use of those variations: "Such an investigation /also/ might be used to better evaluate the position of each manuscript within the entire tradition" (translated from the Danish).

[9]Compare Holzapfel, Det balladeske, pp. 36-37: "When Ebbe Skammelsøn allows himself to 'be fettered hand and foot in irons,' or 'allows himself to be chained in iron fetters,' (DgF 354), we recognize a well-known medieval penance which can be explained by existing conditions. This motif is transferred to the ballad to show that the hero has sinned. Even though the motif appears in several ballads, there is little doubt that it can be traced to one place. It can even be used to date this version of the ballad from 'Catholic' times" (translated from the Danish). I don't, however, agree that we can date this version with the motif.

[10]Danmarks gamle Folkeviser, VI, 244.

[11]Sofus Larsen, Ebbe Skammelsøns Vise (Copenhagen: Carlsbergfondet, Hagerup, 1923).

[12]Recorded in 1870 by Evald Tang Kristensen and published in his Gamle Viser i Folkemunde, IV, Jyske Folkeminder, No. 11 (Copenhagen & Viborg: Gyldendalske & V. Backhausen, 1891).

[13]Erik Dal and Iørn Piø, eds., Danmarks gamle Folkeviser, 10, No. 2 (1960-65; rpt. Copenhagen: Universitets-Jubilæets Danske Samfund, 1967), p. 796.

[14]Bengt R. Jonsson, Svensk balladtradition, I (Stockholm: Svenskt Visarkiv, 1967), p. 755.

[15]Axel Olrik, with Ida Falbe-Hansen, <u>Danske Folkeviser</u>, I (Copenhagen: Gyldendalske, 1899).

[16]H. Grüner-Nielsen, <u>Danske Folkeviser</u>, II (Copenhagen: Dansk Bogsamling, Martins, 1927).

[17]Ernst Frandsen, ed., <u>Danske Folkeviser i Udvalg /A Selection of Danish Folksongs /</u> (Copenhagen: Dansklærer-foreningen & Gyldendalske, 1937).

[18]Jørgen Lorenzen, ed., <u>Danske Folkeviser</u>, I (Copenhagen: G.E.C. Gad, 1974).

[19]Dal, <u>Danish Ballads and Folksongs</u>, p. 273.

[20]Ernst von der Recke, ed., <u>Danmarks Fornviser</u>, II (Copenhagen: Møller & Landschultz, 1928).

Danish Folklore Archives
Copenhagen;

Odense University
The Center for the Study of Vernacular Literature in the
    Middle Ages
Odense, Denmark

Translated from the Danish by Jette Holland Andersen and Carol L. Edwards

SYSTEMS OF CLASSIFICATION

GREEN GROWS THE LAUREL

J. Evans stall print #25242.73 in the Harvard University
Library. Original: Long-Lane, London.

1. I have oftentimes wondered how women loved men,
   But I oftimes have wondered how men could
       love them;
   They will love you a little and give your
       heart ease,
   And when your back's on them, they'll love
       who they please.

Chorus. Then green grows the laurel, and so does the rue;
   How sad's been the day I parted from you!
   But at our next meeting our love we'll renew;
   We'll change the green laurel for the origin blue.

2. Some will love a short love, and others love long,
   Some will love a weak love, and others love strong;
   Some will love a short love, and others love long,
   And some will love an old love till the new
       love comes in.

3. I wrote my love a letter all bounded in pain;
   She wrote me another all bounded the same:
   Say, "You may keep your promise and
       I will keep mine;
   We'll change the green laurel for the origin blue."

4. On the top of yon mountain, where the green
       grass doth grow,
   Way down in yon valley, where the still waters flow,
   I saw my old true love, and she had proved true;
   We changed the green laurel for the origin blue.

TRISTRAM POTTER COFFIN

A METHOD OF INDEXING THE TEXTS OF THE ANGLO-AMERICAN LOVE LYRIC

Ever since the close of World War II, when the late MacEdward Leach began a series of bibliographical and analytical guides to the various forms of American folksong,[1] folklorists interested in such things have found themselves frustrated by the Anglo-American love lyric with its <u>floating stanzas</u>. These are the songs which H. M. Belden, one of the first scholars to give them attention, called "expressions of mood, feeling, not stories."[2] These songs usually contain stanzas such as the following one:

> I wrote my love a letter with roses entwined;
> He wrote me an answer all twisted and twined
> Saying "You keep your letters, I will keep mine;
> You write to your sweetheart and I'll write to mine"

or

> A meeting is pleasure, a parting is grief,
> But an unconstant lover is worse than a thief.
> A thief he will rob you and take what you have,
> But an unconstant lover will lead you to the grave.

Because these lyric songs have no plots and sketch out the most rudimentary situations of parting, inconstancy, or regret, because of the casual fashion in which they mingle and separate, and perhaps because of the huge body of such material, no folklorist has solved the problem of classifying the love lyric in the convenient way in which the forms of the ballad have been classified. This paper is a step toward the correction of this situation. As such, it attempts to offer a method of classification that will bring about an analytical index to the love lyric and perhaps to similar forms such as the Black blues, the play-party, the sea shanty and similar work-gang songs.

The present paper is not the initial effort at solving the problems of love lyric classification. Personally, I toyed with the subject in the early 1950s,[3] and in 1976 made it the topic of a folksong research project at the University of Pennsylvania. At that time, four graduate students came up with what I considered to be workable methods of love lyric classification. The students were Michael Chalmers, Alan S. Forman, Barbara Reimensnyder, and

Etheldreda Vukmanovich. And, if there were marked differences in the methodology used, all four came to a conclusion stated so well in the Reimensnyder paper:

> I am not sure that the name lyric song is as positive an identification as the name ballad, that these songs <u>can</u> be identified as such hard-and-fast, inviolable historical entities as the ballads. Lyric songs, lacking the cohesiveness which the junctures of narrative provide for the ballad, appear, rather as assemblages which cohere through the strength of the emotion which they express.[4]

Moreover, all four nibbled at the idea of a classification system based on music. And all four rejected it.

I repeat, when approaching love lyric classification from the textual point of view one can't use plot to label the various pieces, for by definition no identifiable story exists. Some of the lyrics are, however, relatively easy to deal with because they possess constant stanzas or stanza patterns which are widely used to give them fixed titles: "Green Grow the Lilacs," "Careless Love," "On Top of Old Smokey," "Who's Goin' To Shoe My Pretty Little Feet?" Such songs can be labelled by the widely known title and given a Roman numeral designation much in the way Child and Laws numbers serve for the ballads. And, no matter what floating material associates itself with the variants of these lyrics, the fixed stanzas remain identifiable. It is the lyrics without fixed stanzas (with what I will call <u>inconstant stanzas</u>, where the floating material forms and reforms patterns as if in a kaleidescope) that the real difficulty of love lyric identification comes. What, for instance, do we do with the two lyrics that follow? Particularly when we know that there are dozens similar to them, though not exactly like them or each other?[5] Are they the same song or not?

A Forsaken Lover

O Johnny is on the water,
Let him sink or swim!
For if he can live without me,
I can live without him.

Johnny is a young boy,
But still younger am I;
For how often has he told me
How constant he would be!

I'll take off this black dress,
And I'll flourish in green;
For I don't care if I am forsaken,
I am only nineteen.

O meeting is a pleasure,
But to part with him was grief;
But an unconstant true lover
Is worse than a thief.

A thief can but rob you
And take all you have;
But an unconstant lover
Will take you to your grave.

The grave it will rot you
And turn you to dust;
There is scarce one out of twenty
That a young girl can trust.

They will court you and kiss you
And get your heart warm;
Then, as soon as your back's turned,
They'll laugh you to scorn.

The cuckoo is a pretty bird,
She sings as she flies.
She brings us good tiding,
And tells us no lies.

Forsaken, forsaken,
Forsaken am I!
He will think himself mistaken
If he thinks I'll cry.

* * *

The Cuckoo

The cuckoo, she's a pretty bird,
She sings as she flies,
She brings us glad tidings,
And she tells no lies.

She sucks all the pretty flowers
To make her voice clear,
And she never sings "cuckoo"
Till the spring of the year.

Come all you young women,
Take warning by me,
Never place your affections
On the love of a man.

For the roots they will wither
The branches decay.
He'll turn his back on you
And walk square away.

A meeting, it's a pleasure,
And a parting is a grief,
But an inconstant lover,
Is worse than a thief.

A thief he'll but rob you
And take what you have,
While an inconstant lover
Will lead you to your grave.

The case, it seems, has to be made for an initial identification of such songs through something not, to date, used for song classification: i.e., their emotional situation or, in other words, their emotional core.

"Emotional core" in this case does not differ radically from the emotional core which I argued is the essential ingredient of the ballad when I wrote that

> . . . Anglo-American ballads stress impact over action and retain, in the long run, only enough of the original action or plot to hold this core of emotion in some sort of focus.[6]

Some lyrics, like "Old Smokey,"[7] or the text Albert Friedman labels "Mary Hamilton's Last Goodnight,"[8] are little more than cores surviving from plots of full-fledged ballads ("The Waggoner's Lad" in the case of the former; Child 173 in the case of the latter), even though they may have established traditions in their own rights:

Old Smokey

On top of old Smokey
On the mountain so high
Where the wild birds and turtle doves
Can hear my sad cry.

Sparking is a pleasure
Parting is a grief,
But a falsehearted lover
Is wuss nor a thief.

They'll tell you they love you
To give your heart ease,
And as soon as your back's turned
They'll love who they please.

I wrote him a letter
In red rosy lines.
He sent it back to me
All twisted in twine.

He says, "Keep your love letters
And I'll keep mine.
You write to your love
And I'll write to mine.

I can love little
And I can love long.
I can love an old sweetheart
Till a new one comes along.

I can hug them and kiss them
And prove to them kind,
I can turn my back on them
And alter my mind."

My horses ain't hungry,
They won't eat your hay.
So farewell, my darling,
I'll be on my way.

I'll drive on to Georgia
And write you my mind.
My mind is to marry
And leave you behind.

* * *

Mary Hamilton's Last Goodnight

Yestre'en the queen had four Maries
This nicht she'll hae but three;
There was Mary Beaton an' Mary Seaton,
An' Mary Carmichael an' me.

Last nicht I dressed Queen Mary,
An' pit on her braw silken goon,

An' a' the thanks I've gat this nicht
Is tae be hanged in Edinboro toon.

O little did my mither ken,
The day she cradled me,
The land I was tae travel in,
The death I was tae dee.

O happy, happy is the maid,
That's born o' beauty free;
O it was my rosy dimplin' cheeks
That's been the deil tae me!

They've tied a hanky roon ma een,
An' they'll no let me see tae dee;
An' they've pit on a robe o' black
Tae hang on the gallows tree.

Yestre'en the queen had four Maries,
This nicht she'll hae but three;
There was Mary Beaton, an' Mary Seaton,
An' Mary Carmichael an' me.

The details of those original ballad plots (compressed or omitted) still influence them and give a certain constancy to their moods and conclusions, variant after variant.

However, many more Anglo-American love lyrics, like the best-selling country western and Tin Pan Alley tunes, never had a plot and .owe nothing to a narrative ancestor. This allows them a freedom that lyrics derived from ballads cannot have. Even though they too center about a consistent emotional core, they often develop variants which are rendered quite opposite from one another in mood and conclusion by the capricious addition or withdrawal of a stanza or two. Two common variants of the constant stanza in the tradition of "Green Grow the Lilacs" demonstrate this caprice, for this particular lyric does not have a fully developed narrative in its past to keep it in focus:

Green grow the lilacs all sparkling with dew,
I'm lonely my darling since a-parting with you.
But at our next meeting I hope you'll prove true
And change the green lilacs for the red, white,
 and blue.

* * *

Green grows the laurel and so does the rue,
How lonely was I when I parted from you.
The next happy meeting our love we'll renew
And change the green laurel to the origin blue.

These two texts, coming to opposite conclusions about "our next meeting," express opposite moods, one of questioning hope or despair, one of certainty, even joy. Still, in addition to the identifiable opening stanza, they clearly share the same emotional core: in this case a core centering on parting. Both songs are about parting and the idea of parting binds them together.

The emotional core of the love lyric thus provides a method of definition, a method somewhat less satisfactory than one based on plotting, but a method nevertheless. For instance, Arthur Kyle Davis terms the well-known lyric beginning "Who's to shoe my pretty little feet?" "the hydrogen ion of balladry"[9] because of the readiness of its stanzas to combine with and fill out other material:

> Who's to shoe my pretty little feet?
> And who's to glove my hand?
> And who's to kiss my ruby, red lips
> When you're in a far-off land.
>
> Poppa will shoe my pretty little feet,
> And Momma will glove my hand.
> Sister will kiss my ruby, red lips,
> And I won't need no man.

In this lyric, there may be one speaker or two, the questioner may be male or female, the questions asked may be numerous and varied, and the most compelling one: "Who will kiss my ruby, red lips?" may be answered with "sister," "brother," "sweetheart," "lover," "true love," "friends," "no one," "somebody," even with "I myself." This list alone covers a full spectrum from chastity and innocence to infidelity. There is only one unchanging, constant core: the lyric is asking over and over "Who is going to look after me when you are gone?" and so an emotional core of parting and concern can be identified and used to unite variants. And if the reader will take the time to check those variants listed in The British Traditional Ballad in North America[10] (there are almost five dozen references), he will find that this core is unchanging, regardless of the host of superficial differences. It is from the emotional core of the lyrics, then, that the crux of the present system of classification emerges.

As was mentioned earlier, certain lyrics, like "Green Grow the Lilacs" and "Careless Love," have a convenient fixed stanza (a constant stanza) which can be used for initial identification, and any guide to the love-lyric should list such constant stanzas as follows, printing each in a typical form with a Roman numeral affixed to it:

I - "Green Grow the Lilacs"

Green grow the lilacs all sparkling with dew,
I'm lonely, my love, since a-parting from you,
But at our next meeting I hope to prove true
And change the green lilacs for the red, white,
  and blue.

II - "Shoe My Foot"

Who's to shoe my pretty little feet?
And who's to glove my hand?
  And who's to kiss my ruby red lips
When you're in a far-off land?

III - "Careless Love"

Love, oh love, oh careless love,
Love, oh love, oh carelsss love,
Love, or careless love, how can it be,
To love someone who don't love me?

IV - "On Top of Old Smokey"

On top of Old Smokey
All covered with snow
I lost my true lover
By courtin' too slow.

This method should be followed until all such constant
stanza lyrics have been indexed.

The next step, certainly a subjective one, is to
identify (as was just done for the "Shoe My Foot" lyric) and
then list the emotional cores which appear in the various
love lyrics, setting up a grouping that would look something
like this:

A - Parting
B - Rejection
C - Deception or Inconstancy
D - Interference from Parents, and so forth
E - Pledge of Fidelity

This method seems simple enough, but it is clearly the
most controversial part of the system and will undoubtedly
need some tinkering. Possibly, sub-headings, such as the
following would be useful:

              A - Parting
              a - forever
              b - with reconciliation

Such matters will work themselves out as soon as the listing
of the emotional cores gets underway.

    Finally, a list of the miscellaneous, inconstant
stanzas which fill out the huge canon of Anglo-American love
lyric would have to be drawn up. Each stanza should have an
Arabic number assigned to it (the list would be extensive,
though manageable):

    1 - I wrote my letter with roses entwined;
        He wrote me an answer all twisted and twined
        Saying, "Keep your love-letters and I'll keep mine,
        Write to your sweetheart and I'll write to mine."

    2 - I've oftentime wondered why women like men,
        Just as ofttime wondered why men like them,
        For by my own experience I very well know
        That men are deceitful wherever they go.

    3 - I passed my love's window both early and late,
        The look that she gave me would make your heart
          ache,
        O the look that she gave me was painful to see,
        For she loves another one better than me.

    4 - Come all you young maidens, take warning from me,
        Never place your affections on a green willow tree,
        For the roots they will wither, the branches decay,
        He'll turn his back on you and soon walk away.

    5 - My horses ain't hungry, they won't eat your hay
        So farewell, my darling, I'll be on my way.
        I'll drive on to Georgia and write you my mind.
        My mind is to marry and leave you behind.

    6 - A meeting is a pleasure, a parting is grief,
        But an unconstant lover is worse than a thief;
        A thief he will rob you, and take what you have,
        But an unconstant lover will send you to your
          grave.

    7 - The grave can but moulder you and turn you to dust.
        There is scare one hundred a fair maid can trust;
        They will offer your tongue to deceive.
        There is scarce one in a hundred I can believe.

8 - The cuckoo is a pretty bird, she sings as she
    flies.
    She brings us glad tidings, she tells us no lies.
    She sucks all the flowers to make her voice clear,
    And she never sings "cuckoo" till the spring of
    the year.

9 - I can love little and I can love long.
    I can love an old sweetheart till a new one comes
    on.
    I can hug them and kiss them and prove to them
    kind;
    I can turn my back on them and alter my mind.

Once these three steps were completed, the various forms which the Anglo-American love lyric takes would be identifiable in a rather easy shorthand. The text of "Old Smokey," printed earlier in this paper, would be described as follows, using the letters and numbers above:

    IV-B-6,1,9,5

"The Cuckoo" would be described as follows:

    C-8,4,6.

Under such a system, a field collector could easily label a lyric just recorded and quickly compare its make-up and emotional impact with ones previously printed.

It is true that establishing this particular index would be more complicated and tedious than establishing the indices to the Child ballads or to the narrative obituary verses.[11] Each text of each lyric in collections such as Belden or Davis would have to be coded individually. But the task is imposing, nothing more; and there seems to be no alternative. The love lyric is constant most in the sorrow it causes indexers.

NOTES

[1]Leach started the Bibliographical and Special Series of the American Folklore Society partly for this purpose. See especially, Vols. I, II, VIII.

[2]H. M. Belden, Ballads and Songs Collected by the Missouri Folklore Society, University of Missouri Studies, Vol. XV (Columbia Mo.: University of Missouri Press, 1940), 473.

[3]See my "A Tentative Study of a Typical Folk Lyric: 'Green Grows the Laurel,'" Journal of American Folklore, 65 (1952), 341-52 and "'Green Grows the Laurel': Further Notes," Journal of American Folklore, 67 (1954), 295-96.

[4]"A System for Classifying Native American Songs with Floating Stanzas," an unpublished class report in my possession.

[5]See J. Harrington Cox, Folk-songs of the South (Cambridge: Harvard University Press, 1925), pp. 425-26; Alan Lomax, The Folksongs of North America in the English Language (Garden City, N.Y.: Doubleday, 1960), pp. 217-18.

[6]An article first published under the title "'Mary Hamilton' and the Anglo-American Ballad as an Art Form," Journal of American Folklore, 70 (1957), 208-14.

[7]This is a previously unpublished text in my possession.

[8]Albert Friedman, The Viking Book of Folk Ballads of the English Speaking World (New York: Viking, 1963), pp. 219-20.

[9]Arthur Kyle Davis, Traditional Ballads of Virginia (Cambridge: Harvard University Press, 1929), p. 261.

[10]Tristram Potter Coffin, The British Traditional Ballad in North America, Supplement by Roger deV. Renwick (Austin: University of Texas Press, 1977), pp. 73-74.

[11]See the work on narrative obituary verse, a form somewhat different from the ballad, in Mark Tristram Coffin, American Narrative Obituary Verse and Native American Balladry (Norwood, Pa.: Norwood Editions, 1975).

University of Pennsylvania
Philadelphia

PRETTY POLLY

Sung by Mrs. Levi Langille, Pictou County, Nova Scotia.

1. There was a lord in Ambertown
        Courted a lady fair,
    And all he wanted of this pretty fair maid
        Was to take her life away.

2. "Go get me some of your father's gold
        And some of your mother's fees,
    And two of the best horses in your father's stall
        Where there stands thirty and three."

3. So she mounted on her steed white milk,
        And he on his dappling grey,
    And they rode forward to the sea
        Two hours before it was day.

4. "Light off, light off thy steed white milk,
        And deliver it unto me,
    For six pretty maids I have drownded here,
        And the seventh one thou shalt be.

5. Take off, take off thy bonny silk plaid,
        And deliver it unto me.
    Methinks they are too rich and gay
        To rot in the salt salt sea."

6. "If I must take off my bonny silk plaid,
        Likewise my golden stays,
    You must turn your back around to me
        And face yon willow tree."

7. He turned himself around about
        To face yon willow tree;
    She grasped him by the middle so small,
        And she tumbled him into the sea.

8. So he rolléd high and he rolléd low
        Till he rolléd to the seaside.
    "Stretch forth your hand, my pretty Polly,
        And I'll make you my bride."

9. "Lie there, lie there, you false-hearted man,
        Lie there instead of me,
    For six pretty maids thou has drownded here,
        But the seventh hath drownded thee!"

10. She mounted on her steed white milk,
        And she led her dappling grey,
    And she rode forward to her father's door
        An hour before it was day.

11. The old man he, it's being awoke,
        And heard all that was said.
    "What were you prittling and prattling, my
                pretty Polly,
        And keeping me awake all night long?"

12. "The old cat had got up to my littock so high,
        And I was afraid she was going to eat me,
    And I was calling for pretty Polly
        To go drive the old cat away."

13. "Don't prittle, don't prattle, my pretty Polly,
        Nor tell any tales on me.
    Your cage shall be made of the glittering gold
        Instead of the greenwood tree."

W. Roy MacKenzie. Ballads and Sea Songs from Nova
Scotia. Cambridge: Harvard University Press, 1928,
pp. 7-8, tune p. 391. Reprinted in Bertrand H. Bronson,
The Traditional Tunes of the Child Ballads. Princeton:
Princeton University Press, 1959, I, 65.

W. F. H. NICOLAISEN

"THERE WAS A LORD IN AMBERTOWN":
Fictitious Place Names In The Ballad Landscape

Anybody attempting to write about place names in traditional ballads cannot but acknowledge a debt to W. Edson Richmond. To deal with such a topic without reference to his seminal article on "Ballad Place Names"[1] would be foolhardy, for what one wants, or manages, to say usually turns out to be either an extension or a modification of his basic classification and of the reasons for it. Whether one argues from a fundamental stance of agreement or disagreement, one's arguments are bound to be shaped out of an attitude of response to Richmond.[2]

This brief study is no exception in that respect. It accepts Richmond's triad of reasons for the appearance of place names in traditional ballads: (1) historical events necessitate the recording of particular names, (2) place names lend credibility to ballad stories, and (3) actual or pseudo place names are substituted for an unrecognized place name or for a seemingly meaningless word or phrase.[3] But, viewing the third category of reasons adduced as being somewhat different in nature, it intends to examine the characteristics of the name substitutions in question and to investigate the function of the names thus created through substitution, within the context of individual ballads and as part of the toponymy of the whole ballad corpus. The emphasis will not be so much on the process by which substitutions are made--Richmond mentions phonetic analogy and reduction as two major factors[4]--but on the ways in which the products of this process contribute to the establishment of a recognizable ballad landscape.

It is, in fact, the creation, maintenance and structure of a viable and acceptable ballad nomenclature which is to be the focus of this little essay. The question whether the components of such a nomenclature are genuine or in some way corrupted will not enter into this discussion. It is taken for granted that one of the basic tenets of oral tradition in a folk-cultural register is variation in repetition and that stability in a diachronic sense therefore can not be expected. In synchronic comparison and description, on the other hand, the notion of change is, of course, irrelevant, and what we are left with is the phenomenon of diversity.

For our purposes, the mere occurrence of place names in this category in ballad topography is important while it matters little that <u>in Ohio</u> has developed out of <u>in the choir</u>, <u>Chevy Chase</u> is a reinterpretation of <u>Cheviot</u>, <u>knee breast key</u> seems to be an awkwardly etymologizing transformation of <u>Nebraska</u>, or <u>Olinglunt</u> can be shown to be a nonsensical substitution for <u>Old England</u>.[5] Ultimately it is presumably even immaterial whether a name exists in the actual landscape or not. For listeners not familiar with the Scottish map it must remain doubtful whether such place names as <u>Cowdenknowes</u>, <u>Usher's Well</u>, <u>Carline Sands</u>, <u>Binnorie</u>, <u>Embro</u>, <u>Braidslie</u>, <u>Cargarff</u>, <u>Ochiltree</u>, <u>Auchentrone</u> really exist (actual and fictitious names have been deliberately mixed in the list) or whether <u>Cumbernaud</u>, <u>Comarnad</u>, <u>Skimmerknow</u>, <u>Camernadie</u>, <u>Cummernad</u>, <u>Cambernauld</u>, <u>Cumbernaldie</u>, <u>Cambernaudie</u> or <u>Campernaudie</u> is the correct form of a place name mentioned frequently in variants of Child 232.[6] Since I have elsewhere dealt with the question of knowability, semantic status and metaphorical usage of such ballad place names,[7] I want to concentrate here on the role played in ballads by place names which have no counterpart in the actual world, whether they are semantically accessible to English-speaking listeners or not. Examples will be culled from the whole of the published Child and Bronson corpus of traditional ballads.[8]

In this respect, the name quoted in the title of this paper is probably as good a starting point as any. It occurs in the opening line of a version of Child 4, "Lady Isabel and the Elf Knight," collected in the 1920s in Nova Scotia (Bronson 61), one of several versions in which Lady Isabel has turned into the ubiquitous, alliterating Pretty Polly. Within the tradition of this particular ballad type, <u>Ambertown</u> takes the place of such well worn topographical designations as <u>the north lands</u> (Child E, Bronson 84), <u>the North Land</u> (Child F), <u>the northern land</u> (Bronson 1), <u>the Northlands</u> (Bronson 14, 15, 94), <u>the North Land</u> (Bronson 17, 20a[9], 40, 46, 48, 54, 141), <u>northern lands</u> (Bronson 23), <u>the North Lands</u> (Bronson 28a, 29, 51), <u>the North Countrie</u> (Bronson 31), <u>the North Countree</u> (Bronson 59); <u>the West Countrie</u> (Bronson 3, 93), <u>the South Country</u> (Child D); <u>Scotland</u> (Bronson 126), <u>fair Scotland</u> (Bronson 16), <u>far Scotland</u> (Bronson 101), <u>New Scotland</u> (Bronson 109), <u>Old Scotland</u> (Bronson 110, 123), <u>north of Scotland</u> (Bronson 67), <u>the North Scotland</u> (Bronson 99); <u>Old England</u> (Bronson 140), <u>Old Ingel</u> (Bronson 119), <u>London</u> (Bronson 35), <u>London Town</u> (Bronson 44), and perhaps even <u>North Cumberland</u> (Bronson 74).

All of these names, in some more or less lucid fashion, serve to pinpoint the geographical origins of the threatening stranger in this ballad or the destination of the couple's ride, or both. Apart from the thinly disguised old Ingel, Ambertown is the only place name in the whole set of almost 150 variants which is both fictitious in nature and confidently precise in its locatory capacity; it is, in fact, not only unique in the tradition of Child 4 but also as a toponymic hapax legomenon in the whole Child and Bronson corpus. If one wanted to view it as a phonological misunderstanding, one might think of it as a re-interpreted descendant of Embro-town (Edinburgh-town), but no variant has survived in which this name occurs. Its lexical meaning is clearly fitting, as far as the setting of the ballad story is concerned--the seaside--and might even represent a specific aspect of the northern lands, their sandy ocean beaches where amber may be found. Whether these speculations as to the origin of the name are right or not, Ambertown functions in the Nova Scotia variant of Child 4, in which it occurs, as a convenient, plausible, even persuasive locatory device which, through its denotative, focusing force "lends credibility"--to use Richmond's term-- to the story the ballad tells. If the murderous lord came from Ambertown, his threatening intrusion had sufficient motivation, and one need say no more. Ambertown nobles are like that, and when one of them happens to appear on the scene, our suspicions are aroused.

And yet the very uniqueness of the name's occurrence seems to call into question the necessity for its existence. The much more frequently mentioned northlands and their equivalents are, it would seem, in their ominous vagueness much more immediately menacing than a more precise toponymic reference. The same applies to the several allusions to Scotland and its northern parts, other less frequent directional indications like west and south, or even the urban corruption of London. There is no need for Ambertown to bridge the credibility gap and to account for the cruelties of a mass murderer. Other geographical references would have done as well, especially when, like north and west, their threatening potential is confirmed by other ballad stories. Nevertheless, Mrs. Levi Langille of Pictou County, Nova Scotia, sang Ambertown in the 1920s, and ever since then, perhaps even longer, Ambertown has been on the ballad map, has been part of the ballad landscape. No further proof of its existence is necessary beyond her sung narrative.

Perhaps there are not many fictive place names which are singularly recorded in only one extant version of one particular ballad, but on the other hand, Ambertown is not without company. We only have to think of Salin (2:4,1[1]), Cadrian (2:49, 1[1]), Wearie's Well (4:B, 3[4]), Bunion Bay

(4:D, 8^4), <u>Carline Sands</u> (4:D, 28^3), <u>Leed</u> (6:A, 13^2), <u>Lurk</u> (20:E, 1^1), <u>Marblestone</u> (20:47, 5^5), <u>Strathdinah</u> (24:13, 1^1), <u>Archerdale</u> (47:D, 1^1), <u>Saussif</u> or <u>Sausuf</u> (49:B, 7^3 and 8^3), <u>Fordland</u> (49:F, 14^3), <u>Langford's Town</u> (49:11, 5^3), <u>the Mackintaw woods</u> (49:27, 3^3), <u>the Olgen woods</u> (49:32, 5^3), <u>Starksborotown</u> (49:38, 4^3), <u>Declarn</u> (68:15, 2^3), <u>the Eden land</u> (68:14, 2^3), <u>the Arksund land</u> (68:15, 2^3), <u>Cornersville</u> (68:19, 2^3), <u>Ferrol's land</u> (72:C, 6^4), <u>St. Air</u> (74:36, 1^4), <u>Usher's Well</u> (79:A, 1^1), <u>Portingale</u> ($80:1^3$), <u>Starlings Town</u> (84:147, 1^1), <u>Sittingen's Rocks</u> (87:B, 1^1), <u>Knotingale Castle</u> (87:C, 13^1), <u>Prime Castle</u> (93:B, 13^3), <u>Lillus Town</u> (99:4, 5^3), <u>Crecynbroghe</u> (178:A, 2^3), <u>Auchruglen</u> (178:G, 6^4), <u>Arrow</u> (214:30, 1^4), <u>Ochilberry</u> (217:N, 29^1), <u>Looney Town</u> (279:9, 1^4), and <u>Taperbank</u> (293:D, 12^7). This is, even in its incompleteness, an impressive list.

In certain instances, we may be able to guess from what other place names, real or fictitious, individual names here included may have been derived. In others, we can point to names in other variants of the same ballad which fill the same slots. Such speculation or comparison, however, is not really relevant to our survey, unless we wish to use place names as major evidence in another kind of legitimate onomastic investigation: the elucidation of ballad genealogies and the closely linked search for place and time of origin of a possible original and its paths of diffusion in subsequent oral tradition. This was, of course, Child's own predominant interest in the study of ballad toponymy and he found the pursuit of that interest quite frustrating:

> The topography of traditional ballads frequently presents difficulties, both because it is liable to be changed, wholly, or, what is more embarrassing, partially, to suit a locality to which a ballad has been transported, and again because unfamiliar names, when not exchanged, are exposed to corruption. Some of the places, also, have not a dignity which entitles them to notice in the gazetteers.[10]

The main desire behind this kind of approach is obviously the identification of place names or place nomenclatures in ballads with their equivalents or "ancestors" in actual maps and gazetteers.

And the frequent failure to achieve that goal is here attributed both to the distorting interference of factors involved in the process of transmission and to the lack of refinement in research methods. It is our contention that the place names just enumerated and many others are not accessible to this particular approach, not because of any maddening flaws resulting from faults inherent in the very phenomenon of tradition but because there is, in a very large number of types, no congruency between the landscape of the ballad and the landscape of the actual world. Any attempt at recognition or re-cognition is therefore doomed from the outset.

Naturally, not only does this statement apply to such place names in the ballad topography which have, for one reason or another (some traceable, some bizarre), only been recorded once, but also to those whose occurrence has been noted more often. Any dividing line drawn between these two categories would, in any way, be highly artificial since it would place far too high a premium on chance survival and similar kinds of eccentricities. Fictive place names do not lose any of their fictitiousness through repetition, and the singly recorded toponym is only an extreme manifestation of a general principle. Place names which have been recorded more than once within the corpus of variants of the same ballad type would be, for example, Bin(n)orie (Child 10), Green Willow (24), Broomfield Hill(s) (43), Northumberlee (53), Scarlet Town (84), and so forth.

More often than not such names are subject to extensive variation which, although it has no bearing on the function of the name within the same ballad variant, produces clusters of names which are, in an onomastic sense, cognate with each other, although it is not always clear how and in what sequence they relate to each other phonologically. Child 10, for example, not only has the variants Binorie and Binnorie but also the obviously related Benorrie and Benonie, and in one refrain (94), Bonnery. The refrain of Child 14 has produced Vergeo, Virgie O, Bernio and Barbry-0, as well as the more authentic sounding Fordie and Airdrie O. Child 39 has Kertonha, Charter's ha, Charteris ha, Cartershay, as developments, it seems, of Carterhaugh, as well as the somewhat more distant Chaster's Wood, Charter's woods, and Charter Wood(s). Another set of names in this ballad comprises Rides Cross, Miles Moss and Miles-corse, Blackstock, Blackning Cross, and Crickmagh. In Child 49, Chesley Town, Jesseltown and Jersey School apparently belong together. Child 68 has given us Garlick's Wells, Garlioch Wells, Brandie's Well, and Richard's Wall; Child 72 has Owsenford, Oxenford and Oxenfoord. In Child 75, we find the bells, churches and church-yards of St. Patrick, St. Varney, St. Pancras (!), St. Vincent, St. Bank, St. Clemens, St. Pancrum, St. Pancrus, St. Charles, but also, puzzlingly, King Patsy bells, and, capriciously, St. Charles Hotel. The titular Roch Royal of Child 76 also appears as Rochroyall, Roch Royall, Rough Royal, Ruchlaw Hill, Lochroyan, Lochranline, Locharain and even Aughrim and Ocram.

The Buckelsfordbery of the A version (Bronson 15, 6[1])
of Child 81 has as its equivalents Buchlesfieldberry in B,
Mulberry in E and Dalisberry in F. Barbara Allan's
birthplace or place of residence (in Child 84) is most
frequently (17 times) given as Scarlet Town but, as already
mentioned, Starlings Town also occurs, as do the non-
fictitious names Scotland, Reading, London, and Oxford, as
well as the lexical "scornful town" (61, 1[1]). Dablin takes
its place beside Dublin in Child 85. Sillertoun Town and
Sittingenty Rocks are parallel usages in Child 87, and
Onorie and Onore are obviously variants of the same name in
Child 89, as are Bee Hom and Bahome in Child 92,
Cautheryknowes and Cathery knowes in Child 92, and Winsbury,
Winsburry, Winchberrie, Winsberry, Winesberrie, Winchbury
and Welshberrie in Child 100. Whereas the usual place name
in Child 105 is Islington, phonological or orthographic
variants are Hazel Town, Hazling Town, Hazlingtown, Isling-
town, Islinkton, Oslingtown, and Asle-un-town, while other
versions have Ireland Town, Waterford Town, Dublin Town and
Exeter Town. Similar clusters are found in the remaining
200 ballads in the Child canon of which perhaps Child 243
deserves special mention since its one-hundred-and-a-half
variants included in Bronson, place the Demon Lover's
alluring location on the banks, shores or isle of (sweet) Da
Tee (or Da Lee), Aloe Dee, Tennessee, Lilee, Galilee,
Norlee, Andee, Willie, Haly, Bewlea, Calvary, Willee,
Kiddie, Marie, Relee, Will-lea, Malea, Malee, Treelee,
Dundee, Val Varie, Mawrie, Wiley, Lacolee, Otee, Claudy, and
Vallie. What fertile ground for the ballad comparatist and
genealogist.

There seems to be no doubt that the more versions have
been recorded of a ballad the more variation there is in the
phonological and orthographic shape of the place names it
contains. It is also likely that, if an actual name is the
point of origin, the difference in the distances variants
travel may have a corresponding echo in the amount of
variation observable in the name forms. Be that as it may,
each of the above toponymic variants of a fictitious name
adds a new item to the topography of the ballad types in
question, creating an ever-growing place nomenclature that
belongs to the world of the ballad and to it alone.

There are, however, also a few instances of fictive
names which have crossed the boundaries between types and
are consequently found in more than one, sometimes several,
ballads included in the Child canon. The most ubiquitous of
these is probably St. Mary's Kirk (with its variants Mary's
Kirk, Marie's Kirk, Mary Kirk and St. Mary's Church) which
makes an appearance in at least nine ballads (Child 7, 64,
66, 74, 76, 85, 110, 254 and 255), giving ballad aficionados

the impression that its churchyard has become the final, and certainly formulaic, resting place of many a lover. There are <u>Strawberry Castles</u> in three ballads (Child 65, 87 and 109) and there is a <u>Strawberry Lane</u> in a fourth (Child 2: 23, 1[1] and 35, 1[1]). While <u>Lyne</u> and its cognates <u>Lynn</u>, <u>Line</u> and <u>Linne</u> may originally have represented the Northumberland <u>Lyne</u> or similar place names elsewhere on the map of Britain, repeated references to them in several different ballads (Child 2, 5, 47, 53, 88, 267 and 304) make it more than likely that these names, too, may be categorized as fictive in the sense that singers and listeners alike may well regard them as expected ingredients of ballad topography rather than of the actual landscape. They are, one might say, both as real and as unreal as the <u>Clydes</u>, <u>Tweeds</u>, <u>Edinburghs</u>, <u>Yarrows</u>, <u>Scarboroughs</u>, <u>Dublins</u> which are dotted on many a ballad map, often, of course, with metaphorical as well as immediate geographical implications.

Apart from the stereotyped place nomenclature of the Robin Hood cycle of ballads, the rather detailed and meticulous recording of place names on both sides of the Scottish-English border in some of the historical ballads, and the equally faithful toponymic depiction of the landscape of the Scottish Northeast in others, traditional ballads rely, whenever necessary, on an extensive corpus of place names that belong exclusively to their own sense of topography. They not only rely on it but invent it and, through such innovative creation, produce a mental ballad map which, despite its proven partial fictitiousness, serves admirably and efficiently in the provision of plausible, though illusory, space and spatial relationships. The place names incorporated in this map serve as deictic signposts pointing to places of birth and of residence, of the origin of the stranger and of the interference of the supernatural, to places of delight and despair, of departure and destination, of stern prohibition and seductive invitation, to places of heartache and of heartbreak, of deceit and revenge, of fulfillment and of dissolution, to places of love requited and of love thwarted, of innocence and malice, of sweet joy and bitter jealousy, to places of wholesome fun and of sinister contest, of murder and of interment, of temporal separation and of eternal union. While some of the names involved smack of secondary re-interpretation in their semantic suggestiveness (<u>Strawberry Castle</u>, <u>Bonny Moor Hill</u>, <u>Ambertown</u>, <u>Temple Hill</u>, <u>Broomfield Hill</u>, <u>Kirkland</u>, <u>Merrytown</u>, <u>Oxenford</u>), most of them derive their locatory efficiency from the very nature of names which do not require lexical meaning in order to function adequately, which is why names can so easily be substituted for, or interchanged with, meaningless vocables in ballad refrains.

Thus ballad landscapes are both extensions of and
complements to actual landscapes. The place nomenclatures of
fiction and of reality both interweave and find their own
appropriate spaces, so that in the world of sung folk
narrative the most outrageously fictive place name becomes
as persuasive in locatory force as the best known name of an
actual city or river. After all, a good ballad story does
not primarily thrive on credible historicity but on the
power, felicity and emotional appeal of its narrative. If
it does not entertain, in both words and tune, no number of
historical facts, including attested historical localities,
will rescue it from oblivion; but when names, fictive and
actual, are given an opportunity to focus and confirm, even
to intensify an entertaining story in song, they become, as
it were, an enriching part of that story and somehow enhance
its enjoyment and believability, and therefore its survival.

NOTES

[1]W. Edson Richmond, "Ballad Place Names," _Journal of American Folklore_, 59 (1946), 263-67.

[2]See, for example, my own articles "Place-Names in Traditional Ballads," _Folklore_, 84 (1973), 299-312, reprinted with slight revisions, in _Literary Onomastics Studies_, 1 (1974), 84-102; and "Personal Names in Traditional Ballads: A Proposal for a Ballad Onomasticon," _Journal of American Folklore_, 94 (1981), 229-31.

[3]Richmond, p. 263.

[4]Ibid., p. 266.

[5]These are Richmond's examples. See "Ballad Place Names" (note 1).

[6]The reference here is to a place the name of which appears as _Cumbernauld_ on the modern Scottish map--yet another form not quoted in the Child and Bronson variants.

[7]W. F. H. Nicolaisen, "Place-Names in Traditional Ballads."

[8]Francis James Child, _English and Scottish Popular Ballads_, 5 vols. (Boston: Houghton-Mifflin 1882-1898); Bertrand Harris Bronson, _The Traditional Tunes of the Child Ballads_. 4 vols. (Princeton, N.J.: Princeton University Press, 1959-1972). References to Child variants will be prefaced by the appropriate capital initial and references to Bronson by the relevant number. Thus B, 1^3 means Child's B version, stanza one, line three, whereas 84, 2^7 indicates Bronson's version No. 84, stanza two, line seven.

[9]So in the third line of the stanza; line one has a puzzling _the North South_.

[10]Child IV, 156, commenting on his inability "to settle the whereabouts of the House of Marr, in the vicinity of which the scene /of 213, "Sir James the Rose"_7 is laid."

State University of New York
Binghamton

HISTORICAL SURVEYS

VENEESEEN PYRKIVÄ NEITO

THE EMBARKING MAID

Sung by Anni Tenisova (Tenesseinen) nee Karhunen, born 1879 at
Vuokinsalmi in Archangel Karelia. Recorded by Lauri Simonsuuri
and Jouko Hautala 1952 at Helsinki (SKSÄ A 196. 1952).

1. An - ni tyt - tö ae- nut nei - to   is - tu- pa tu- run ko- rol - la,

tu - run ko- ron kor-vasel-la,   kat-tšou y-lös, kat-tšou   a - les,

y - lä-hä - nä päe-vä paistaa,   a - la-ha - na ve - no sou-taa.

1. Anni tyttö aenut neito
   istupa turun korolla,
   turun koron korvasella,
   kattšou ylös, kattšou ales,
   ylähänä pävä paistaa,
   alahana veno soutaa.

2. "Ota toatto venehehe!"
   "Empä jouva enkä ole,
   sulkut verkot venehessä,
   lohikala munimassa
   ruuvikossa, heinikössä,
   kaunehessa kaeslikossa."

3. Anni tyttö aenut neiti
   istupa turun korolla,
   turun koron korvasella,
   kattšou ylös, kattšou ales,
   ylähänä päeva paestaa,
   alahana veno soutaa.

4. "Ota muamo venehehe!"
   "Empä jouva enkä ole,
   sulkut verkot venehessä,
   lohikala munimassa
   ruuvikossa, heinikössä
   kaunehissa kaeslikoessa."

1. Pretty Anni, that fair maid
   Is sitting up upon a bluff
   High above the square.
   She looks up, she looks down.
   Up above the sun is shining,
   Down below a boat is rowing.

2. "Father, take me into the boat!"
   "I can't, haven't got the time,
   The silk nets are in the boat,
   The salmon is a-spawning,
   In the reeds, in the weeds
   In the lovely water grass."

3. Pretty Anni, that fair maid
   Is sitting up upon a bluff
   High above the square.
   She looks up, she looks down.
   Up above the sun is shining,
   Down below a boat is rowing.

4. "Mother, take me into the boat!"
   "I can't, haven't got the time.
   The silk nets are in the boat,
   The salmon is a-spawning,
   In the reeds, in the weeds,
   In the lovely water grass."

5. Anni tyttö aenut neiti
   istupa turun korolla,
   turun koron korvasella,
   kattšou ylös, kattšou ales,
   ylähänä päevä paestaa
   alahalla veno soutaa.

6. "O, ota veikko venehehe!"
   "Enkä jouva enkä ole,
   sulkut verkot venehessä
   lohikala munimassa
   ruuvikossa, heinikössä
   kaunehessa kaeslikossa."

7. Anni tyttö aenut neiti
   istu vaan turun korolla.
   turun koron korvasella,
   kattšou ylös, kattšou ales,
   alahana veno soutaa.
   alahana veno soutaa.

8. "Ota tsikko venehehe!"
   "Empä jouva enkä ole,
   sulkut verkot venehessä
   lohikala munimassa
   ruuvikossa, heinikössä
   kaunehessa kaeslikoessa."

9. Anni tyttö aenut neiti
   istu häin turun korolla.
   turun koron korvasella.
   kattsou ylös, kattsou ales.
   ylähänä päevä paestaa.
   alahana veno soutaa.

10. "Ota ämmö venehehe,
    ota ämmö venehehe!
    Aa, toattoni hevone hävitköhö
    parahana kyntöaikana!
    Äitini lehmät hävitköhön
    parahana lypsyaikana!
    Veikkoni miekka katetkohon
    parahana sojintaikan!
    Sikkoni niekla katetkohon
    parahana ompeluaikan."

5. Pretty Anni, that fair maid
   Is sitting up upon a bluff
   High above the square.
   She looks up, she looks down.
   Up above the sun is shining,
   Down below a boat is rowing.

6. "Oh Brother, take me into the boat!"
   "I can't, haven't got the time.
   The silk nets are in the boat.
   The salmon is a-spawning
   In the reeds, in the weeds,
   In the lovely water grass."

7. Pretty Anni, that fair maid
   Just sits alone upon the bluff
   High above the square.
   She looks up, she looks down.
   Down below a boat is rowing,
   Down below a boat is rowing.

8. "Sister, take me into the boat!"
   "I can't, haven't got the time.
   The silk nets are in the boat.
   The salmon is a-spawning,
   In the reeds, in the weeds,
   In the lovely water grass."

9. Pretty Anni, that fair maid,
   Is sitting up upon a bluff
   High above the square.
   She looks up, she looks down.
   Up above the sun is shining,
   Down below a boat is rowing.

10. "Granny, take me into the boat,
    Granny take me into the boat!
    Let my father's horse up and off
    When the time is best for ploughing!
    Let my mother's cows up and off
    When the time is best for milking!
    Let my sister's needle break
    When the time is best for sewing."

ANNELI ASPLUND

THE FINNISH NARRATIVE FOLK SONG:
A Changing Genre

"As customs and life have changed in other respects too, we may not wonder at the change from the former song to the present, for songs, if they are natural and not contrived, depict the times in which they are born as well as or perhaps even better than many other forms of description." Thus wrote Elias Lönnrot in his foreword to the Kanteletar in 1840. He went on to point out that it is ridiculous not to value what the present day has to offer: "Each era has its own character, life and other existence, and past times cannot be made to return. . . ." Lönnrot does, however, say that he hopes the modern Finnish song, wretched and insignificant as it is, may in time develop in a more favourable direction.

These comments show what the pioneers of folk research thought of the contemporary folk song in the mid-nineteenth century. It did not, they thought, stand comparison with the old song culture that went before it, only fragments of which were at that time to be found in the eastern-most parts of the country. Its era was irrevocably past. The transition had been made to a completely new way of singing marked by rhyming verses and different musical elements and--so it was claimed--a poverty and paltriness of content. The models for the new song came from elsewhere, chiefly Sweden. It was universally regretted that the basic elements of the true Finnish song had been discarded: alliteration, parallellism, the four-foot trochaic meter and the unique, pentachordic melody. But Lönnrot, realizing that natural renewal is part of the essence of tradition, wished to show that he approved of a state of affairs that could not be changed. But in comparing the new song with the old he could not help finding it in every way inferior: "If we take a closer look at these modern songs compared with the old ones, we may in general say that they are poorer in quality, not only in their language but also in their charm in general." This attitude has in fact continued well into this century and is clearly evident in research into the Finnish folk song. It has chiefly been aimed at the Kalevala song. There is far less objective information on the songs of the new stratum.

Narrative songs have always been the most interesting and most highly-valued genre of folk songs both in Finland and in other parts of the world. The ballad has attracted the song-maker most often in Scandinavia, Central Europe and the Anglo-American language area. The Russians speak of ballads and also of the byliny, the Spanish of the romancero, the Finns of the ancient epic. The terms may vary but the object itself does not: the narrative folk song has belonged to the highest caste in the folk song hierarchy.

The Kalevala epic contains archaic, mythical elements, songs of heroes in the pagan days of the Vikings and legend songs and ballads from the Catholic Middle Ages.[1] The linguistic, stylistic and contentual richness of these songs has aroused continual interest among different generations of researchers, and attempts to explain their message continue. "Modern man, if not a child or a barbarian deaf to poetry, has an intuitive assurance as to the significance of ancient messages," writes Matti Kuusi.[2] Since the new song stratum did not seem to contain anything comparable to this, it was understandable that the interest of researchers was, for a long time, slight. Alongside the archaic, poetic language of the Kalevala song, the unconstrained slang used by the new song, and in particular the vulgar expressions typical of mocking songs, gained in emphasis and easily led to the disparagement of this whole new song genre. "The ancient poem enshrouded in myths and the dimness of history is open to idolization; the everyday realism revealed by the new folk song in sharp close-up is not valued," wrote Matti Hako.[3]

The new rhyming folk songs were characteristically lyrical: love songs and satirical songs of mockery and derision. They were written in four lines, varying in tone from airiness to melancholy and with themes reflecting the whole way of life of the nineteenth-century country village. They resounded through the village lanes and at young people's games or other common meeting places. The verse was comprised of two pairs of rhyming lines, each with seven feet, and this verse model was, in the language of the people, called a rekilaulu or roundelay, originally from the German Reigenlied.[4] The tunes had a greater ambitus than those of the Kalevala song and were melodically more varied. It was, in fact, precisely the melodies alone that were approved by the researchers. "Only in the diversity of their tunes are they superior, and because of this they have in fact become so common," Lönnrot points out.[5]

Alongside the oral song tradition there also existed a popular written song, the content of which was chiefly narrative. Broadsides had been printed from the seventeenth century onwards, but they did not gain any notable significance until the mid-nineteenth century. Broadsides were then published in rapid succession and they became an important part of the song repertoire of the ordinary person. For a long time they were not, however, regarded as belonging to the folklorist's field of research, for they were not folk songs--products of tradition handed down by word of mouth. They tended rather to be classified, along with peasant poetry, under literary research. (Peasant poetry was the term used to describe the products of literate peasant poets; it was also published as broadsides and sung.) Such poems were either in Kalevala metre or rhyme.[6]

The new folk song stratum, then, was not completely without the oral, narrative folk song, though viewed quantitatively there seem to have been very few compared with the lyric and the epic broadside song. Lönnrot had already paid attention to a few ballads which, he mentions, were of Swedish origin. In his foreword to the Kanteletar he published, among others, "Velisurmaaja" ("The Brother-Slayer," cf. Child No. 13 in the British tradition and TSB D 320 in the Scandinavian tradition[7]) and "Morsiamen kuolo" ("The Death of the Bride," cf. TSB D 280), which were later also published in broadside editions. It was, however, some time before the rhyming, narrative folk song became the object of research. It was 1901 before Kaarle Krohn's studies of the Kanteletar appeared.[8] In them he looks into the foreign background of three rhyming ballads. The original form of the song "Kreivin sylissä istunut" ("The Maiden in the Count's Lap") he found in the ballad "Graf und Nonne" from Germany. Similarly he found counterparts in the Scandinavian and Central European traditions to the ballads "The Death of the Bride" and "Lunastettava neito" ("The Maid Freed from the Gallows," cf. Child No. 95), and to a few other ballads of the newer stratum. The emphasis in his examination is, however, on the fact that some of these themes were already known in the older era of song culture. The same ballad had found its way to Finland by two routes at different times. Like Krohn, J. J. Mikkola suggested the original source of the ballad in studying the song "Vesmanviiki" and compared it with the Scandinavian ballad "Sven Svanevit" (cf. Child 1, TSB E 52).[9]

These were typical research results produced by the geographical-historical method. An examination was made of the routes of transmission, the origins, and the original form of traditional items. Some fifty years later Martti Haavio examined the same ballads from the phenomenological approach, placed the Finnish songs against an international background, and found in them basic universal elements that have interested man ever since ancient Egypt and the Greece and Rome of antiquity.[10]

The first extensive study of broadsides was published by Eino Salokas in the 1920s and deals with Finnish secular broadsides that appeared during the period of Swedish rule (up to 1809). He divides his material into narrative, lyrical, humorous, educational, and historical songs; examines them mainly from a cultural-historical perspective; and looks into their sources.[11] Matti Vilppula studied Finnish broadside ballads on the Demon Lover theme and their relationship with the British and German traditions.[12] A few general treatises on the new folk song have appeared, along with some studies that throw light on the rhyming narrative song from the perspective of the melodies, the formal structure, and the interaction of the oral and the written. Generally speaking the narrative song tradition of the new song stratum has, however, come in for little study.

One of the reasons for the small amount of attention paid to the narrative song tradition of the new song stratum is that the recording of tradition in Finland in the last century was much in the nature of a rescue operation, and it was organized by the Finnish Literature Society.[13] Every effort was made to record whatever could still be rescued of the old song tradition. Thus only the oldest people were asked about songs. This was not, of course, a failing of Finnish collectors alone. It is known that Cecil Sharp, for example, rarely collected from anyone under sixty.[14] As a result, the most vital tradition at the moment of collection was in danger of being left undocumented with sufficient thoroughness. In Finland the old Kalevala songs or poems, as they were usually called, were among the most sought after. Songs of the new stratum were written down if performed spontaneously, but they were not particularly asked for, especially since they were to a great extent part of the repertoire of the younger people.

Towards the end of last century more careful attention was, however, paid to collection, and gradually attempts were made to document the more recent song tradition too. In 1883 the Finnish press published a summons to collect, mentioning the more recent songs alongside the old ones and asking people to send in other folk items too, such as fairy tales, riddles, proverbs, tales, incantations.[15] By 1900 the Society had a collection of 14,000 new songs. Although many other traditional genres were being collected by special inquiries, songs were not collected in this way. The reason was presumably that they seemed to be finding their way to the Society in any case, and the collections were being added to by the Society's own researchers and collectors and also by many amateurs. Since there was no systematic program for recording newer songs, the narrative song in the new meter was not thoroughly documented in time. Thus some songs have only one or two recorded variants. An example is "Sisarukset" ("The Sisters," cf. TSB A 38), for which only one variant, an incomplete one, is known. Only two variants have been recorded of the ballad "Wilhelmi ja Liisunen" ("Wilhelm and Little Lisa," cf. Child 5, TSB D 288).

Not until 1953 did the Folklore Archives of the Finnish Literature Society organize the first project to add specifically to the collection of songs. The result was good: 17,000 songs. Five years ago new material comprising more than 4,000 songs was again obtained, a third of it on sound tapes.

Although systematic recording was begun late, there is nevertheless a very considerable collection of folk songs in the new meter in the archives. The number of items in the manuscript material alone runs to about 130,000. In addition there are several thousand tapes both in the folklore Archives and at the Institute for Folk Tradition at Tampere University, which was founded in the 1960s. The proportion of narrative song cannot be estimated at the moment for technical archive reasons: written material used not to be included at all in the archive numbering; thus broadside ballads, for example, are not included at all in the figures on the earlier material. In any case there is sufficient material for research centering on the genre, but archive material such as this cannot provide an answer to many of the problems of modern research, such as the study of performance or the process by which tradition is passed on.

W. Edson Richmond, in dealing with the narrative folk song, points out: "Each culture in which such poetry has lived, however, has produced its own prosodic patterns, and these, in turn, have undergone their own evolution."[16] Over the centuries the Finns created their own prosodic patterns. These emerged out of the framework created by the language itself, the musical and verbal elements adjusting to one another. Forgetting the old way of singing and giving birth to the new meant a radical breakthrough in vocal expression as a whole. It meant discarding the traditional formulaic language and structural models and developing and assimilating a prosodic and musical pattern of a new type, i.e., a completely new vocal language. The influences were, however, taken from a linguistic and musical form of expression completely foreign to the Finns, and assimilating them did not happen in a flash, but took its own time. Thus the language of the song went on developing right up to the end of the eighteenth century. By then it had developed into an oral mode of expression operating through formulas and certain structural and stylistic basic patterns, a skill comparable to the Kalevala song as it existed in everyone's repertoire. This pattern, called a roundelay, presumably did not even exist in the seventeenth and early eighteenth centuries.

The old manner of singing was not, of course, universally forgotten by different people or different singers even simultaneously. The old style influenced the emergence of the new language of expression in many different ways. Proof of this is the many songs from the seventeenth and eighteenth centuries that contain features of the old type of song. These songs do not seem to have had an established form. The poetic meter varied; it did not keep to the even trochaic meter of the old song, and the number of syllables varied. Often there was alliteration, and on top of this a tendency towards rhyme. As a result verses became established. There were a number of verse and end-rhyme constructions and rhyme was not used with the same regularity as in the nineteenth century. The melodies expanded considerably from the pentachord to tunes spanning an octave or more. There was also a gradual transfer to the minor and major tonalities. Songs such as these, containing features of both types, can be called transitional songs.[17]

One type of transitional song is the ballad. A vital factor in borrowing ballads from the Swedes was melody; some songs appear to adhere slavishly to their Swedish model both in their melody and their text. Sometimes both the words and the melody have been borrowed simultaneously in the same ballad variant, in which case they are the same as in the Swedish variant model. It was, however, more usual for the words and the melody to be lifted from different sources. Sometimes the first part of a song might have been taken from a Swedish song but the last part was an independent Finnish development. There was, however, no original, creative composition proper, and counterparts can be found for all ballads in the Swedish language. The world of values and the message contained in them is naturally also in line with the Scandinavian ballad tradition.

Thematically the majority of ballads can be classified under love or domestic tragedies. Examples are the ballads "The Death of the Bride," "The Brother-Slayer," "Kaksi kuninkaanlasta" ("The Two Royal Children," Erk-Bohme 83-85),[18] and The Maid Freed from the Gallows," which were popular all over Finland. There are two types of riddling ballads, "Vesmanviiki" (TSB E 52, cf. Child 1) and "Vanha muori ja nuori mies" ("The Old Hag and the Young Fellow"). The latter is a counterpart to the ballad, seldom met with in the Scandinavian or British traditions, which Child mentions as number 3: "The False Knight upon the Road." Eight variants of this are, however, known in the Finnish tradition. In the ballad "Herra Petteri" ("Sir Peter"), the theme is human sacrifice (Child 57, TSB D 361); and "The Maiden in the Count's Lap" is by nature a pastorale, where the narrative is in the first person and the dramatic approach is weaker.

Since the new-meter folk song developed into a vital oral tradition among lyric songs, it is surprising that the narrative song remained, as it were, unfinished in regard to its prosodic patterns. Although the few ballads of the new stratum known to us were in fact very popular, the ballad as a genre did not progress beyond the translation stage and did not begin a strong Finnish creative tradition. Faulty documentation can be blamed partly for this, but not even this alters the fact that no oral tradition of narrative song similar to that of the roundelay ever came into being. Certain signs, however, indicate that this potential existed, and in different circumstances a living oral tradition might have ensued. A few men of common renown in the nineteenth century--robbers and murderers--became popular heroes, and there were numerous verses on the roundelay pattern telling of their deeds. They lacked a uniform thematic scheme, however; the verses remained disjointed and were used in the same way as the lyrical roundelay.

In seeking the reasons for the absence of the Finnish oral narrative song, reference was made above to the written song, which took on the role of the oral tradition. Just as the conditions for the original narrative song were forming, it became drowned in the flood of written songs.[19]

The greatest part of the flood of written songs was provided by the broadside. As in other parts of the Nordic countries, in Finland, too, the broadside became a medium having a tremendous influence on the song repertoire of the average person, and also in changing people's attitudes to songs assimilated orally. Since booklearning and books in general were highly valued, so the printed song was regarded as more valuable and correct than its oral form.[20] Most of the boradsides were, however, songs that were translated directly from Swedish, or else they were Finnish compositions with no oral tradition behind them. In Finland broadsides began to be published from the seventeenth century onwards. At the outset, they were only religious, but ones with a secular content gradually became more common. The heyday of broadside literature in Finland came in the latter half of the nineteenth century, and they were still popular even in this century, right up to the First World War.

In Salokas' study of early secular broadsheet literature, songs were divided into five groups; the same classification applies equally well to later material too. The biggest group contains epic songs, but there is also narrative material in the historical and educational songs. The songs classified as historical were in the nature of news, tellings of events such as wars or fires or other misfortunes. Murders were also served up in sensational style and often had a moral twist at the end. Many of these were fated to be forgotten quickly once the event had lost its news value or its effect on people's lives. For example, the murder of the Russian Czar Alexander II began a flood of dirges in Finland. The Czar's policy towards Finland had been favourable and he was generally looked on as a good ruler. An earlier attempt on the Czar's life had caused the Finnish songsters to break out in hymns of praise and thanks because of the happy ending. The murder then inspired a host of broadside poets to put pen to paper and turn out songs in memory of the Czar. All in all nearly forty songs have been classified.[21] They did not, however, take root in oral tradition, and by the beginning of the twentieth century they were seldom sung. Natural catastrophes and accidents were also popular themes for songs. The sinking of the Titanic provided the subject for some twenty or more Finnish songs, and some of them are still in the repertoire of the older generation. Similarly, accidents in Finnish waters were recorded in song.

Many songs classed as educational also have narrative content. Many of the songs telling of the lives of prisoners have strong moral pathos, warning the listener. These are of purely Finnish origin. There are also educational songs which have a foreign origin; for example, one of the most common songs published by way of a warning is "Pommerin piika" ("The Servant Girl of Pomerania"), originally a German song, which tells the tale of a girl who longed for finery and was finally swallowed up by the earth. The song was published for the first time in 1761 and was subsequently published in more than forty editions right up to the end of the nineteenth century.[22] It is still known even today.

By far the most popular from the latter half of the nineteenth century onward, however, have been the entertaining narrative songs, ballads or ballad imitations, and sentimental romances. They tell of the relationship between two young people who are usually of different social status. The maidens are daughters of the nobility or of rich traders or ship-owners; or they are heiresses to a great manor; or else they are orphans, fishermen's daughters, serving girls, or sometimes factory workers. The young men are sons of princes, nobles, only sons or students (which in nineteenth-century Finland meant they belonged to the upper class: a student was a future man of consequence). On the other hand, they might be poor sailors or farm hands. The young people's parents, usually the father, opposed the marriage and parted the lovers. The young people remained faithful to one another and the result was often death. Sometimes the hard-hearted father would soften at the last moment; death would be avoided and the song would have a happy ending.

Social inequality is the basic premise in these songs, and the idea is to stress the power of faithful love. Woe betide the man who breaks his promise. Often disaster also befalls anyone who tries to prevent the union of lovers. The motif of the lover returning to his former bride, either incognito or as a spirit, is repeated in a number of ballads. One of the most popular is "Haamu ja Marjaana" ("The Ghost and Marjaana," cf. Child 77), which took root in the Finnish tradition through five broadside editions in 1902-1905. It was recorded on a gramophone record very early on, in 1924. It was reissued on record in 1950 and met with great popularity; thus this ballad is one of the songs familiar to almost every middle-generation Finn today.[23] Another popular song on the theme of the demon lover is "Aalonksi ja Emueli" ("Aalonksi and Emueli"), which is based on M. G. Lewis' poem Alonzo the Brave and Fair Imogine.[24] This song is likewise in the repertoire of many older Finns today.

Social equality and social injustices are given even more emphasis in a few songs in which love is not the central motif. These already point to the class conflicts and themes recorded with far greater thoroughness in the songs of the workers; they did not clearly emerge in Finland until after the Civil War of 1918.[25]

One of these earlier narrative songs clearly containing social criticism is "Matti ja Pappi" ("Matti and the Clergyman"). The criticism is aimed at the priest who, in accordance with the ancient privileges of the Finnish clergy, is paid for his services at a funeral in the form of a cow. This time the price of the service seems grotesque, because it was the last cow belonging to the man burying his wife. Usually the clergy or the Church hold a position of trust in the eyes of the Finns, and seldom have they been placed in such an unfavourable light in songs as in this case. Jests, on the other hand, bring out the attitudes of the Finns towards the clergy with far greater thoroughness.[26]

The texts to the first broadsides published in Finland were mostly translations of Swedish songs. The proportion of Finnish songs did, however, increase in the latter half of the nineteenth century. Finnish broadside poets learned to make use of their foreign examples to compose new songs using their own topical themes and motifs. These poets also had a command of certain opening and closing formulas. Among the most common were: "Let me now take up my pen," "Let me begin to tell you," "Let me sing to you of, . . ." "As I sit humming sadly," "A man of sorrow, I sing to you, . . ." and so on. Formulas such as these often go with songs telling news and containing sensational material. Ballads or ballad imitations and songs in the style of a romance more often began without any phrase suggesting a personal opinion by stating simply, "There was a merchant in India," "There was a handsome soldier and a maiden fair," "There was a rich house."

In the latter half of the nineteenth century the most common verse form for broadsides became the verse with four lines divided into two pairs of rhyming lines, corresponding in rhythm to the lyrical roundelay verse. Although broadside songs came into being and were spread in written form, they nevertheless observed the verse models of the oral tradition. This model had, from the end of the eighteenth century onwards, already become so engraved on public awareness that the broadside poets, too, naturally were skilled in it. Although the narrative song in the nineteenth century remained a transitional form in oral tradition, failing to develop into a genre producing independent song types, it still lives on in written form within the broadside song tradition. New types of song were still being invented even in the twentieth century.

The bulk of Finnish broadside poetry came into being in the nineteenth century and thus reflects the world as it was viewed at that time. The rational overall impression is far less colorful than the world of the Kalevala song, with its nuances and fairy-tale, mythical, and supernatural elements. True, supernatural themes and motifs do appear in the songs of the new stratum too, but the emphasis nevertheless lies elsewhere: on erotic problems. Examination of its various manifestations in different strata has shown that the values regulating life in the period of the old song had given way to new ones by the beginning of the nineteenth century. The all-vanquishing power of romantic love was emphasized in songs as the counterbalance to the authority of the family. This outlook also corresponded to historical developments in Finnish society. In the nineteenth century the power of the family in the forming of marriage alliances gave way to freer attitudes and the right to choose one's own husband or wife. The wealth of songs telling of young romantic love and the way in which aspects of this love are stressed are evident against precisely this background.[27]

What remains of the narrative folk song in the mind of the modern Finn? Does he still have any command of the traditional narrative song, and if he has, then what sorts of songs are in his repertoire? In order to answer these questions, I studied the material acquired by the Folklore Archives as the result of collection organized in 1978-1979.[28] I chose twelve singers from the material, the ones with the biggest repertoires. The singers live in different parts of Finland (one from Western Finland, one from Central Finland, one from Northern Finland and the rest from various parts of Eastern Finland). The oldest was born in 1900 and the youngest in 1923. The biggest collection obtained from one singer comprised 242 songs. Four singers provided 100-200 songs and the rest 40-100 songs. The total variants numbered 1054. This material does not, even so, give a complete picture of what they knew, for it was recorded using spontaneous collection. No special inquiry lists were used, nor were singers asked about individual songs; the tradition bearers performed what they remembered at the time of recording. Thus obtained, the material represents the repertoire best known to the singers.

Study of the percentage of narrative songs revealed that they represented 9% of the total common repertoire. There were great differences between singers. The eighty-four-variant repertoire of one singer included no narrative songs at all--only lyrical roundelays. For five singers narrative songs accounted for only a few per cent (2-6%), whereas for some they represented as much as 30%. Fifty-six different types of songs were included in this sample, thirty-nine appearing only once. Of the remaining songs, nine appeared twice, two songs three times, three songs four times, three songs five times and one song seven times. The song known by seven singers was the broadside ballad "Kauppias Intiasta" ("The Merchant in India"), as it is most often called, and it tells of Juliaana, the daughter of a rich merchant who tries to prevent his daughter from marrying a poor sailor by sending him across the ocean. The daughter dies of grief while her loved-one is away. When the sailor receives the message telling of the girl's death, he speedily returns and finds his beloved dead. However, because of the strength of his great love the girl suddenly comes back to life again.

Ballads such as this of sentimental love (romantic tragedies) are the largest category within the collected material, representing twenty-six types. The other themes

are: domestic tragedies--six, accidents and disasters--six,
ballads of the supernatural--four, religious ballads--four,
songs connected with criminals--two, satirical and jocular
themes--three, political songs connected with the Civil War
of 1918--two, pastorales--one and others--three.

The majority of the songs are broadsides; most were
published between 1880 and 1920, but there are also some
published before and after these dates. There are three
transitional songs known in the oral tradition even before
they were printed ("The Two Royal Children," "Sir Peter,"
and "The Maiden in the Count's Lap"). There are two ballads
on the demon lover theme ("The Ghost and Marjaana" and
"Aalonksi and Emueli"). There are, further, three ballad
imitations composed by writers in folk style. The Titanic is
the subject of three variants and smaller shipwrecks, of a
further three. The repertoire of one singer further included
two compositions of his own--songs in a humorous style on
love themes.

Quantitatively this material is not particularly large.
A sample of just over one thousand songs is relatively
slight compared with all the Folklore Archives in fact
contain. What is more, the collection method is not suitable
for studying, for example, the singing activity or total
repertoire of people in general. But this material
nevertheless brings out a few points sufficiently clearly.
The older generation of singers--people of about sixty or
more, who were young in the 1920s and 1930s--were to some
extent familiar with traditional narrative songs. The bulk
of their repertoire did, however, constitute songs other
than narrative ones. The percentage of narrative songs
depended on individual factors. Most narrative songs are
written products that spread as broadsides; in many cases,
nevertheless, they were learned verbally, being passed on
from mouth to mouth. The singer did not necessarily always
have a printed sheet or hand-written song book, though the
latter were common among young people in the 1920s and
1930s. By far the most common were romantic and tragic
themes telling of young love. Secondary motifs criticizing
society are included in many songs, however, and they point
the way to the assimilation of class-consciousness typical
of the worker song, which later comes out mostly as epic-
lyrical songs. Jocular and humorous themes account for only
a few: they did not seem to appeal to Finnish singers of
narrative songs. Satire and derision are better suited to
media other than the narrative song.

It is also important to note that most of the singers
in question came from the country and learned their
repertoire there. Thus this material reflects the situation

among the rural population exclusively. A surprising amount of the traditional song repertoire seems to have been preserved among young country people right up to the 1930s; many of the broadside ballads already in fashion in the 1880s were still being sung by young people in the 1930s. A record song in this respect is "The Servant Girl of Pomerania," which appeared as a broadside in Finland as early as 1761.

It should, however, be remembered that these songs represent specifically one genre still in fashion in the 1920s and 1930s. The majority of young people today are not interested in these songs and do not even know of their existence. The only exception is a small group of youngsters interested in traditional folk music and its revival. Over the past ten years their ranks have shown signs of growing; but this interest cannot, of course, be compared to the trends that dominate young people's music today.

The Second World War is a dividing line, after which the former folk song known in its day as the "new song" and the popular song can no longer be spoken of as a viable genre. Instead, great changes were taking place. After the First World War the pop song had already conquered the market as the gramophone record gradually became more and more popular. But even in the 1930s the practice of ring-games, for example at evening socials, still kept up the roundelay tradition. The song book custom in turn helped the learning of broadsides. But by the end of the 1940s ring-games were only something for school festivals, and the era of the hand-written song book was over. If anything, it was full of pop songs.

In the early 1950s Finland's biggest publisher of sheet music and records began to issue an annual booklet called "Toivelaulut" ("Song Requests"), containing the most popular recorded songs and hits from each month. The booklets immediately caught on, running to many editions, often with many thousands of copies (a large number for Finland). Each booklet contained sixty to eighty songs and several booklets were issued a year. The first ones contained both Finnish and foreign folk songs, operetta songs, opera arias, Finnish and foreign hits and light-hearted ditties. The contents thus varied greatly, and as examples of the foreign songs in the first booklet we may take "Loch Lomond," "Old Black Joe," "Carry Me Back to Old Virginny," "Perhaps, Perhaps, Perhaps," "Heartaches," and "Riders in the Sky." At the beginning of the 1950s Finnish hit production was still suffering from the after-effects of the War, and the emphasis was to a great extent on foreign material. The contents of "Song Requests" were tied to commercial needs and thus also to foreign fashionable trends. Only 28% of the songs in the first booklet were Finnish. With a few exceptions, the narrative songs had vanished and the remaining songs consisted of lyrical and epic-lyrical love or comic songs.

"Song Requests" continues to appear, and for example the four booklets published in the course of 1981 contained 153 songs. Now the ratio between Finnish and foreign songs is the reverse of what it was at the start of the 1950s; nearly 70% are now Finnish. As before, love lyrics are still the central element of the words of pop songs, but these have been joined by a radically new element. This element is most evident in the programs of bands that produce music separate from the big recording companies and which usually come from some part of Finland other than the area around the capital, Helsinki. These bands play rock music and perform their own compositions and pieces.

Rock and Roll had already reached Finland by the 1950s, and since then the Finns have of course tried to follow the same trends as in the rest of the world. Only in recent years, however, has rock taken on new dimensions in Finland. People speak in this context of a New Wave. No longer do they simply imitate Anglo-American culture; now young people are creating songs about the Finnish way of life, songs that state opinions on matters that in recent years have come in for considerable debate in Finland. Admittedly the songs of the New Wave do contain much that is universal, on themes of topical importance the world over, but the way of handling these themes is Finnish and the message is not always fully revealed to anyone who has not lived in precisely this society. Many well-known phrases and references to particular customs hover in the background along with doctrines of the Protestant Church and Biblical myths.

Although Finland lies in one of the most peaceful corners of the world, this does not mean that world events do not affect the Finns too. The mass media take care to see that it is impossible not to form some opinion of world events. Uneasiness at the state of the world and the preservation of peace, the fear of nuclear weapons, and growing unemployment are matters to which young people in Finland, as elsewhere in the world, have readily reacted. Faith in politicians' promises, and likewise in the weapons of both East and West, has vanished. "Farewell to arms / Farewell to the lies people believed / Farewell to the speeches by which sins were atoned for / farewell to the arms with which life is protected / Farewell to the arms with which life is destroyed," proclaims one pacifist singer of the new wave (Jyrki Siukonen).[29]

These songs are not narrative. They do not tell a particular story or series of events, nor are they by nature objective. They are reminiscent of the lyric in that they take a personal stand at the level of me and you. But they go far beyond the normal, conventional, Finnish hit lyric in their choice of subject matter and the way this subject matter is treated. Without being narrative in a traditional way, these songs nevertheless speak in clear terms of the modern world and bring out the atmosphere of insecurity, uncertainty, and fear that prevails not only in the Third World but also amid the ostensible well-being of western man. "Go to hell freezer chests, into the grave all you cars / Color TV's are out, are out, stereos fit for the marsh," shouts a singer scorning the status symbols of the modern Finnish man-in-the-street. These songs do not serve any propaganda purpose; they speak of the lack of illusion and the Weltschmerz of today's young: "The trumpets of the gods sound not for the new generation / as deaf and dumb it grovels in the steps of the fathers" (Ismo Alanko).

But even amid all this anxiety and fear, the lust for life is powerful: "Listen, plant that apple tree even though the fire is already licking your hair / Though tomorrow the fall-out will descend upon us/though tomorrow the sun will die / Be there, it's easier that way / be there when the flames start to lick me. Be there and shout your torment to the skies only when the sun dies. / There you can stand beside me and wave / as the world limps into its grave" (Juice Leskinen).

One unique feature is the strong moral pathos of many songs. A host of generally accepted directions concerning love of one's neighbour and the Christian view of the world come out, for example, in the following song: "Take care of yourself / and those who suffer. / Give alms to those who need them to live. / Remember to build / where home has collapsed. / Try to encourage those / who in their decisions waver / For anyone who receives help / will one day think to give it" (Pave Maijanen). Morality is even a fundamental element in the repertoire of one band.[30] They concern themselves repeatedly with the last judgment and the question of whether we are all sinful. The line of the traditional hymn that sounds over the Finnish cemetery from one generation to another, "Wretched am I, worm, pilgrim on earth" is slipped in by a rock singer among his own moral teachings: "Man of God, grab hold of the lamb / Wretched am I, worm, pilgrim on earth, Resurrection, when it's all over, resurrection, the new day / Resurrection, there's only one chance, Be human, be human" (Juice Leskinen).

The songs of the New Wave are of course only one part of modern Finnish pop culture. The bulk of it is conventional and commercial, containing platitudes both in content and message. The songs of the New Wave differ from normal songs both in the concern of their content and in their language. They use broken everyday language, young people's slang, and also, often, expressions of a sexual nature. They have in fact aroused deep moral indignation in many listeners because of an assumed atheism and the mocking of sacred values. In fact some songs have even been banned from radio and television. When a rock singer reiterates in a husky voice: "It's good to be a bum / no troubles, no headaches," the middle-aged Finn frowns and switches the radio off. He does not hear what the singer is trying to say: "If being a bum means loving / making the most of the moment and not wanting to kill / it's good to be a bum" (Ismo Alanko).

We do not have to search far to find a corresponding phenomenon some hundred and fifty years ago. The "new folk song" that spread after the Kalevala song was regarded by the intelligentsia as having negative features. The new folk song nevertheless developed in its own way into a viable song culture. True, it was completely different and did not appear to be as deep or as rich in nuance as the old song, but it fulfilled the needs of the people using it at that time. They created their songs to satisfy their own needs. We may, however, ask where the epic song has vanished to from the repertoire of today's young singer. Whereas a representative of the older generation can still compose a narrative song himself on the basis of the traditional song models he has at his command, the contemporary song writer does not. The content of the song is expressed in a more concise way than in the narrative song, using the devices of the lyrical, or at most the epic-lyrical song. The composer does not draw on epic. Or is this just the outcome of a narrowness and shortness of perspective in examining songs? Is there something quite new and different on the way, just as there was a hundred years ago when the Finns, having lost the tradition of the oral epic song, learned to create new popular songs in a different way, on paper?

The music of modern youth cannot yet be expressed objectively nor by using the same criteria as those that applied to the old folk song. An open mind is needed to listen to what the husky, wailing voice amid the din created by the electric guitars and drums is trying to say. Sometimes the composer may be a virtuoso of verbal expression who has succeeded in crystallizing ideas about our age perhaps better than many contemporary poets. And as W. Edson Richmond said, "Only where such virtuosi still

exist is folk poetry a living tradition."31 In saying this
Richmond was referring in particular to the folk song.
Without expressing in this context any opinion in general
about how far rock culture or pop music goes in constituting
folk song, it is nevertheless clear that the phenomenon in
question is one that the folklorist cannot, in examining the
changing song, overlook.

[1]The most complete general treatise on Kalevala poetry is by Matti Kuusi in the work "Kirjoittamaton kirjallisuus," Suomen kirjallisuus I (Helsinki: Suomalaisen Kirjallisuuden Seura ja Kustannusosakeyhtiö Otava, 1963), 31-417. See also Finnish Folk Poetry: Epic: An Anthology in Finnish and English, ed. and trans. by Matti Kuusi, Keith Bosley, Michael Branch, Publications of the Finnish Literature Society No. 329 (Helsinki: Finnish Literature Society, 1977).

[2]Matti Kuusi, "Ikkuna kalevalaiseen muinaisuuteen," in Kalevalaista kertomarunoutta, toim. Matti Kuusi, Suomalaisen Kirjallisuuden Seuran toimituksia, No. 362 (Helsinki: Suomalaisen Kirjallisuuden Seura, 1980), p. 23.

[3]Matti Hako, "Riimilliset kansanlaulut," Suomen kirjallisuus I ed., Matti Kuusi (Helsinki: Suomalaisen Kirjallisuuden Seura ja Kustannusosakeyhtiö Otava, 1963), p. 418.

[4]It is difficult to find a corresponding term in English for the term rekilaulu. The nearest term would be "roundelay." For the etymology of the term rekilaulu see Mikko Saarenheimo, "Sananen suomalaisen rekivirren alkuperästä," Kirjallisuuden tutkijain seuran vuosikirja, 16 (1958) 220-24; Lauri Kettunen, "Rekilaulu-kansanetymologia," Kalevalaseuran vuosikirja, 42 (1962), 265-71.

[5]Elias Lönnrot, "Alkulause," in Kanteletar elikkä Suomen Kansan Vanhoja Lauluja ja Virsiä (Helsinki: Suomalaisen Kirjallisuuden Seura, 1840), p. xxxii.

[6]Vihtori Laurila, Suomen rahvaan runoniekat sääty-yhteiskunnan aikana, I, Suomalaisen Kirjallisuuden Seuran toimituksia 249 (Helsinki: Suomalaisen Kirjallisuuden Seura, 1956), 35-58.

[7]James Francis Child, ed. The English and Scottish Popular Ballads (1882-98; rpt.: New York: Folklore Press, 1956), pp. 167-170, The Types of the Scandinavian Medieval Ballad, ed. by Bengt R. Jonsson, Svale Solheim and Eva Danielson (Oslo and Stockholm: Universitetsforlaget, 1978), p. 164.

[8] Julius and Kaarle Krohn, "Kahdenlaisella runomitalla," in Kantelettaren tutkimuksia (Helsinki: Suomalaisen Kirjallisuuden Seura, 1900), pp. 253-348.

[9] J. J. Mikkola, "Balladi Wesmanviikistä," Virittäjä, 9 (1905), 57-63.

[10] Martti Haavio, Kansanrunojen maailmanselitys (Helsinki: Werner Söderström Osakeyhtiö, 1955), pp. 76-120, 204-445.

[11] Eino Salokas, "Maallinen arkkirunoutemme Ruotsin vallan aikana," Suomi, 5, No. 3 (1927), 255.

[12] Matti Vilppula, "Aalonksi ja Emueli: Erään arkkiballadin taustaa," Suomi 114, No. 3 (1969), 84.

[13] For early activities of the Finnish Literature Society see Jouko Hautala, "The Folklore Archives of the Finnish Literature Society," Studia Fennica 7 (1957), 1-36 and for later activities, "The Folklore Archives of the Finnish Literature Society," in A Guide to Nordic Tradition Archives, ed. by Gun Herranen and Lassi Saressalo, NIF Publications No. 7 (Turku: Nordic Institute of Folklore, 1978), 32-42.

[14] Ray M. Lawless, "Some Problems and Definitions," in Folksingers and Folksong in America: A Handbook of Biography, Bibliography and Discography (New York: Duell, Sloan, and Pearce, 1960), p. 3.

[15] Martti Haavio, "Kansanrunouden keruu ja tutkimus," Suomi 5, No. 12 (1935), 70.

[16] W. Edson Richmond, "Narrative Folk Poetry," in Folklore and Folklife: An Introduction, ed. by Richard M. Dorson (Chicago: University of Chicago Press, 1972), p. 90.

[17] Anneli Asplund, "Riimilliset kansanlaulut" in Kansanmusiikki, toim. Anneli Asplund ja Matti Hako, Suomalaisen Kirjallisuuden Seuran toimituksia, 366 (Helsinki: Suomalaisen Kirjallisuuden Seura, 1981), 64-68.

[18] Ludwig Erk and Franz Böhme, Deutscher Liedhort (Leipzig: Breitkopf und Härtel, 1893), I, 289-304.

[19]Anneli Asplund, "Balladen i den finska folkvisetraditionen," in Sumlen 1982, Årsbok för vis-och folkmusikforskning (Stockholm: Svenskt Visarkiv, 1983), pp. 17-35.

[20]Anneli Asplund, "The Oldest Finnish Broadside Ballads and Their Influence on the Oral Tradition," Studia Fennica, 18 (1974), 134-37.

[21]Anneli Asplund, ed., "The Finnish Broadside Tradition," Broadside Songs: Finnish Folk Music 2. A textbook for record SFLP 8566 (Helsinki: Suomalaisen Kirjallisuuden Seura, 1976), pp. 9-10, 32.

[22]Asplund, "Broadside Tradition," p. 31.

[23]Urpo Haapanen, ed., "Catalogue of Finnish Records: 1902-1945," Finnish Institute of Recorded Sound. Publication No. 4 (Helsinki: Suomen Äänitearkisto, 1970), p. 33; Id., Publication No. 1 (Helsinki, 1967), p. 338.

[24]Vilppula, pp. 10-57.

[25]For workers' songs in Finland see Ilpo Saunio, Veli sisko kuulet kummat soitot: Työväenlaulut eilen ja tänään (Helsinki: Kansankulttuuri Oy, 1974), pp. 235-341.

[26]Seppo Knuuttila, "Kaskut ja vitsit," in Kertomusperinne: Kirjoituksia proosaperinteen lajeista ja tutkimuksesta, toim. Irma-Riitta Järvinen ja Seppo Knuuttila. Tietolipas, 90 (Helsinki: Suomalaisen Kirjallisuuden Seura, 1982), 106-25.

[27]Anneli Asplund, "Kansanlaulustomme eroottisten asenteiden muutoksista," Kotiseutu, 1 (1972), 32-38.

[28]The collection was arranged jointly by the Folklore Archives of the Finnish Literature Society and the Rural Education Association, and it yielded both manuscripts and sound material. The research material was selected from the material recorded on sound tapes only.

[29]The texts quoted in this section have been published in Toivelauluja, 119-21 (Helsinki: Musiikki Fazer, 1981) and have been recorded by Poco Records, Pälp 17.

[30]Interview by Seppo Knuuttila and Marja Niiniluoto, published in <u>Uusi Suomi</u>, 31 (1982), 27.

[31]Richmond, p. 86.

<u>Finnish Literature Society</u>
<u>Helsinki</u>

Translated from the Finnish by Susan Sinisalo

EL CONDE ARNALDOS*   COUNT ARNALDOS

Martin Nuncio, Cancionero de romances, Antwerp, c. 1548.
Tune from Diego Pisador, Libro de musica de vihuela,
1552.

Qvien vuiesse tal ventura
sobre las aguas de mar

2 como vuo el conde Arnaldos
la mañana de san juan
con vn falcon enla mano
la caza yua cazar

4 vio venir vna galera
que a tierra quiere llegar
las velas traya de seda
la exercia de vn cendal

6 marinero que la manda
diziendo viene vn cantar
que la mar fazia en calma
los vientos haze amaynar

8 los peces que andan nel hondo
arriba los haze andar
las aues que andan bolando
nel mastel las faz posar

10 alli fablo el conde Arnaldos
bien oyreys lo que dira
por dios te ruego marinero
digas me ora esse cantar

Who might have such good fortune,
On the waters of the sea,

As had Count Arnaldos
On the morning of St. John!
With a falcon upon his hand,
He went to hunt for game.

He saw a ship come sailing,
Striving to reach the land:
Its sails were all of silken cloth;
Its shrouds of silken thread;

The mariner who is steering it
Comes singing a magic song,
That made the sea become all calm;
It makes the winds die down;

The fish that swim down in the deep,
To the surface it makes them rise;
The birds all flying through the air,
It makes them perch on the mast.

Then spoke Count Arnaldos,
Well will you hear what he says:
"In God's name, I beg you, mariner,
Teach me now that song."

respondiole el marinero	To him the mariner answered,
tal respuesta le fue a dar	Such an answer he gave to him:
yo no digo esta cancion	"I will teach that song to no one,
sino a quien comigo va	But to him who goes with me."

Tune reprinted in G. Morphy, <u>Les Luthistes espagnols</u> . . .
(Leipzig: Breitkopf and Härtel, 1902), II, 176-77.

SAMUEL G. ARMISTEAD

HISPANIC BALLAD STUDIES:
Recent Trends in Criticism

The Hispanic ballad is in many ways quite similar to its counterparts in other European culture areas, yet, in other ways it is quite different, a highly distinctive form of traditional narrative poetry. Many of the general definitions and overall characteristics of ballads in other speech communities could just as well apply to the Hispanic romance in its Spanish, Portuguese, Catalan, and Judeo-Spanish modalities and their extra-European extensions.[1] Roderick Beaton's perceptive description of Greek tragoúdia could be shifted to their Hispanic counterparts without fear of misrepresenting essential features:

> Very few Greek songs . . . are either charming or simple. Most are formal and highly organised although . . . these characteristics are not always immediately apparent. The ideas they express are complex, often hauntingly elusive; and alongside their lyricism and fine imagery there is a violence and an uncompromisingly pragmatic outlook which are not easily sentimentalised.[2]

Conversely, many of the features identified by Colin Smith in his insightful appraisal of the Spanish ballad-- "stylistic compression, . . . terseness and dramatic power, . . . extreme plainness of language bereft of elaborate simile, metaphor and other rhetoric, . . . implicit rather than explicit, . . . not exemplary or didactic, . . . lack/ing in/ religiosity, . . . /with a/ unique ability to touch a great variety of universal human emotions"--would obviously strike a note of recognition in anyone familiar with Anglo-American or any other European ballad tradition.[3] Many Hispanic ballad types, whether genetically related or coincidentally similar (Husband's Return, Evil Mother-in-Law, Baffled Knight, Adulteress, Brother finds Lost Sister, Girl Poisons Lover, Warrior Maiden, and numerous others) are also shared in common with the Pan-European tradition.[4]

Yet in several of its characteristics and circumstances--its form, its complex origins and current cultural situation--the Hispanic ballad seems at variance with neighboring traditions. A majority of Hispanic narrative songs are not strophic, as is the case with other Western European ballads, but consist rather of a single series, of indeterminate length, of 16-syllable verses divided into two 8-syllable hemistichs, with one consistent assonant rhyme in the even hemistichs throughout the poem. Ostensibly, such uniform formal characteristics should, in theory at least, make the definition of a ballad in the various Hispanic sub-traditions a relatively easy task, but in practice, a number of hexasyllabic, strophic, and polyassonant narrative songs are also habitually included in the corpus.[5]

The Hispanic ballad also differs from its European relatives in its pedigree, in that both its verse form and a number of its narrative themes derive from the medieval Spanish epic and from Spanish adaptations of medieval French chansons de geste.[6] The connection between epic and ballad is direct and genetic. Some of the earliest romances derive from narrative fragments of the longer epic poems. Without doubt, however, there are also other elements in the Hispanic ballad's complex genealogy: The primitive lyric, thematic borrowings from European--chiefly French--balladry, and early use of the emergent epic-ballad meter in compositions independent of both epic or imported balladry are all factors which undoubtedly played essential roles in the development of the genre.[7] The Hispanic ballad's origins must, then, have been multiple and complex. Distinctive too is the Spanish romance's peculiar relation to learned literature. In the very first printed collection there are already poems of learned authorship written in ballad verse,[8] and even before, there is evidence that ballads, written down from oral tradition, were adapted to the peculiar artistic intent of an individual literate poet.[9]

The Hispanic ballad is also outstanding, if not unique, in Europe at least, as regards the relative vigor with which it has survived down to the present time. While several of the once most brilliant and productive ballad traditions of medieval Europe are now essentially dead, the Hispanic ballad, though admittedly in grave danger of extinction in many areas, can still be collected abundantly in its different geographic sub-traditions throughout the Hispanic world.[10] It is symptomatic that the earliest known ballad-- "The Lady and the Shepherd," written down by Jaume Olesa, a Catalan law student, in Florence, in 1421--was until recently still sung in the oral tradition of Spanish Jews in Morocco and the Near East.[11] Various other narrative themes have survived in direct oral tradition from the Middle Ages down to the present day. Perhaps the most striking characteristic of the Hispanic tradition is its chronological and geographic continuity. It is impossible to study the early ballads without constant reference to the modern tradition in all its different branches: A fifteenth- or sixteenth-century text may very well be clarified by another now sung in Northern Portugal, in Asturias, in

Catalonia or in North Africa; at the same time, no one of these modern sub-traditions can be thoroughly studied to the exclusion of any of the others (or of the early evidence either). The consistent correlation of ballads to Hispanic languages is another factor worthy of note. It is safe to say, as Menendez Pidal theorized years ago, that romances will be found wherever Spanish, Portuguese, Catalan and Judeo-Spanish are spoken thoughout the world.[12]

Modern Hispanic ballad scholarship had its origins in the brilliant and vigorous initiatives of the great Spanish philologist, Ramón Menéndez Pidal, who, during the early decades of this century, established rigorous modern methodology in Spanish medieval scholarship, philology, dialectology, historiography, and related disciplines.[13] Ballad studies continued to be one of Menendez Pidal's major interests throughout his long and extraordinarily productive scholarly career.[14] He laid the groundwork for the study of early manuscript and printed evidence of ballads and, at the same time, rediscovered the modern tradition in all its geographic diversity, personally conducting field work both in Spain and in Spanish America. Through personal contacts and an extensive correspondence, he inspired disciples and colleagues to explore the tradition in every corner of the Hispanic world.[15]

Ballad studies have burgeoned in the last fifteen years and to this period we must, with certain exceptions, limit the present survey, for obvious reasons of space.[16] Recent Hispanic ballad criticism testifies to a healthy and expanding variety of scholarly concerns and perspectives. These can, very roughly, be grouped under the following headings (allowing, of course, for numerous overlaps): Historical studies; Pan-European analogues; geographic studies; ballad music; bibliography and cataloguing; linguistic studies; literary criticism; creativity in oral tradition; ideology and sociology; semiotics; formulism; and computer-based studies.

The early stages of ballad criticism, under the aegis of Menendez Pidal, were primarily, though not exclusively, historical in orientation and concerned with the urgent task of locating the Romancero in its relation to other literary and folk-literary genres and of tracing and identifying its historical, literary, and folkloric sources. Such important work is still far from completed and has continued apace in recent years. Note, for example, the contributions of Manuel Alvar,[17] S. G. Armistead and J. H. Silverman,[18] Juan Bautista Avalle-Arce,[19] Francisco Caravaca,[20] Julio Caro Baroja,[21] Diego Catalan,[22] Antonio Cid,[23] Manuel da Costa Fontes,[24] Joanne B. Purcell,[25] Juan Torres Fontes,[26] and Edward M. Wilson,[27] among others.

The study of the <u>Romancero</u>'s relationship to its Pan-European analogues has barely begun. Menéndez Pidal was, of course, well aware of the problem. He discussed a number of important thematic agreements in his <u>Romancero hispánico</u>.[28] In general, however, Hispanic balladry's Continental contacts have not been systematically explored. In the apparatus of our various editions of Judeo-Spanish ballads we have attempted to cross-reference all Pan-European analogues that have come to our attention, using an extensive bibliography in a variety of languages.[29] Edith Rogers' important investigations also co-ordinate a broadly international spectrum of ballad collections.[30] Florette Rechnitz's comparative study of Hispanic and Rumanian narrative poetry has uncovered interesting new parallels.[31] Such a comparative approach could profitably be applied to other European sub-traditions as well. Monographic studies of individual ballad themes will doubtless refine our knowledge of Hispano-Continental ballad relationships.[32]

Investigations of ballad geography, patterned on the techniques of the Finnish school of folklore studies, were brilliantly launched by Menéndez Pidal in his 1920 article on the dynamic geographic diffusion of the ballads of "Gerineldo" and "El conde Sol."[33] His study was expanded and renovated by Diego Catalán and Alvaro Galmés in 1954.[34] More recently, Manuel Alvar has applied similar methods to the study of another widely diffused ballad: "Tamar y Amnón."[35] Francisco Martínez-Yanes has used the geographic approach in studying "La Blancaniña," a ballad of even more complex Pan-Hispanic distribution.[36] Suzanne H. Petersen has recently programmed computer-generated maps, producing dramatic new evidence which makes possible a more accurate characterization of the various sub-traditions.[37] More geographic studies are an obvious desideratum.

Ballad music, long neglected, is now receiving more attention, though certainly here (as elsewhere) many more scholars are urgently needed to carry forward the work. Note the recent publications on early ballad music by Charles Jacobs and Jack Sage.[38] Israel J. Katz's abundant contributions are fundamentally important and highly innovative.[39] His monographic article on "The Traditional Folk Music of Spain" surveys all work on traditional ballad music up to 1974.[40]

Bibliographical work and cataloguing must go hand in hand. Some of the major bibliographical sources are: Manuel García Blanco, for the <u>Romancero</u> in general;[41] for Spanish America, Merle E. Simmons;[42] for the Judeo-Spanish tradition, several primarily linguistic bibliographies, aside from the apparatus of various recent editions, provide

indispensable prime materials;[43] for Portugal, Benjamim Enes
Pereira;[44] for Brazil, Braulio do Nascimento;[45] and for
Catalonia, Joan Amades and Josep Massot i Muntaner.[46] Much
of this material has been brought together and supplemented
in BRO. Note also Armistead's "Critical Bibliography . . .
(1971-1979)." Such surveys of recent scholarship as those
published by Rina Benmayor, Judith Mauleón, and Merle E.
Simmons provide further useful information.[47]

The cataloguing of Hispanic ballads is just beginning.
Its antecedents lie in such useful collecting manuals as
Menéndez Pidal's "Catálogo del romancero judío-español,"
María Goyri's Romances que deben buscarse en la tradicion
oral, and the Romancerillo canario compiled under the
direction of Diego Catalán.[48] Armistead's Catálogo-Indice of
Jewish ballads in the Menéndez Pidal Archive sorts out
almost all narrative themes in that particular tradition and
bridges into the major collections from other Hispanic
areas, as well as major European ballad collections (Child,
Grundtvig, Meier, Nigra, and so forth). The classification
system is traditional, being bound to that used in the
Archive.[49] Paloma Díaz Mas' splendid studies on Judeo-
Spanish luctual poetry include a definitive classification
and bibliography of Sephardic dirge ballads.[50]

The collaborative Catálogo general descriptivo del
Romancero pan-hispánico (CGR), directed by Diego Catalan,
will embody an exhaustive coverage in which ballad
narratives are analyzed at various levels of meaning (fabula
/ intriga / discurso = story /récit7 / plot / discourse) to
provide a thorough synoptic presentation of each text-
type.[51] Needless to say, text-type indices for individual
areas, such as that augured for the Portuguese tradition in
the apparatus of Manuel da Costa Fontes' various
collections, will still be urgently needed and eminently
useful.[52]

The problems of ballad language--the genre's
conservation of archaisms and the development of a
specialized poetic diction in ballads--have not received the
attention they warrant. In this regard, Rafael Lapesa's
pathfinding study is crucial.[53] Manuel Alvar's interesting
investigation of the varied linguistic texture of sixteenth-
century ballad collections is an important contribution.[54]
Armistead and Silverman have studied certain archaic lexical
items present in the Judeo-Spanish romances and Iacob M.
Hassán has explored the use of Hebraisms in Moroccan
Sephardic traditional poetry (including ballads).[55]
Obviously much remains to be done. Stephen Gilman's
brilliant study of the romance as a special poetic

language[56] and the discourse analysis embodied in <u>CGR</u> point the way toward new regions to be explored.[57]

Literary criticism applied to Hispanic balladry has recently, at long last, come into its own. We might note, especially, Cesare Acutis' interesting study of fragmentism;[58] Edmund De Chasca's penetrating analyses of individual ballads ("Alora la bien cercada"; "Cabalga Diego Laínez"; "El sueno de doña Alda");[59] Mercedes Díaz Roig's fine investigations of ballad style and its connections with the traditional lyric;[60] Carmelo Gariano's sensitive study on "Rosaflorida";[61] Guido Mancini's splendid reading of "La pérdida de Alhama";[62] Patricia Pogal's perceptive treatment of light imagery in ballads;[63] Edith R. Rogers' pathfinding investigations of ballad symbolism and its literary and mythical functions;[64] and Colin Smith's excellent characterization of the <u>romances</u>' ethos,[65] among many others that could be named. Giuseppe Di Stefano's anthology includes, as an appendix, some of the most insightful recent commentary on individual ballad texts.[66] N. D. Shergold's interesting collaborative collection of essays, <u>Studies of the Spanish and Portuguese Ballad</u>, includes important and perceptive literary studies of both learned and traditional ballads, though the traditionalist will doubtless note here a decidedly individualist perspective.[67] Various scholars have been concerned with the beginnings and endings of ballads: Giuseppe Di Stefano, David W. Foster, Francisco Martinez-Yanes, Aurelio González Pérez, and Ruth House Webber.[68] Problems of time, verb tense, and temporal perspectives, following up a path-finding book by Stephen Gilman on tense usage in the <u>Poem of the Cid</u> and an important monograph by Joseph Szertics on ballad tenses,[69] have continued to concern scholars and have lead to interestingly divergent conclusions by Jean-Claude Chevalier, Giuseppe Di Stefano, and Manfred Sandmann.[70] The role of ballads in the early theater and their literary functions, long a subject of investigation,[71] has recently been illuminated by stimulating new perspectives: Jesús Antonio Cid, Luciano García Lorenzo, Marsha H. Swislocky, Gustavo Umpierre, Edward M. Wilson and Jack Sage.[72]

Inseparable from the literary problems of the <u>Romancero</u> are the numerous recent studies concerning the oral tradition as a dynamic creative process, analogous, over time and through the intervention of innumerable traditional singers, to the creative art of the individual poet. Paul Bénichou's pathfinding monograph established new directions in this important field.[73] Subsequent articles by Diego Catalán, Mercedes Díaz Roig, Oro A. Librowicz, Braulio do Nascimento, Suzanne H. Petersen, Antonio Sánchez Romeralo, and Joseph H. Silverman, among others, have brought important new perspectives to bear upon the problem.[74]

The ballad as a vehicle of ideology has received considerable attention. Note, for example, the studies of Françoise Cazal, Michelle Débax, Georges Martin, and Julio Rodríguez-Puértolas.[75] Ballads as a reflection of social values have been penetratingly explored by Rina Benmayor, Manuel da Costa Fontes, Manuel Gutiérrez Esteve, and Candace Slater.[76]

Semiotic approaches to Hispanic balladry are as yet scarce. B. Pelegrín and David Quinn have analyzed two early learned ballads.[77] Diego Catalán and a number of his students have developed semiotic analyses of numerous romances collected from oral tradition.[78] The on-going CGR is based on semiotic criteria.[79]

Formulaic studies were initiated by Ruth House Webber, years before the Parry-Lord theory was applied to the medieval Spanish epic.[80] Professor Webber has continued her formulaic work on both epic and ballad.[81] Other important studies are those of Bruce A. Beatie, John S. Miletich, and Oreste R. Ochrymowycz.[82]

Computer-based research has been auspiciously begun by Diego Catalán and Suzanne H. Petersen.[83] Computer-generated maps and computerized analysis of certain text-types have already yielded important and sometimes surprising new discoveries. Computers have been instrumental in printing and compiling the indices of BRO and AIER, I-II, and in elaborating CGR.[84] Computer technology holds forth perhaps the only viable method for cataloguing, editing and analyzing the gigantic corpus of Pan-Hispanic balladry.

Every one of the approaches I have just mentioned could well be continued and expanded to the benefit of Hispanic ballad scholarship. However, several areas of activity suggest themselves as being in particularly urgent need of further exploration.[85] In documentary and historical studies, there is a need for extensive investigation of what might be called the Spanish ballads' "minor documentation": a scrutiny of late medieval and Golden Age literature in search of allusions and fragmentary ballad quotations that may help us to document the early ballads' textual diversity in oral tradition.[86] Likewise a catalogue of early ensaladas (miscellany poems composed of quotations from variegated sources) would clearly teach us much about the early ballad repertoire.[87] Continued work on ballads in the theater is also greatly to be desired: As we learn, through field work, ever more about the modern oral tradition, we will be better equipped to perceive ballad allusions and relationships that would have gone unnoticed earlier on.[88]

The study of Hispano-Continental ballad relationships, in terms both of entire repertoires and individual narrative themes, offers the possibility of numerous exciting discoveries. Scholarship on ballad music, so essential to the editing and study of the oral tradition, is at present gravely "understaffed." The cataloguing and typological indexing of the various sub-traditions has barely begun, with Spanish America offering perhaps the thorniest bibliographical thicket of all.[89] Linguistic studies of the ballads have recently been neglected and renewed efforts in this field would doubtless produce important results. In line with ideological and sociological approaches, the need for contextual studies and an exploration of the ballads' functions and performance[90] and their significance to the singers themselves is of major importance.[91] Here a semiotic approach to ballad poetics can offer important new perspectives. Computer-based research clearly provides the only methodology that can cope with a vast and ever expanding textual corpus.

Field work, though, for reasons of space, we have not been able to discuss it here, remains without doubt one of the highest priorities of Hispanic ballad research. Recent field work throughout the Hispanic world has been (or at least should be) marked by a sense of urgency, a feeling of the tragically ephemeral quality of human life and of its cultural traditions; a knowledge that the present is a moment of critically perilous transition and the future is an unknown quantity; a realization that what is here today must be recorded today and saved before it is too late. The ballad may perhaps, against all odds, survive, at least in some of its geographic modalities, but if indeed it does, it will never again be quite what it has been up to now. A precious literary monument is dying or being transformed before our eyes and time is all too short for us to save what can still be saved.

Ballad studies have, in recent years, emerged as a recognized and notably productive sub-discipline of Hispanic scholarship (as is attested, for example, in the over 450 pertinent publications to appear between 1971 and 1979 alone).[92] That Romancero studies are now the province of an extended fellowship of scholars, working in a cordial spirit of international collaboration, bodes well that we may indeed not only be able to salvage the remaining "relics" of the living tradition, but also confer upon them and their printed congeners the multi-faceted scholarly analyses warranted by such an ancient, rich, and creatively dynamic balladic heritage.

NOTES

*Since my contribution to the present volume is a review of scholarship on the Hispanic ballad and no specific texts are commented on in any detail, it is difficult to relate our textual example very specifically to the article which follows it. The best solution has been to present a ballad, which, at one and the same time, represents one of the major stylistic tendencies in the early Spanish tradition and is also a thoroughly excellent poem, undoubtedly the most famous and most beloved of all romances. The ballad in question is, of course, "El conde Arnaldos." There are at least three, perhaps four, known early versions of "Arnaldos": One is in a late fifteenth- or early sixteenth-century MS in the British Library; another was printed in an early broadside; a third is included in the undated Cancionero de romances published by Martín Nucio at Antwerp around 1548; and a fourth is doubtless represented by verses added to the amplified 1550 revision of Nucio's anthology (and subsequent reprintings). For the early versions of "Arnaldos" and to scholarship on the ballad, see S. G. Armistead, Judeo-Spanish Ballads in the Menéndez Pidal Archive, 3 vols. (Madrid: C.S.M.P., 1978), I, no. H15, and "A Critical Bibliography of the Hispanic Ballad in Oral Tradition (1971-1979)," The Hispanic Ballad Today: History, Comparativism, Critical Bibliography (Madrid: C.S.M.P., 1979), pp. 199-310 (index, p. 330). For English translations, see J. M. Cohen, The Penguin Book of Spanish Verse (Baltimore: Penguin, 1966), p. 94, and W. S. Merwin, Spanish Ballads (Garden City, N.Y.: Anchor, 1961), p. 57.

[1]Compare, for example, the various definitions of "ballad" in William J. Entwistle, European Balladry (Oxford: Clarendon, 1951), pp. 16-32; M. J. C. Hodgard, The Ballads (New York: Norton, 1962), pp. 9-13; David Buchan, The Ballad and the Folk (London: Routledge & Kegan Paul, 1972), pp. 1, 173, 272-73.

I use the following abbreviations in this article: -- BRO-I = Bibliografía del Romancero Oral, ed. Antonio Sánchez Romeralo, Samuel G. Armistead, and Suzanne H. Petersen (Madrid: CSMP, 1980); -- CGR = Catálogo General Descriptivo del Romancero Pan-Hispánico, ed. Diego Catalán, et al. (in press); -- CSIC = Consejo Superior de Investigaciones Científicas (Madrid); -- CSMP = Cátedra-Seminario Menendez Pidal (Madrid); -- ExTL = Explicación de Textos Literarios (Sacramento, California); -- HBT: Frontiers = The Hispanic

Ballad Today: New Frontiers, ed. A. Sanchez Romeralo, et al. (Madrid: CSMP, 1979); -- HBT: History = The Hispanic Ballad Today: History, Comparativism, Critical Bibliography, ed. S. G. Armistead, et al. (Madrid: CSMP, 1979); -- HBT: Poetics = The Hispanic Ballad Today: Poetics, ed. D. Catalán, et al. (Madrid: CSMP, 1979); -- LeL = Linguistica e Letteratura (Pisa); -- NRFH = Nueva Revista de Filología Hispánica (Mexico City); -- RFE = Revista de Filología Española (Madrid); -- RTOM = El Romancero en la Tradicion Oral Moderna, ed. D. Catalan, et al. (Madrid: CSMP, 1972).

[2]R. Beaton, Folk Poetry of Modern Greece (Cambridge: Cambridge University Press, 1980), p. 13. See my review: Comparative Literature, 35, No. 1 (1983), 89-95.

[3]C. C. Smith, "On the Ethos of the 'Romancero Viejo,'" in Studies of the Spanish and Portuguese Ballad, ed. N. D. Shergold (London: Tamesis, 1972), pp. 5-24, at 7, 19, 24.

[4]See S. G. Armistead, "Judeo-Spanish and Pan-European Balladry," Jahrbuch für Volksliedforschung, 24 (1979), 127-38; Id., "The Portuguese Romanceiro in its European Context," in Portuguese and Brazilian Oral Traditions in Verse Form, ed. Joanne B. Purcell, et al. (Los Angeles: /University of Southern California/, 1976), pp. 178-200; Id., with Israel J. Katz, "The New Edition of Danmarks Gamle Folkeviser," Yearbook of The International Folk Music Council (1977), 9 (1978), 89-95.

[5]See, for example, S. G. Armistead, et al., El romancero judeo-español en el Archivo Menéndez Pidal (Catálogo-índice de romances y canciones), 3 vols. (Madrid: CSMP, 1978), I, 56, n. 66.

[6]See S. G. Armistead, "Epic and Ballad: A Traditionalist Perspective," Olifant, 8 (1981), 376-88.

[7]Cf. Alan D. Deyermond, Historia de la literatura española: La Edad Media (Barcelona: Ariel, 1976), pp. 220-22.

[8]See Kathleen V. Kish, "Los romances trovadorescos del Cancionero sin año," Actas del Sexto Congreso Internacional de Hispanistas (Toronto: Paul Malak, 1980), pp. 427-30. On the stylistic continuity of the Romancero viejo and Romancero nuevo, and even of learned eighteenth-century ballads, see Judith H. Mauleón, "Oral Theory and the

Romancero Nuevo," in HBT: History, pp. 49-62, and K. V. Kish, "The Spanish Ballad in the Eighteenth Century: A Reconsideration," Hispanic Review, 49 (1981), 271-84.

[9]See Therese Meléndez Hayes, "Juan Rodríguez del Padrón and the Romancero," in HBT: History, pp. 15-36.

[10]See, for example, Diego Catalán, "El romancero de tradición oral en el último cuarto del siglo XX," HBT: Frontiers, pp. 217-56; Flor Salazar and Ana Valenciano, "El Romancero aún vive: Trabajo de campo de la CSMP: 'Encuesta Norte-77,'" in HBT: Frontiers, pp. 361-421; for some current threats to the modern tradition: S. G. Armistead and I. J. Katz, "In the Footsteps of Kurt Schindler: Ballad Collecting in Soria," in HBT: Frontiers, pp. 257-66.

[11]See Ramón Menéndez Pidal and María Goyri de Menéndez Pidal, Romancero tradicional de las lenguas hispánicas (Español-portugués-catalán-sefardí), ed. D. Catalán et al., 11 vols. (Madrid: Gredos, 1957-1978), X, 23-57.

[12]Ramón Menéndez Pidal, Romancero hispánico, 2 vols. (Madrid: Espasa-Calpe, 1953), II, 358-59. Ballads have turned up even in the most isolated communities. See S. G. Armistead, " Existió un romancero de tradición oral entre los moriscos?" in Actas del Coloquito internacional sobre literatura aljamiada y morisca, ed. Alvaro Galmés (Madrid: Gredos, 1978), pp. 211-36; Id., "Spanish Romances in Tunisia in 1746," Neophilologus, 63 (1979), 247-49; Id., "Romances tradicionales entre los hispanohablantes de Luisiana," NRFH, 27 (1978), 39-56; Id., "Más romances de Luisiana," NRFH, 32 (1983), 41-54.

[13]See D. Catalán, "Menéndez Pidal y la formación de la 'escuela de Madrid,'" in Lingüística íbero-románica (Madrid: Gredos, 1974), pp. 22-32.

[14]See Ruth House Webber, "Ramón Menéndez Pidal and the Romancero," Romance Philology, 5 (1951-1952), 15-25; Henry V. Besso, "Don Ramón Menéndez Pidal and the Romancero sefardí," Sefarad, 21 (1961), 343-74.

[15]Menéndez Pidal's articles of a more theoretical emphasis have been brought together in Estudios sobre el Romancero (Madrid: Espasa-Calpe, 1973). On Don Ramón's correspondence with potential ballad collectors, see Armistead, Catálogo-índice, I, 44-48 (espec. n. 22).

[16]Note my bibliographical surveys, "A Critical Bibliography of the Hispanic Ballad in Oral Tradition (1971-1979)," in HBT: History, pp. 199-310; "Romancero Studies (1977-1979)," La Corónica, 8, No. 1 (1979), 57-66; also Rina Benmayor, "Current Work on the Romancero viejo tradicional," La Corónica, 4, No. 1 (1975), 49-54; Judith H. Mauleón, "Recent Work on the Romancero Nuevo: Editions and Studies since 1950," La Corónica, 5, No. 1 (1976), 26-30. For extensive coverage, see BRO. For reasons of space, I have been unable to survey here important recent work on the documentation of the early Romancero and have likewise had to make no mention of the latest, very productive developments in field work. Concerning the latter, see my "Recent Field Work on the Hispanic Ballad in Oral Tradition," in HBT: Frontiers, pp. 53-60; S. G. Armistead, et al., "Hispanic Ballad Field Work during the summer of 1980," La Corónica, 9, No. 1 (1980), 29-36. For a compact survey of ballad scholarship, see my entry on "Medieval Spanish Ballad," Dictionary of the Middle Ages (New York: Scribners, in press). In the present article, obviously, not all critical publications can be mentioned or discussed.

[17]M. Alvar, El Romancero: Tradicionalidad y pervivencia, 2nd ed. (Barcelona: Planeta, 1974).

[18]A number of studies are brought together in En torno al romancero sefardí: Hispanismo y balcanismo de la tradición judeo-española (Madrid: CSMP, 1982).

[19]J. B. Avalle-Arce, "El cantar de La niña de Gómez Arias," "Los romances de la muerte de Don Beltrán," and "Bernal Francés y su romance," Temas hispánicos medievales (Madrid: Gredos, 1974), pp. 83-92, 124-34, 135-232.

[20]See F. Caravaca, "Hermenéutica del Romance del Conde Arnaldos, . . ." Boletín de la Biblioteca Menéndez Pelayo, 47 (1971), 191-319, among other valuable studies.

[21]J. Caro Baroja, "La Serrana de la Vera, o un pueblo analizado en conceptos y símbolos inactuales," Ritos y mitos equívocos (Madrid: Istmo, 1974), pp. 259-338.

[22]See D. Catalán, Siete siglos de Romancero: Historia y poesía (Madrid: Gredos, 1969); Id., Por campos del Romancero: Estudios sobre la tradición oral moderna (Madrid: Gredos, 1970), among numerous other important studies.

[23] J. A. Cid, "Calderón y el romancillo de El bonetero de la trapería," Hispanic Review, 45 (1977), 421-34.

[24] M. da Costa Fontes, "Dona María and Batalha de Lepanto: Two Rare Luso-American Ballads," Portuguese and Brazilian Oral Traditions, pp. 147-57; Id., "D. Duardos in the Portuguese Oral Tradition," Romance Philology, 30 (1976-1977), 589-608; Id., "Lizarda: A Rare Vicentine Ballad in California," Romance Philology, 32 (1978-1979), 308-14; Id., "The Batalha de Lepanto in the Portuguese Oral Tradition," Hispanic Review, 47 (1979), 487-503; Id., "A Sephardic Vestige of the Ballad Floresvento," La Corónica, 10, No. 2 (1982), 196-201.

[25] J. B. Purcell, "Recently Collected Ballad Fragments on the Death of Don Fernando I," Portuguese and Brazilian Oral Traditions, pp. 158-67.

[26] J. Torres Fontes, "La historicidad del romance Abenámar, . . ." Anuario de Estudios Medievales, 8 (1972-1973), 225-56.

[27] E. M. Wilson, "On the romanze . . . mi padre era de Ronda," in Medieval Hispanic Studies Presented to Rita Hamilton, ed. Alan D. Deyermond (London: Tamesis, 1976), pp. 267-76. A much neglected aspect of romancero studies, until now, concerned the ballad's situation in the eighteenth century. Kathleen V. Kish's incisive article opens new perspectives on the problem: "The Spanish Ballad in the Eighteenth Century: A Reconsideration," Hispanic Review, 49 (1981), 271-84.

[28] Romancero hispánico, I, 317-34.

[29] See especially S. G. Armistead and J. H. Silverman, The Judeo-Spanish Ballad Chapbooks of Y. A. Yoná (Berkeley: University of California Press, 1971); also nn. 4-5 above.

[30] See n. 64 below.

[31] See F. M. Rechnitz, "Hispano-Romanian Ballad Relationships: A Comparative Study with an Annotated Translation of A. I. Amzulescu's Index of Romanian Ballads," Diss. University of Pennsylvania, 1978; Id., "Hispano-Romanian Ballad Correspondences," in HBT: History, pp. 141-49.

[32]See, for example, Therese Meléndez Hayes, "A Study of a Ballad: The Continuity of 'El caballero burlado,'" Diss. University of California, San Diego, 1977; Beatriz Mariscal de Rhett, "La balada occidential moderna ante el mito: Análisis semiótico del romance de 'La muerte ocultada,'" Diss. University of California, San Diego, 1978.

[33]"Sobre geografía folklórica: Ensayo de un método," RFE, 7 (1920), 229-338.

[34]R. Menéndez Pidal, D. Catalan, and A. Galmés, Cómo vive un romance: Dos ensayos sobre tradicionalidad (Madrid: CSIC, 1954).

[35]M. Alvar, "El romance de Amnón y Tamar," Cuadernos Hispanoamericanos, 238-40 (1969), 308-76; reproduced in El Romancero: Tradicionalidad y pervivencia (1970) and (1974).

[36]F. Martinez-Yanes, "El romance de 'La Blancaniña': Estudio comparativo de sus variantes," Diss. University of Pennsylvania, 1976.

[37]S. H. Petersen, "Representación cartográfica de datos complejos mediante ordenador," Revista de la Universidad Complutense, 25 (1976), 205-19; Id., "Computer-Generated Maps of Narrative Affinity," in HBT: Poetics, pp. 167-228.

[38]Ch. Jacobs, ed., Luis de Milán, El Maestro (University Park: Pennsylvania State University Press, 1971); Id., Miguel de Fuenllana, Orphénica Lyra (Seville 1554) (Oxford: Clarendon, 1978); J. Sage, "Early Spanish Ballad Music: Tradition or Metamorphosis," in Medieval Hispanic Studies Presented to Rita Hamilton, pp. 195-214.

[39]See especially his Judeo-Spanish Traditional Ballads from Jerusalem: An Ethnomusicological Study, 2 vols. (Brooklyn: Institute of Mediaeval Music, 1971-1975).

[40]I. J. Katz, "The Traditional Folk Music of Spain: Explorations and Perspectives," Yearbook of the International Folk Music Council, 6 (1974), 64-83. Note the detailed treatment of musical components in such recent collections as Joaquin Díaz, et al., Romances tradicionales: Catálogo folklórico de la provincia de Valladolid, 2 vols. (Valladolid: Institución Cultural Simancas, 1978-1979), and Maximiano Trapero and Lothar Siemens Hernández, Romancero de

Gran Canaria, Vol. I, Zona del Sureste (Las Palmas: Mancomunidad de Cabildos de Las Palmas-Instituto Canario de Etnografía y Folklore, 1982).

[41]M. García Blanco, "El Romancero," Historia general de las literaturas hispánicas, II, ed. Guillermo Díaz-Plaja (Barcelona: Vergara, 1968).

[42]M. E. Simmons, A Bibliography of the "Romance" and Related Forms in Spanish America (Bloomington: Indiana University Press, 1963).

[43]The most exhaustive coverage so far is in S. G. Armistead and J. H. Silverman, Judeo-Spanish Ballads from New York (Berkeley: University of California Press, 1981). Note the extensive listings of ballad bibliography in the following works: Michael Studemund, Bibliographie zum Judenspanischen (Hamburg: Helmut Buske, 1975); Marius Sala, Le Judéo-espagnol (The Hague: Mouton, 1976); David M. Bunis, Sephardic Studies: A Research Bibliography (New York: Garland, 1981).

[44]B. Enes Pereira, Bibliografia Analítica de Etnografia Portuguesa (Lisbon: Instituto de Alta Cultura, 1965).

[45]B. do Nascimento, Bibliografia de Folclore Brasileiro (Rio de Janeiro: :Biblioteca Nacional, 1971).

[46]J. Amades, Folklore de Catalunya: Cançoner (Cançons-refranys-endevinalles) (Barcelona: Selecta, 1951); J. Massot i Muntaner, "Aportació a l'estudi del Romancer balear," Estudis Romànics, 7 (1959-1960), 63-155.

[47]See n. 16 above and M. E. Simmons, "Folklore Research in Spain and Spanish America," The American Hispanist, 1, No. 5 (1976), 2, 4-5.

[48]R. Menéndez Pidal, "Catálogo del romancero judío-español," Cultura Espanola, 4 (1906), 1045-77; 5 (1907), 161-99; reproduced in slightly abbreviated form in El Romancero: Teorías e investigaciones (Madrid: Paez, /1928/), pp. 101-83, and in Los romances de América y otros estudios (Buenos Aires: Espasa-Calpe, 1948), pp. 121-88; M. Goyri de Menendez Pidal, Romances que deben buscarse en la tradición oral, 2d ed. (Madrid: Centro de Estudios Histõricos, /1929/); an expanded edition, without the author's name, is represented by Romances tradicionales y canciones narrativas

existentes en el folklore español (Barcelona: Instituto Español de Musicología, 1945); Mercedes Morales and María Jesús López de Vergara, Romancerillo canario: Catálogo-Manual de recolección (La Laguna: Universidad, 1955).

[49]See n. 5 above.

[50]M. P. Díaz Mas, Poesía luctuosa judeo-española ("Memoria de Licenciatura," Universidad Complutense, Madrid, 1977); Id., "Temas y topicos en la poesía luctuosa sefardí," Diss. Universidad Complutense, Madrid, 1981; see also her "Romances sefardíes de endechar," in Actas de las Jornadas de Estudios Sefardíes, ed. Antonio Viudas Camarasa (Cáceres: Universidad de Extremadura, 1981), pp. 99-105.

[51]See, for now, Jesús Antonio Cid, et al., "Towards the Elaboration of the General Descriptive Catalogue of the Pan-Hispanic Romancero," in HBT: Poetics, ed. D. Catalán, et al. (Madrid: CSIC, 1979), pp. 335-63. The first three volumes of CGR are currently in press.

[52]M. da Costa Fontes, Romanceiro Português dos Estados Unidos, II: Califórnia (Coimbra: Universidade, 1983); Id. Romanceiro da Ilha de São Jorge (Coimbra: Universidade, 1983); Id., Romanceiro de Trás-os Montes (in preparation).

[53]R. Lapesa, "La lengua de la poesía épica en los cantares de gesta y en el Romancero viejo," in De la edad media a nuestros días (Madrid: Gredos, 1967), pp. 9-28.

[54]M. Alvar, "Transmisión lingüística en los romanceros antiguos," Prohemio, 3, No. 2 (1972), 197-219. The article is reproduced in the 2nd ed. of El Romancero: Tradicionalidad (1974).

[55]S. G. Armistead and J. H. Silverman, "Jud.-Sp. alazare: An Unnoticed Congener of Cast. alazán," Romance Philology, 21 (1967-1968), 510-12; Id., "J.-esp. algüeca 'trompetilla,'" Estudios Sefardíes, 1 (1978), 143-45. (Both studies are now reedited and expanded in our book, En torno al romancero sefardí); I. M. Hassán, "Más hebraísmos en la poesía sefardí de Marruecos: Realidad y ficción léxicas," Sefarad, 37 (1977), 373-428.

[56]S. Gilman, "On Romancero as a Poetic Language," Homenaje a Casalduero, . . . ed. Rizel Pincus Sigele and Gonzalo Sobejano (Madrid: Gredos, 1972), pp. 151-60.

[57]See n. 51 above.

[58]C. Acutis, "Romancero ambiguo Prenotorietà e frammentismo nei romances dei secc. XV e XVI," Miscellanea di Studi Ispanici, 28, No. 1 (1974), 43-80.

[59]E. De Chasca, "Alora la bien cercada: Un romance modelo," ExTL, 1, No. 1 (1972), 29-37; Id., "Pluralidades anaforicas en . . . Cabalga Diego Laínez, . . ." Revista de Estudios Hispánicos, 2 (1972), 21-32; Id., "Algunos aspectos de la ordenación con números correlativos en el . . . Romancero del Cid," Studia Hispanica in Honorem R. Lapesa, II (Madrid: CSMP-Gredos, 1974), 189-202.

[60]M. Diaz Roig, "Un rasgo estilístico del Romancero y de la lírica popular," NRFH, 21 (1972), 79-94; Id., El Romancero y la lírica popular moderna (Mexico City: El Colegio de México, 1976).

[61]C. Gariano, "Estructura y lirismo en el Romance de Rosaflorida," ExTL, 5, No. 2 (1976), 133-38.

[62]G. Mancini, "Proposta di lettura di un romance fronterizo," LeL, 1, No. 1 (1976), 57-73.

[63]P. Pogal, "Light Imagery in the Romancero," Diss. Harvard University, 1977; Id., "The Poetic Function of Light Imagery in the Romance," in Essays in Honor of Jorge Guillén, . . . ed. Martha G. Krow-Lucal (Cambridge, Mass.: Abedul Press, 1977), pp. 133-40.

[64]E. R. Rogers, The Perilous Hunt: Symbols in Hispanic and European Balladry (Lexington: University Press of Kentucky, 1980). See the review by Kathleen V. Kish, La Coronica, 9, No. 1 (1980), 76-79.

[65]See n. 3 above.

[66]G. Di Stefano, El Romancero (Madrid: Narcea, 1973). Other recent ballad anthologies, superseding S. Griswold Morley's classic and still most useful Spanish Ballads (New York: Holt, 1938), are C. Colin Smith, Spanish Ballads (Oxford: Pergammon, 1964); Juan Alcina Franch, Romancero antiguo, 2 vols. (Barcelona: Juventud, 1969-1971); Manuel Alvar, El Romancero viejo y tradicional (Mexico City: Porrúa, 1971); Germán Orduna, Selección de romances viejos

de España y de América (Buenos Aires: Kapelusz, 1976);
Mercedes Díaz Roig, El Romancero Viejo (Madrid: Cátedra,
1976); Michelle Débax, Romancero (Madrid: Alhambra, 1982).
An important recent trend has been to include substantial
material from the modern oral tradition alongside the
established favorites from the early cancioneros. Among
ballad anthologies, Menéndez Pidal's Flor nueva de romances
viejos, 1st ed. (Madrid: "La Lectura," 1928; and many
subsequent eds.), a synthesis of the most attractive
readings from hundreds of texts in his unedited Archive,
occupies a very special position.

[67] See n. 3 above; note my review article, "Neo-
Individualism and the Romancero," Romance Philology, 33
(1979-1980), 172-81. On the Traditionalist-Individualist
polemic, see Charles B. Faulhaber, "Neo-traditionalism,
Formulism, Individualism, and Recent Studies on the Spanish
Epic," Romance Philology, 30 (1976-1977), 83-101; S. G.
Armistead, "The Mocedades de Rodrigo and Neo-Individualist
Theory," Hispanic Review, 46 (1978), 313-27; C. Colin Smith,
"Epics and Chronicles: A Reply to Armistead," Hispanic
Review, 51 (1983), 409-28; also n. 6 above.

[68] G. Di Stefano, "Un exordio de romances," in HBT:
Poetics, pp. 41-54; D. W. Foster, "Closure in Early Spanish
Ballad," Ballads and Ballad Research, ed. Patricia Conroy
(Seattle: University of Washington, 1978), pp. 136-46; F.
Martínez-Yanes, "Los desenlaces en el romance de la
Blancaniña: Tradición y originalidad," in HBT: Poetics, pp.
132-55; A. González Perez, Formas y Funciones de los
principios en el Romancero viejo, "Tesis de Licenciatura"
(Universidad Nacional Autónoma, México City, 1981); Ruth H.
Webber, "Ballad Openings: Narrative and Formal Function," in
HBT: Poetics, pp. 55-64.

[69] S. Gilman, Tiempo y formas temporales en el "Poema
del Cid" (Madrid: Gredos, 1961); J. Szertics, Tiempo y verbo
en el romancero viejo, 2nd ed. (Madrid: Gredos, 1974); note
also Szertics' "Observaciones sobre algunas funciones
estilisticas del pretérito indefinido en el Romancero
viejo," ExTL, 2, No. 3 (1974), 189-97.

[70] J. C. Chevalier, "Architecture temporelle du Romancero
tradicional," Bulletin Hispanique, 73 (1971), 50-103; G. Di
Stefano, "Discorso retrospettivo e schemi narrativi nel
Romancero," LeL, 1 (1976), 35-55; M. Sandmann, "La 'mezcla
de los tiempos narrativos' en el Romancero viejo,"
Romanistisches Jahrbuch, 25 (1974), 278-93.

[71]See, for example, Ernest H. Templin, "Carolingian Heroes and Ballad Lines in Non-Carolingian Dramatic Literature," Hispanic Review, 7 (1939), 35-47; Jerome A. Moore, The "Romancero" in the Chronicle-Legend Plays of Lope de Vega (Philadelphia: University of Pennsylvania, 1940); Angel López, El cancionero popular en el teatro de Tirso de Molina (Madrid: Artes Gráficas H. de la Guardia Civil, 1958).

[72]See n. 23 above; L. García Lorenzo, El tema del conde Alarcos . . . (Madrid: CSIC, 1972); Id., "Entremés del Conde Alarcos," Prohemio, 5, No. 1 (1974), 119-35; Id., El teatro de Guillén de Castro (Barcelona: Planeta, 1976); M. H. Swislocki, "Lope, the Romancero and the Comedia," Diss. Harvard University, 1976; Id., "Ballad Formation in the Plays of Lope de Vega," in HBT: History, pp. 63-73; G. Umpierre, Songs in the Plays of Lope de Vega: A Study of their Dramatic Function (London: Tamesis, 1975); E. M. Wilson and J. Sage, Poesías líricas en las obras de Calderón (London: Tamesis, 1964); Id., "Addenda, . . ." Revista Canadiense de Estudios Hispánicos, 1, No. 2 (1977), 199-208. Note also Francisco Porrata, Incorporación del Romancero a la temática de la comedia española (Madrid: Plaza Mayor, 1973).

[73]P. Bénichou, Creación poética en el Romancero tradicional (Madrid: Gredos, 1968). See also his "El romance de la muerte del príncipe de Portugal en la tradición moderna," NRFH, 24 (1975), 113-24.

[74]Among various other studies by D. Catalán, see especially his "Memoria e invención en el Romancero de tradición oral," Romance Philology, 24 (1970-1971), 1-25, 441-63; Id. (with Teresa Catarella), "El romance tradicional, un sistema abierto," in RTOM, pp. 181-205; Id. "Los modos de producción y 'reproducción' del texto literario y la noción de apertura," in Homenaje a Julio Caro Baroja, ed. Antonio Carreira, et al. (Madrid: Centro de Investigaciones Sociológicas, 1978), pp. 245-70; Id., "El Romancero hoy," Boletín Informativo (Fundación Juan March), No. 106 (July-August 1981), pp. 36-40. Other important contributions to the study of oral creativity are: M. Díaz Roig, "Palabra y contexto en la recreación del Romancero tradicional," NRFH, 26 (1977), 460-67; Oro A. Librowicz, "Creación poética en tres versiones sefardíes del romance de Espinelo," La Corónica, 10 (1981), 59-64; B. do Nascimento, in "Eufemismo e Criação Poética no Romanceiro Tradicional," RTOM, pp. 233-75; Suzanne H. Petersen, "Cambios estructurales en el Romancero tradicional," in RTOM, pp.

167-79; A. Sánchez Romeralo, "Razón y sinrazón en la creación tradicional," in <u>HBT: Poetics</u>, pp. 13-28; J. H. Silverman, "La contaminación como arte en un romance sefardí de Tánger," in <u>HBT: Poetics</u>, pp. 29-37. Also pertinent are the studies of individual ballads in such collections as P. Benichou, <u>Romancero judeo-español de Marruecos</u> (Madrid: Castalia, 1968); Rina Benmayor, <u>Romances judeo-españoles de Oriente</u> . . . (Madrid: CSMP, 1979); O. A. Librowicz, <u>Florilegio de romances sefardíes</u> . . . (Madrid: CSMP, 1980); and S. G. Armistead and J. H. Silverman, <u>The Judeo-Spanish Ballad Chapbooks</u>, and <u>Romances judeo-españoles de Tánger</u> . . . (Madrid: CSMP, 1977).

[75]F. Cazal, "L'Idéologie du compilateur de romances: . . . Juan de Escobar (1605)," <u>L'Idéologique dans le texte</u> . . . (Toulouse: Université, 1978), pp. 197-209; M. Débax, "Problèmes idéologiques dans le <u>Romancero</u> traditionnel," ibid., pp. 141-63; G. Martin, "Idéologique chevauchée, . . ." ibid., pp. 165-96; J. Rodríguez-Puértolas, "El Romancero, historia de una frustación," <u>Philological Quarterly</u>, 51 (1971), 85-104; also Carlos Blanco Aguinaga, et al., <u>Historia social de la literatura española</u>, 3 vols. (Madrid: Castalia, 1978-1979), I, 140-54, 188-89.

[76]R. Benmayor, "Social Determinants in Poetic Transmission, . . ." in <u>HBT: History</u>, pp. 153-65; M. da Costa Fontes, "As Funções Sociais dos Romances," <u>Atlântida</u>, 19, No. 2 (1975), 211-22; M. Gutiérrez Esteve, "Sobre el sentido de cuatro romances de incesto," in <u>Homenaje a Julio Caro Baroja</u>, pp. 551-79; C. Slater, "The <u>Romance</u> of the Warrior Maiden, . . ." in <u>HBT: History</u>, pp. 167-82.

[77]B. Pelegrín, "Flechazo y lanzada, Eros y Tánatos (Ensayo de aproximación al <u>Romance de don Tristán</u> . . .)," <u>Prohemio</u>, 6 (1975), 83-115; D. Quinn, "El 'A caza va el caballero' de Lope de Vega," <u>ExTL</u>, 6, No. 2 (1978), 215-24. (Note, however, that here <u>monte</u> means "forest," not "mountain," so some of Quinn's conclusions involving Freudian symbolism need to be modified.)

[78]See D. Catalán, "Análisis semiótico de estructuras abiertas: El modelo 'Romancero,'" in <u>HBT: Poetics</u>, pp. 231-49, and the studies by Francisco Romero, Beatriz Mariscal de Rhett, Kathleen D. Lamb, Cynthia Steele, Marguerite Mizrahi Morton, and Sandra Robertson. See also n. 32 above.

[79]See n. 51 above.

[80]Ruth H. Webber, "Formulistic Diction in the Spanish Ballad," University of California Publications in Modern Philology, 34, No. 2 (1951), 175-278. L. Patrick Harvey first suggested the application of Parry-Lord methodology to the Spanish epic. His article, "The Metrical Irregularity of the Cantar de Mio Cid," Bulletin of Hispanic Studies, 40 (1963), 137-43, was followed by that of Alan D. Deyermond, "The Singer of Tales and Mediaeval Spanish Epic," ibid., 42 (1965), 1-8. For more on formulaic studies of Spanish traditional poetry, see my review of E. R. Haymes, A Bibliography of Studies Relating to Parry's and Lord's Oral Theory (Cambridge: Harvard University, 1973), in Modern Language Notes, 90 (1975), 296-99.

[81]Among her latest contributions: "Lenguaje tradicional: Epopeya y Romancero," Actas del Sexto Congreso Internacional de Hispanistas (Toronto: Paul Malak, 1980), pp. 779-82.

[82]B. A. Beatie, "Oral-Traditional Composition in the Spanish Romancero of the Sixteenth Century," Journal of the Folklore Institute, 1 (1964), 92-113; John S. Miletich, "The South Slavic Bugarstica and the Spanish Romance: A New Approach to Typology," International Journal of Slavic Linguistics and Poetics, 21, No. 4 (1975), 51-69 (among many other important articles); Oreste R. Ochrymowycz, Aspects of Oral Style in the "Romances Juglarescos" of the Carolingian Cycle (Iowa City: University of Iowa Press, 1975).

[83]D. Catalán, "Análisis electrónico de la creación poética oral, . . ." in Homenaje a la memoria de Don Antonio Rodríguez-Moñino (Madrid: Castalia, 1975), pp. 157-94; Id. "Análisis electrónico del mecanismo reproductivo en un sistema abierto, . . ." Revista de la Universidad Complutense, 25, No. 102 (1976), 55-77; Suzanne H. Petersen, "El mecanismo de la variacion en la poesía de trasmisión oral: Estudio de 612 versiones del romance de 'La Condesita'," . . . Diss. University of Wisconsin, Madison, 1976; Id., "A Computer Aided Analysis of the Mechanics of Orally Transmitted Poetry," in Ballads and Research, pp. 88-100. See also n. 37 above. An extensive study of computerized ballad scholarship, by Suzanne H. Petersen, is included in the present volume.

[84]See n. 51 above. AIER is the Archivo Internacional Electrónico del Romancero. The first two volumes have just appeared: Voces nuevas del Romancero castellano-leonés, ed. Suzanne H. Petersen, et al. (Madrid: CSMP-Gredos, 1982).

Concerning the projected "International Electronic Archive of the Romancero," see D. Catalan, et al., "International Cooperative Research on the Hispanic Ballad, . . ." La Coronica, 8, No. 2 (1980), 180-81.

[85]For suggestions concerning innovative approaches to Romancero studies, see Rina Benmayor, "Oral Narrative and the Comparative Method, . . ." Romance Philology, 31 (1977-1978), 501-21, and "New Directions in the Study of Oral Literature," La Corónica, 7, No. 1 (1978), 39-42; also Candace Slater's suggestions in Armistead, et al., "Hispanic Ballad Field Work . . . 1980," pp. 29-31. Note Ruth H. Webber's stimulating evaluation of structural approaches: "Prolegomena to the Study of the Narrative Structure of the Hispanic Ballad," in Ballads and Ballad Research, pp. 221-30.

[86]Such a formidable undertaking was carried out long ago for the early ballad in Portugal: Carolina Michaëlis de Vasconcelos, Romances Velhos em Portugal (1934; rpt., Oporto: Lello & Irmão, 1980). On the various types of fragmentary and allusive evidence that might be looked for, see my review article cited in n. 67 above (Romance Philology, 33, pp. 175-76).

[87]For some discoveries in this regard, see Antonio Rodríguez-Moñino, "Tres romances de la 'Ensalada' de Praga (Siglo XVI)," La transmisión de la poesía española en los siglos de oro (Barcelona: Ariel, 1976), pp. 231-40; S. G. Armistead and J. H. Silverman, "El romance de Celinos: Un testimonio del siglo XVI," NRFH, 25 (1976), 86-94; Id., "Una variación antigua del romance de Tarquino y Lucrecia," Thesaurus, 33 (1978), 122-26.

[88]See, for example, J. A. Cid's recent Calderonian discovery (n. 23 above).

[89]See my review article, "The Romancero in Spanish America: Perspectives and Priorities" (in preparation for Romance Philology.)

[90]Could such a study as Dan Ben-Amos' innovative monograph, Sweet Words: Storytelling Events in Benin (Philadelphia: ISHI, 1975), be attempted for Hispanic ballads? The romance is, of course, essentially non-professional, and it is usually much less public, more intimate and personal, sometimes even solitary in its performance than are many other genres (Ben-Amos' Nigerian

stories, in particular). Yet, till now, performance studies have been totally lacking. Though such a study would be fraught with difficulties, it would be interesting to see what could be done. A basic problem is that very few ballads, if any, have been recently collected under spontaneous conditions. The performance of harvest ballads in Tras-os-Montes might offer a possible starting point.

[91]Note Diego Catalán's splendid comment: "/El7 romance de La muerte del príncipe don Juan (composed circa 1497), . . . sin . . . perder ninguna de las connotaciones que los contemporáneos introdujeron en su valoración objectiva y subjetiva del evento/ ,_7 . . . se ha ido adecuando al medio en que cada día se canta, y se reproduce buscando nuevas interpretaciones de la información recibida y reorganizándola de tal forma que su mensaje no sólo pueda seguir siendo significativo hoy, sino abierto siempre a nuevas reinterpretaciones en el mañana" ("El Romancero hoy," Boletin Informativo /Fundación Juan March7, No. 106 /July-August 1981/, p. 36).

[92]See my "Critical Bibliography . . . (1971-1979)" (n. 16 above.)

University of California
Davis

RE-CREATION OF NARRATIVE SONG

THE MURDER OF MARIA MARTEN

By W. Corder

Tune, as sung by M. J. Whitby of Tilney All Saints,
Norfolk, collected by R. Vaughan Williams 7 January,
1905.

1. Come all you thoughtless young men, a warning take by me,
   And think upon my unhappy fate to be hanged upon a tree;
   My name is William Corder, to you I do declare,
   I courted Maria Marten, most beautiful and fair.

2. I promised I would marry her upon a certain day,
   Instead of that, I was resolved to take her life away.
   I went into her father's house the 18th day of May,
   Saying, my dear Maria, we will fix the wedding day.

3. If you will meet me at the Red-barn, as sure as I have life,
   I will take you to Ipswich town, and there make you my wife;
   I then went home and fetched my gun, my pickaxe and my spade
   I went into the Red-barn, and there I dug her grave.

4. With heart so light, she thought no harm, to meet him she
     did go;
   He murdered her all in the barn, and laid her body low:
   After the horrible deed was done, she lay weltering in
     her gore,
   Her bleeding mangled body he buried beneath the
     Red-barn floor.

5. Now all things being silent, her spirit could not rest,
   She appeared unto her mother, who suckled her at her breast,
   For many a long month or more, her mind being sore
     oppress'd,
   Neither night or day she could not take any rest.

6. Her mother's mind being so disturbed, she dreamt three
      nights o'er,
   Her daughter she lay murdered beneath the Red-barn floor;
   She sent the father to the barn, when he the ground
      did thrust,
   And there he found his daughter mingling with the dust.

7. My trial is hard, I could not stand, most woeful was
      the sight,
   When her jaw-bone was brought to prove, which pierced my
      heart quite;
   Her aged father standing by, likewise his loving wife,
   And in her grief her hair she tore, she scarcely could
      keep life.

8. Adieu, adieu, my loving friends, my glass is almost run,
   On Monday next will be my last, when I am to be hang'd.
   So you, young men, who do pass by; with pity look on me,
   For murdering Maria Marten, I was hang'd upon the tree.

From the broadside of 1828 printed by J. Catnach. This text,
resolved into ballad quatrains, and collated with the other
broadside texts, is reproduced as version A in Appendix II.
Tune published in Folk Song Journal, 2 (1905-6), 118.
Printed by kind permission of Mrs. Ursula Vaughan Williams.

FLEMMING G. ANDERSEN AND THOMAS PETTITT

"THE MURDER OF MARIA MARTEN":
The Birth of a Ballad?

Maria Marten, of Polstead in Suffolk, by most accounts a young woman of somewhat dubious morality, met a brutal and bloody end at the hands of her latest and last paramour, William Corder, in May, 1827.[1] From the moment her body was discovered (under quite extraordinary circumstances) in the following April, public interest in this sensational case was amply catered to by the press and popular entertainment businesses, accounts and re-enactments being offered in newspapers, cartoons, peep-shows, stage melodramas, puppet-shows, and broadside ballads. One of these ballads, "The Murder of Maria Marten," issued by the Catnach Press on the occasion of Corder's execution at Bury St. Edmunds in August, 1828, offers invaluable and hitherto unappreciated insights into the genesis and evolution of popular narrative song.[2] As Holger Nygard has remarked, study of the origins of ballads, "or transitions from something to the ballad form" is usually prevented by "incompleteness of record."[3] But "Maria Marten" provides the full range of the information which is needed to observe these processes in action, information which we do not have, for example, for any song within the received canon of traditional balladry. We have the original text of the song (so that its own way of handling its story can be compared with that of other contemporary accounts), later re-issues on broadsides, and versions of the song recovered from oral tradition some three-quarters of a century subsequent to its composition and initial publication.[4] Before proceeding to a closer inspection of this material, however, it will be pertinent to examine some of the problems of ballad scholarship on which this song might be expected to shed some light.

At the heart of the heated debates which characterized ballad studies in the early part of this century was the question of ballad origins: this question, indeed, remains unresolved, although the debate has cooled. A good deal of confusion and misunderstanding was removed when in 1932 Gordon Hall Gerould separated the problem of origins into three distinct, although evidently inter-related, questions: the origin of the narrative form, the origin of the melodic or poetical form, and the origin of the individual ballads.[5] On the second of these questions "Maria Marten" has nothing to offer; it is sung to a traditional tune (variously known as "Lazarus" and "Come All Ye Worthy Christians"),[6] and in consequence its text, while printed and recorded in a variety of stanzaic arrangements, resolves itself easily into the familiar ballad quatrains. "Maria Marten" proves only that a newly-composed journalistic ballad can be written to fit "a melodic or poetical form" the origins of which lie far beyond the scope of the present inquiry.

An answer to the first of Gerould's questions naturally requires a precise notion of just what characterizes the narrative form of the ballad. This Gerould provided in a concise and influential definition:

> A ballad is a folk-song that tells a story with stress on the crucial situation, tells it by letting the action unfold itself in event and speech, and tells it objectively with little comment or intrusion of personal bias.[7]

In subsequent discussion Gerould adds that what he calls the ballad's rhetoric is characterized by repetitions and a commonplace phraseology.[8] Viewed in the light of work on the ballad since Gerould wrote, his characterization of its narrative form requires adjustment in one respect and more fundamental re-assessment in another. David Buchan, in a thorough and spirited analysis, has amply demonstrated that the ballad's commonplaces, and particularly its complex verbal and conceptual patternings (of which repetition is merely one aspect), rather than being merely ornamental, as Gerould implied, are really of basic structural significance for the dynamics of ballad narration.[9] It should also be appreciated that Gerould provided not so much a definition of a genre as a description of a particular way of telling a story in song. Indeed, speaking in terms of a ballad genre is an inappropriately academic approach to popular traditions: there is little indication that the scribes, printers and singers who preserved popular song in manuscript, broadsides or oral tradition, respectively, distinguished between what we call ballads and other varieties of popular song.[10] It is hard to see how they could make such a distinction, since the songs display a range of narrative styles in varying degrees of conformity with Gerould's ballad-model (and the same applies to versions of the same song collected in different times and places). It would evidently be better to speak not so much of ballads as a specific genre for which there can be established a strict canon, but rather of a balladic narrative style, which popular songs can display to a greater or lesser extent. Deciding where to draw the line between the acceptably and the insufficiently balladic (or between ballads and mere narrative songs) is an artificial,

arbitrary, and therefore inevitably controversial
exercise.[11]

Gerould's first question, "the origin of the narrative
form peculiar to the ballads,"[12] may therefore be taken to
mean "the origin of the balladic narrative style," and any
solution offered should account for the uneven incidence of
this style between different songs and between different
versions of a song. Gerould himself suggested that the
balladic style was an inevitable result of the harnessing of
narrative to a short, repeated melodic vehicle:

> The singing of a narrative to a melody is the
> kernel of the whole matter. Wherever and whenever
> that adaption was made, the ballad as we know it
> came into being. . . . the peculiarities of ballad
> structure are explicable if we remember that the
> stories are moulded to fit a recurrent melody.
> Their compression, their centralization, with the
> impersonality that results from the dramatic
> treatment of a theme, and, above all, the swiftly
> moving action, are precisely the qualities that
> would arise, almost inevitably, from the practice
> of singing stories to brief tunes.

Gerould adds that the ballad's dramatic character and its
frequent repetitions are to be similarly explained.[13] As it
stands this is unsatisfactory, implying that all traditional
narrative songs must "almost inevitably" be ballads (i.e.,
be uniformly and predominantly balladic). In later
discussion, however, Gerould suggests that the process,
while inevitable, is gradual (and hence can be recorded in
various stages of development), but he is not consistent on
the exact nature of the process involved. On the one hand,
Gerould speaks of his intent to explore "how and why songs
launched on the tide of popular tradition acquire the
characteristics by virtue of which they are a genre apart"[14]
(i.e., ballads), implying that the balladic style is
gradually evolved in the individual song in the course of
transmission. On the other hand his discussion concludes
that ballads have been shaped by "two equally important and
inter-related factors":

> /T/he development, at least as early as the twelfth
> century, of a traditional art in folk-song, which
> included the composition of ballads that were
> sharply focused, dramatic, impersonal; and
> secondly, the constant reshaping of ballads, once
> they were launched on the stream of tradition, by
> the co-operation of later generations, each of

which learned the popular art and passed it on to the generation following.[15]

Here it is the <u>art</u> of composing songs in the balladic style which undergoes a historical development; the subsequent reshaping of the individual ballads in oral transmission occurs within this already established framework: the songs change, but in so doing they do not necessarily become more like the ballad as Gerould defines it.

Each of these scenarios has been elaborated on in subsequent work on the ballads. David C. Fowler, as the provocative title of his <u>Literary History of the Popular Ballad</u> implies, follows the second scenario, suggesting a gradual (although much later) evolution in the art of composition towards the fully-fledged balladic style, in response to the shifting balance of power between the narrative and musical elements.[16] Fowler's model of generic evolution has been criticized, however, because it fails to take account of the possible role of oral transmission in shaping the ballads.[17] That this role is indeed significant is the view of a number of scholars who follow the first of the elaborations offered by Gerould: songs acquire their balladic features only in the course of transmission. In an influential study, Tristram P. Coffin suggests that any ballad starts life merely as a narrative song, marked by literary features characteristic of the time of its composition and the stylistic idiosyncracies of an individual author. In the course of oral transmission, however, the song loses what Coffin calls these "frills of sub-literary style," details of the action are lost, and altogether it is knocked into balladic form.[18] M. J. C. Hodgart suggests similarly that "communal recreation /the remoulding of the text by the singers who transmit it/ is the means by which a ballad, however learned, loses the signs of individual authorship and takes on impersonality and other ballad characteristics."[19] This scenario adequately explains why not only some songs, but some versions of a song, are more balladic than others. It is vulnerable, however, in being based on a theory of oral transmission which has never been adequately demonstrated and the validity of which has recently been strongly challenged.

Oral transmission, in the view of Gerould and the other scholars discussed above, is an essentially memorial process. A singer learns the words of a song and reproduces them as best he can in his own performances. He may consciously introduce alterations of his own, but then it is this revised text he remembers and performs. More usually, changes are made less deliberately, lines or whole stanzas being altered, replaced, or simply omitted. It is this process of memorization adjusted by conscious or unconscious alteration which, in the course of oral transmission, affects the communal re-creation of folk songs in general,[20] and which, some suggest, gradually transforms narrative songs into ballads. A radically more dynamic relationship between text and transmission has been proposed by the oral-formulaic school of ballad scholars, who seek to apply to traditional balladry the findings of Milman Parry and Albert Bates Lord about the performances of the _guslars_ of Yugoslavia.[21] Transmission and performance, in this view, are improvisational: a singer learns not a text but a story, and he recreates a text anew at each performance. To do so he uses a series of improvisational techniques, prominent among them being formulas and a complex of structural patternings. These and other features of balladic style, it is argued, are inevitable qualities of a text improvised in performance.[22]

None of these competing theories on the mechanisms of oral transmission has been based on adequate or reliable empirical evidence: it is not enough merely to note the features of a song, or even of many songs, and offer a hypothesis on how and why such features got there. When empirical evidence is invoked in support of the one theory or the other it usually takes the form of comparing different versions of a particular ballad to assess the extent and nature of the textual variation between them. But conclusions are inevitably contradictory: the versions vary so much, says Jones, that they must be the result of improvisation; they vary so little, says Friedman, that they must be the result of memorization.[23] Such confusion is the inescapable consequence of comparing quantities whose relationship is unknown. We do not have the original from which the variant texts may be supposed to have diverged, and we do not know their relative placings along the complex chains of transmission. A rough and ready alignment can sometimes be achieved on the basis of external criteria, such as date and place of recording. Comparison of an early version with later versions, for example, permits very broad conclusions to be hazarded about the evolution of a particular song.[24]

More reliable insights into the workings of tradition may be achieved by the study of multiple performances: that is, by comparing texts recorded in several performances of a song by one singer. Here at least we know the relative alignment of the texts, and in particularly favourable circumstances the approach can be extended to cover more than one singer: for example when we have versions of a song as sung by several members or generations of a singing family and can be sure it was passed on from singer to singer in an unbroken sequence.[25] But while the study of multiple performances is a useful and uniquely reliable way of exploring such vital questions as the interplay between tradition and the individual singing talent,[26] its significance for the purpose in hand is limited: it uncovers too short (and perhaps too late) a segment of a song's tradition to help in assessing the theories of ballad genesis and evolution under discussion. For this we need much more: we need in particular the original text of a song (and ideally the historical events or fictional narrative which form its source) as a fixed point of reference for analysis of the later versions which must all ultimately derive from it. These conditions are not fulfilled for any ballad in Child's collection,[27] and outside it they are also extremely rare.[28] It is with particular interest therefore that one turns to the broadside ballads. A large proportion of the songs recovered from oral tradition have appeared on broadsides at one time or another,[29] and many of them, we may suppose, actually descend from broadside ballads composed by the hacks and minor poets in the employ of the printers.[30] We cannot, however, simply take a broadside text of a song, even an early one, and assume that it is the original from which all the oral versions ultimately derive. English folk songs have moved in and out of print and oral tradition throughout their recorded history,[31] and we have no way of telling which, if any, of the surviving versions, printed or oral, is the original.[32]

This reservation does not apply, ironically, to those journalistic broadside ballads, the despair of scholars in quest of authentic tradition, which offer sensational relations and revelations on current events in the news.[33] Here at least the alignment of broadside and oral texts is ascertainable: the text of a journalistic broadside ballad which appears at the time of the events it relates has not been transmitted from earlier oral versions, and any oral version recorded subsequently must derive ultimately from the broadside. Divergences between an oral text and the broadside original must have been introduced in the course of transmission, and features shared by the oral versions against the original reveal the impact of tradition on the song. Since many journalistic broadsides have a strong narrative element, such material offers our best hope of accurate assessment of the respective roles of composition and transmission in the molding of traditional narrative song.

It is not to be expected that the amount of material available for such analysis is very great. Few folk songs

recovered from oral tradition, we imagine, can with
certainty be traced back to identifiable and available
journalistic broadsides. This may be, as is sometimes
suggested, because such songs are short-lived in tradition;
it is just as likely that they were simply not recorded: a
collector offered such a piece by a singer would recognize
the obviously popular source of the text and decline to
record it unless perhaps it was set to an interesting tune.
We have probably lost many oral versions of our popular
songs--say from the music halls--for similar reasons.[34] Much
remains to be done in matching the broadside and traditional
song collections to determine the number of suitable
instances available for analysis. In the meantime we offer
the results of what must be considered a pilot project along
these lines, our consideration of the afterlife of the song
which relates the end of the life of poor Maria Marten.

The press of James Catnach of Seven Dials, London,
followed the case from the beginning. In the April of 1828,
immediately after the inquest (referred to as opening "on
Sunday last"), Catnach issued a broadside giving a long
prose account. It contained the headlines, "Atrocious Murder
of a Young Woman in Suffolk. Singular Discovery of the Body
from a Dream" and was illustrated by a woodcut depicting
"The Red Barn. The Scene of the Murder, and where the Body
of Maria Marten was found concealed." It relates the girl's
disappearance, the remarkable circumstances that occasioned
the discovery of her body and reports that efforts were in
hand to apprehend Corder. The arrest of Corder is duly
reported (as having occurred "yesterday") in a sequel where
the headlines of the first account are supplemented by
"Apprehension of the Murderer at Ealing, Middlesex"--another
lengthy prose account this time illustrated by an
unprepossessing woodcut of Corder. Finally in August, after
Corder's conviction ("on Friday last") and execution,
Catnach issued a third prose account (without illustration)
headed "Confession and Execution of William Corder, the
Murderer of Maria Marten".[35] It includes what purports to be
Corder's eve-of-execution confession, duly witnessed by the
gaol chaplain and under-sheriff, and a description of his
demeanor at the execution. The bottom half of the
broadside's second column is taken up by the text of the
song which is the subject of the present inquiry. It is
headed "The Murder of Maria Marten. By W. Corder," a rather
ambiguous formulation which might mean simply that Corder
committed the murder but which as punctuated was probably
designed to give the impression that Corder had composed the
song itself. This is of course quite in keeping with the
conventions of this classic broadside genre, for the song is
a "Goodnight" or "Sorrowful Lamentation," in which the

condemned murderer is purported to relate and regret his crimes and warn others to avoid his example.[36]

The song, which refers to the murder, the discovery of the body, and the trial, and--accurately--anticipates the execution ("on Monday next"), was evidently composed and issued in close association with the events of early August, 1828, perhaps even during the weekend between the conviction and the execution, in order to exploit the widespread interest in these extraordinary and public events. Its appearance, together with the prose account of the execution, makes it virtually certain that here indeed is the original text of this particular journalistic ballad,[37] a text which may have been composed by James Catnach himself.[38]

The song was apparently a success, at least if we can trust accounts that it sold in over a million copies.[39] It was certainly successful enough to warrant further issues. The Catnach Press printed it again, with the slightly less misleading title, "Murder of M. Marten, by W. Corder," on an undated broadside together with another song, "Wilt Thou Say Farewell, Love,"[40] and it was also issued by the printer H. Such on an undated broadside together with "Barney Buntline to Billy Bowline; or a Sailor's Consolation in a Storm," with the title, "Murder of Maria Marten by W. Corder, at the Red Barn May 18th, 1824 $\underline{/\ sic\ \underline{7}}$."[41] Its appearance on broadsides with other songs suggests that "Maria Marten" had an appeal independent of its news value in connection with the events it relates. The song was successful too in a way which is highly significant for the present investigation. A. L. Lloyd has observed, ominously,

> . . . the countless Sorrowful Lamentations of hanged men did not become anchored in tradition, . . . perhaps because the song-sheets having these effusions are of late appearance and the texts, in consequence, turgidly literary--if not always very literate--and hard for folk tradition to absorb despite the sturdiness of its digestive system.[42]

Lloyd may be right about the text of "Maria Marten," but he is wrong, fortunately, about the ability of folk tradition to digest it:[43] between 1904 and 1920, this song was recorded from fourteen different singers, in the counties of Cambridgeshire, Surrey, Sussex, Norfolk, Lincolnshire, Ely, Essex and Yorkshire.[44] In the majority of cases, unfortunately, the collectors, probably recognizing the text for what it was, recorded only the tune. In a few precious instances, however, they swallowed their prejudices sufficiently to record the words as well, with the result that "Maria Marten" provides us with the invaluable opportunity of observing the mechanisms of tradition at work by comparing the original Catnach broadside with four fragments (Appendix II, Nos. B, C, E and F)[45] and three complete versions (Appendix II, Nos. D, G and H), recovered from oral tradition 70-90 years later.

"Maria Marten," as issued by the Catnach Press in connection with the execution of William Corder in 1828 (Aa) is a song in what many would consider the worst tradition of sensational and sentimental journalistic broadside balladry. The narration of the events which led to Corder's condemnation is prefixed by the typical "Come all ye" incipit and concluded by his sorrowful valediction to his "loving friends" (st. 15) and all "young men who do pass by" (st. 16). The narrative thus packaged comprises two main sections which we shall designate as the Crime (sts. 4-8) and the Discovery (sts. 9-12). This narrative center is further encapsulated by a brief introduction which sets the scene and presents the protagonists (sts. 2-3) and by a brief evocation of the scene at the trial (sts. 13-14). The narrative is detailed and circumstantial, revealing Corder's aims at the outset (st. 3) and providing such specific information as the date on which they made their assignation (May 18th, st. 4^2), their place of rendezvous (the Red Barn, st. 5^1), and their supposed destination (Ipswich, st. 5^3). The song carefully reports that Corder collected all the implements he would need, "my gun,/ my pickaxe and my spade" (st. 6^{1-2}) to both kill and bury his victim. Each quatrain of which the narrative is composed provides new information, steadily carrying the matter forward. The Crime: Corder goes to the house (st. 4), makes the assignation (st. 5), prepares for the crime (st. 6), commits the crime (st. 7), buries the body (st. 8); the Discovery: the spirit walks (st. 9), the mother is restless (st. 10) and has a dream (st. 11) which leads to the discovery (st. 12). This steady, informative progression is in what might properly be termed the journalistic ballad style, and indeed the song is largely a precis of the narrative already provided in the three prose accounts printed by Catnach:

> Maria Marten, a fine young woman, . . . formed an imprudent connection . . . with a young man named William Corder.
>
> ("Atrocious Murder"; cf. st. 2)
>
> . . . He appeared much attached to her, and was a frequent visitor at her father's house. On the 19th of May last she left her father's house, stating . . . that she was going to the Red Barn to meet

William Corder, who was to be waiting there with a
chaise to convey her to Ipswich, where they were to
be married.

("Atrocious Murder"; cf. sts. 4-5)

When we left her father's house, we began
quarrelling . . . I took the pistol from the side
pocket of my velveteen jacket and fired. She fell,
and died in an instant. . . . The body fell . . .
on the floor of the barn. A vast quantity of blood
issued from the wound.

("Confession and Execution"; cf. sts. 7-8[2])

Having determined to bury the body in the
barn . . . I was obliged to go home for a pickaxe
and a better spade, with which I dug the hole, and
then buried the body.

("Confession and Execution"; cf. sts. 6, 8[3]-[4])

The parents became more and more disturbed, . . .
and these fears were still more strongly agitated
by the mother dreaming, on three successive nights
. . . that her daughter had been murdered, and
buried in the Red Barn.

("Atrocious Murder"; cf. sts. 10-11)

She insisted that the floor of the barn should be
upturned. On Saturday, Marten, the father, . . .
went to examine the barn, and soon . . . turned up
a piece of shawl . . . and . . . part of a human
body.

("Atrocious Murder"; cf. st. 12)

This factual narrative is colored in a number of ways
by the balladist. As comparison with the prose accounts
shows, he has Corder prepare for the murder by taking his
gun and tools to the barn and even digging the grave (st. 6)
before Maria arrives, instead of afterwards as Corder
confessed, so that the crime is now a pre-meditated murder
(cf. also st. 3) rather than the fatal outcome of a quarrel.
The innocence of Maria, and hence the heinousness of the
crime, is enhanced by omitting any reference to the
illegitimate child she had by Corder which the two of them
may have murdered (mentioned in Corder's "Confession"). The
narrative is similarly intensified by attributing thoughts

and emotions to the protagonists: Corder is "resolved" (st. 3^3), Maria comes "with heart so light" and she "thought no harm" (st. 7^1); and her mother's mind is "sore oppress'd" (st. 10^2), and Corder's heart is "pierced" (st. 13^4) at the trial. In particular, the journalist-cum-balladist has provided the story with some striking, almost gothic visual images: the "bleeding mangled body" of the victim, "weltering in her gore" (st. 8^{2-3}--cf. the prose account's more restrained "a vast quantity of blood issued from the wound"); the spirit of Maria suckled at the breast of her mother in a grotesque _Pieta_ (st. 9); and Maria's jaw-bone produced as an exhibit at the trial (st. 13^3).

This sensational and sentimental journalism is a far cry from the bare, impersonal manner of the balladic style. But before going on to examine the later versions it would be wrong not to point out such traditional features as this Catnach text, which is the point of departure for subsequent comparisons, already possesses. Despite its sub-literary features, "Maria Marten" is a narrative song. Its narrative centre (sts. 4-12) tells the story of a young girl who is enticed away from her parents' home by a lover who promises marriage, but who instead makes a brutal assault on her life.

Thus baldly summarized, the narrative resolves itself into the kind of story--romantic intrigue with strong leavenings of sex and violence--which is well-represented in the received corpus of traditional balladry. And if the story of Maria Marten has in it the stuff that ballads are made of, the manner of its telling, even in this broadside, has something of the balladic about it. In particular, the narrative shows signs of those conceptual patternings, sometimes reinforced by verbal repetitions, which are generally recognized as one of the hallmarks of traditional balladry. At the heart of the narration is a triad of visits to that fatal Red Barn: by Corder (st. 6), Maria (st. 7) and by her father (st. 12). Maria's movement to the barn balances Corder's instruction to her to do so (st. 5). Another triad is formed by the burial of the body under the floor of the barn (st. 8^{3-4}), the mother's dream of it being there (st. 11^{2-4}), and the father's discovery of it in the same place (st. 12); in the first two instances the conceptual pattern is reinforced by the verbal repetition, "beneath the Red-barn floor" (sts. 8^4 and 11^4). The section of the narrative we have called the Crime is framed by Corder's visit to the parental home (st. 4) and the visitation of the same house by Maria's spirit (st. 9). The restlessness of which this visit is a symptom ("her spirit could not rest," st. 9^2) is balanced by the restlessness it causes in her mother ("she could not take any rest," st.

10^4). This anxiety ("her mind being sore oppress'd," st. 10^2) in turn provokes the revelatory dream ("Her . . . mind being so disturbed, / she dreamt, . . ." st. 11^{1-2}), giving two--overlapping--balances, each reinforced by a degree of verbal repetition. There is a general tendency to render similar events in parallel terms (cf. also "I went into, . . ." sts. 4^1 and 6^3). The whole story, finally, is framed by the narrator's reference to the gallows-tree (sts. 1^4 and 16^4).

While it would be absurd to speak of formulas in such a context, even a journalistic ballad, it would seem, can display a certain commonplace element in its phraseology. The "Come all ye" opening stanza is of course a familiar broadside convention, but other lines too recur in other crime or execution ballads:[46]

Most beautiful and fair (st. 2^4)
-- cf. "So beautiful and sweet"
   ("A Ballad from the Seven Dials Press")

I promised I would marry her (st. 3^1)
-- cf. "And I promised I would marry her"
   ("The Berskhire Tragedy")

I went into her father's house/the 18th day of May (st. 4^{1-2})
-- cf. "I went unto her sister's house/at eight o'clock that night":
   ("The Lexington Murder")

After the horrible deed was done (st. 8^1)
-- cf. ". . . a cruel deed has done"; "Who did the horrid deed"
   ("Trial of Good"; "Mary White")

She lay weltering in her gore (st. 8^2)
-- cf. ". . . lay weltering in her gore"; ". . . reeking in their gore"
   ("Outrage and Murder"; "Trial of Good")

She could not take any rest (st. 10^4, cf. st. 9^2)
-- cf. "For I could take no rest"
   ("The Berkshire Tragedy")

Even an expression apparently specific to the story, like
I will take you to Ipswich town,
   and there make you my wife (st. 5^{3-4})

could be used of another lover with vile intentions:
I brought her up to London Town,

To make her my dear wife.
("A Ballad from the Seven Dials Press"; in both
cases, ominously, "wife" is rhymed with "life".)

In one instance a line startlingly echoes the formulaic
diction of traditional balladry: "And laid her body low"
(st. 7[4]) is a phrase recurring in the formulaic stanza which
is used in connection with a sexual assault upon a young
girl, as in "Tam Lin":

He took her by the milk-white hand,
  And by the grass green sleeve,
And laid her low down on the flowers,
  At her he asked no leave.   (Child No. 39D 7)

Or in "The Wylie Wife of the Hie Toun Hie":
  One of them took her by the milk-white hand,
    And he's laid her body on the ground,
  And aye she sighed, and said, Alass,
    'T is a sin to do me wrong!   (Child No. 290A 7)

Catnach's "The Murder of Maria Marten" is evidently
something of a stylistic mixture. Its broadside packaging of
incipit and Valediction and its circumstantial and
occasionally melodramatic account mark it as a piece of
journalistic versification belonging to a specific sub-
literary tradition. However, it belongs equally clearly to a
sub-type of the broadside crime-and-execution ballad in
which the narrative of events, as opposed to emotional or
moral response to them, is a dominant feature.[47] This
narrative at the song's core, and the structural patternings
which inform its telling, undeniably have something of the
balladic about them; and while the phraseology is scarcely
formulaic, it does seem to derive from a style traditional
to the narration of this kind of material. It is the
handling of these diverse and unevenly distributed
characteristics in subsequent tradition which will now be
examined.

That subsequent tradition has two streams, printed and
oral, the first of them represented by the two re-issues of
the broadside. The two streams undoubtedly crossed from time
to time: oral tradition, we may be sure, was occasionally
reinforced by the availability of one or other of the
broadsides, and conversely oral tradition may well have
affected the broadside reissues. While we might expect that
the compositors setting up the new prints worked with the
original before them, there are changes in textual detail
which go beyond what could reasonably be attributed to mere
typographical error, even in a notoriously careless trade,
suggesting that the compositors may have been working in

part from memory.[48] The changes are not large and do not affect the overall structure of the song: both the re-issues (Ab and Ac) reproduce all sixteen stanzas of the original (Aa) in their correct order. Most changes indeed are restricted to single words, for example "unto" for "into" (a preference shared by the oral versions), and "on" for "upon," but on occasion such small changes can affect the sense of a line (e.g., st. 14^{1-2}). Some changes in a line are more radical, although the rhyme-word is retained, as in Ac's "and let us fix the day" (st. 4^4) for Aa's "we will fix the wedding day." The most significant changes, however, are those which are related to the conceptual patternings in the narrative just discussed. Those patterns, it seems, are instrumental in provoking and controlling verbal change. Two parts of the narrative linked by such a pattern are the burial of Maria's body "beneath the Red-barn floor" (Aa 8^4) and her mother's dream that indeed the body lay "beneath the Red-barn floor" (Aa 11^4), the pattern here reinforced by verbal repetition. Ab alters the first instance to relate that Corder "threw" the body "under" the floor,[49] and the second moves automatically into line, the mother dreaming of the body "under" the floor. More remarkably, Ac has Corder throw the body "upon" the floor, and it is still there when the mother dreams, "Her daughter she lay murdered / upon the Red-barn floor," even though the father still has to dig her up in the next stanza. Verbal alteration at one point in a conceptual pattern, it seems, provokes parallel alteration at another point in the pattern.

In other instances textual alterations add verbal reinforcement to existing conceptual patterns. In both re-issues the restlessness of Maria's spirit is described with the line, "she could not take no rest" (Ab, Ac 9^2; cf. Aa "her spirit could not rest"), which exactly reproduces the phrase used in all three broadsides at st. 10^4 to describe the parallel restlessness of the mother. Similarly the visitation by Maria's spirit is related in Ab and Ac with the line "She appeared in her mother's house" (st. 9^3; cf. Aa "She appeared unto her mother"), adding a verbal parallel to the conceptual balance with the earlier visit by Corder to "her father's house" (st. 4^1). The process involved here is probably best characterized as "internal contamination," as a line at one point in the narrative is altered to produce a verbal echo of a line at another point; the significance of the phenomenon is that the points involved in the process are those already linked through the conceptual patternings in the song's narrative structure. A simpler form of direct contamination can occur between adjacent lines (e.g., "bleeding" for "weltering" in Ab, Ac 8^2, cf. st. 8^3).

The changes in the oral texts, to which we now turn, are by comparison much more complex, and it will be convenient to treat them in terms of the sensible headings suggested by Tom Burns, which replace and subsume the often chaotic vocabulary applied previously to the discussion of verbal change in tradition. Burns's categories are, quite simply: <u>addition</u>, <u>subtraction</u>, <u>rearrangement</u>, and <u>substitution</u> (subtraction plus addition).[50] We shall discuss changes first at the stanzaic and then the linear levels.[51] Considering the fate of the sixteen stanzas of which the broadside is composed, it is immediately apparent that the overwhelming impact of oral transmission, as we might expect, is subtraction. While there are some alterations on the linear level, there is no stanza in any of the oral versions which does not have an equivalent in the original broadside: there are no stanzaic additions or substitutions. Nor are there any significant rearrangements: with a single exception, the oral versions present such stanzas of the broadside as they do retain in their original order.

The material does not permit us to determine whether the stanzaic substractions were deliberate or merely the result of defective memorization; but it is abundantly clear that they are not haphazard. Certain parts of the song are evidently more prone to subtraction than others, and it is interesting to observe which parts they are. For example the opening and closing business, what we have called the <u>incipit</u> (A 1) and the Valediction (A 15-16), are decidedly vulnerable. Of the six oral versions which might have opened with the "Come all ye" <u>incipit</u>, only two (E 1, G 1) retain it.[52] The three versions which reach the Valediction all render it imperfectly: D has only A 16 (D 9), G concludes with a composite stanza (G 11),[53] and H, while alone retaining A 15 (H 9), follows it with a stanza (H 10) mostly derived from A 1 (thus qualifying as the one example of stanzaic rearrangement in the oral versions). The narrative introduction (A 2-3) survives nearly intact; but the broadside's narrative section suffers unevenly at the hands of tradition, which seems to pick and choose from the material offered to it in a remarkably consistent way. Of the two sections of the narrative proper, the Crime is most faithfully reproduced. All three complete versions retain its first four stanzas (A 4-7) fairly accurately and in their correct order (and are here joined by C, whose three stanzas correspond to A 5-7), but they are unanimous in omitting A 8, which describes the burial of the body. It may be that its sensational style ("horrible deed," "weltering in her gore," "bleeding mangled body") was not to the taste of the singers;[54] or perhaps they rejected its lack of narrative economy (1. 3 largely repeats 1. 2) and redundancy --the burial of the body is sufficiently signalled by st. 6.

The Discovery (A 9-12), in contrast, consistently suffers stanzaic subtraction. The stanza in which Maria's father uncovers her body (A 12) is retained in all three complete versions, but the preceding relation is imperfectly reproduced in each case. Such stanzas as are retained suffer considerable disturbance at the linear level, and a distinct lack of interest is evinced in the stanza (A 9) describing the walking and suckling of the girl's spirit: it is omitted in D and H, and in G (st. 8) it is garbled and evidently not fully understood. This again may be because of the melodramatic content (although revenants are not unknown in traditional songs) or because the stanza performs no essential narrative function: the mother has reason enough to be disturbed already, and this stanza, in bringing the girl and the mother together, in fact functions as a transition between the Crime and Discovery sections of the narrative. Without it we have a rather balladic leap between the two. Finally, the narrative aftermath (A 13-14), which provides a brief glimpse of the trial, is uniformly omitted. In this third instance, too, the omission may be because of the melodramatic tone and content ("her jaw-bone," "pierced my heart," "her hair she tore"),[55] or because the stanzas lack an essential narrative function. These two stanzas do not, in Gerould's words, "let the action unfold itself"; rather, they sketch the scene at the trial and describe the emotional responses of the participants. And as our term implies, they concern the judicial aftermath, not the tragedy of "Fair Maria and Sweet William" itself.

From this complex of detail there emerge some significant trends. The impact of tradition on a narrative song evidently involves stanzaic subtraction, but neither omission nor retention is purely arbitrary. The packaging of incipit and Valediction with which the broadside presents its story is particularly vulnerable, as are those stanzas not essential to the narrative--supplying redundant information, providing transition between scenes, or reporting the aftermath of the narrative proper.[56] In consequence, the narrative itself becomes more compressed and efficient. At the same time, by accident or design, we lose most of the song's sub-literary, melodramatic descriptions, expressions of the feelings of the narrator, and much that links the song to a specific criminal case. It may not be too much to suggest even at this stage that the song is shedding much that characterizes it as a journalistic ballad of a particular type and period and acquiring distinctly balladic features.

Further hints along these lines are revealed by examination at the linear level. A line which is already reminiscent of traditional phraseology (such as A 7^4) is characteristically preserved intact (cf. C 3^4, D 6^4, G 7^4 and H 6^4), while elsewhere we encounter quite comprehensive linear revision, for example:

D 7

Her mother dreamed three dreams
    one night,
    she ne'er could get no rest
She dreamed she saw her daughter
    dear
    lay bleeding at the breast.

A 11

Her mother's mind being so
    disturbed
    she dreamt three nights
    o'er
Her daughter she lay murdered
    beneath the Red-barn floor.

G 9

Her mother had a dreadful
    dream,
    She dreamed it three
    nights o'er,
She dreamed that her dear
    daughter
    Lay beneath the Red Barn
    floor.

H 7

Her aged mother dreamt
    three nights
    all o're and o're and
    o're -
That her daughter, she lay
    murdered,
    beneath the red barn
    floor.

We are presented here with the results of what is evidently considerable re-creation in the course of transmission. The recreation is successful in that all three new stanzas make tolerably good sense, and it is achieved in a variety of ways. Partly, there is a form of rearrangement as lines or phrases from otherwise lost stanzas at vulnerable points of the song find a last refuge elsewhere. Thus D 7^2 preserves A 10^4 (or Ab, Ac 9^2); D 7^4 may preserve bits of A 9^4 and A 8^3. Other lines result from the process of _internal contamination_, producing the verbal parallels discussed earlier--this process applies to D 7^3 (cf. D 8^3) and perhaps G 9^3 (cf. G 10^3). The remainder are generally reformulations or rearrangements of material already present in A 11. Least successful at reformulation is H 7, where the first line manages to summarize A 11^{1-2} but leaves an awkward gap, one filled by the infelicitous, if mathematically accurate, "all o're and o're and o're" (H 7^2). Rather more interesting is the tendency of D 7 and G 9 to repetition, particularly of "dream" and "dreamed," producing alliterative formulations frequently encountered in traditional balladry:

Yestreen I dreamd a dolefu dream (Child No. 214E 10^1)
I dreamed a dreary dream this night (Child No. 214A 1^1)
I dreamed a dream, my dear lady (Child No. 74A 8^1)
I have dreamed a dreary dream, she says (Child No. 88B 10^1)

All these dreams are associated with death and blood.

The subtractions on the stanzaic level already discussed have inevitably disrupted a number of the conceptual patternings observed in the narrative structure of the original, although it is noticeable that those already verbally reinforced tend to be retained. But by way of compensation new patterns can emerge: for example, the traditional narrative mechanism that we saw at work in the broadside version at this point--the verbal balance between A 8^4 and A 11^4--is retained in the oral versions: D 7^{3-4} and D 8^{3-4}, G 9^{3-4} and G 10^{3-4}, which instead of marking a balance between the burial and the dream of the original text, establishes a similar connection between the dream and the discovery. In particular, substitutions on the linear level often reinforce such conceptual patterns as there are with verbal repetition as well. The density and impact of these patternings and repetitions, moreover, are increased by the subtractions of non-essential material that have occurred at the stanzaic level. As in the case of the broadside reissues, this is achieved by internal contamination, as a line in the song affects the formulation of a line at the other end of a structural pattern. The parallel movements of Corder and Maria to the barn, for example, acquire in H a verbal parallel as well:

A	H
st. 6^3:	st. 5^3:
I went into the Red-barn	And to the Red Barn he did go
st. 7^2:	st. 6^2:
to meet him she did go	to meet him she did go.

This feature is particularly prominent in D, which displays a complex pattern of verbal-conceptual repetitions involving all the stanzas in its narrative section:

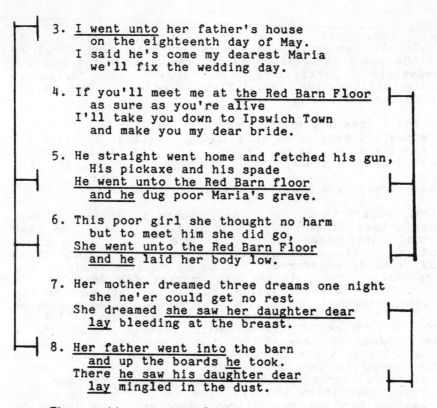

3. I went unto her father's house
    on the eighteenth day of May.
    I said he's come my dearest Maria
    we'll fix the wedding day.

4. If you'll meet me at the Red Barn Floor
    as sure as you're alive
    I'll take you down to Ipswich Town
    and make you my dear bride.

5. He straight went home and fetched his gun,
    His pickaxe and his spade
    He went unto the Red Barn floor
    and he dug poor Maria's grave.

6. This poor girl she thought no harm
    but to meet him she did go,
    She went unto the Red Barn Floor
    and he laid her body low.

7. Her mother dreamed three dreams one night
    she ne'er could get no rest
    She dreamed she saw her daughter dear
    lay bleeding at the breast.

8. Her father went into the barn
    and up the boards he took.
    There he saw his daughter dear
    lay mingled in the dust.

The patterns displayed here are not incremental repetition, but rather simpler forms of repetition which are nonetheless equally characteristic of balladic style. They play two distinct roles in this text. There are, first, verbal repetitions corresponding to similar or parallel actions by the protagonists: Corder to the house (st. 3^1), Corder, Maria, and her father to the barn (sts. 5^3, 6^3, 8^1). "Maria Marten" here shows putative forms of a kind of repetition familiar in ballads:

When she came to her father's yates,
    She tirled gently at the pin:
    . . . .

When she came to Earl Crawford's yates,
    She tirled gently at the pin:
    . . . .

When he came to Lady Crawford's yates,
    He tirled gently at the pin:
    (Child No. 229B 10^{1-2}, 20^{1-2}, 28^{1-2})

In addition, there are repetitions in which a narrative step is expressed in words similar to those in which it was earlier prefigured: Maria's movement to the barn (st. 6^3) echoes Corder's instruction (st. 4^1); the discovery of the body (st. 8^{3-4}) echoes the mother's vision of its location (st. 7^{3-4}). Again the song seems to be moving towards the generation of a familiar balladic form of repetition:

> "O turn you about, O false Sir John,
> And look to the leaf of the tree,"
> . . . .
> He turned himself straight round about,
> To look to the leaf of the tree.
> . . . .   (Child No. 4C 8^{1-2}, 9^{1-2})

The balladic quality of the oral versions is further enhanced by small-scale additions and substitutions, some of them, probably, to fit the words more neatly to the tune.[57] Their general effect is to bring the text closer to familiar folk song idiom:

> all on a certain day   (D 2^2; A, upon. Cf. G 3^2)
> ... 'twas my intent   (E 3^3; A, I was resolved)
> I went down to her father's house   (H 3^1; A, into)
> all mingling with the dust   (H 8^4; an addition)
> daughter dear (D 7^3, 8^3; G 9^3, 10^3; an addition).

Some of them seem motivated by the desire to achieve internal rhyme:

> I'll take you down to Ipswich Town (D 4^3, cf. G 5^3, H 4^3)
> I promised her I'd marry her (D 2^1, cf. E 3^1, G 3^1, H 2^1)

Here, finally, belong the changes in the names of people and places, which, together with the subtractions already discussed, show the song slowly severing its connection with the events that inspired its composition: "William Cornwell" (B 1^2), "William Cordewood" (H 1^1), "Peddewick town" (H 4^3), and perhaps "Maria Martin" (Ab 16^3, B 1^3, D 1^3, E 2^3, F 1^3).

From these analyses of the printed and oral texts of "Maria Marten" there emerge some general trends which may provide a useful vantage point from which to review the ballad problems outlined at the beginning of this study. Most easily resolved, perhaps, is the question of the mechanisms involved in oral transmission. While our discussion has not examined the matter explicitly, it will have been evident throughout that "Maria Marten" has been preserved in oral tradition by a process of memorization rather than improvisation. The text has been memorized, but parts of it have been forgotten: the oral versions present

such stanzas of the original as they preserve in their
original order and with a large degree of verbal stability.
There is some re-creation on the linear level, but this is a
far cry from the full-scale restructuring and reformulation
of the text which are the concomitants of the oral-
improvisational theory. If further demonstration were
required, it is adequately provided by the two fragmentary
texts supplied by Joseph Taylor (C) and John East (E).
Joseph Taylor's version, indeed, may be not so much a
fragment as the most radically altered of all the oral
texts; it is arrived at by the subtraction of all but three
of the broadside's sixteen stanzas. These three are,
however, a consecutive sequence from the original (A 5-7,
incl.) and are rendered with considerable verbal fidelity.
The choice of these three stanzas looks deliberate, since,
astonishingly, they manage to summarize the entire tragedy.
This is perhaps an extreme form of the creative
forgetfulness evinced by many of the oral texts.[58]

Equally indicative of memorial transmission is the less
creative forgetfulness of John East. He reproduces
accurately the broadside's first three stanzas, but the
identity of rhyme and one of the rhyming words between
stanzas 3 and 4 betrays him into an error:

        I went unto her father's house
            On the 18th day of May
        And I promised her I'd marry her
            Upon a certain day   (E 4)

The third and fourth lines repeat st. 3^{1-2} rather than
moving the story forward as the original does:

        Saying, my dear Maria,
            we will fix the wedding day.   (A 4^{3-4})

Having made the text double back on itself, East is
evidently at a loss; and the "etc., etc." in Sharp's
notebook probably represents the singer scratching his head.

It will be objected by proponents of the oral-
improvisational theory of ballad transmission that all this
is no more than could be expected of a song like "Maria
Marten." It enters tradition at a time when the transmission
of songs was decisively affected by the widespread
availability of printed texts, and of course itself derives
from a broadside. It therefore belongs to the verbal phase
of tradition, long after the improvisational techniques of
the oral phase have been ousted by memorization-by-rote and
when singers reproduce their songs in the state of "mental
sleepwalking" regretted by Bronson.[59] But as we have noted

elsewhere, for balladry in England this postulated oral (improvisational) phase is, in the technical sense of the term, pre-historic; we have very few ballads indeed from the period before the substantial impact of broadsides in the sixteenth century, and even at this early period rates of literacy among the ballad-singing strata of society were by no means negligible.[60] It would be reasonable to suggest rather that what "Maria Marten" can tell us about ballad transmission will be broadly applicable to the tradition in England throughout most of its recorded history.

"Maria Marten" makes it possible, perhaps for the first time, to assess the relative contributions of composition and transmission to the characteristic balladic narrative style. On the one hand, it will be recalled, it has been suggested there developed a tradition of song-making in the balladic mode, its characteristics intimately related to the conjunction of narrative and short, melodic vehicle. "Maria Marten" suggests that there is some truth in this assertion: for all its sub-literary stylistic features it is built around a strong narrative core. The matter of this narrative is determined by the real-life tragedy of Maria Marten and William Corder, but comparison between the broadside and other accounts (such as the Catnach prose accounts and newspaper reports) shows the balladist selecting and rearraging his received material to produce a forceful, dramatic narrative formulated to accompany an existing traditional tune. The narrative is built up of a sequence of significant events arranged to form distinct conceptual patternings which are on occasion reinforced by verbal parallels. There are, furthermore, signs of the use of a number of commonplace formulations apparently conventional in this tradition of broadside balladry.

"The Murder of Maria Marten," beneath its literary frills, has some features in common with the songs now habitually designated ballads, and, furthermore, is traditional in the sense that it shares these characteristics with other broadside ballads on similar themes. The conventional quality of the diction has been illustrated above; the conventional quality of its matter presumably needs no illustration; what does merit demonstration is the conventional quality of its narrative mode, its patterned structuring of significant events.

This feature is shown, for example, by the song, or "Copy of Verses" accompanying the undated prose account on a broadside of "A Horrible Murder, A Father Cutting his Child's Head off!"[61] As in the case of "Maria Marten," comparison of the song with the prose account shows the balladist, in the narrative section of the song (packaged

between a florid _incipit_ and conclusion), selecting only the
most significant events and presenting them in a neatly (in
this case, chiastically) structured sequence: the mother
leaves--description of the living baby--the murder--
description of the murdered baby--the mother returns.
Significantly, the father's departure after the crime, which
is important in a journalistic sense (as it explains why he
is not yet arrested) and of which much is made in the prose
account, is omitted in the song, perhaps precisely because
it would disturb this structure. Another Catnach broadside,
describing the murder of "Sarah Spriggens" by "Richard
Wilbyforce" similarly presents a careful (again chiastic)
arrangement of its material: Richard courts Sarah (described
as "an angel bright")--journey to London--murder--journey
from London--Sarah (as a "ghost in burning fire") haunts
Richard.[62]

Just when and how this narrative mode developed is
beyond the scope of this study and is a matter on which
"Maria Marten" can shed no light. To judge by "The Berkshire
Tragedy"[63] it was applied to this kind of matter by the
eighteenth century. The degree to which its appearance in
broadside texts is influenced by already existing
traditional songs (which is very likely) is a question
difficult to discuss without circular argument, a contortion
this study has been at pains to avoid. Rather, it is more
profitable to recall that there is still much in the
broadside versions of "Maria Marten" which is alien to the
balladic mode but that these features are radically reduced
in the course of oral transmission, which must therefore
also be given its due credit in the generation of the
balladic style. The broadside packaging is systematically
reduced, as are parts of the song more important to the
journalistic accumulation of facts rather than the progress
of the narrative. Much of the local literary quality is
similarly shed. Such features as are already reminiscent of
traditional balladic style are, however, resolutely
retained. The result is a more economical, prominent and
concentrated narrative, the verbal rendition of which is
increasingly characterized by phrases and formulations from
the general folk song idiom, and the conceptual patternings
of which, through the process we have labelled internal
contamination, are reinforced by verbal repetition. These
are the features which distinguish the texts shaped by
tradition from the original broadside. Although not
entirely traditional in nature, the oral versions of "Maria
Marten" evidently demonstrate a traditional ballad in the
making, and the comparative analyses undertaken here reveal
many of the forces at work in that process. Oral
transmission, if not exactly the incubator of folk poetry,[64]
still appears to be one of the main generators of the

balladic narrative mode, operating in terms of preservation of existing traditional material, elimination of foreign elements, and alteration of lines to create traditional structural patternings.

"Maria Marten": List of Sources

Broadside Texts

Aa. "The Murder of Maria Marten. By W. Corder," together
with "Confession and Execution of William Corder, the
Murderer of Maria Marten" /prose account/; printed by
J. Catnach, n.d. /1828/. Facsimile reprint in Charles
Hindley, The Life and Times of James Catnach (London,
1878; rpt. Detroit: Singing Tree Press, 1968), p.187.

Ab. "Murder of M. Marten, by W. Corder," together with
"Wilt thou Say Farewell Love," printed by J. Catnach,
n.d., sold by Bennett, Brighton. Facsimile reprint in
Leslie Shepard, The History of Street Literature
(Newton Abbot: David & Charles, 1973), p. 195.

Ac. "Murder of Maria Marten by W. Corder, at the Red
Barn. May 18th, 1824 / sic /," together with "Barney
Buntline to Billy Bowline; or a Sailor's Consolation
in a Storm," printed and sold by H. Such, n.d.
Vaughan Williams Memorial Library, Broadwood Ballad
Sheet Collection, p. 117.

Oral Versions

B. Vaughan Williams Memorial Library, Vaughan Williams
MSS. vol. 3, pp. 128-9, as sung by Mr. J. Whitby, of
Tilney All Saints, Norfolk, 8 January, 1905. Fragment
of two quatrains. Printed by kind permission of
Mrs. Ursula Vaughan Williams.

Ca. Vaughan Williams Memorial Library, Grainger MS.
Collection of English Folk Songs, No. 193, as sung by
Joseph Taylor of Saxby, Lincolnshire, collected by
Percy Grainger and Lucy Broadwood on several
occasions in 1905 and 1906, including a phonograph
recording on 28 July, 1906. Fragment (?) of three
quatrains. Printed by permission of Percy Grainger
Library, New York.

Cb. English Traditional Folk-Songs, Gramophone Company
G.C. 3-2971(a), 1908, sung by Joseph Taylor of Saxby
All Saints, Lincolnshire, recorded by Percy Grainger,
July, 1908; reissued on Unto Brigg Fair. Joseph
Taylor and other traditional singers recorded in 1908

by Percy Grainger, L.P., Leader LEA 4050 mono., 1972, A-side No. 10. Fragment (?) of three quatrains. Printed by permission of Percy Grainger Library, New York.

Cc. Vaughan Williams Memorial Library, Broadwood MSS. p. 171, as sung by Joseph Taylor of Saxby, Lincolnshire, 7 March, 1906. Fragment of one quatrain. Printed by permission of the English Folk Dance and Song Society.

D. Vaughan Williams Memorial Library, Sharp MSS. 2211, as sung by William (or Robert) Feast at Ely Union, 11 September, 1911. Text of nine quatrains. Printed by permission of the English Folk Dance and Song Society.

E. Vaughan Williams Memorial Library, Sharp MSS. 2798, as sung by John East at Dunmow Union, 14 September, 1912. Fragment of four quatrains. Printed by permission of the English Folk Dance and Song Society.

F. Vaughan Williams Memorial Library, Sharp MSS. 4811, "sent me by Miss (?) Karpeles," 1920. Fragment of one quatrain. Printed by permission of the English Folk Dance and Song Society.

G. Birmingham Reference Library, MS No. 661164, as sung by George Hall of Hooton Roberts, Yorkshire, collected by R. A. Gatty; rpt. in Everyman's Book of English Country Songs, ed. Roy Palmer (London: Dent, 1979), No. 61. Text of eleven quatrains.

H. Vaughan Williams Memorial Library, LIB/COLL/MPS 50(31)34, typescript of unknown provenance. Text of ten quatrains. Printed by permission of the English Folk Dance and Song Society.

Other Recordings (tune only)

Vaughan Williams Memorial Library, Vaughan Williams MSS. vol. 1, p. 106, as sung by Mr. Flack of Foulmere, Cambridgeshire, 10 August, 1907.

Ibid., vol. 1, p. 254, as sung by Mr. Burrage of Capel, Surrey, April and August, 1908.

Ibid., vol. 1, p. 435, as sung by Harry Malyon of Fen Ditton, Cambridgeshire, 27 August, 1906.

Ibid., vol. 2, p. 274, as sung by Mr. and Mrs. Verrall of Horsham, Sussex, 8 October, 1904.

Ibid., vol. 3, p. 74, as sung by Mr. Booker of Kingsfold, Surrey, 23 December, 1904.

Ibid., vol. 3, p. 398, as sung by Harry Malyon of Fen Ditton, Cambridgeshire, 27 August, 1906.

Ibid., 4to I, p. 44, as sung by Mr. Christopher Jay of Acle, Norfolk, 18 April, 1908.

Vaughan Williams Memorial Library, Broadwood MSS. p. 169, as sung by Joseph Taylor of Saxby, Lincolnshire, n.d.

Ibid., p. 249, collected by Ella Bull from Charlotte (?) Fen of Cottenham, n.d.

Vaughan Williams Memorial Library, Clive Carey MS. Ex. 104, as sung by Mrs. Yeldham and Mrs. Challis of Thaxted, Essex, 1911.

We should like to express our gratitude to Malcolm Taylor, Librarian of the Vaughan Williams Memorial Library, Cecil Sharp House, London, for his kind and invaluable help in locating this material.

APPENDIX II

"Maria Marten": Texts

A

The Catnach broadside of 1828 (Aa), collated with the later re-issues (Ab and Ac). The collation records only those variations which can be <u>heard</u>: a number of typographical errors in Ab, which is carelessly printed with many letters broken, omitted or displaced, are ignored.

1

Come all you thoughtless young men,
   a warning take by me,
And think upon my unhappy fate
   to be hanged upon a tree.

2

My name is William Corder
   to you I do declare,
I courted Maria Marten
   most beautiful and fair.

3

I promised I would marry her
   upon a certain day,
Instead of that, I was resolved
   to take her life away.

4

I went into her father's house
   the 18th day of May,
Saying, my dear Maria,
   we will fix the wedding day.

5

If you will meet me at the Red-barn,
   as sure as I have life:
I will take you to Ipswich town,
   and there make you my wife.

6

I then went home and fetched my gun,
    my pickaxe and my spade,
I went into the Red-barn
    and there I dug her grave.

7

With heart so light, she thought no harm,
    to meet him she did go.
He murdered her all in the barn,
    and laid her body low/⁻:_7

8

After the horrible deed was done,
    she lay weltering in her gore,
Her bleeding mangled body
    he buried beneath the Red-barn floor.

9

Now all things being silent,
    her spirit could not rest,
She appeared unto her mother,
    who suckled her at her breast.

10

For many a long month or more,
    her mind being sore oppress'd,
Neither night or day
    She could not take any rest.

11

Her mother's mind being so disturbed,
    she dreamt three nights o'er
Her daughter she lay murdered
    beneath the Red-barn floor;

12

She sent the father to the barn,
    when he the ground did thrust,
And there he found his daughter
    mingling with the dust.

13

My trial is hard, I could not stand,
  most woeful was the sight,
When her jaw-bone was brought to prove,
  which pierced my heart quite;

14

Her aged father standing by,
  likewise his loving wife,
And in her grief her hair she tore.,
  she scarcely could keep life.

15

Adieu, adieu, my loving friends,
  my glass is almost run,
On Monday next will be my last,
  when I am to be hang'd.

16

So you, young men, who do pass by,
  with pity look on me,
For murdering Maria Marten,
  I was hanged upon the tree.

13³ upon) on, Ab; of, Ac.
4¹ into) unto, Ac.
4³ Saying) O come, Ab,c.
4⁴ and let us fix the day, Ac.
6¹ then) straight, Ab,c.
7² him) me, Ac.
8¹ The horrid deed that he had done, Ab,c.
8² weltering) bleeding, Ab,c.
8³ . . . bleeding and mangled, . . . Ac.
8⁴ buried beneath) threw under, Ab;
    threw on, Ac.
9² she could not take no rest, Ab,c.
9³ . . . in her mother's house, Ab,c.
10² sore) sorely, Ab,c.
10³ or) nor, Ab,c.
10⁴ any) no, Ab,c.
11¹ mind) night, Ac.
11⁴ beneath) under, Ab; upon, Ac.
12¹ the father) her father, Ab,c.
12² when in the ground he thrust, Ab,c.
13⁴ . . . me to the heart, Ac.

141¹ <u>His aged mother</u>, . . . Ab,c.
143³ in) <u>with</u>, Ab,c.
154⁴ hang'd) <u>hung</u>, Ac.
161¹ So you) <u>All</u>, Ab. who) <u>that</u>, Ab.
163³ murdering) <u>the murder of</u>, Ab.
    Marten) <u>Martin</u>, Ab.
164⁴ the) <u>a</u>, <u>Ab</u>,c.

- / -

In the texts from oral tradition, which follow, the quatrains are numbered consecutively in their order of occurrence. Supplementary figures in brackets indicate the corresponding quatrains/lines of the broadside text (A).

<u>B</u>

J. Whitby

1(A2)

My name is William Cornwell
    to you I do declare
I courted Maria Martin
    most beautiful and fair

2(A3)

I promised her I'd marry
    on the 18th day of May
Instead of that I was resolved
    to take her life away.

- / -

<u>C</u>

Joseph Taylor

(Ca, collated with Cbc)

1(A5)

If you'll meet me at the Red Barn,
    as sure as I have life,
I will take you to Ipswich town
    and there make you my wife.

2(A6)

I straight went home & fetched my gun,
  my pickaxe & my spade,
I went into the Red Barn
  and there I dug her grave.

3(A7)

With her heart so light she thought no harm,
  to meet her love did go;
he murdered her all in the barn,   ·
  and he laid her body low.

In Ca we have regularized Grainger's
  spelling and orthography.
1^1 meet me at) <u>go down to</u>, Cc, as an
  alternative.
2^1 I straight) (?) <u>this lad</u>, Cb.
2$^{1-2}$ my) <u>his</u>, Cb.
23-4 I) <u>he</u>, Cb.

- / -

<u>D</u>

William Feast

1(A2)

My name is William Corder
  to you I do declare,
I courted Maria Martin
  so beautiful and fair.

2(A3)

I promised her I'd marry her
  all on a certain day
Instead of that I was content
  to take her life away.

3(A4)

I went unto her father's house
  on the eighteenth day of May.
I said he's come my dearest Maria
  we'll fix the wedding day.

4(A5)

If you'll meet me at the Red Barn Floor
    as sure as you're alive
I'll take you down to Ipswich Town
    and make you my dear bride.

5(A6)

He straight went home and fetched his gun,
His pickaxe and his spade
He went unto the Red Barn floor
    and he dug poor Maria's grave.

6(A7)

This poor girl she thought no harm
    but to meet him she did go,
She went unto the Red Barn Floor
    and he laid her body low.

7(cf. A10-11)

Her mother dreamed three dreams one night,
    she ne'er could get no rest
She dreamed she saw her daughter dear
    lay bleeding at the breast.

8(A12)

Her father went into the barn
    and up the boards he took.
There he saw his daughter dear
    lay mingled in the dust.

9(A16)

Now all young men do you beware,
    take a pity look on me,
For the time is past to die at last
    all on the gallus tree.

- / -

E

John East

1(A1)

Come all you thoughtless young men
    And a warning take by me

And think upon an unhappy fate
  To be hung upon a tree

2(A2)

For my name is William Corder
  The truth to you I'll tell
I (?)cosied Maria Martin
  Most beautiful & fair

3(A3)

I promised her I'd marry her
  Upon a certain day
Instead of that 'twas my intent
  To take her life away.

$4(A4^{1-2}, 3^{1-2})$

I went unto her father's house
  On the 18th day of May
And I promised her I'd marry her
  Upon a certain day.

etc., etc.

- / -

F

Singer Unknown

1(A2)

My name is William Corder
  the truth I'll now declare
I murdered Maria Martin
  So beautiful and fair.

- / -

G

George Hill

1(A1)

Come all you bold young thoughtless men,
  A warning take by me;
And think of my unhappy fate
  To be hanged upon the tree.

2(A2)

My name is William Corder,
  The truth I do declare;
I courted Maria Marten,
  Most beautiful and fair.

3(A3)

I promised her I'd marry her,
  All on one certain day;
Instead of that I was resolved
  To take her life away.

4(A4)

I went unto her father's house
  Upon the eighteenth day of May,
"O come my dearest Ria,
And we'll fix the wedding day.

5(A5)

"If you will meet me at the Red Barn,
  As sure as I have life,
I will take you down to Ipswich Town
  And there make you my wife."

6(A6)

He straight went home and fetched his gun,
  His pick-axe and his spade;
He went unto the Red Barn,
  And there he dug her grave.

7(A7)

With heart so light she thought no harm
  To meet him she did go;
He murdered her all in the barn,
  And he laid her body low.

8(A9)

And all things being silent,
  They could not take no rest,
Which appeared in her mother's house
  When suckled at her breast.

9(A11)

Her mother had a dreadful dream,
   She dreamed it three nights o'er,
She dreamed that her dear daughter
   Lay beneath the Red Barn floor.

10(A12)

They sent her father to the barn,
   And in the ground he thrust;
And there he found his daughter dear
   Lay mingling with the dust.

11(A1^1, 16^2, 15^3, 1^4)

Come all you young thoughtless men,
   Some pity look on me;
On Monday next will be my last,
   To be hanged upon the tree.

- / -

H

Singer Unknown

1(A2)

My name is William Cordewood
   to you I do declare;
I courted Maria Marten--
   most beautiful and fair;

2(A3)

I told her I would marry her
   upon a certain day--
But instead of that I was resolved
   to take her life away.

3(A4)

I went down to her father's house
   the eighteenth day of May,
Saying "Come my dear Mariah--
   let's fix the wedding day/⁻._7

4(A5)

If you will meet me at the Red Barn,
  as sure as I'm alive;
I'll take you down to Peddewick town
  and there I will make you my bride."

5(A6)

He went back home and fetched his gun,
  his "pitax" and his spade,
And to the red Barn he did go--
  and there he dug her grave.

6(A7)

With her heart so light she thought no harm,
  to meet him she did go,
He mudered $/\overline{\text{sic}}\,/$ her all in the barn
  and laid her body low.

7(A11)

Her aged mother dreamt three nights
  all o're and o're and o're--
That her daughter, she lay murdered,
  beneath the red barn floor.

8(A12)

She sent her husband to the place
  and in the ground he thrused $/\overline{\text{sic}}\,/$
And there he found his daughter--
  all mingling with the dust.

9(A15)

Adieu, Adieu, my loved friend
  my race is almost run
And Monday next is my last day
  when I have to be hung.

10(A1$^{3-4}$)

Fair well to you faithless fellows
  and a warning take by me--
And think of my unhappy fate
  to be hung up in a tree.

- / -

[1]The real-life tragedy of Maria Marten and its impact
on popular culture at large, which will not be discussed at
length here, is thoroughly explored in Donald McCormick's
The Red Barn Mystery (London: John Long, 1967). See also
Leslie Shepard's essay, "Murder in the Red Barn: In Drama
and Verse," prefaced to Great Newspapers Reprinted, No. 12,
Special Issue, Sunday Times 150th Anniversary (1972), p. 3.
This issue also includes long accounts of the trial and
execution of Corder from The Sunday Times, August 10th and
17th, respectively, 1828.

[2]The present essay expands and corrects some earlier
observations, based on one text of the broadside and one
oral version of the song. See Thomas Pettitt, "The Later
English Ballad Tradition: 'The Outlandish Knight' and 'Maria
Marten,'" in The Ballad as Narrative, ed., Flemming G.
Andersen, et al. (Odense: Odense University Press, 1982),
pp. 71-84.

[3]Holger Olof Nygard, "Popular Ballad and Medieval
Romance," in Ballad Studies, ed. E. B. Lyle, Mistletoe
Series (Cambridge: D. S. Brewer, 1976), p. 19.

[4]All the texts are given above, Appendix II, and their
sources listed in Appendix I.

[5]G. H. Gerould, The Ballad of Tradition (Oxford, 1932;
rpt. New York: Gordian, 1974), p. 193.

[6]See Ralph Vaughan Williams, "Come All Ye Worthy
Christians," Folk Song Journal, 2 (1905-06), 118-123. The
tune can be heard in the recording of a Lincolnshire
singer's performance of "Maria Marten" made by Percy
Grainger in 1908 and recently reissued on an LP. See
Appendix I, No. Cb.

[7]Gerould, Ballad of Tradition, p. 11.

[8]Gerould, pp. 105-117.

[9]David Buchan, The Ballad and the Folk (London:
Routledge & Kegan Paul, 1972), chs. 9-12. This is the
undeniable achievement of Buchan's study, whether or not one

171

agrees with his hypothesis on the improvisational function of these phenomena in ballad tradition.

[10]There are occasional signs of such a distinction being made by recent singers, although the question has not been thoroughly explored, and we cannot be sure that the singers have not been influenced indirectly by academic ballad scholarship. See for example Roger D. Abrahams, "Creativity, Individuality, and the Traditional Singer," Studies in the Literary Imagination, 3 (1970), 5-34 (Almeda Riddle is said to distinguish between classic songs--mostly Child ballads--and others); Herschel Gower & James Porter, "Jeannie Robertson: The Child Ballads," Scottish Studies, 14 (1970), 35-58 (Jeannie Robertson is said to distinguish Child ballads as "big ballads").

[11]Hence the persistent and growing dissatisfaction with F. J. Child's collection of "every known ballad," The English and Scottish Popular Ballads, 5 vols. (1882-98; rpt. New York: Dover, 1965)--the phrase quoted occurring in the "Advertizement to Part I," I, vii. See Thelma G. James, "The English and Scottish Popular Ballads of Francis James Child," Journal of American Folklore, 46 (1933), 51-68, reprinted in The Critics and the Ballad, ed. MacEdward Leach & Tristram P. Coffin (Carbondale: Southern Illinois University Press, 1961), pp. 12-19; James Reppert, "F. J. Child and the Ballad," in The Learned and the Lewed: Studies in Chaucer and Medieval Literature, ed. Larry D. Benson (Cambridge: Harvard University Press, 1974), pp. 197-212; Dave Harker, "Francis James Child and the 'Ballad Consensus,'" Folk Music Journal, 4 (1980), 146-64.

[12]Gerould, p. 193.

[13]Gerould, pp. 211-12.

[14]Gerould, p. 225.

[15]Gerould, pp. 231-32.

[16]David C. Fowler, A Literary History of the Popular Ballad (Durham, North Carolina: Duke University Press, 1968). The thesis is summarized in chapter 1, "The Evolution of Balladry."

[17]See for example W. Edson Richmond's review, "The Development of the Popular Ballad: A New Theory," Genre, 3 (1970), 198-204.

[18]Tristram P. Coffin, "'Mary Hamilton' and the Anglo-American Ballad as an Art Form," Journal of American Folklore, 70 (1957), 208-14, reprinted in The Critics and the Ballad, ed. Leach and Coffin, pp. 245-56; see particularly pp. 248-49. Subsequent to this "ballad stage," Coffin suggests, the song is further reduced, according to circumstances, to an "emotional core" or a nonsensical fragment.

[19]M. J. C. Hodgart, The Ballads (New York: W. W. Norton, 1962), p. 96. See also A. B. Friedman, The Ballad Revival (Chicago: University of Chicago Press, 1961), p. 61:

Since 1550 at least, if not before, the ballad people have not so much been making ballads as remaking into ballads poetry and songs originally of another nature. By a process of creative variation, such pieces were gradually, under the superintendence of the ballad pattern, being approximated to folksong.

[20]See, for example, Cecil J. Sharp, English Folk Song: Some Conclusions, 4th ed., rev. Maud Karpeles (Wakefield: EP Publishing, 1972), pp. 12-20; Maud Karpeles, An Introduction to English Folk Song (London: Oxford University Press, 1973), Ch. 1.

[21]Albert B. Lord, The Singer of Tales (Cambridge: Harvard University Press, 1960).

[22]James Jones, "Commonplace and Memorization in the Oral Transmission of the English and Scottish Ballads," Journal of American Folklore, 74 (1961), 97-112; D. J. McMillan, "A Survey of Theories Concerning the Oral Transmission of the Popular Ballad," Southern Folklore Quarterly, 28 (1964), 299-309; Wolfhart Anders, Balladensänger und mündliche Komposition: Untersuchungen zur englischen Traditionsballade (Munich: Wilhelm Fink, 1974); David Buchan, The Ballad and the Folk.

[23]Jones, "Commonplace and Memorization"; A. B. Friedman, "The Formulaic Improvisation Theory of Ballad Tradition: A Counter-statement," Journal of American Folklore, 74 (1961), 114.

[24]As Cecil Sharp does, for example, with "Robin Hood and the Tanner" (Child No. 126), English Folk Song, p. 22,

and Gerould with "Sir Lionel" (Child No. 18), The Ballad of Tradition, pp. 173-74. For a more detailed analysis of the latter instance, see Thomas Pettitt, "'Bold Sir Rylas' and the Struggle for Ballad Form," Lore and Language, 3, No. 6 (1982), 45-60.

[25]For example, in the case of ballads recorded from the Scottish singer Jeannie Robertson, her daughter Lizzie Higgins, and her nephew Stanley Robertson. See also W. Edson Richmond, "Rhyme, Reason and Re-creation," in Ballads and Ballad Research, ed. Patricia Conroy (Seattle: University of Washington, 1978), pp. 58-67.

[26]For example, John Quincy Wolf, "Folk Singers and the Re-creation of Folksong," Western Folklore, 26 (1967), 101-11; Eleanor R. Long, "Ballad Singers, Ballad Makers and Ballad Etiology," Western Folklore, 32 (1973), 225-36; Roger D. Abrahams, "Creativity, Individuality, and the Traditional Singer."

[27]The nearest approach is perhaps provided by "The Battle of Otterburn" (Child No. 161) and "The Hunting of the Cheviot" (Child No. 162), where in each instance we have external evidence on the events they describe, fairly early texts of the ballads, and later versions from broadsides and oral tradition. See Douglas Joseph McMillan, "Five Traditional Medieval Historical Ballads and the Nature of Oral Transmission," Diss. University of Maryland, 1963.

[28]Phillips Barry has pointed to the intriguing case of the poem "Olban," written by Thomas (later Professor) Coggswell Upham in 1818 and published in a Boston magazine, the Columbia Centinel. At some stage it was set to music and entered oral tradition, eventually turning up in the song repertoires of the Texas cowboys and the woodsmen of the American Northeast: "It has even undergone a certain amount of re-creation," notes Barry, but does not elaborate. "The Part of the Folk Singer in the Making of Folk Balladry," in The Critics and the Ballad, ed. Leach and Coffin, pp. 68-71, and see also p. 74. Oddly, Barry has elsewhere studied in detail variations between versions of a song whose author is known but whose original text is beyond recovery. "William Carter: the Bensontown Homer," Journal of American Folklore, 25 (1912), 156-68. Danish tradition offers some interesting instances, examined by Sven Hakon Rossel, of literary poems from the late eighteenth and early nineteenth centuries which, via early broadside printings, have entered oral tradition. Rossel checks the broadsides, early oral versions and versions from modern oral tradition against the original

poems, and notes all changes and omissions, adequately demonstrating that the texts are moulded and re-moulded in tradition. Rossel does not, however, consider the role of transmission in the generation of generic features. Sven Hakon Rossel, Den litterære vise i Folketraditionen (Copenhagen: Akademisk Forlag, 1971).

[29] For example, of the 47 Child ballads in Cecil Sharp's Collection of English Folk Songs, ed. Maud Karpeles, 2 vols. (London: Oxford University Press, 1974), at least 25 appear on surviving broadsides.

[30] For comment along these lines, see Alfred Williams, ed., Folk-Songs of the Upper Thames (London: Duckworth, 1923), pp. 16, 23; James Reeves, ed., The Idiom of the People, 2nd ed. (London 1958; rpt., New York: W. W. Norton, 1965), pp. 21-22.

[31] A. L. Lloyd, Folk Song in England (London: Lawrence & Wishart, 1967), p. 30.

[32] This is a fundamental uncertainty in a number of otherwise highly significant studies of textual variation in transmission based on comparison of printed and oral versions, such as G. Malcolm Laws's essay on "Ballad Recomposition" in American Balladry from British Broadsides (Philadelphia: American Folklore Society, 1957), pp. 104-22; Louis C. Jones, "Folk Songs of Mary Wyatt and Henry Green," Bulletin of the Folk Song Society of the Northeast, 12 (1937), 14-18; Edwin Capers Kirkland, "The Effect of Oral Tradition on 'Robin Hood and Little John,'" Southern Folklore Quarterly, 4 (1940), 15-21; and Edwin Shepard Miller, "Nonsense and New Sense in 'Lord Thomas,'" Southern Folklore Quarterly, 1 (1937), 25-37.

[33] Victor E. Neuburg, Popular Literature: A History and Guide (Harmondsworth: Penguin, 1977), pp. 127 ff.

[34] Sharp, English Folk Song, pp. 138-39.

[35] All three are reprinted in Charles Hindley, The Life and Times of James Catnach (London, 1878; rpt. Detroit: Singing Tree Press, 1968), pp. 180-82, 183-85, and 187 (facsimile), respectively.

[36] For full text, see above, Appendix II, No. Aa.

[37]It clearly cannot have been written before the trial, and McCormick, The Red Barn Mystery, pp. 15-16, is wrong in citing the text as an example of those ballads sung and sold at Polstead Cherry Fair the preceding July, complained of by Corder's counsel at the trial.

[38]Hindley, pp. 185-86.

[39]Lloyd, pp.29-30.

[40]Facs. repr. in Leslie Shepard, The History of Street Literature (Newton Abbot: David & Charles, 1973), p. 195. This text is collated above, Appendix II, as No. Ab.

[41]Collated above, Appendix II, from a copy in the Vaughan Williams Memorial Library, as No. Ac.

[42]Lloyd, p. 31.

[43]Compare Sharp, p. 122: "'Execution Songs' . . . possess a strange fascination for the peasant singer."

[44]Listed in Appendix I.

[45]A fragment of four quatrains sung by George Digweed of Michel Delver, Hampshire (Vaughan Williams Memorial Library, Gardiner MS, H. 214) is not considered in the following analysis. Its lines are all unique to this version and can hardly have evolved from the broadside or any other version by any imaginable process of memorial or improvisational transmission.

[46]Parallels are cited from the following broadsides: "A Ballad from the Seven Dials Press /The Murder of Sarah Spriggens by Richard Wilbyforce7," in The Common Muse, ed. Vivian de Sola Pinto and A. E. Rodway (Harmondsworth: Penguin, 1965), No. 89; "The Outrage and Murder on a Little Child at Purfleet," in Leslie Shepard, The History of Street Literature, p. 193; "Trial of Good for the Murder of Jane Jones," and "The Life, Trial, and Execution of Mary White," in Print and the People, 1819-1851, ed. Louis James (Harmondsworth: Penguin, 1978), pp. 256 and 259, respectively; "The Berkshire Tragedy" and "The Lexington Miller," in Laws, American Balladry, pp. 104-09 and 109-11, respectively.

[47] "The Murder of Maria Marten" shares this narrative preponderance with, for example, "The Berkshire Tragedy," "The Lexington Miller," and "A Ballad from the Seven Dials Press." The lyrical element dominates, in contrast, in "Trial of Good" and "Mary White" (see n. 46 above).

[48] For similar observations on the working of the broadside printers, see John Holloway and Joan Black, eds., Later English Broadside Ballads (London: Routledge & Kegan Paul, 1975), I, 3.

[49] This change in Ab, like some of the formulations in Aa, may reflect the traditional phraseology of crime-and-execution broadsides. Cf. "And then the bleeding body threw / All underneath the bed" ("A Horrible Murder, A Father Cutting his Child's Head off!,") in Print and the People, p. 251.

[50] Tom Burns, "A Model for Textual Variation in Folksong," Folklore Forum, 3 (1970), 49-56.

[51] By "stanza" we mean the common-measure quatrains into which we have resolved all the texts of "Maria Marten."

[52] In the case of the fragments B, E and F, which all start with A 2, we consider the omission significant: the singer may be expected to have started with the first stanza he knew. Omissions after the end of the fragments are, in contrast, not treated as significant: either the singer could remember, or the collector could stomach, no more. The three-stanza text of Joseph Taylor (C), which may or may not be a fragment, is reserved for separate treatment later.

[53] This stanza significantly preserves and regularizes the traditional balance already present in A between the opening and closing references to hanging "upon the tree."

[54] But cf. Child No. 90A 14^{3-4}, ". . . the bonny boy, / Lay weltering in her blude." Mrs. Brown is alone in using precisely this formulation.

[55] But cf. Child No. 191, "Hughie Grame," where the parents of the condemned hero similarly tear their hair; e.g., 191A 19^{3-4}: "... his father dear, / Came tearing his hair most pittifully," and cf. A 21^{3-4}, C 13^{3-4}, D 11^{3-4}. A and D are broadsides; C is from Scott's Minstrelsy.

[56] It is worth noting as well that the non-traditional absolute constructions in A 9^1, 10^2, 11^1, which provide explicit explanations for the ensuing events, all disappear in oral tradition (apart from G 8^1).

[57] See Sharp, p. 137, for remarks on this phenomenon.

[58] It may be worth noting in passing that Taylor preserves what might be termed the "narrative core" of the ballad, rather than the "emotional core" as predicted by Coffin, "'Mary Hamilton' and the Anglo-American Ballad," pp. 249-50.

[59] Bertrand H. Bronson, "Mrs. Brown and the Ballad," The Ballad as Song (Berkeley: University of California Press, 1969), pp. 73-74. On the oral and verbal phases of tradition, see Buchan, The Ballad and the Folk, particularly chs. 1 and 20.

[60] Flemming G. Andersen & Thomas Pettitt, "Mrs. Brown of Falkland: A Singer of Tales?" Journal of American Folklore, 92 (1979), 23. For the scale of early English broadside balladry, see Hyder E. Rollins, "The Black-Letter Broadside Ballad," PMLA, 34 (1919), 258-339, and for literacy in early modern England, see, e.g., David Cressy, "Levels of Illiteracy in England, 1530-1730," Historical Journal, 20 (1977), 1-23.

[61] Print and the People, p. 251.

[62] "A Ballad from the Seven Dials Press, . . ." in The Common Muse, ed. Pinto and Rodway, No. 89. This broadside is particularly significant in illustrating the narrative conventions of the crime-and-execution broadsides, for it is almost certainly a "cock," i.e., a ballad on a fictitious story catering to the same market as the genuine "Goodnights" but which could be sold when there were no convenient executions pending. It is thus in a sense a parody of the genre and may be taken to exemplify its typical characteristics. See Hindley, pp. 355 ff.

[63] Discussed by Laws, "Ballad Recomposition," in American Balladry.

[64] W. Edson Richmond, "Narrative Folk Poetry," in Folklore and Folklife, ed. Richard M. Dorson (Chicago: University of Chicago Press, 1972), pp. 85-97, p. 86.

Odense University
Odense, Denmark

GRAF UND NONNE

Recorded: Bessarabien, 1966; Künzig-Werner, <u>Balladen aus ostdeutscher Überlieferung</u> (1969), No. 22.

1. Stand auf hohen Berigen, schau runter ins tiefe Tal.
   Ich sah ein Schifflein fahren, darin es drei Grafen
   warn.

2. Dar jingste, der da drunten war, der in dem Schifflein
       war,
   Er tut es miar winken mit einem goldnen Glas.

3. "Was tust du mir winken, was bietst du mir den Wein?"
   "Das tu ich aus lauter Liebe, weil wir zwei Liebchen
       sein."

4. "Ich weiß von keiner Liebe und auch von keinem Mann,
   Ins Kloster will ich gehen, will werden eine Nonn."

5. "Willst du ins Kloster gehen, willst werden eine Nonn,
   So will ich die Welt durchreisen, bis daß ich zu dir
       komm."

6. Da sprach er zu dem Reitsknecht sein: "Sattel mir und
       dir zwei Pferd,
   Ins Kloster wollen wir reiten, der Weg ist
       reitenswert."

7. Als sie vors hohe Kloster kamen, wohl vor das hohe
       Haus,
   Da schaut sein Herzallerliebste zum hohen Fenster raus.

8. "Gebt raus die jingste Nonne, die letzt gekommen ist
       an!"
   "Es ist noch keine gekommen und darf auch keine raus!"
   "So will ich das Kloster anzinden, das schene
       Nonnehaus!"

9. Da kam sie angeschritten, schneeweiß war sie gekleidt,
   Die Haar warn kurz geschnitten, zur Nonne war sie es
       bereit.

10. Da setzt der Graf sich nieder auf einen hohen Stein,
    In zweimal dreizehn Stunden sprang ihm sein Herz
        entzwei.

11. Mit ihren zarten Händen zog sie's den Glockenstrang,
    Mit ihrem bleichen Munde sie ihm sein Todlied sang,
    Mit ihrem bleichen Munde sie ihm sein Todlied sang.

The Nobleman and the Nun

1. _/ I _7 stood on the high mountains, looked down into the
   deep valley.
   I saw a little ship sailing, in it were three noblemen.

2. The youngest of those who were down there in the little
   ship,
   He beckoned to me, with a golden glass.

3. "Why do you beckon to me, why do you offer me wine?"
   "I do it entirely out of love, because we are two
   lovers."

4. "I know nothing of any love, nor of any man;
   I shall enter a nunnery and become a nun."

5. "If you enter a nunnery and become a nun,
   Then I shall ride through all the world until I come to
   you."

6. Then he spoke to his groom, "Saddle two horses for me
   and you;
   We'll ride to the nunnery--the road is worth riding."

7. When they came before the nunnery, in front of that
   high house,
   Then his sweetheart looked out of the high window.

8. "Deliver to me the youngest nun, she who came in last!"
   "None has come as yet, and none may come out."
   "Then I shall set fire to the cloister, this fine
   nunnery."

9. Then along she came walking, she was dressed in snow-
   white,
   Her hair was cut short, she was ready to become a nun.

10. Then the nobleman sat him down on a high rock;
    In twice thirteen hours his heart broke in two.

11. With her tender hand she pulled the bell-rope;
    With her pale lips she sang his dirge,
    With her pale lips she sang his dirge.

Flemming G. Andersen, ed., et. al., The Ballad as Narrative.
Odense: Odense University Press, 1982.

OTTO HOLZAPFEL

"GRAF UND NONNE":
An Analysis of the Epic-Formulaic Elements in a German
Ballad

Within the genre of folk ballad, German tradition
recognizes different types. Previous research has repeatedly
discussed the problems of type as such, especially since the
wide range of ballad narrative styles at times threatens to
collapse the carefully fixed frame of ballad definition.
Such variation is certainly not an "error" in tradition;
instead, it indicates narrowness, deficiency, and rigidity
in our definitions and our boundaries. In attempting to
characterize ballad narration more precisely, and in
attempting to sketch these characteristics by analyzing the
epic-formulaic narrative style of the folk ballad, we come
closer to these limits. At this point we must decide for or
against the label ballad. By evading such a step as being
tedious, I would not wish thereby to shirk a definition; on
the contrary, I would like to concentrate on those
characteristics of narrative style typical of the genre.
(For the ballad, I understand this style to be an epic-
formulaic one.) If we view the ballad with these
characteristics in mind, the entire genre and its sub-types
are easier to survey and describe. I'm more concerned with
analyzing the specifics of type through which the essence of
the balladic is to be described and understood.

Finally, in this area of folk tradition, rather than
being closed and bounded, a definition indicates the spheres
around which a song oscillates and toward which it moves as
an optimal form (Zielform) of balladic narration. Since we
here concern ourselves with oral tradition, we must,
correspondingly, observe the formulaic elements. And, since
we also examine a type of narrative song, the epic element
comes into play. Both elements combined, that is, the epic-
formulaic style, seem to me to characterize the folk ballad.
The requirement of presenting a song text to the listener as
a comprehensible development of interactions, as a
consequence of dramatic events, allows us to observe
particularly the roles of scene sequences, of dramatic
scenes, and of a typical narrative process in a chain of
events. That observation permits us to approach the analysis
of oral tradition, the understanding of the ballad as an
object of oral communication; it is an understanding of a
characteristic of the type which classicism, from its view

of an <u>aesthetic</u> of the ballad, previously outlined via Goethe's model of the epic-lyric-dramatic.

A second fundamental aspect of the problem appears: if there is such a thing as a "folk ballad genre," then we must assume from the contents of the songs a definite, close relationship between song-fables and narrative material as well as a correspondingly close relationship between the narrative <u>style</u> of ballads--one which transcends national linguistic boundaries. It appears to me to be thoroughly justified, on the basis of the analysis of each epic-formulaic narrative style in English and Scottish, in Scandinavian, and in German traditions, to suppose a common conception of the balladic, at least in these linguistic regions; this is true even though tradition presents itself differently in each concrete, individual case. The so-called "sterling examples" of epic-formulaic narrative styles are to be found among the ballads in the Scandinavian tradition. In connection with this tradition, we can now, in the case of the Danish sources, work with a large body of traditional ballads--ballads which date from the middle of the sixteenth century.

If on this basis we can prove with any certainty the proposed system of epic-formulaic narrative styles of folk ballads, then the conclusions must have wide-ranging significance both for the tradition of folk ballads in the English and Scottish areas and in the German areas. Many previous investigations and the increasing volume of research undertaken in this area confirm such an acceptance (and also support the significance of older research in this direction--research since Herder, Böhme, Grundtvig and Child). The far-reaching genre of folk ballad, one which extends beyond middle- and north-European boundaries, does exist; it not only has similar narrative material but also similar performance styles. The assumption of this genre's existence has also already been made on the basis of common prototypes in late medieval tradition.

If we consider German tradition, we can choose among various versions of different degrees of importance, among versions of a particular ballad type in its relation to ideally constructed balladic optimal forms (<u>Zielformen</u>). The song "Winterrosen" (DVldr No. 145) belongs to the type of lyric ballad characteristic for German tradition. While this type has governed tradition since the seventeenth and eighteenth centuries, its sources date back as far as the sixteenth century. We cannot, therefore, unconditionally maintain that the lyric ballad is a more recent development, one which has diverted the song from its basic narrative substance. But the tenor of the lyrical element in general supports the notion that the German folk ballad loses length and epic breadth; it becomes considerably shorter than the average length of, for example, its Scandinavian parallels. Occasionally the ballad's narrative is reduced to the elaboration of a single scene; and so, it seems to me, it enters into the periphery of the ballad type. In this case we must speak increasingly of a narrative love song. That the balladic narrative style also functions as the optimal form (Zielform) within the genre, however, is verified by examples like the ballad "Nachtjäger" (DVldr No. 133), where an original material foreign to the genre (a love allegory) became recast as a narrative and thereby took ·on balladic features. In a later variation entitled "Glücksjäger" (DVldr No. 134), it even gained further narrative elements. From such examples of songs one can judge the far-reaching influence of balladic remodeling, a remodeling which set the tone for the pre-romantic epoch of the eighteenth century and defined the conception of the German genre of folk ballad as a song of epic-lyric-dramatic character. The situation with regard to German ballad tradition suggests that here we should investigate less the origin of ballad narration styles (for even in comparison with that of Old Norse, Danish material is preferable for posing such an hypothesis) than examine the process of transformation which, here in the medium of an almost non-literate culture (yet not in pure oral tradition), has determined the life of a song in recent tradition.

As an example of such an examination, let us consider the song "Graf und Nonne" (Erk-Böhme No. 89). While this ballad is found, to be sure, in the nearly overpowering abundance of over two thousand versions in the German folk song archives, in its concise balladic form it exhibits variation within a relatively narrow framework. Here the ballad has already been transformed to such a degree and has been so completely perfected that scarcely anything has been omitted from or added to this astonishingly stable type. This stability exists in even the broadest regional tradition. In illustrating the tendency in oral tradition to fluctuate between variation and stability, "Graf und Nonne" provides an outstanding example of stability. In my opinion, the reasons for this characteristic lie, above all, in an epic-formulaic style which appears to be relatively fixed, and which, because of its fixed nature, can be analyzed especially well for the German tradition. For purposes of the inquiry under discussion, I present a text which was first recorded in 1966 from Bessarabien German settlers from Russia and became available on a musical recording by Johannes Künzig and Waltraut Werner-Künzig in 1969. This eleven-stanza version must serve here as a representative of many recordings, the treatment of which in the German work on ballads, <u>Deutsche Volkslieder mit ihren Melodien</u>, is still in progress. I used this recording in a larger context elsewhere and, similarly, for the analysis of its epic-formulaic frame.[1]

Graf und Nonne

1. Stand auf hohen Berigen, schau runter ins tiefe Tal.
   Ich sah ein Schifflein fahren, darin es drei Grafen warn.

2. Dar jingste, der da drunten war, der in dem Schifflein war,
   er tut es miar winken mit einem goldnen Glas.

3. "Was tust du mir winken, was bietst du mir den Wein?"
   "Das tu ich aus lauter Liebe, weil wir zwei Liebchen sein."

4. "Ich weiß von keiner Liebe und auch von keinem Mann,
   ins Kloster will ich gehen, will werden eine Nonn."

5. "Willst du ins Kloster gehen, willst werden eine Nonn,
   so will ich die Welt durchreisen, bis daß ich zu dir komm."

6. Da sprach er zu dem Reitsknecht sein: "Sattel mir und dir zwei Pferd,
   ins Kloster wollen wir reiten, der Weg ist reitenswert."

7. Als sie vors hohe Kloster kamen, wohl vor das hohe Haus,
   da schaut sein Herzallerliebste zum hohen Fenster raus.

8. "Gebt raus die jingste Nonne, die letzt gekommen ist an!"
   "Es ist noch keine gekommen und darf auch keine raus!"
   "So will ich das Kloster anzinden, das schene Nonnehaus!"

9. Da kam sie angeschritten, schneeweiß war sie gekleid,
   die Haar warn kurz geschnitten, zur Nonne war sie es bereit.

10. Da setzt der Graf sich nieder auf einen hohen Stein,
    in zweimal dreizehn Stunden sprang ihm sein Herz entzwei.

11.   Mit ihren zarten Händen zog sie's den Glockenstrang,
        mit ihrem bleichen Munde sie ihm sein Todlied sang,
        mit ihrem bleichen Munde sie ihm sein Todlied sang.

        Bessarabien, 1966; Künzig-Werner, Balladen aus
        ostdeutscher Überlieferung, 1969, No. 22.[2]

/1. I stood on the high mountains and looked down into the deep valley. / I saw a small ship sailing in which there were three counts. 2. The youngest of those who were below in the small ship, / waved at me with a golden glass. 3. "Why do you wave, why do you offer me wine?". / "I do it entirely out of love, because we are two lovers." 4. "I know nothing of love and also nothing of any man; / I wish to go into the cloister, I_wish to become a nun." 5. "If you go into the cloister, /and/ you become a nun, / I will travel throughout the world until I come to you." 6. He spoke to his groom: "Saddle two horses for me and for you; / we will ride to the convent; the way is worthy of a ride." 7. As they came before the high cloister, right before the high house, / his beloved looked out from a high window. 8. "Let the youngest nun out, the one who has most recently arrived!" / "No one has come in yet, and no one may go out!" / "Then I will set fire to the cloister, the beautiful convent!" 9. Then she came stepping forward, dressed in snow white, / her hair cut short; she was ready to become a nun. 10. The count sat down on a high stone; / in twice thirteen hours his heart broke in two. 11. With her tender hands she pulled the bell chord; / with her pale lips she sang his death song to him; / with her pale lips she sang his death song to him./

In characterizing this ballad, we see that it appears not as the report of a palpable historical event, but rather as the mirroring of a universally valid fate. In spite of this appearance, however, to the singer it appears no less true and realistic. On the contrary, for each person it becomes didactic, representing a moral precept: there are social barriers that even lovers cannot transgress-- symbolized here by the contrasting images of mountain and valley. The ballad becomes an exemplum. On this plane the dramatis personae quickly lose any kind of identification by name and by association with an historical event. As an optimal form (Zielform) the ballad overemphasizes this universal validity by beginning rather personally with "I."

Not until the ballad shifts to third person in stanzas 7 and 9 does this perspective of immediate experience disappear. And so, with the semi-raised index finger of the singer who identifies with the "I," the ballad probably recalls its performance in an older tradition; that is to say, this approach is not just a recent lyrical addition. We can trace "Graf und Nonne" back as far as the fifteenth century (and perhaps even as far as the fourteenth); the song also belongs to the ballads which Goethe heard in Alsace in 1771 and which gave him his first introduction to folk song.

A closer analysis of the text shows that we are dealing with a four-part stanza construction, single parts of which at times form syntactic closings or pauses. Those acquainted with the quatrains of Scandinavian tradition, and, similarly, those of English and Scottish tradition, know that the second line is a filler composed of stereotypical formulas. Similarly, in this ballad we invariably recognize here in the second halves of stanzas 9 and 10 such common formulas as: "sie war schneeweiß gekleidet" and "er saß auf einem hohen Stein." Also, in these few lines we can sense the familiar, all-pervading structure of balladic narrative style: the saddling stanza in stanza 6 and the resultant pattern of the Confrontation Schemata in stanza 7, "er kommt vors hohe Haus" and "sie schaut aus dem Fenster." These are well-known epic formulas, formulas which are widely used to stylize a plot and are independent of the individual character of a song.

As a phenomenon of oral tradition, these formulas are characteristic of the balladic style of narration. Because these epic formulas are used automatically, we accept any implied contradictions without question: here, for example, between stanzas 7 and 8 there is a definite break in the flow of the plot. As he arrives at the cloister, she, "seine Herzallerliebste," is looking out. "Gebt raus die jungste Nonne" (stanza 8) cannot, of course, be the proper sort of address to the true love of stanza 7. Truly she--if we take the ballad literally (too literally)--arrives at the cloister only during stanza 9. But a linear unfolding of ballad plot resists the attempt to introduce more characters than absolutely necessary, and so the addressee in stanza 8 and the apparent female speaker of stanza 7 coincide. Not only does the epic formula blur any sense of the individual unfolding of action; but also, in combination with the confrontation pattern, it heightens the dramatic climax of this stereotyped plot. This climax even requires a change of scene and both separates and links together the two sections characterized by dialogue (stanzas 3 to 5 and stanza 8).

As a result, we have a linear plot that appears so self-contained, universally valid, and thoroughly formulaic that nothing can be added or supressed. The ballad has arrived at a stable form which makes it exceptionally resistant to alteration in oral tradition. An essential means to this extreme stability is its structure. This structure, permeated by formulas, comes out of the simplest and most common patterning. Here, for example, confrontation and description of the problem already exist in the opposition between mountain and valley in stanza 1. This pattern, which is supposed to define the later conflict underlying the social difference between a count and a simple maiden destined for the convent, is also used in other German ballads.

A characteristic example of this patterning is "Ritter und Magd" (DVldr No. 55). There is no way of determining whether the maiden decides to enter the convent because of a previous fateful experience; she embodies no particular fate but rather a universal one. Universality is also supported by the presentation of the "youngest count," following Axel Olrik's epic law of three with stress on the last. Here, however, it is an utterly irrelevant motif: there is no reference to another count nor to the special place of the youngest. The ballad's central events are presented in the form of dialogue (sts. 3 to 5), and here the linked enjambment continues even in the repetition of words: Schifflein (1-2), winken (2-3), Liebe (3-4) and Kloster (4-5). The climax of the ballad, the so-called turning point, like a hinge that snaps together, is clearly set forth in the previously-mentioned Saddling stanza and in the Confrontation stanza (sts. 6-7).

The plot is rapidly brought to an end. The maiden is brought foward to the threshold of the cloister (st. 9); the unlucky count commits suicide (st. 10); and the maiden mourns at the grave (st. 11). No intertwining of rose and briar at the grave mitigates hard, inevitable fate: whoever is destined for a separate life never does join his beloved. The ballad therefore conforms well to a conservative peasant population's attitude toward life. The plot is straight-forward, decisive, and easily comprehended; at most it arouses grief. It does not arouse opposition. Even the narrative style of this ballad is conservative and stabilizingly rigid, tradition-bound, and popular. This ballad, therefore, also occupies an important place within the moral outlook of a relatively self-contained community, one such as that represented by the former German colonists in Russia.

A further investigative step would be the comparison of motifs of single German-language versions. For the entire tradition that cannot yet be done, but for the tradition that is apparently significant within Germany proper, the collected variants from Franconia will be analyzed more closely and compared to the versions from the Volga-German

settlement district already discussed. "Das epische
Volkslied in Franken um 1900" was the subject of a Wurzburg
dissertation in 1974.[3] At that time thirty-three variants
(all together, 109 variants) from oral tradition (A numbers)
were cited by Norbert Richter for Franconia--as defined by
its present boundaries. (See below.) These variants were
then more closely analyzed for their motifs.[4] Hans Helbron
completed his Kiel dissertation in 1936 with, all together,
fourteen variants from Franconia made available in his
study.[5] The two works compliment each other and need not be
discussed in more detail here.

The wine motif belongs to introductory stanzas using
the I-form as support for the suitor's offering (Richter:
eighteen variants), or else is interchangeable with the
offer of a ring--the ring motif (Richter: fourteen
variants). For the Saddling stanza Richter mentions twenty-
six occurrences; and these numbers, in comparison with the
entire group of thirty-three references, indicate what is
meant by a "stable balladic technique of composition." But
we cannot pursue this argument directly, since the remaining
Franconian versions, and indeed the majority of them
(seventy-six out of 109), put entrance in the cloister and
dialogue with the beloved together.[6] The more explicit
explanation of the cause of the count's death is certainly
quite diverse (ranging from poisoned wine to "ihm bricht das
Herz entzwei"), but fundamentally the ballad strives toward
this tragic end (Richter: over fifty variants). There,
however, the clear mark of a dramatic caesura is missing and
opens the way to compressing the song into, simply, one
episode of dialogue (conversation in front of the cloister).

In his second most important category, Richter places
all the texts having the introduction "Es welken alle
Blätter" together.[7] Here a short version has been
formulated, influenced by other songs (for example, compare
Erk-Böhme No. 683), which exhausts in a single, epically
unmotivated episode, the wish to enter the cloister. In the
center stands the encounter, heavily laden with feeling, at
the cloister's gate; and this version (parting drink and
separation) we might consider a "late lyrical remodeling."[8]

Die Nonne

1.   Alle welken Blätter,
      sie fallen herab auf mich;
      ja weil michs mein Schatz verlassen hat
      das kränket, kränket mich.

2. Ins Kloster will sie gehen,
   will werden eine Nonn.
   So muß ich die Welt durchreisen,
   bis daß ich zu ihr komm.

3. Ins Kloster angekommen
   ganz leise klopft ich an.
   Gebt heraus die jüngste Nonne,
   die zuletzt ins Kloster kam.

4. 'S ist keine reingekommen
   und's kommt auch keine raus.
   So muß ich das Kloster stürmen,
   das schönste Nonnenhaus.

5. Da kam sie rausgeschritten,
   ganz weiß war sie gekleid',
   ihre Haar' waren abgeschnitten,
   zur Nonn' war sie bereit.

6. Sie trug unter ihrer Schurze
   eine Flasche guten Wein.
   Nimm's hin mein Herzallerliebster,
   dies soll der Abschied sein.

Geldersheim, Unterfranken, 1913 (DVA A 200
740).

/1. All the withered leaves, / they fall down on me; / because my beloved has abandoned me, / that grieves me, grieves me. 2. She wishes to go into the cloister, / wishes to become a nun. / So I must travel throughout the world / until I come to her. 3. Arriving at the cloister, / I knocked very softly. / Let the youngest nun out, / the one who came into the cloister last. 4. No one came in / and no one comes out. / So I must storm the cloister, / the beautiful convent. 5. Then she came stepping out; / all in white she was clothed; / her hair was cut off; / she was ready to be a nun. 6. She carried under her skirt / a bottle of good wine. / Take it, my beloved; / this shall be the parting./

Because of this investigation's scope, I must forgo a closer analysis of "Es welken die Blätter" and concentrate on the previously-mentioned form in order to characterize the common framework of balladic narration. A closer comparison between the ballad "Ich stand auf hohem Berge" and the narrative love song "Es welken alle Blätter" would have to depend upon the relationship between the numerous variants of the ballad in Germany proper and the more conservative type in the surrounding German-speaking areas and in former German colonies. That must be reserved for a later investigation.

Though my conclusions are tentative, another argument already suggests itself for further pursuit. Beside the image of the wine-drinking and waving with the glass-- Richter calls it a motif--appears the other interchangeable epic formula: the offering of the ring. The two elements have the same function in the narrative structure, yet each certainly has very different associations. In the first case the wine-drinking appears more as a temptation by the lover, a temptation which the maiden destined to be a nun must resist.

She therefore says, "Ich weiß von keiner Liebe." Such explicit dialogue between count and nun appears important for the dramatic unfolding of the presented events and is the core of the first scene of the ballad in the Bessarabien version; it constitutes an essential element of the ballad. Only if this first scene remains stable does a dramatic development, in the sense of balladic narration, follow from the change of scene--a development which is emphasized by the formulaic, contrasting pattern in the second scene in front of the cloister.

In the second case the offer of the ring is an unequivocal promise of marriage and therefore differs in degree of importance in the song's progression of argument. The gift of the ring certainly belongs to the general pool of common motifs found in German folk songs. It is often formulaic in the sense of being put in an interrogative form at a moment of surprise and in itself suggests the presentation of a scheme of contrast out of which dramatic events develop.

> 3. Was zog er von dem Finger?
> Ein goldnes Ringelein.
> "Nimm's hin du Hübsche, du Feine,
> das soll dir ein Denkmal sein."
> > "Graf und Nonne," Kürnach,
> > Unterfranken, 1913 (DVA A 200 754).

/What did he take from his finger? / A small gold ring. / "Take it, you beauty, you elegant one; / it shall be a remembrance for you."_7

On the other hand, the offer of the ring seems to be such a common formula that it does not necessarily provide the background for dramatic action. Quite the contrary, the ring scene may be simply an inducement for shortening the complex ballad to a single scene in a love song. This path evidently was followed when a typical version of "Graf und Nonne" was translated into Danish.[9] The motif of offering the ring was further developed using the equally common motif that the maid should not be at a loss for an excuse about the ring: she found it in the green meadow. We should not, however, overlook the ambiguity of her excuse; to have found the ring on the green meadow indicates that the maiden has already been seduced. Accordingly, the Danish version continues with the image of tender love in the forest and finally with the longing of the beloved, who contemplates, from the high mountain, the ship in the deep valley. A purely physical separation develops out of this image of social contrast, and out of the ballad, in which the impetus for dramatic narrative development is the need to offer motivation for a thwarted romance, develops a narrative love song focusing on a seduction scene.

Jomfruen og greven[10]

1. Jeg stod mig og på højen bjerg,
   så ned i dyben dal,
   da så jeg et skib kom sejlende, kom sejlende,
   hvori tre grever var.

2. Den alleryngste greve,
   som udi skibet var,
   han ville mig trolove, trolove,
   så ung som han end var.

3. Så tog han af sin finger
   en ring af røden guld;
   "Se her, se her, min pige, min pige,
   den vil jeg give dig."

4. "Og hvad skal jeg med denne ring,
   i fald min moder spørg?"
   "Så sig blot, du har fundet den,
   har fundet den ud i den grønne eng."

5. "Du lær' mig godt at lyve,
   det står mig ikke an,
   langt heller vil jeg sige, ja sige
   en ungkarl elsker mig."

6. Vi fulgtes ad til skoven,
   i græsset sad vi blødt,
   han skænked mig sin kærlighed, sin kærlighed,
   og taled ømt og sødt.

7. Jeg står så tit på højen bjerg,
   ser ned i dyben dal,
   mon ej det kommer sejlende, ja sejlende,
   det skib, hvori han var.

/1. I stood on a high mountain, / saw down in the deep valley / when I saw a ship come sailing, come sailing, / in which there were three earls. 2. The youngest earl, / who was in the ship, / he wants to be my true love, true love, / as young as he then was. 3. So he took from his finger / a ring of red gold; / "See here, see here, my maid, my maid, / this I will give to you." 4. And what shall I /do/ with this ring / in case my mother asks?" / "Simply say that you found it, / found it out in the green meadow." 5. "You teach me well to lie; / that doesn't please me; / rather will I say, yes say, / a bachelor loves me." 6. We went together to the forest; / we sat softly in the grass; / he gave me his love, his love, / and spoke tenderly and sweetly. 7. I stand so often on the high mountain, / look down in the deep valley; / I wonder if it comes sailing, yes sailing, / that ship, in which he was./

Consequently, the perspective of the singer or narrator has also changed. The identification with universally tragic events as in the Bessarabian German version generally disappears; the "I" of the new form is, throughout, unequivocally the maiden, who yearns for her beloved. Because the action is single-stranded, without dramatic break and without confrontation, the epic formulas become functionless and can disappear. No confrontation pattern is necessary; no dramatic development needs to be outlined. The true balladic style of narration becomes superfluous. The above version of "Alle Blätter welken . . ." might be interpreted in this way also. Thus the material, in my opinion, takes a direction which moves clearly away from the ballad; and as a result the Danish version stands out as alien to the Scandinavian ballad tradition. Indeed, it is no longer recognizable as a ballad and instead probably aligns itself very closely with the popular art song of the nineteenth century.

NOTES

[1]The Ballad as Narrative, in collaboration with Flemming G. Andersen and Thomas Pettitt (Odense: Odense University Press, 1982). For comparison, see also my most recent presentation about Danish tradition (with references to further sources) in Det balladeske (Odense, 1980), English Summary. For German tradition especially, see "Die epische Formel in der deutschen Volksballade," Jahrbuch für Volksliedforschung, 18 (1973), 30-41.

[2]Johannes Künzig and Waltraut Werner, Balladen aus ostdeutscher Überlieferung, Quellen zur deutschen Volkskunde, 4, No. 22 (Freiburg: Institut für ostdeutsche Volkskunde, 1969).

[3]Norbert Richter, "Das epische Volkslied in Franken um 1900," Diss. Würzburg 1973 /1974/.

[4]Richter, p. 21 and pp. 112-24.

[5]Hans Helbron, "Das Lied vom Grafen und der Nonne," Diss. Kiel 1936, 6, 22 ff.

[6]Compare Richter, p. 116.

[7]Compare Richter, p. 116, n. 3.

[8]Richter, pp. 119 ff. Gottfried Habenicht investigated thoroughly a third form, which he understands as a transitional version from "Graf und Nonne" to "Es welken alle Blätter," in "Die Nonnenballade: Zu einem Sondertyp mit vornehmlich ost- und sudostdeutscher Verbreitung," Jahrbuch für ostdeutsche Volkskunde, 23 (1980), 83-147.

[9]See Otto Holzapfel, Folkevise und Volksballade, Motive, No. 6 (München: Wilhelm Fink, 1976), pp. 116 ff.

[10]Iørn Piø, ed., Folkesangerens Visebog (København: Morten Levy, 1966), pp. 94 ff.

Deutsches Volkliedarchiv
Freiburg

Translated from the German by Kathleen E. B. Manley

THE COMPUTER AND THE BALLAD

EL HIJO PÓSTUMO

THE POSTHUMOUS SON

Sung by Bernardo García Pérez, 60
Cuiñas (Lugo), 1929-1930

Hoy se marcha nuestro rey	Today our king is leaving,
de Madrid para Granada;	Leaving Madrid for Granada;
2 también se marchó la reina	The queen left with him as well,
de nueve meses preñada.	Nine months pregnant 'though she was.
Indose por el camino	Travelling along the road·
encontró con gran batalla;	He found himself in great battle;
4 toda era gente negra,	The enemy were all dark skinned,
cristiana non era nada.	No Christian was there among them.
Y a la buena de la reina	And our beloved queen,
le dieron una puñalada.	She was stabbed with a dagger.
6 Y le sacan un niño vivo	They remove a living child
por medio de una illarga,	From the wound where the blade entered;
y lo fueran' bautizar	they took him to be baptized
a la iglesia más cercana.	To the nearest church there about.
8 Y de padrinos le dieran	For god-parents they gave him
una gente muy honrada:	A very honorable couple:
o Santo Cristo de Burgos,	The Lord Jesus Christ of Burgos,
y la Virgen Soberana;	And the Holy Virgin Mary;
10 y lo dieran a criar	And they gave him to be nursed
a una niña que por allí estaba,	To a young girl they found there,
delgadita de cintura	A young girl small in the waist
y algo morena de cara.	And a bit dark of complexion.
12 Medráballe mais n'un dia	He grew more in just one day
que o outro n'unha semana.	Than another grows in seven.
Al cabo de nueve meses	After nine months had gone by
regia capa y espada,	He was wearing cape and sword,
14 y al cabo de nueve años	And after nine years had passed
era rey por toda España.	He was king in all of Spain.

SUZANNE H. PETERSEN

A COMPUTER-BASED RESEARCH PROJECT ON THE ROMANCERO

For the past eleven years the "Instituto Menéndez Pidal" (IMP) research team and its numerous collaborators have been working on a long-range, computer-based research project on the oral Hispanic ballad tradition.[1] The ultimate objectives of this project are: 1) to make available the entire corpus of all versions of Romances sung in the four Hispanic languages (Spanish, Portuguese, Catalan and Judeo-Spanish) and their dialects, collected throughout the world from the fifteenth century to the present, and 2) to define the structural properties of the Romancero through the analysis and subsequent description of the reproductive patterns and the "language" of this particular model of oral poetic discourse.[2] In view of the scope of the project and its continued dependence on outside funding, these goals have been reformulated and distributed over consecutive work phases, each with its own more immediate objectives. In pursuing long-range goals through stages of interrelated short term projects the use of computer technology provides the required continuity and largely eliminates unnecessary duplication of effort, in addition to its more creative role in the analysis of oral discourse. In the following pages I will outline briefly and illustrate where appropriate, past and current IMP-sponsored, computer-assisted research activity on the modern Hispanic ballad.[3] The first part of the paper describes the computer-based information systems we are currently working with, while the second reviews briefly an earlier system of computer-aided analysis of the Romancero and illustrates, also in brief, how we are now attempting to analyze and process data stored in one of the information systems to elaborate an ideological dictionary of the poetic language of the Romancero.

To facilitate our own ballad research and in general to foment theoretical activity through the dissemination of information among students of the Romancero, the IMP recently created three new computer-based information systems. The first to become operational was a computer-based bibliographic data file of references to primary sources and studies of the Romancero in modern tradition, from 1700 to 1980.[4] While numerous catalogues and bibliographies on the Romancero already existed, no single source was available which adaquately served the wide variety of theoretical interests focused in recent years on this model of traditional poetic discourse.

A bibliographic documentation system available at the University of Wisconsin Madison Academic Computing Center (MACC) and supporting software prepared by the University of Wisconsin's Seminary of Medieval Spanish Studies for their computer-based <u>Bibliography of Old Spanish Texts</u>, Volume I, were adapted and used to generate a relatively complete file of bibliographic entries (or citations) on the modern oral <u>Romancero</u>.[5] By distributing the information in each entry of the bibliographic file (BRO) over eight separate fields, the file could be easily accessed for editing and then automatically re-sorted and cross-indexed on the basis of one or a combination of fields. A copy of the main citation file, comprised of 1624 alphabetically ordered, consecutively numbered, complete bibliographic descriptions in standard form, each accompanied by three additional informational fields (specifying the area(s) of the tradition referred to in the work described, the designation of one or more libraries in possession of the work, and a reference to the source of the bibliographic information given) was then formatted for photo-composition. It was subsequently published, together with six indexes which cross-reference the citations by author, journal and periodical, place of publication, date of publication, area of the oral tradition, and library or achive.[6]

Even as the first edition of the <u>Bibliography</u> went to press the original BRO file was reloaded for updating and modification. While a second edition of other reference works overlooked in <u>BRO I</u>, or published since 1980 would be a relatively simple undertaking, we have given priority to a revised, expanded version of <u>BRO I</u>, in which the most significant modification is the addition of a new descriptive field. This "contents" field lists by ballad and in the order of appearance, all traditional texts contained in each bibliographic reference. It also includes the following information for each text described: assonance(s), meter, text number or page in the publication in which the text appears, number or page of the musical transcription, if applicable, and various brief notations on the origin of the text cited in the publication. The <u>Descriptive Bibliography of the Hispanic Ballad in Oral Tradition</u>, I (<u>BIDRO</u>), will only describe reference works published since 1700 in journals, periodicals, and books of critical studies by one or more authors.[7] In the contents field we describe only the first edition of each bibliographic reference unless later editions include additional ballad texts. For those sources which contain no traditional ballad texts the contents field simply states "no texts."[8] A cross-index generated on the basis of ballads listed in the contents field will provide an extensive inventory of all the versions of nearly all traditional Hispanic ballads to have appeared in print since 1700. This index (which, when necessary, may be used in conjunction with the field that identifies at least one library in possession of the publication) will do much to overcome a problem that has long frustrated those who work in traditional balladry: the difficulty of locating and compiling bodies of evidence suitable for the types of analyses one would like to do.

The identification of the ballad texts each reference work contains is proving to be by far the most time-consuming aspect of the revision process. A significant number of the _romances_ cited in Latin American publications are unknown in the oral traditions of other areas, while others differ considerably from their counterparts in the rest of the tradition. As a result, much of this material has never been adequately identified. A similar problem exists for the religious ballads in general. In nearly all areas of the tradition, ballads on religious themes have been largely ignored by modern criticism, and efforts to classify and identify these materials are just now getting underway. To this end IMP researchers are at work cataloguing the entire ballad collection (over 25,000 texts) in the Menéndez Pidal Archive. As each ballad is identified, it is assigned a permanent identification number which will be incorporated into the BIDRO descriptive field and used to generate the index of bibliographic entries by ballad.[9]

The _Descriptive Bibliography_, projected for publication in 1984, will include one further improvement over its earlier version: the breakdown of the modern tradition into geographic areas will be redefined to reflect a more rigorous application of linguistic and logical criteria. Consequently, the index by areas of the tradition, one of the most useful to scholars interested in ballad geography, will provide a more valid means of establishing comparisons.

A second information system, the "International Electronic Archive of the _Romancero_" (AIER), provides a centralized mechanism for storing all primary data on the _Romancero_. The ultimate goal is to incorporate into this cooperative data bank all available Hispanic ballad texts, each classified geographically, chronologically, and idiolectically and coded to identify and classify the narrative, discursive and poetic paradigmatic units it manifests. Once completed, this classification will permit a wide variety of exhaustive studies of the _Romancero_, but even prior to any analytical encoding, the mere incorporation of minimally classified ballad texts into the electronic archive creates a data base that is easily reorganized and open to all for consultation. The entire contents of the AIER, any individual contribution to it or any subset selected on thematic, geographic, or temporal criteria can automatically be made available for analysis. Since particularly in the early stages the utility of the AIER is to some extent proportionate to its volume, we encourage others working in the field to contribute their own individual ballad collections by offering them, in exchange, access to all ballad materials stored in the AIER and in the Menendez Pidal Archive. The primary advantage of the AIER as a research tool is that all reorganizations of the material are compatible with each other. In addition, the geographic extension and administrative complexity of the Hispanic world creates a pressing need to establish a focal point for a broad network of interested scholars. By providing access to a vast amount of information normally difficult, if not impossible to consult, the AIER can effectively encourage collaboration, minimize duplication of effort and, in general, accelerate the rhythm of publications of new texts and the preparation of critical studies.

In an effort to complete the vast collection of ballads in the Menéndez Pidal Archives with materials collected by the IMP during recent field trips and, at the same time, organize and facilitate consultation of the thousands of traditional texts rapidly accumulating as a result of this work, we selected as the first file in the AIER the 687 ballad texts collected during the 1977 IMP "Encuesta-Norte."[10] Other individual collections such as the very sizeable one gathered in 1969-70 by Joanne B. Purcell ("Romanceiro português das Ilhas Atlânticas") are also being prepared in machine-readable form for incorporation into the AIER.

Aside from the facility with which electronically stored ballad texts lend themselves to a wide variety of analyses, another benefit of considerable advantage in times of rising editorial costs is the possibility of publishing these materials with very little additional effort. In order to guarantee for the future the economic feasibility of computer-generated ballad publications the IMP initiated, simultaneous with the creation of the AIER, a new publication series based on the AIER data files. With the corpus of ballad texts subsequently published as the first two volumes in the AIER-Texts series and with the assistance of a systems analyst at MACC we designed a computer-based system that could thereafter be used to prepare phototypeset copy of any corpus of ballad materials stored in the electronic archive.[11]

The original MACC photocomposition system, developed specifically to meet our relatively complex formatting requirements, involves the following basic steps:

1. Preparation of the input tape: transcription of the original text together with control or mark-up commands for the particular typesetter processor used.

2. Composition of the text: processing the input to interpret its typesetter mark-up commands. The output of this step is an intermediate disk file that serves as the input to the next step--that of generating the original magnetic tape (final typesetter output tape) with all the mark-up necessary for photo-composition. Although this intermediate output can be converted directly to the tape used by the typesetter to make typeset copy, in practice it is far more economical to first make one or as many proof copies as are necessary to avoid having to reset or patch-up errors on photocomposed pages. For this reason, the final typesetter phase normally involves two steps:

3. Correction of the output of step two on the basis of a pseudo-formatted proof-listing which simulates with a line printer the final formatted output in all its formal characteristics: composed pages with appropriate centering, margins, leading, running heads, pagination, and typefaces (simulated with overprinting and underscoring), together with numerical notations in the margin indicating the exact page length and, line by line, the pointsize(s) and precise leading used.[12]

4. Typeset (camera-ready typeset copy)

Having developed the format mark-up, special character codes and the programs capable of producing a publication of Hispanic ballad materials analogous in form to the established Romancero Tradicional series, we can now use this cost-effective system to prepare new editions of ballad texts. The purpose of AIER-Texts, which can be prepared without laborious prior study and without the aid of professional printers, is to facilitate the reading and handling of a small but significant portion of the ballad materials stored in the AIER.[13] However, even if not published in this series, collections that have been incorporated into the electronic archive will have entered into circulation and can be used and quoted by specialists.

In the preparation of texts for their inclusion in the AIER the initial transcription and editing is normally done off-line using data entry and editing equipment and is then transferred to a magnetic tape for permanent storage in the AIER tape library.[14] Additional editing to update, encode for analysis or format for publication can be done off-line as needed on a microcomputer system. Interactive use of the computer is required only for final processing of the data. The flexibility and high degree of independence from a large computer facility that this centralized electronic ballad data bank offers is particularly desirable for a cooperative project which depends on extensive collaboration among a widely dispersed group of Romancero scholars of very diverse, individual research interests. The contribution the AIER can make to the preservation and study of a vast, but fleeting popular culture will ultimately depend on the extent to which others perceive it as a useful research tool.

The most ambitious and by far most complex of the computer-based information systems developed by IMP researchers is the "General Descriptive, Bilingual Catalogue of the Pan-Hispanic Romancero" (CGR).[15] The CGR differs radically from more conventional catalogues that generally provide succinct summaries of ballad narratives, classified and indexed by theme and motif. In its descriptive conventions this catalogue proposes a theoretical model and an analytical apparatus designed to take into account the essential, distinctive property of oral poetic discourse: its potential for continual, unlimited variation at all levels of articulation of a message. With a view to accomodating the dynamic, open structure of orally transmitted narratives, in the preparation of catalogue entries each and every version of the ballad being described is treated as an equally valid re-creation of a potential model or program. Accordingly, each descriptive summary or abstract attempts to faithfully record at various levels of organization of the narrative the underlying structural elements common to all its versions, and, at the same time, to register at each level all significant variants manifested in one or more of its versions.[16] Through the use of diacritical marks each abstract reflects the interrelation of three hierarchically structured levels of articulation (tale or fabula, plot, and discourse) and maintains a balance between the two perspectives (invariant/variant). This mode of presentation allows the reader to perceive the invariant units of plot and fabula and to comprehend the base text without sacrificing the multifold diversity manifested at all three structural levels.

The summary, itself a restatement of the plot, is fragmented and organized so as to reflect the succession of narrative sequences that constitute the <u>fabula</u>. At the level of coherence in which the <u>fabula</u> is the invariant semantic content of the particularized expressions of the plot the narrative sequence is defined as an event (action or psychological process) whose realization substantially modifies the interrelationship of <u>dramatis personae</u>, the subjects and objects of the sequential phrase.[17] In the abstracts, narrative sequences are consecutively numbered and set off between triple diagonal bars (1///...///, 2///...///, and so on). In addition to the numbered sequences essential to a faithful reconstruction of the <u>fabula</u>, the summaries include supplementary sequences that register information present only in a minority of the versions of a ballad (normally in one version or one branch of the tradition), but which do not alter the basic <u>fabula</u> of the narrative. These sequences are of two types and are coded to signal their accessory nature. Those that are borrowed from other ballads appear as ⟨⟨+X///...///⟩ when incorporated at the beginning of the narrative, as ⟨⟨+Y///...///⟩⟩ when inserted in the middle, and as ⟨⟨+Z///...///⟩⟩ when tacked on at the end. In all cases the contaminating ballad is identified by number and footnoted. When on the other hand one or more versions of a ballad offer a commentary marginal to the narrative itself (often in the form of a declaration, warning or moralizing <u>sententia</u>), one of two self-explanatory conventions is used:

Ex///   (exordium) or   PS///   (<u>Post Scriptum</u>)
Ap//...   (apostrophe)   Epit//... (epitaph)

In spite of the essential simplicity of the sequential phrase's underlying message, the constant effort on the part of those who participate in the oral transmission of ballad narratives to more effectively express those messages normally results in considerable variation of both plot and, to a lesser extent, <u>fabula</u>. The descriptive summaries, for purely practical reasons and without any chronological or aesthetic implications, present one traditional plot variant as the base text. For each narrative sequence all alternatives present in the remaining versions (be they additions, omissions or substitutions) are embedded in the base text between the symbols ⟨...⟩. Inside these diacritical marks, if an alternate consists of functionally analogous but semantically different segments of plot, the variant is preceded by a single diagonal bar ⟨/ ...⟩ (the bar to be read "or"). When the alternating variants result from the absence of a particular detail, the bar is followed by a crosshatch ⟨/#⟩ ("empty"). In both cases a vertical bar is used in the base text to signal the point at which the divergence begins. Informative elements not present in the base text which are purely discursive and do not affect the plot/<u>fabula</u> relationship are introduced by a plus sign: ⟨+ ...⟩. The abstract can be read equally well choosing any one of the often numerous alternating plot variants.

Not infrequently the extent of intra-sequential variation is so great that the variants cannot be represented with embedding techniques. In such cases the functionally equivalent variants are enumerated separately using decimals and double diagonal bars:

        1///
        1.1// ...//
        1.2// ...//

The same convention is employed to represent non-equivalent sequential alternates, that is, those variants which manifest semantic differences that can only be resolved at the more abstract level of the ballad's functional model.[18] In the graphic representation of alternates which constitute variants in the <u>fabula</u> the consistent use of decimal digits serves to identify related variants in successive narrative sequences (e.g., variant 1.2//... corresponds with 2.2//..., 3.2//..., so that 1.1//... + 2.1//... + 3.1//... constitute the plot of a given group of versions.

While the descriptive summary itself contains no actual discourse, the relationship between the invariant semantic content of plot (each motif) and its expressive plane is maintained by appending to each element or motif a letter code /(:a), (:b)/ which points to the location in the discourse field where all the specific verbalizations of each detail of the plot are registered. (e.g., the motif registered in the abstract as sequence 1/// ...(:a) is expressed in the oral tradition with one of the several units of discourse registered in the DISC field under 1///:a. The geographic origin of each unit of discourse is appended to the unit in square brackets. As this convention serves to mark the end of a poetic phrase, it can be used to automatically fragment the corpus of poetic discourse in the CGR into discrete units for future processing.[19]

The units of poetic discourse vary in length from one to, occasionally, as many as five or six hemistichs, depending on the degree of expressive economy with which the individual singers dramatically concretize a particular element of content.[20] Each hemistich recorded in the discourse field, whether one of several octosyllables of a larger unit or a discrete unit of discourse in and of itself, is preceded either by the symbol "$<$", identifying it as a first hemistich in the sixteen syllable verse, or by the symbol "$>$", denoting a second (rhyming) hemistich.[21]

Within a single series of discourse variants grouped together and linked to an element of plot, diacritical marks are used both within and between units of discourse to preserve the invariant/variant distinction at the discourse level and to indicate the precise relationship the poetic phrases bear to the common element of plot they express. Internal verbal variation manifested in generatively related structures is recorded inside parentheses within the traditional poetic phrase chosen as the "base text" of a unit of discourse. The lexical-syntactic variation that can be accomodated through the embedding convention is necessarily limited (addition, omission or substitution of articles, pronouns, nouns, synonymic subsitition of adverbial phrases, anastrophe, and so forth). When more radical transformations are involved and the resulting variation can not be represented internally, we record textual variants as separate, alternative units of discourse, linking all alternative forms with the equivalent symbol ($\sim\ <...$ or $\sim\ <...$). Functionally equivalent alternating units which, unlike those just described, are not manifestations of the same base structure, are introduced with the diagonal bar ($/\ <...$ or $/\ >...$). Finally, we use the plus sign ($+\ <...$ or $+\ >...$) to record additional poetic phrases which, while they may be highly effective, do not affect the plot.

Each CGR entry is comprised of fourteen fields that may be grouped by function into three main categories: the first four fields identify the ballad and indicate the number and geographic dispersion of the versions used in the elaboration of the description. The next six fields provide the description, registering the invariants and the variants of _fabula_, plot and discourse that the corpus offers. The last four reference other information that further identifies the ballad being described.

Because of the complexity and innovative nature of this catalogue, a sample entry will help illustrate the CGR's components and their relationship to one another (see Appendix I).[22] The description of El hijo póstumo (The Posthumous Son) was chosen for its relative brevity and limited structural complexity and because the ballad has analogues in the Pan-European tradition.[23] Following the sample, in the exegesis of the contents of each field, diacritical marks not yet discussed will be explained.

In addition to the title, the first field, TITU, contains the permanent identification number assigned to this ballad (0030) and its assonance (a-a). The next field, GEOG, gives the size of the corpus of versions used (26) and specifies the total number of fragmentary versions (2) and of published versions (8: 4 in their entirety; 4 only in their variant hemistichs), followed by a geographic breakdown of this same information. The third field, INCO (incorporations), indicates, where applicable and identifiable, the presence in other ballads of segments belonging to the ballad being described. It further specifies the geographic origin of the versions which have borrowed these segments. (As elsewhere, the crosshatch signifies "empty.") The last identification field, TRAV (travestia), references, where relevant, other re-creations of the ballad described which, while they use significant portions of the discourse of this ballad, offer a substantially different fabulistic content (e.g., ballads reinterpreted in a religious context, that is, "vueltos a lo divino").

Following the narrative description proper (RESU and SUMM), the next field, CONT, gives the identification number and title of other ballads which contaminate or are contaminated by the one being analyzed. The fourth field in this group, NOIN (notes to the intrigue), records the geographic origin of the plot and fabula variants registered in the descriptive summary. The discourse field (DISC) gives an inventory of all the various ways in which the details of the plot are manifested in each of the geographic areas for which we have one or more traditional versions of the ballad. The last field in the descriptive section, NODI (notes to the discourse), further breaks down, where needed, the geographic specifications footnoted in the discourse field.

In the final group of fields the first, BIBL, details bibliographic data on all traditional versions published to date, distinguishing between those versions actually used in the description (i.e., those counted in GEOG) and versions of other ballads that include segments of the one being described (i.e., those enumerated in INCO). The old title field, OTIT, lists other names used in the past to identify the ballad under consideration. It also includes references by number and title to the two nineteenth-century collections universally cited by scholars for purposes of identification as well as to three modern ballad catalogues.[24] The next field, IANT, enumerates the ballad's incipit (or in its absence, the first verse known) in the old tradition, while the last field, IMOD, records the ballad's most common _incipit_ in the various branches of the modern oral tradition.

Both as a model for the description of oral discourse and as a systematic guide to Hispanic ballad themes the "General Descriptive, Bilingual Catalogue of the Pan-Hispanic _Romancero_" should prove a useful research tool to students of traditional poetic narratives. While the ultimate and as yet distant goal of the project entails the description of all _romances_ known to exist or to have existed in the oral Hispanic tradition since the fifteenth century, for the present the IMP has limited the scope of the project to the central nucleus of the modern _Romancero_ (nineteenth and twentieth centuries). The 82 entries included in the three volumes of the Catalogue completed to date describe all of the ballads of national-historical themes documented in the modern tradition. Although thematically limited, this corpus constitutes a substantial body of evidence, one that is sufficiently broad in scope to begin testing the analytical potential of the Catalogue and, in particular, the validity of some of our hypotheses concerning the system of poetic communication of the oral _Romancero_.

The theoretical principles on which the IMP Catalogue is based and the projected analysis of the poetic discourse it contains grow out of an earlier attempt to design a system of computer-aided analysis for the study of oral creative processes in the _Romancero_.[25] The database for this pilot project consisted of 612 versions of one Hispanic ballad, "La Condesita" (~ "El conde Sol"), documented in the oral tradition from 1825 to 1970. In order to observe the processes of transformation operating at various levels of organization of the narrative, the entire "Condesita" corpus was fragmented into several smaller units of analysis: the version, the hemistich, the word, the dramatic scene, the thematic segment, and the element of narrative content. Additional codes were used to generate other paradigmatic groupings related either to the poetic system (metric, modal, syntactical, and grammatical classifications) or to the temporal and spatial classification of the corpus. The following diagram illustrates the general organization of the primary and secondary data and its sub-classification at the appropriate level:

The system's basic operational procedure consisted of repeated massive sorting and tabulating operations performed on selected significant sub-sets of the total database (612 versions, 34,233 hemistichs, 170,978 words). While some of the data pertains primarily to one level of analysis, in effect, it is all retained and available at all levels and

Level of analysis	Paradigmatic classifications (Subscripts)	Subscript breakdown	Number of entries in each Subscript	Coded in or generated from columns
WORD	A) BY GRAPHEMIC VARIANTS (words grouped by graphic form)	"A" + "A-" + "Abajo" + "Aballo" +...	170,978	7-44
	B) ARCHETYPAL /INVARIANTS7 (words gped by lexemes)	°A + °Abajo + °Abandonar + ...	6,418	7-44
	C) GRAMMATICAL I (words gped by grammatical classes)	0 + 1 + A + J +....	36	65-74
	D) GRAMMATICAL II (words gped by parts of speech)	(0,1,A,J,) + (4,D,U,N,5,V,6) + ...	9	65-74
	E) GRAMMATICAL III (words gped by type: functional vs. content)	(0,1,A,J,4,U,...) + (2,B,K,3,...)	2	65-74
	F) BY METRIC FUNCTION (words gped by rhyme function: rhyming vs. non-rhyming)	(Last word, 2nd hemist.) + (other words)	2	65-74 & 6
HEMISTICH	G) BY VARIANTS (hemist. gped by verbal expression)	Each hemistich in the chain of discourse not identical to another	19,403	7-44
	H) ARCHETYPAL /INVARIANTS7 (hemist. gped by archetypal hemistiches)	10:150:111( ) + 10:150:112( ) + ...	1,937	54-61
	I) BY SYNTACTIC STRUCTURE (hemist. gped by syntax patterns)	(T+J+4) + (A+A) + (D+6=5) + ...	?	65-74
	J) BY MODE OF DISCOURSE (hemist. gped by mode of presenting inform: narration vs. direct discourse)	(C,H,I,...) + (B,A) + (W,Y) + ...	10	45
	K) BY METRIC FUNCTION (hemist. gped by presence or absence of assonance)	A + B	2	6
ELEMENT	L) BY NARRATIVE FUNCTION (hemist. gped by archetypal narrative elements)	101 + 102 + 103 + ...	250	48-53
SEGMENT	M) ARCHETYPAL (expository units gped by archetypal segments)	10 + 11 + 12 + ...	19	46-47
SCENE	N) ARCHETYPAL (dramatic units gped by archetypal scenes)	1 + 2 + 3 + ...	4	46
VERSION	O) SPATIAL I (versions gped by province)	LC + PO + LU + ...	52	75-76
	P) SPATIAL II (versions gped by region)	(LC+PO+LU+OV+ST) + (LN+ZM+OR) +...	10	75-76
	Q) TEMPORAL (versions gped by period of collection)	(before 1900) + (1901-1920). + ...	4	77-80
	R) TYPOLOGICAL (vers. gped according to mode of transmission: auton, double, lit., derived from Flor nueva....)	(001-130,132-320) + (501-627,631-765) +..	4	1-3
	S) TESTIMONIAL (versions gped according to the quality of testimony: fragmentary vs. complete)	(001-022,024,027-047,...) + (023,048,049,...)	2	1-3

can therefore be used in conjunction with any of the various units of analysis /Ā-S̲/ or sub-sets thereof. With this ability to take into account simultaneously all the simple and complex variables operating at the different organizational levels, many aspects of the structural transformation of a dynamic model can be plotted, measured and defined.

In order to test as extensively as possible the viability of the system, rather than concentrate on an exhaustive study of one level of analysis, we preferred to address a wide variety of problems involving each of the different units of analysis. In pursuing that objective we focused in particular on those problems that required either a multilevel analysis or the interpretation of large batches of mechanically sorted and tabulated data as these involved transformational processes that had consistently defied analysis with more traditional methodologies.

Among the studies of the total lexicon of the ballad, simple frequency and dispersion listings of both lexical variants and invariants revealed an unexpectedly rich vocabulary and a surprising correlation between the semantemes of maximum diffusion and the functional structure of the ballad. Other studies of verbal variation exemplified the play between the internal pressure of the verbal heritage and the ecological interference or external pressure of the environments in which the ballad moves. In evaluating the pressures of the metric and rhyme schemes, an analysis of the relationship between rhyme and lexical stability produced statistics that cast serious doubt on the supposed mnemonic function of rhyme in the traditional Hispanic ballad.[26]

In another series of analyses which used the archetypal or invariant hemistichs as a frame of reference, we investigated the lexical-syntactical, semantic, and functional transformation of the variant hemistichs of a common base structure. In addition to less extreme phenomena, variation at this level was found to produce both semantic continuity with unlimited formal variation and formal continuity with radical semantic transformation. Evidence of syntagmatic reorganization of parts of the narrative as a result of the mobility and functional transformation of archetypal hemistichs suggested the need to study the reproductive mechanisms operating within larger segments of the narrative.

Analyses of the distortion of natural order in the sequence of thematic segments and narrative elements, modifications in the absolute and relative length of thematic segments and dramatic scenes, and extreme variation in the proportionate use and distribution of direct discourse and narration all indicated that the poem adjusts itself to a number of very different poetic molds with particular structural characteristics dominating in certain regions, certain periods and certain ballad types. In order to observe the synchronic and diachronic transformation of the overall narrative, a series of programs was used to determine and cartographically represent (by means of a shading system based on overprint symbols) varying degrees of narrative affinity among all 612 spatially and temporally classified versions of the ballad.[27]

During the pilot study on the "Condesita" we were able to interpret only a fraction of the secondary data made available through various reorganizations of the corpus. Poetic formulas received relatively little attention. We had in fact alloted space in the coding sequence to identify variant hemistichs which, based on our prior experience and familiarity with the "Condesita" corpus, seemed formulaic. Each formula identified was assigned a number based on its semantic definition, but because of the thematic limitation of the corpus the field was largely overlooked in subsequent analyses. In spite of this practical neglect there was a growing awareness that: 1) poetic formulas vary considerably in both form and length, 2) when inserted in different contexts they can acquire new meaning, and 3) more than being just occasional or characteristic of certain moments of the tradition, they express many of the actions with which Hispanic ballad narratives throughout the tradition are constructed. A few abbreviated examples from the "Condesita" corpus illustrate these observations:[28]

SALIDA (DEPARTURE).

    Ya se parte el conde Arco, ya se parte, ya se va
    Ya se marcha el conde Bado, hoy se marcha y se va
    Hoy se despide don Badio, hoy se despide y se va
    Don Belardo, don Belardo, Don Belardo ya se va
    El senor conde de Flores ya se fue, ya se venia
    Y el conde Flores se va (~se ha ido ~se ha marchado)
    Y el conde nino (~romero ~Bado) se ha ido (~se fue)
    Ya se marcho el general
    Se despide el rey Lumbardo

PASAR DEL TIEMPO (PASSAGE OF TIME)

    Pasan tres, pasan cuatro, pasan cinco y pasan mas
    Pasan siete, pasan ocho, cerca de los nueve estan
    Pasan dias, pasan meses, pasan anos por alla

ENCUENTRO SUBITO O FORTUITO (SUDDEN OR FORTUITOUS ENCOUNTER)

```
Al bajar por la escalera
Al subir una escalera
N'el medio de la escalera
En el medio de la calle (~del camino ~de una sierra)
Y en medio de aquel camino
Quan es a mitjan cami
Andando (~Yendo) por el camino
Al revolver una esquina (~un cerrito)
Y al pasar por un camino
Al pasar los siete arroyos
Al subir un peno arriba  y al bajar un penascal
Subiendo un peno arriba  y bajando un penascal
A la salida de un monte,  al entrar n'un arenal
A las entradas de un monte,  a las salidas de un mar
A la pasada de un rio  y a la colada de un mar
Al subir un alto cerro, al bajar un arenal
Ha subido una muralla,  ha bajadito un castillo
```

These examples comprise but a fraction of the poetic formulas identified in the "Condesita" corpus. Like the "call for silence," "order to withdraw," "(emphatic) request," "(emphatic) denial," "(emphatic) refusal," "impatient wait," or "fruitless search," they are common to many ballads. However, any attempt to thoroughly explore and ultimately define the formulaic language of the Romancero requires a much more representative sample of its discourse encompassing as many versions as possible of numerous ballad themes. The CGR project was conceived in part to provide just such a database.

Since the work of Parry and Lord, studies of oral formulaic composition and research on formulaic diction in the Romancero in particular have identified poetic formulas (and formulaic expressions) on the basis of form and frequency, considering formulaic only those verbal expressions with a relatively fixed lexical-syntactical verse structure recurring in several texts within a particular oral tradition.[29] Yet few if any of those who have worked with this aspect of the Romancero would deny formulaic status to at least some of the poetic phrases cited above. If it is generally agreed that "En medio (~al subir ~bajando) la escalera" (Sudden Encounter) is formulaic, then why not "En el medio del camino," "Yendo (~andando) por el camino," "Al subir un peno arriba y al bajar un penascal," or "Ha subido una muralla, ha bajado un castillo"? If all or even if only some are formulaic, it is certainly not because of a fixed lexical-syntactical structure. Very few if any of the generatively related variants from the preceding lists, when considered together with all their related variants, manifest anything approaching a fixed form.

Rather than considering formulaic language as a verbal structure, if we view it from the level in which discourse is the signifier and plot the signified, each group of formally variable poetic formulas share a constant semantic value.[30] Seen in this light, as lexicalized expressions of a given content, poetic formulas function at the scenic level (the level of discourse), concretizing a more generic, abstract idea. When the female protagonist of "La condesita" sets out in search of her long absent husband traveling "seven years (~leagues, ~days, ~months) on land and another seven by sea," ("Sete anos andou por tierra e outros sete no mar") or taking care that she go "by night along the roads, by day through a thicket" ("de noche por los caminos, de dia por un jaral"), or all the while "weeping in the lowlands and singing in the high" ("Por los bajos va llorando por los altos cantando iba") and journeying with such speed that "running down a plain she resembles a sparrow-hawk" ("Por unas vegas abajo, corre mas que un gavilan"), all we are told at the level of the plot is that she travels far, in secrecy, hiding her passion or with great speed. The literal meaning of the phrases, the specific actions described, exist only at the level of discourse. At this level the formulas constitute the figurative language with which the qualified actions of the plot (go with speed, in secrecy, in solitude, together) are made perceptible. The formula's length is irrelevant to the plot. Discourse modality, level of dramatic intensity, and aesthetic value all vary in the extreme. When the abandoned wife in "La condesita" assumes a pilgrim's disguise, the action signified is the same. This conclusion is true whether it is graphically visualized in a series of acts:

> Se ha marchado pa su case, se ha empezado a desnudar;
> se quita traje de seda, se le pone de sayal,
> se quito zapato blanco, se le pone cordoban,
> se quito media bordada, se le pone sin bordar

requested in a dramatic dialogue between daughter and father:

> Hagame un vestido, padre, que me lo voy a buscar;
> no se lo pido de seda, ni de gro que cuesta mas,
> que se lo pido de esparto, de eso que llaman sayal

offered as advice:

> deja el zapato de seda y ponte el de cordoban,
> deja el vestido de seda y pontelo de sayal

or simply narated in a consise, straightforward manner:

Se vistio de peregrina

As the lexicon of the <u>Romancero</u>, poetic formulas have an extratextual semantic definition, but their denotative value is susceptible to modification when inserted in different contexts. Thus, for example, in a rare modern version of the ballad "Durandarte Sends his Heart to Belerma" the final lines inform us of the literal death of Belerma:

(Al oir esta palabra, Guillerma cae desmayada,)
ni con vino ni con agua no fueron a recordarla.

The same formula is used in other ballads (most notably in "The Death of Prince John") with the same meaning. It also reappears in 68 versions of "La Condesita," but here, with the addition of an extra formula, it implies a much less definitive passing. Such is the count's shock on discovering the pilgrim's identity on the eve of his projected second marriage that he faints dead away and can be revived by none but his long-lost first love:

(Al oir estas palabras don Belardo cae pa atras,)
ni con agua ni con vino le pueden resucitar,
solo con palabras tiernas que la romera le da.

The potential for lexical-syntactical variation of an invariant hemistich is so great that the formula can easily be accomodated in ballads with different assonant rhymes.[31]

Much more characteristic of the <u>Romancero</u> than its language at the verbal level is its poetic language at the level in which discourse manifests itself in organized content. From this point of view, essentially all oral Hispanic ballad discourse is formulaic. Recurrence of a particular formula in numerous texts is not essential, although in fact it is difficult to identify with any assurance even one that does not recur. For any action conceived, a formula can be found or readily invented. In spite of this fact, just as the number of conceivable human actions is limited, so too the number of poetic formulas which express them must be finite. An inventory of the totality of poetic phrases in the <u>Romancero</u>, classified on the basis of their semantic function, would provide a global overview of its figurative language and a basis from which to evaluate its use of that language.

This project, only recently begun, involves at present merely the development of a workable model for an

ideological dictionary of the poetic language of the
Romancero. In matter of fact an ideological dictionary which
pretends to define at the paradigmatic level the denotative
value of the poetic phrases of the Romancero can be realized
only after a careful examination of all the contexts in
which each phrase appears. In practice, however, we are
forced to work with the materials at hand which, even in the
best of cases, comprise but a small portion of the whole--
more or less representative, but a mere sample nonetheless.
The corpus of some 5500 poetic phrases currently registered
in the CGR electronic data file derives solely from the 82
historical-national ballad themes surviving in the modern
tradition. While this particular corpus represents perhaps
the most venerable portion of the oral Hispanic ballad
tradition, its very thematic coherence results in a
relatively high degree of coincidence of plot elements.
Consequently the semantic definition of our poetic formulas
cannot at this point be other than contextual.

In theory it might seem preferable at this early stage
to attempt to avoid contextually determined semantic
definitions by settling for a broader classification system,
identifying formulas of poetic discourse on the basis of
general semantic fields (e.g., "hunt," "wound," "dreams,"
"death," "physical beauty," or "sickness"). In practice,
however, even a classification by ideological key words
cannot be carried out without first determining the
contextual meaning of the poetic phrase. This becomes
immediately apparent once the entire corpus of CGR discourse
has been prepared for classification by dividing it into
isolated units of discourse (each retaining the information
necessary to identify and locate it in the corpus). For
example, isolated from its context the following phrase can
tell us little: "Una vez que tu lo vias (~dices eso), tu
eres el que lo harias" ("Having seen it /~said that7, you
are the one who would do it"). It is not inconceivable that
there are three or four Romancero specialists sufficiently
familiar with the Sephardic versions of "The Death of the
Duke of Gandia" to recognize this formula. Those working on
the project have little recourse but to consult the
appropriate CGR descriptive abstract where the corresponding
phrase of the plot summary, "the king unjustly accuses the
poor fisherman of being responsible for the crime," clarifies the semantic function of the otherwise uninterpretable
unit of discourse.

Even if comprehensible, the apparent meaning of a
formula, when isolated from its context, can be misleading.
By itself the following phrase, for example, might well be
taken as a formula of masculine gallantry: "Donde estuvieran
mujeres, hombres no beban primero" ("Where women are

present, let men not drink first"). Its functional meaning
in the context of the ballad could not be more at odds with
this interpretation. In the two versions of "The Treacherous
Countess from Castile" which include this formula, following
the queen mother's aborted attempt to poison her son, the
poem concludes with this precept warning of the need to be
mistrustful of women.

Regardless of whether we chose to interpret the
figurative language of the Romancero with precise
definitions of semantic content or with labels identifying
each phrase with a broad semantic category, if we want to
classify poetic formulas not on the basis of what the words
say or might be saying, but by their intended semantic
content, the "text" must be read in its context. And surely
it must be the poetic intention that concerns us.

At least in the early developmental stage of the
Romancero ideological dictionary project a double
classification seems desirable. Definition of units of
poetic discourse on the basis of contextually determined
semantic function is unavoidable if we are to determine
meaning at all, and will ultimately be required to arrive at
the paradigm. By maintaining as well the more superficial
classification by semantic fields we retain the possibility
of regrouping the formulas to confront those that allude to
a particular general concept. Moreover, the double classification will help us to anticipate and perhaps resolve some
of the inevitable problems encountered in determining the
internal organization and reference system of an ideological
dictionary.

The first experimental attempt to define and append
appropriate semantic labels to the poetic discourse
registered in the CGR brought into focus the specific
problems involved in the classification of coded discourse.
While I am far from able to suggest definitive solutions at
this point, I can illustrate through example where some of
the important decisions must be made and, in some cases,
weigh the relative merits of what seem to be the
alternatives.

Unquestionably the most important issue affecting the
structure of the dictionary and eventually its very function
is the level of abstraction at which we operate in
establishing the entries or headings. One readily apparent
option is to resort to logical concepts as is the custom in
most dictionaries of this sort. In this case we organize the
dictionary on the basis of such headings as "love,"
"rescue," "seduction," "horses," "games," or "weddings."
From a practical standpoint a classification by logical

concepts has two advantages. On the one hand it facilitates handling of the dictionary as a reference source. The reader knows how to locate what he is looking for. On the other, it greatly facilitates classification of the semantic, poetic materials of the Romancero. In view of the signifier/signified relationship obtaining between our poetic formulas and elements of plot, a logical concept can readily be found to define the actions expressed in the units of discourse. However, in the hierarchical structuring of the narrative the semantic content at the level of plot is in turn a specification of the invariant content of the fabula. Thus the actions expressed in the units of poetic discourse have meaning at a higher level of abstraction. Consequently, the danger of organizing the dictionary on the basis of logical concepts is that quite possibly we lose sight of the deepest and most important poetic message--that most intimate and most exact meaning the singer is trying to express. The point can be illustrated with a single formula from the ballad "The Battlements of Toro": "Por las almenas del toro (~oro ~moro) se pasea una donzella" ("Along the walls of Toro a maiden strolls"). Taken out of context the logical concept that defines the action might be "se pasea," but in context the semantic function of the formula is rather "mujer vista" ("woman seen"). However, in the last instance and at a higher level of abstraction, what it actually signifies is "mujer inaccesible."

An ideological dictionary organized on the basis of entries that refer to the heart of the poetic message ("dama inaccesible," for example) could prove difficult to use and thus of questionable utility. On the other hand, if we sacrifice the underlying message, we stand to lose or not express in our dictionary of poetic formulas of the Romancero precisely that which makes them poetic--the very reason for our interest in them. Therefore, it would seem that we must attend to two criteria: one logical and the other poetic. To implement this requires dividing the dictionary into two parts: the dictionary itself and the index. In the body of the work units of discourse are classified on the basis of their semantic, poetic content: "Inaccessibility" (and under that heading: "of a city," "of women," and so forth). The index then classifies according to logical concepts: "knights," "love," "death," and so forth. Structuring the dictionary in this way requires, if not a complete second index, at least a rather detailed synoptic diagram of the scheme of entries.

Another theoretical consideration that further complicates the reordering of the formulas and the structure of the dictionary is that of multiple semantic meanings at

the same level of classification. The units of discourse can
have more than one relevant semantic content. In principle
there should be but one primary content, but often two or
more coexist and both (or all) ought to be represented in a
dictionary of this sort. Three parallel formulas exemplify
this phenomenon:

En la vega os espero hasta las seis de la tarde

Compte Sano, surt al camp, que amb tu venc a peleiar;
si ins una hora no hi et, quedara por afrentado

Tres horas te doy buen rey, para ensillar tu caballo;
si a las tres horas no sale, quedara por afrentado

The primary semantic content of all three is a challenge and
they should be so classified under the heading "Desafiar"
(~"Retar"). But the secondary semantic content "plazo" (set
time limit) is surely of interest to students of oral
literature. The obvious solution is to resort to an ample
system of cross-references to register multiple coexisting
senses. The only difficulty lies in carefully determining
the limits of secondary semantic content.

Although in general the dictionary attends primarily to
semantic content and not to expressive form, it cannot
entirely ignore verbal formulas--those which traditionally
have attracted most attention. These formulas usually have a
certain semantic content as well, but that content is often
variable. They readily take on more than one semantic
function. The list of formulas in Appendix II[32] enumerates
all the formulas constructed around the expression "calla,
calla, . . ." "calledes, . . ." and so forth. As indicated
by the labels, they can be used to interrupt a message,
protest against something said, say "no" emphatically, calm
or console an interlocutor, or butt in on another's speech,
but the idea of "mandar callar" (order to silence) is also
in the formula and is of interest for itself. These formulas
can easily be incorporated into the dictionary, but only
those whose primary meaning is "order to silence" should be
listed in the body of the dictionary under the idea of
"mandar callar." ("Mandar callar" will be a sub-category of
"callar," just as "mandar matar" must be of "matar"). Other
verbal formulas of "callar," however, will logically appear
under those headings which best allude to their most
profound semantic content. Only in the index will the
locations of all be enumerated.

Any list of formulas we consult offers examples of the
theoretical considerations discussed above. Those chosen to
give an indication of what an ideological dictionary of our

poetic formulas might look like also provide an opportunity
to evaluate on a slightly larger scale the implications of
some of the most problematical aspects of the dictionary.

Appendix III, classifying formulas under the general
heading of "Desafiar," reflects in its length the importance
of this semantic function in the historical-national
romances. The appended semantic definitions, used
provisionally to sub-classify this group of poetic phrases,
distinguishes among formulas that allude to the challenge in
a narrative form (e.g., "he challenged," "he accepted the
challenge"), those that verbalize the challenge itself
(e.g., "I challenge you," "I accept your challenge"), others
which express the challenging attitude of the speaker and,
finally, a few whose semantic content is not a challenge per
se, but a threat. Quite possibly this last group must
ultimately be eliminated, but it serves to point out that in
this context the idea of challenge and that of threat are
closely akin. The difficulty is drawing the line between
related concepts. In the historical-national context many of
the formulas which express the idea of "to challenge" are
closely related to several other ideas, such as "to
threaten," "to insult," "to offend," "to reproach."
Nevertheless, these related ideas appear as well in contexts
not involving knights and warring nobility: the wife who
reproaches her husband, the rivals for a lady's hand who
insult each other, and so forth. The example illustrates
both the difference between syntagmatic and paradigmatic
semantic definitions and the need to organize the dictionary
on the basis of sufficiently precise and individualized
semantic content. The connotative affinity of one idea with
another in a particular context will require extensive and
careful use of cross-references in the index.

Assuming that the difficulty of avoiding contextual
meanings can be overcome, once the dictionary headings
define denotative values (e.g., all formulas whose
paradigmatic value is "to threaten," are grouped together),
it might be appropriate to mark with some convention those
formulas which assume different functional meanings in other
contexts. Another possibility is to assign a permanent
number to each formula in the dictionary and in the index
remit directly to those numbers in order to identify all
formulas which, regardless of their paradigmatic value, take
on a particular contextual meaning. In the case of our
present list of challenge formulas, for example, with a
number system those which must eventually be grouped instead
under "to threaten" in the dictionary, will be cited by
number twice in the index: once under their paradigmatic
definition "to threaten" (e.g., "To threaten": 1027-1355)
and once under the contextual semantic definition (e.g., "To

challenge": 2397-2512; see also, 1100, 1105, and so forth).
While this system offers maximum clarity and precision, it
does not very readily lend itself to a dictionary that will
be periodically enriched with the incorporation of new
corpora of poetic phrases. Numbers will have to be revised
repeatedly.

One of the most famous challenges included in this
group of formulas is the one that appears in the ballad "Don
Manuel and the Moor Muza" (ballad #66). It will be noted
that the acceptance of this challenge is in some cases
explicit (ballad #61 /00617 2: b 020-021), and in others
implicit (66 /00617 2: c & d 023-028), but there is always a
unit of discourse in which the acceptance is expressed. The
formulas that manifest this idea can, at the same time,
include other semantic content also registered in the
dictionary. For example, the "d" formulas signify
additionally "to arm with haste." As noted above, these
poetic phrases will be classified in the dictionary on the
basis of their denotative value, with the contextual
semantic definition referenced only in the index.

In spite of the numerous problematical aspects that
have as yet to be worked out in practical terms, the
Ideological Dictionary of the Poetic Language of the
Romancero promises to be far more than a research tool for
future investigations. Even in the elaboration of the model
we stand to gain new understanding of the inimitable
language of an oral poetic genre whose art has for too long
been thought elemental, natural and spontaneous.

APPENDIX I

TITU: **El hijo postumo (a-a)** /The Posthumous Son (a-a)7

GEOG: 26 /2 fr. 8 ed: 4 en var7. Lugo 2; Leon 4; Madrid 1; Avila 2; Caceres 12 /1 fr, 5 ed: 4 en var7; Badajoz 4 /1 fr, 3 ed7; Huelva 1.

INCO:#

TRAV:#

RESU:

SUMM:

+X1/// 0104... *[1]///

1///

1.1// As Don Alonso ⟨/ the king[1]⟩ (:a) and the queen ⟨/ his wife[2]⟩, far along in her pregnancy (:b), travel toward Zaragoza[3] /⟨Granada[4]⟩, in order that she may give birth in her own land[3] ⟨/ #[4]⟩ (:c), they are over-taken on the road (:d) by an infidel army (:e)[5] ⟨/ by misfortune (:f)[6]⟩. Don Alonso / the king[1] / Barcelona[7] is killed with all those in his company (:g), and the queen is mortally wounded (:h)*[8]//

1.2// While Don Alonso (:a) and the queen, far along in her pregnancy (:b), are travelling (:d), he stabs her (:i)*[9]///

2///

2.1// The child is born from the wound (:a) ⟨+ without the aid of his mother (:b)[1]⟩ ⟨+ with the help of a villager who performs a caesarean on the dead (:d) mother (:c)[2] / with the help of some passersby (:e)[3]⟩ *[4]//

2.2.//#*[5]///

3///

3.1// Those present at[1] ⟨/ the villager who helps with[2]⟩ the posthumous birth of the child baptize him (:a), entrusting him to supernatural godparents (:b),[1] and ⟨/ #[2]⟩ /give[3] ⟨/ gives[2]⟩ him to a young and healthy peasant woman (:c)[4] to be raised ⟨/ #[5]⟩*[6]//

3.2// The queen, near death, entrusts those present ⟨/ a servant[7]⟩ to see that her son is raised by an unmarried nurse (:d)[8] ⟨/ by one of the child's aunts[9] / by the child's grandmother[10]⟩, who would devote herself exclusively to him (:e), | who would lavish him with maternal affection (:f) and would keep alive the memory of his unfortunate birth (:g)[11] ⟨/ |#[12]⟩. | Furthermore she requests that, if the child dies[13] ⟨/ furthermore she requests that, if she dies[14] / the newborn himself demands that, if he dies[15]⟩ (:h), he ⟨/she[14]⟩ / be buried in an open field (:i) to proclaim his ⟨/her[14]⟩ misfortune (:j)[16] ⟨/ to lie forgotten (:k)[17] / to proclaim the parricide (:1)[10]⟩ ⟨/ |#[18]⟩*[19]//

3.3// The queen, near death, beseeches those present to take the child (:m) and to make him a shepherd when he is grown (:n), but to keep his father's memory alive (:o)*[20]///

4///

4*1// The posthumous son matures precociously (:a) and, in a prodigious manner, achieves during childhood the demeanor and habits of a knight (:b); finally, before reaching adolescence, he occupies the throne (:c)*[1]//

4.2// #*2///

CONT: 0101 El pastor desesperado /The Desperate Shepherd/
    0104 La flor del agua /The Water Flower/

NOIN::

X1/// *1 Madrid///

1/// 1 Lugo; 2 León (mayoría); 3 León, Ávila, Cáceres, Badajoz, Huelva; 4 Lugo; 5 Lugo, Madrid, León (1 ver); 6 León (mayoría), Ávila, Cáceres, Badajoz, Huelva; 7 Madrid; *8 Toda la tradición (salvo 1 ver); *9 Cáceres (1 ver: Herrera de Alcántara)///

2/// 1 León (1 ver), Madrid; 2 León (mayoría); 3 Lugo; *4 Toda la tradición (salvo 2 ver); *5 Cáceres (2 ver: Alcuéscar)///

3/// 1 Lugo, Madrid; 2 León; 3 Lugo; 4 Lugo, León; 5 Madrid; *6 Lugo, Madrid, León; 7 Ávila, Cáceres (mayoría), Badajoz; 8 Ávila (1 ver), Cáceres (1 ver), Badajoz; 9 León (1 ver), Ávila (1 ver), Cáceres (mayoría); 10 Cáceres (1 ver: Herrera de Alcántara); 11 León (1 ver), Ávila, Cáceres (minoria), Badajoz (1 ver); 12 Cáceres (mayoría), Badajoz (1 ver); 13 Ávila (1 ver), Cáceres (mayoría), Badajoz (mayoría); 14 León (1 ver), Cáceres (1 ver); 15 Ávila (1 ver), Cáceres (2 ver),

Badajoz (1 ver); 16 Leon (1 ver), Avila, (1 ver), Caceres, (mayoria), Badajoz; 17 Avila (1 ver); 18 Caceres (1 ver: Talavan); *19 Leon (1 ver: Cabanillas), Avila, Caceres, Badajoz; *20 Huelva///

4/// *1 Lugo, Leon (mayoria); *2 Madrid, Leon (1 ver: Cabanillas), Avila, Caceres, Badajoz, Huelva///

DISC:

1///

:a) ⟨Caminaba don Alonso, ⟩a caballo (~don Alonso) caminaba /Leo, Avi, Cac, Bad7 / ⟨Ya se salió don Alonso ⟩ya se salió de su casa /Cac, Hue7 / ⟨Hoy se marcha nuestro rey ⟩de Madrid para Granada /Lug7

:b) ⟨También caminó la reina ⟩de nueve meses preñada /Lug7 ⟨Lleva la reina (~su mujer) consigo ⟩de nueve (~siete ~ocho) meses preñada /Leo, Avi, Cac, Bad, Hue7

:c) ⟨Fue a parir a Zaragoza ⟩siendo ella (~porque era ~que linda) zaragozana /Leo, Avi, Cac, Bad, Hue7 / ⟩De Madrid para Granada /Lug7

:d) ⟨En el medio del (~índose por el ~a la vuelta del) camino /Lug, Leo, Avi, Cac, Bad, Hue7~ ⟨Y en el camino se encuentra /Mdd7

:e) ⟩Se encontró con gran battalla /Lug7 + ⟨toda era gente negra, ⟩cristiana non era nada (~nadia) /Lug7~ ⟩A los moros en battalla /Mdd7~ ⟩Le salió mala compana /Leo7

:f) ⟩La fortuna desgraciada /Leo7^2~ ⟩Le (~les) sucedió una desgracia /Leo, Cac, Bad, Hue7^3

:g) ⟨Mataron a don Alonso (~a Barcelona) ⟩y a la gente que llevaba /Mdd, Leo, Avi, Cac, Bad, Hue7

:h) ⟨Y a la buena (~triste) de la reina ⟩le dieron de puñaladas /Lug, Mdd, Leo, Avi, Cac, Bad, Hue7

:i) ⟩Le ha dado de puñaladas /Cac7^4///

2///

:a) ⟨Por donde el puñal (la daga) entró ⟩la mano el niño asomaba (~⟩el niño la mano saca) /Mdd, Leo, Avi, Cac, Bad, Hue7^1 ~⟨Por donde el puñal entró un tierno (~blanco) niño

asomaba /̄Ca̱c̱7² / Le sacan un nino vivo por medio de una
illarga /Lu̱g̱7

:b)   ⟨El niño quiere nacer, ⟩su madre no le ayudaba
(⌐dejaba) /Le̱o̱, Mḏḏ7³

:c)   ⟨Pasó (⌐vino) por allí un pastor (⌐hombre), ⟩que la
gracia de Dios haya (⌐⟩que guardaba ovejas blancas) /Le̱o̱7⁴
+ abre el cuerpo a la mujer ⟩y el niño vivo lo saca /Le̱o̱7⁴⁻

:d)   Quédate con Dios, el cuerpo, (⌐⟨el cuerpo se quedó
allí) San Miguel te pese (⌐le pesa) el alma /Le̱o̱7⁴

:e)   Vid 2:a (Lug)///

3///

:a)   ⟨Lo llevaron bautizare ⟩a la eirexa más cercana /Lu̱g̱7

:b)   ⟨Y de padrinos le dieron ⟩una gente muy honrada: ⟨al
santo Cristo de Burgos ⟩y la Virgen soberana /Lu̱g̱7 / ⟨Le
nombraron por madrina ⟩a la gloriosa Santa Ana, ⟨le
nombraron por padrino ⟩a San Juan de las Montañas /M̄ḏḏ7

:c)   ⟨El nino lo llevo yo (⌐⟨este niño que aquí llevo) ⟩le
tengo de buscar ama, ⟨aunque sea morenita ⟩tenga la lecha
delgada (⌐⟨que sea rosa del pecho ⟩y de la leche liviana)
/Le̱o̱7¹ / ⟨Y lo dieron a criar ⟩a una niña que allí estaba,
⟨delgadina de cintura ⟩y algo morena de cara /Lu̱g̱7

:d)   ⟨Toma a criar a este niño, ⟩toma a criar a este alma
/̄Ca̱c̱7² ⌐⟨Toma, criada, (⌐criada, toma) este niño ⟩dale a
criar a un ama /Āvi, Cac, Ba̱ḏ7³ ⌐⟨Toma, criada, este nino
⟩llévamelo a tierra extraña /̄Ca̱c̱7⁴

:e)   ⟨No se lo des a víuda, ⟩tampoco a recién casada,
⟨dáselo a una solterita ⟩que le quiera más que al alma /Āvi,
Cac, Ba̱ḏ7⁵⌐ ⟨No se lo des a víuda, ⟩ni a soltera ni a
casada, ⟨dáselo a una tia suya⁶ (⌐ se lo darás a su abuela)⁷
⟩que lo quiera más que al alma /Le̱o̱, Avi, Ca̱c̱7⁶

:f)   ⟨Y cuando le dé la teta ⟩que le diga estas palabras:
⟨Mama la teta, mi vida, ⟩mama la teta, mi alma /Le̱o̱7⁸ / ⟨Que
le diga: Hijo mío, ⟩hijo de las mis entrañas (⌐⟩hijo de toda
mi alma⌐ ⟩hijo de la desdichada) /Āvi, Cac, Ba̱ḏ7⁹

:g)   ⟨Que naciste por los montes (⌐en campos verdes)
⟩pudiendo nacer en casa /Le̱o̱, Avi, Cac, Ba̱ḏ7¹⁰

:h)   ⟨Si acaso (⌐y si) se muere el niño (⌐mi hijo) (⌐⟨este
niño si se muere) /Āvi, Cac, Ba̱ḏ7¹¹ ⌐⟨Si acaso yo me

muriera /Leo, Cac/[12]   Madre, si yo me muriese /Avi, Cac, Bad/[13]

:i)   >No le (~me) entierren en sagrado, <entiérrenle (~me) en campo (~prado) verde >donde pazga (~no pazca ~no pase ~pise ~no llegue) el ganado (cfr 0101) /Leo, Avi, Cac, Bad/

:j)   <Y a la cabecera (~en cada esquina) pongan >un Cristo crucificado (~>un letrero colorado) <con letras de oro (~unas letras) que digan >aquí murió un desdichado (~desgraciado) (cfr 0101) /Leo, Avi, Cac, Bad/ +<No murio de calentura >ni de dolor de costado, <que murió de mal de amor (~murió de una puñalada) >que es un mal desesperado (cfr 0101) (~que su majestad le ha dado ~>porque Dios se lo había dado~>que don Santiago le ha dado~>que a mi madre le habían dado) /Avi, Cac, Bad/

:k)   <Sólo las cabras de San José >que pasen al rastrojado <y la mas pequeña de ellas >lleve un changarro <que vaya diciendo >chimilimingo, chimilimango /Avi/[14]

:l)   <No ha muerto de calentura >ni de dolor de costado (cfr 0101), <que murió de puñaladas, >su padre se las ha dado /Cac/

:m)   <Arrecogerme este niño >en el pico de esta capa /Hue/

:n)   <Y cuando sea grandecito >me lo mandáis guardar cabras /Hue/

:o)   <No vaya a monte ni a sierra, >sino a una peñita blanca, <que la pintó don Alonso >con la punta de su espada /Hue/////

4///

:a)   <Medraballe mais n-un día >que o outro n-unha semana /Lug/ / <No tenía el niño un año, >cuando padre y madre llama; <no tenía el niño dos, >cuando se viste y se calza /Leo/

:b)   <Al cabo de nueve meses >regia capa y espada /Lug/~ <No tenía el niño tres, >cuando regia (~ceñia) la espada /Leo/

:c)   <Y al cabo de los diez meses (~nueve años) >era rey por toda España /Lug/~ <No tenía el niño cuatro, >cuando era rey de Granada /Leo/////

NODI:

1/// 1 Leo (1 ver: Millaró); 2 Leo (2 ver); 3 Leo (1 ver: Cabanillas); 4 Cac (1 ver: Herrera de Alcántara)///
2/// 1 Cac (mayoría); 2 Cac (3 ver); 3 Leo (1 ver: Millaró); 4 Leo (mayoría)///

3/// 1 Leo (mayoría); 2 Cac (1 ver: Valencia de Alcántara); 3 Cac (mayoría); 4 Cac (1 ver: Aliseda); 5 Avi (1 ver: Sotalvo), Cac (1 ver: Talaván); 6 Leo (1 ver: Cabanillas), Avi (1 ver: Aliseda de Tormes), Cac (mayoría); 7 Cac (1 ver: Herrera de Alcántara); 8 Leo (1 ver: Cabanillas); 9 Cac (4 ver), Bad (1 ver); 10 Leo (1 ver: Cabanillas), Avi (1 ver: Aliseda), Cac (1 ver: Talaván), Bad (1 ver: Villanueva de la Serena); 11 Avi (1 ver: Aliseda), Cac (mayoría), Bad (mayoría); 12 Leo (1 ver: Cabanillas), Cac (1 ver: Malpartida); 13 Avi (1 ver: Sotalvo), Cac (1 ver: Alcuescar), Bad (1 ver: Villanueva de la Serena); 14 Avi (1 ver: Aliseda)///

BIBL: Berjano 1903, 340; García Plata 1903, 401-402; Gil, B. 1931, I-55-56 + 35 (mel); Gil, B. 1944-47-48; Menéndez Pidal 1910, 371-373 (1 fact, a base de 5 ed ined, + 4 en var).

OTIT: Goyri 1ª, num 83; Goyri 2ª, num 57 / Nacimiento de Sancho Garcés.

IANT: # (Cfr. Por los mas espessos montes y lugares de Navarra).

IMOD: Hoy se marcha nuestro rey de Madrid para Granada;
    Caminaba don Alonso, a caballo caminaba;
    Don Alonso, don Alonso, don Alonso caminaba;
    Ya se salió don Alonso, ya se salió de su casa.

MANDAR CALLAR

1400026	a 044A		<Cala a boca, mê filho Rodrigues, >p|
1400026	a 044B		'a tu sês bem ensinado. <Na corte d'el-|
1400026	a 044C	interrumpir un	rei Fernandes >ũ bof'tão me era dado|
1400026	a 044D	mensaje	<do conde Lisardo (˜<passaram-me pela |
1400026	a 044E		barba) >e também fui resondado [Mad]|

1400028	a 088A		<O menino, cale a boca, >p'ó menino |
1400028	a 088B	protestar algo	sê bem ensinado, <qu'ũ menino de qui|
1400028	a 088C	dicho	nze anos >não era p'ra ser tão mal cri|
1400028	a 088D		ado [Mad]|

14000216	c 157A		<Cala a boca, mê filho Rodrigues, >p|
14000216	c 157B	protestar algo	'a tu sês bem ensinado, <pois então va|
14000216	c 157C	dicho	i dar parte ao rei >que o conde tinhas m|
14000216	c 157D		atado [Mad]|

14000219	b 175A	tranquilizar	<Cállese, mi padre, calle >esto no le d|
14000219	b 175B		é cuidado [Ovi]|

1900012	a 015A	protestar algo	<Calla, calla tú, Ximena, >no seas de m|
1900012	a 015B	dicho (reprochar)	al hablare [Mar]|

2000043	d 038A		<Cállate tú, hija mía, >que no te ten|
2000043	d 038B		go olvidada [Zam]|

3900475	a 094A	interrumpir un	<Vamos, vamos, Isabel, >déjese de tanto|
3900475	a 094B	mensaje	hablar (˜tant parlar) [Ler, Bar]|

3900475	a 095A	interrumpir un	˜ <Vagi, vagi, Isabela, >es cuidi de ta|
3900475	a 095B	mensaje	nt rondar, <no en gastem tant amb romanc|
3900475	a 095C		os [Ger]|

3900475	a 096A	interrumpir un	˜ <Remate, doña Isabel, >remate usted |
3900475	a 096B	mensaje	de hablar [Hca]|

225

3900475	a 097A	interrumpir un		\<Vaites, vaites, Caralinda (~\<baja, b|
3900475	a 097B	mensaje		aja, Carolina), >déjate de (~non sea) |
3900475	a 097C			tanto hablar [Cor]|

6500665	a 024A	No enfático	\<Calléis, calléis, mi señor rey, >|
6500665	a 024B		que yo tal eso no haría [Mar]|

6800693	b 047A	protestar algo	/ \<Calae-vos, minha mulher, >não me dob|
6800693	b 047B	dicho (consolar?)	res o meu mal [Aço]|

710006X1	f 014A	maldición	\<Mala (~cala,) filla, mala (~cala,) fil|
710006X1	f 014B		la (~\<calla tu, hija traidora), >siemp|
710006X1	f 014C		re fuche (~ para mí fue) desdichada (~\<
710006X1	f 014D		calla tú, hija malvada) [Lug, Leo]|

710006X2	a 024A	protestar algo	\<Cale, cale, ay mi padre, >non diga mala|
710006X2	a 024B	dicho	palabra! [Lug]|

710006X2	a 026A	protestar algo	\<Calle, calle, la mujer, >no diga la |
710006X2	a 026B	dicho	tal palabra [Leo]|

710006X2	b 028A	protestar algo	\<Calle, la mi madre, calle, >de eso no d|
710006X2	b 028B	dicho	iga usted nada [Ovi]|

710006X2	d 031A	protestar algo	\<Calle, la mi suegra, calle (~\<no diga u|
710006X2	d 031B	dicho	sted, doña Juana) >no diga usted tal pa|
710006X2	d 031C		labra (~>no sea desvergonzada ~>no se h|
710006X2	d 031D		alle incomodada) [Lug, Ovi, Leo]|

710006X2	d 033A	tranquilizar	\<Calle, calle, la viudina, >qu'eo con|
710006X2	d 033B		ella me casara (=0253 [Ovi]|

7300063	d 012A	tranquilizar	\<Cala lá, dona Maria, >não na pasar a |
7300063	d 012B		teu cargo, \<passará-la a meu lado, >mo|
7300063	d 012C		ntado no meu cavalo [Port]|

DESAFIAR

| 0500275 | b 030A | amenaza | >De aquí no te escaparás; >con la vida| |
| 0500275 | b 030B | | pagarás >por ser delito mayor (L) [Chi]| |

0500278	b 038A	desafiante /	<Quietos se me estén, señores, >que ni	
0500278	b 038B	amenaza	nguno se me mueva, <que el que intente m	
0500278	b 038C		enearse >le he de cortar la cabeza [Cad,	
0500278	b 038D		Sev]	

05002710	a 047A	desafiante	<En chanza lo tomé, tío [Cad, Sev]	
05002710	b 048A		>Porque a tomarlo de veras <no queda gen	
05002710	b 048B		te en palacio >ni en vuestros hombros ca	
05002710	b 048C		beza [Cad, Sev]	

05002710	b 049A	desafiante	+<Mira esta espada >que tiene filos crud	
05002710	b 049B		eles <que ha hecho muchas hazañas >y h	
05002710	b 049C		a matado algunos reyes [Sev]	

| 1400027 | j 072A | desafiante | +<a ver si alguno le dice: >Ahí va el h| |
| 1400027 | j 072B | | ijo del villano [Sev] |

| 1400027 | l 076A | reto | <Compte Sano, surt al camp, >que t'esper| |
| 1400027 | l 076B | | per peleiar [Ibi]| |

1400027	l 077A	reto	/ <Ê te desafio, conde, >ê te desafio,	
1400027	l 077B		diabo, <p'a tu is àquele campo, >	
1400027	l 077C		àquele campo escampado, <and' ê brig'	
1400027	l 077D		e mais homes, >quer a pé, quer a cavalo	
1400027	l 077E		[Mad]	

1400027	n 081A	reto + plazo	<Tres horas le doy, buen rey, >para ensi	
1400027	n 081B		llar su caballo; <si a las tres horas no	
1400027	n 081C		sale, >quedará por afrentado [Ovi]	

1400029	b 095A	reto + plazo	<Compte Sano, surt al camp, >que amb tu	
1400029	b 095B		venc a peleiar; <si dins una hora no hi	
1400029	b 095C		ets, >et tractaré de covart [Ibi]	

1400029	b 097A	reto	/ <Ê te desafio, conde, >ê te desafio,	
1400029	b 097B		diabo, <p'a tu is àquele campo, >	
1400029	b 097C		àquele campo escampado, <and' ê brig'	
1400029	b 097D		e mais homes, >quer a pé, quer a cavalo	
1400029	b 097E		[Mad]	

| 1400029 | b 098A | reto | / <Que con ser Rodrigo y todo >tengo de | |
| 1400029 | b 098B | | salir al campo [Ovi]| |

```
14000210 a 101A   aceptación reto   / <Eu te convido, Rodrigues,  >para ir a |
14000210 a 101B                      Campo Largo,  <adonde vão os mais homens|
14000210 a 101C                      ,  >ir a pé, ir a cavalo [Mad]|

14000210 a 103A   aceptación reto   +<Eu hei de matar Rodrigues,  >na corte f|
14000210 a 103B                      ui desafiado [Mad]|

14000210 a 104A   aceptacíon reto   / <Também te desafio, Rodrigues,  >seja |
14000210 a 104B                      a pé, seja a cavalo [Mad]|

14000217 c 166A   reto              <Si està per avenjado  >un patge pot e|
14000217 c 166B                      nviar;  <si no basta un, dos, tres, quatr|
14000217 c 166C                      e  >poden venir a peleiar;  <i si no esta|
14000217 c 166D                       satisfet,  >surti el rei des seu pala|
14000217 c 166E                      u [Ibi]|

14000217 c 167A   reto              / <Hay alguno entre vosotros,  >primos, p|
14000217 c 167B                      arientes o hermanos  <que salgan a la dem|
14000217 c 167C                      anda?  >aquí para el campo aguardo (L) (|
14000217 c 167D                      =0036) [Mal]|

14000226 b 205A   reto              <Venha tres, ou venha quatro,  >ou o rei |
14000226 b 205B                      com mil diabos (=0067) [Mad]|

1700361  a 001A   reto              <Hay alguno entre vosotros  >primos, pari|
1700361  a 001B                      entes o hermanos,  <que salgan a la deman|
1700361  a 001C                      da?  >Aquí para el campo aguardo [Mal]|

2100325  c 038A   amenaza           <O primeiro qu'atirar  >morrera logo ao |
2100325  c 038B                      pé dela [TrM]|

2100325  c 039A   amenaza           ~<Todo el que a esa niña toque  >le co|
2100325  c 039B                      rtaré la cabeza [Mar]|

2100325  c 040A   desafiante        / <Se m'a vós mandais caçar  >eu ficare|
2100325  c 040B                      i a par d'ela [TrM]|

2800452  a 008A   retar             / <Allí viene un perro moro  >a todos de|
2800452  a 008B                      safiando [Leo]|

2800452  h 026A   retar (implícito) / <Antes que a Valencia llegue  >un bille|
2800452  h 026B   + enviar carta    te ha mandado [Mar]|

28004510 l 260A   reto              <Mais antes que me lo seas  >hemos de xog|
28004510 l 260B                      ar la espada [Zam]|
```

```
28004510 m 262A  reto (ironía)      ~<Ó vem tu cá, ó meu genro  >vem-te |
28004510 m 262B                     ca coraço meu ( ~ó meu genro mais amad|
28004510 m 262C                     o), <que até agora fosteis paz, >agora|
28004510 m 262D                     es genro meu [Mad]|

3200532 e 024A  reto                <Si no me los quieres dar, >a las armas,|
3200532 e 024B                      moro perro ( caballero) [Lug, Ori]|

3200532 e 025A  reto                <Vamos a la lucha, moro, >vamos a la |
3200532 e 025B                      lucha, perro [Lug]|

3200533 a 026A  reto + aceptación  <A las armas, dijo el moro. >El cristian|
3200533 a 026B       reto           o: Bien las quiero! [Ori]|

3200533 a 027A  reto                ~<A las armas, cristianillo, >a las ar|
3200533 a 027B                      mas, non che hay medo [Lug]|

3200533 a 028A  aceptación reto     ~<A la lucha sí por cierto, >a la luc|
3200533 a 028B                      ha no le temo [Lug]|

6400703 e 019A  reto                <Apercíbete a batalla >que aquí te agu|
6400703 e 019B                      ardo en el campo (L) [Cad]|

6600611 i 009A  retar               ~<Ya salía el moro Muza [San]|

6600611 i 010A  retar               ~<Ahí viene el perro moro [Ovi]|

6600611 j 012A  retar               <Corneta de oro en su boca >ciertamente |
6600611 j 012B                      amenazando [San]|

6600611 j 013A                      ~>Ricamente amenazando [San]|

6600611 j 014A                      / >A todos desafiando [Ovi]|

6600611 k 015A  reto                <Salid, valientes de España, >que vos e|
6600611 k 015B                      stoy aguardando [San]|

6600611 k 016A  reto                +<Salga uno, salgan dos, >salgan tres y |
6600611 k 016B                      salgan cuatro <y si no basta con ( ~todo|
6600611 k 016C                      ) eso, >salga el mismo rey Fernando ( ~d|
6600611 k 016D                      on Manuel Fernando) (=0067) [San]|

6600611 k 017A  retar               ~<Salga uno, salgan dos ( ~<De esa ciud|
6600611 k 017B                      ad de Burgos) >salgan ( ~vengan) tres o |
6600611 k 017C                      salgan ( ~ y vengan) cuatro, <venga ese d|
6600611 k 017D                      on ( ~y también salga) Manuel >que es g|
6600611 k 017E                      ran hombre ( ~valiente) de a caballo [Leo|
6600611 k 017F                      , Ovi]|
```

```
6600612  b 020A  aceptar reto    <Si no ser ( ~saliendo) un don Manuel  >q|
6600612  b 020B                  ue de heridas está malo [San]|

6600612  b 021A  aceptar reto    ~<Bien lo oyera don Manuel, >de altas |
6600612  b 021B                  torres ha bajado [Leo]|

6600612  c 023A                  <Bien lo oía ( ~ya lo oyera) don Manuel |
6600612  c 023B                  ( ~<don Manuel lo estaba oyendo) >que en|
6600612  c 023C                  la cama está muy malo ( ~echado) [San]|
                 aceptar reto
6600612  d 025A  (implícito)     <Aprisa pide ( ~aprisa,) el vestido ( ~la|
6600612  d 025B  + acudir        ropa), >aprisa pide ( ~aprisa,) el calz|
6600612  d 025C  apresuradamente ado [San, Leo, Ovi]|

6600612  d 026A  aceptar reto    +<Aprisa ( ~a vuelo) pide las armas ( ~la|
6600612  d 026B  (implícito)     silla) >y su ligero ( ~para ensillar su|
6600612  d 026C  + acudir apres. ) caballo [San, Leo, Ovi]|

6600612  d 027A  aceptar reto    ~<De prisa ( ~pronto) pide el vestido, |
6600612  d 027B  (implícito)     >de prisa ( ~pronto) pide el calzado [Sa|
6600612  d 027C  + acudir apres. n]|

6600612  d 028A  acudir apres.   +<Si de prisa ( pronto) lo ha pedido, >|
6600612  d 028B                  más deprisa se lo han dado [San]|

6600612  d 029A  aceptar reto    ~<No bien lo acabó de oir >cuando ya |
6600612  d 029B  + acudir apres. pidió el caballo; <por aprisa que lo pi|
6600612  d 029C                  de, >más aprisa se lo han dado [San]|

6700672  d 010A  retar           / <Allí viene un ( ~el) perro moro >a t|
6700672  d 010B                  odos desafiando [0045 + 0061 Leo, Ovi]|

6700672  j 024A  reto            <Salga uno, salgan dos, >salgan tres y (|
6700672  j 024B                  ~o) salgan cuatro, <si no quisiere ( ~s|
6700672  j 024C                  aliere) ninguno ( ~<si no bastan todos es|
6700672  j 024D                  os) >salga el mismo ( ~aquí el) rey ( ~|
6700672  j 024E                  rey don) Fernando [0045 Mar +0003 Mar +00|
6700672  j 024F                  61 San]|

6700672  j 025A  reto            ~<Salgan, si han quedado algunos, >de |
6700672  j 025B                  los Manriques Guzmanes (L) [Cad]|

6700672  j 026A  reto            +<Salga ese Portocarrero, >señor de Par|
6700672  j 026B                  ma nombrado, <o salga don Manuel Ponce, |
6700672  j 026C                  >ése de Leon llamado [Cad]|
```

```
6700672  j 027A  reto      +<Salga uno, salgan dos,  >salgan tres o |
6700672  j 027B            salgan cuatro [Cad]|

6700672  j 028A  reto      +<Y si acaso a todos juntos  >ánimo y va|
6700672  j 028B            lor les falten,  <salga el mismo don Fern|
6700672  j 028C            ando,  >de ánimo y valor se arme (L) [Ca|
6700672  j 028D            d]|

6700672  j 029A  reto      / <Salga uno, salgan dos,  >salgan tres o|
6700672  j 029B            salgan cuatro,  <y también salga Manuel|
6700672  j 029C            ,  >que es valiente de a caballo [0061 Ov|
6700672  j 029D            i]|

6700672  j 030A  reto       ~<De esa ciudad de Burgos  >vengan tres|
6700672  j 030B            y vengan cuatro,  <venga ese don Manuel |
6700672  j 030C            >que es gran hombre de caballo [0061 Leo|
6700672  j 030D            ]|

6700672  q 037A  retar     <Corneta de oro en su boca  >ciertamente |
6700672  q 037B            amenazando [0061 San]|

6700672  q 038A             ->Ricamente amenazando [0061 San]|

6700672  t 041A  reto      ...<A todos os reto y trato  >de viles y |
6700672  t 041B            de cobardes (L) [Cad]|

6700672  u 042A  reto      <Salga Pulgar, porque pudo  >fijar en Gra|
6700672  u 042B            nada el Ave,  <a ver si él sabe librarle|
6700672  u 042C            >de este nebrí que la trae (L) [Cad]|

6700672  w 044A  reto + plazo   <En la vega os espero  >hasta las seis de|
6700672  w 044B            la tarde (L) [Cad]|

6700672  x 045A  reto + insulto  <Cobrad vuestro Ave María,  >cristianos,|
6700672  x 045B            viles cobardes! (L) [Cad]|

8001123  g 062A  desafiante  +<empenhando as suas barbas ( ~<vinha pux|
8001123  g 062B            ando pelos vagos)  >Dom João lh'o pagari|
8001123  g 062C            a [Aço]|

8001123  g 063A  desafiante   ~<Perro mouro vem jurando  >que Dom Joã|
8001123  g 063B            o le pegaria,  <que a barba de Dom João|
8001123  g 063C            >na mão dele ficaria [Mad]|

8001123  g 064A  desafiante  +<Perro mouro vem jurando  >que Dom João|
8001123  g 064B            le pagará,  <que a barba de Dom João  |
8001123  g 064C            >na mão dele ficará [Mad]|
```

NOTES

[1] The Instituto (formerly, Catedra) "Seminario Menéndez Pidal" of the Universidad Complutense of Madrid (hereafter the Institute is referred to as the IMP, regardless of chronology) has carried out this work under the supervision of its Research Director, Diego Catalan, and in collaboration with a number of institutions and researchers affiliated with other centers. Cooperating institutions include the IMP, the Center for Iberian and Latin American Studies, an organized Research Unit of the University of California, San Diego, and the University of Wisconsin Madison Academic Computing Center. Specialists and members of the IMP research team are associated with the Universidad Complutense de Madrid, the University of California, San Diego, the Colegio de Mexico, the University of Washington, Seattle, the University of Wisconsin, Madison, the University of California, Davis and the University of Pennsylvania.

[2] In terms of its temporal, geographic, and numerical amplitude the Romancero corpus is in many ways ideally suited to the study of oral poetic discourse. In the case of many romances the re-creative process can be observed over the course of five centuries and, occasionally, in as many as a thousand or more versions of a single ballad theme collected directly form the oral traditions of all areas where one of the Hispanic languages is spoken (from Argentina, Chile, and Brazil to Costa Rica, Cuba, and Mexico; from Texas, New Mexico, and California to Washington and New York; from Portugal and Spain to the Azores and the Canary Islands; from Bosnia, Salonica, and Smyrna to Rhodes and Morocco). While the size and continuity of this corpus allows for exhaustive synchronic and diachronic comparisons of hundreds of versions of one or more ballad themes, the vast quantity of data that must be analyzed and interpreted can only be adaquately processed with the aid of a computer.

[3] In these early stages we have concentrated primarily on the modern tradition in an effort to expand, organize and make available the wealth of largely unedited ballad materials housed in the Menéndez Pidal Archive--the largest single modern collection of Hispanic ballad materials in existence.

232

[4]The original file comprised three major private collections of bibliographic information: the holdings of the Menéndez Pidal Archive in Madrid, the materials collected for the Armistead-Silverman-Katz Judeo-Spanish ballad project and the sources compiled by A. Sánchez Romeralo. To this corpus were added bibliographic materials cited in published sources or uncovered while examining the holdings of two Spanish research institutes.

[5]Edited by Anthony Cárdenas, John Nitti and Jean Gilkison (Madison: Hispanic Seminary of Medieval Spanish Studies, 1975).

[6]Antonio Sánchez Romeralo, Samuel G. Armisted, and Suzanne H. Petersen, eds., Bibliografía del Romancero oral / Bibliography of the Hispanic Ballad in Oral Tradition, I (BRO), (Madrid: CSMP/Gredos, 1980). One advantage of using computer-aided techniques in a publication of this sort is reflected in the overall time involved in its preparation: less than a year elapsed between the moment when initial transcription of the entries was begun and production of phototypeset copy of the file was completed.

[7]Large published collections of oral Hispanic ballads (Romanceros and Cancioneros containing numerous romances) will be described in a second edition of BIDRO.

[8]In order to acknowledge the contributions of all who collaborate in the preparation of BIDRO the complete bibliographic citation includes the name and institutional affiliation of the person responsible for the description.

[9]These permanent, arbitrarily chosen, identification numbers are used in all studies and publications by the IMP and its collaborators. Our hope is that they will be accepted and used henceforth by others in the field, thereby minimizing the confusion resulting from the use of various titles and first verses in referring to Hispanic ballads.

[10]The "Encuesta-Norte, 1977," the second of seven major IMP field trips to date, covered a broad arc along the Cantabrian Cordillera from northern Palencia and southern Santander, through the entire northern portion of Leon and into eastern Lugo and Zamora. Four of the five subsequent annual IMP field trips have concentrated on completing the exploration of the entire northwestern part of the Peninsula.

[11]For more background on the AIER, the publication series and the technology used in the preparation of the first two volumes, see my edition of Voces nuevas del Romancero castellanoleones, AIER-Textos, I-II (Madrid: Gredos, 1982), xxxiii-xlviii.

[12]The diagnostics provided at this stage are particularly valuable in dealing with foreign language texts requiring accents and with any material in fixed format, such as poetic verse. Diagnostic messages alert the proofer to the location of any illegal character combinations, of verses which exceed the width of the print block, and so forth. Effective use of the galleys obtained with the Prooflister program both accelerates the rate and holds down the cost of production. One can generate and correct two or three proof copies in as many days and the per-page cost of a proof listing ($.03) compares very favorably to that of a photo-composed page ($2.50-$3.50 / linear foot).

[13]The selection of ballad materials for publication in the AIER-Texts series is done on the basis of their scholarly interest and the availability of supplementary funding.

[14]Collaborators who have access to an off-line system or who can work interactively with a text editor program at a computer facility are encouraged to submit machine-readable transcriptions of their ballad materials on digital cassettes, 8 inch single density floppy disks or on a magnetic tape that meets the following tape specifications: an ASCII (or in its absence, EBCDIC), 9 track, 1600bpi, unlabeled tape with fixed record length and fixed blocking.

[15]The project was first described in a collective paper, Jesus Antonio Cid, et al., "Towards the Elaboration of a General Descriptive Catalogue of the Pan-Hispanic Romancero," in El Romancero hoy: Poética / The Hispanic Ballad Today: Poetics, ed. Samuel G. Armistead, Diego Catalán, et al. (Madrid: Gredos, 1979), pp. 335-63. A reformulation of the theoretical principles on which the CGR is based appears in Diego Catalán's article "Descripción de modelos translingüísticos dinámicos: a propósito del Catálogo general del Romancero Pan-Hispánico," in Studia Linguistica in Honorem Eugenio Coseriu (1921-1981), No. 5, (Madrid, Berlin: Gredos, W. de Gruyter, 1981), 245-254. In the following, necessarily brief, review of the project I attempt only to summarize some of the more central theoretical notions informing the Catalogue in order to pave

the way for a discussion of the proposed analyses of poetic discourse (in the second part of this paper). I refer the interested reader to the latest and definitive redaction of the criteria and purposes of the CGR in the editors' introduction to the first volume of the Catalogue (D. Catalán, et al., Catálogo general descriptivo del Romancero Pan-Hispánico, 3 vols /Madrid: Gredos/, 1984).

[16]In the structural analysis of traditional poetic narratives we are concerned with four levels of coherence of the text: discourse, plot, tale or fabula, and functional model, although only the first three are represented in the CGR. Like the linguistic sign, each of these generatively related structural levels is a union of a signifier and a signified. Accordingly, discourse is viewed as the expressive plane (signifier) of the invariant semantic content of the plot (signified), plot, in turn, as the signifier of the invariant content of the fabula. Thus, in addition to the traditional distinction between plot and fabula (articifial, aesthetic ordering of events versus their causal, chronological ordering), plot is viewed as a specification of the essential elements of content of the fabula.

[17]Characters modified in one segment automatically become subjects of the next sequence (although the subjects and objects of the fabula's sequential phrase may not coincide with those of the corresponding segment of the plot). For example, at the level in which plot constitutes the expressive plane of the invariant narrative content of the fabula, the object of the sequential phrase, the persona modified by an event, quite often functions as the subject of the plot.

[18]An example of variation at the level of the fabula occurs in the first narrative sequence of the sample catalogue entry given below. In that instance, in one version of the Posthumous Son the loss of four hemistichs, included in some form in all other versions, results in the transformation of the pregnant queen's husband, her natural protector, into traitor and instrument of her death. Defective narration through the accidental loss of a part of the narrative, although common, is one of the least interesting of the numerous phenomena causing fabulistic complication.

[19]The open brace actually identifies the end of a discourse variant, but once the CGR corpus of discourse is fragmented on this basis, the geographic data itself can be

used as a variable in sorting the poetic phrases registered in the catalogue.

[20]While the traditional Hispanic ballad consists of a series of 16 syllable verses divided into two octosyllabic hemistichs with a single assonant rhyme in the even-numbered hemistichs, the octosyllable is the basic unit of composition. For the present I limit my observations on the units of discourse to the conventions used to register invariants and variants at this more superficial level of semiotic organization of the texts in order that the contents of the discourse field may be read correctly. Further theoretical considerations on the units of discourse as the lexicon with which the plot is re-created in scenic form will be taken up at a later point in the paper.

[21]These two symbols, $\langle$ and $\rangle$, together with the open brace, can be used to fragment and reorganize the entire contents of this field into a corpus of 8 or 16 syllable verses.

[22]A model for an ideological dictionary of oral poetic discourse, to be discussed in the second part of this paper, requires the total fragmentation of the discourse field. A complete catalogue entry, in which the units of poetic discourse can be viewed in their proper, recognizable context, will make that discussion more meaningful.

[23]The entry is reproduced here by permission of the editors from the final photo-typeset copy of a portion of the catalogue. To save space I have suppressed the descriptive resume in Spanish (RESU) as it is identical in content to the English summary (SUMM).

[24]References are to Wolf's _Primavera_ or, failing this, Duran's _Romancero_ and to the Maria-Goyri, Menéndez Pidal and Armistead catalogues.

[25]For a description of the project and of its more significant results, see D. Catalan, et al., "Analisis electronico de la creacion poetica oral: El programa Romancero en el _Computer Center_ de UCSD," in _Homenaje a la memoria de don Antonio Rodríguez-Moñino (1910-1970)_ (Madrid: Castalia, 1975), 157-194, and S. H. Petersen, "El mecanismo de la variacion en la poesia de trasmision oral: Estudio de 612 versiones del romance de 'La condesita' con ayuda de un ordenador," Diss. University of Wisconsin, 1976.

[26]See my article "A Computer-Aided Analysis of the Problematic Relationship between Rhyme and Lexical Stability in the Traditional Hispanic Romancero," in Ballads and Ballad Research: Selected Papers of the International Conference on Nordic and Anglo-American Ballad Research, University of Washington, Seattle May 2-6, 1977, ed. Patricia Conroy (Seattle: University of Washington, 1978), pp. 88-100.

[27]See my article "Computer-Generated Maps of Narrative Affinity," in El Romancero hoy: Poética, 20 Coloquio internacional, University of California, Davis, eds. D. Catalan, S. G. Armistead and A. Sanchez Romeralo (Madrid: CSMP-University of California, Gredos, 1979), pp. 167-228.

[28]To illustrate both the extent of formal variation of a single base structure and the potential for functional transformation with limited formal variation the examples (which often encompass less than one-twentieth of the variant 8 and 16 syllable verses) include both unrelated and generatively related phrases. Where space permits I have indicated some lexical variants in parenthesis.

[29]Ruth House Webber's fine study, Formulistic Diction in the Spanish Ballad, University of California Publications in Modern Philology, Vol. 34, No. 2 (Berkeley: University of California Press, 1951), 175-278 is the corner-stone of Romancero scholarship in this area.

[30]The hierarchical structure of the Catalogue descriptions requires just such a focus. The process of extracting the narrative content from the total corpus of poetic discourse of each ballad was instrumental in our reformulation of the concept of poetic formula. The theory was first described by D. Catalán in a paper read as part of a lecture series sponsored by the Fundacion Juan March in the summer of 1981 and is fully developed in the introduction to the first three volumes of the CGR (see n. 15). In reviewing here the more essential aspects of our redefinition of poetic formulas I rely heavily on these sources.

[31]For a discussion of the problems of lexical-syntactical variability in conjunction with rhyme function see my article, "A Computer-Aided Analysis."

[32]The formulas are not internally sorted in this case but listed in order of appearance. The numbers and letter codes to the left are deciphered as follows: The first two digits are the sequential numbers of the ballad in the present corpus. The next four correspond to the permanent ID number of the ballad. The final part of that series registers the narrative sequence number (corresponding to the descriptive summary sequences). The column of single letters is the formula letter (keyed to an element of narrative content). The final four alphanumeric codes are machine generated and number the lines of each formula. The space between these numbers and the text provides a slot for appending semantic definitions. It will be noted that the text itself breaks at the seventy-ninth character position in the line, regardless of word boundaries. The vertical bar in the eightieth column is machine inserted to mark this position. The convention allows for the material to be safely copied to diskettes, edited offline and read back to magnetic computer tape for major processing.

University of Washington
Seattle

CULTURAL AND FUNCTIONAL STUDIES

BARBARA ALLEN

Sung by Mrs. J. E. Schell, Banner Elk, N. C., July 1933.

1. One bright day in the month of May,
   When all the flowers were blooming,
   This young man was taken sick
   For the love of Barbara Allen.

2. He sent his servant to her town;
   He sent him to her dwelling,
   Saying, "Here's a message for the lady fair,
   If your name be Barbara Allen."

3. Slowly, slowly she got up
   And slowly she went to him,
   But all she said when she got there
   Was, "Young man, I think you're dying."

4. "Oh, yes, I'm sick, very sick,
   And I feel very much like dying.
   I shall never see my time again
   If I don't get Barbara Allen."

5. "Oh, yes, you're sick and very sick,
   And you look very much like dying,
   You never shall see your time again
   For you'll never get Barbara Allen.

6. "Oh, don't you remember at yonders town,
   At yonders place of tavern,
   You treated all the ladies 'round
   And slighted Barbara Allen?"

7. "Oh, yes, I remember at yonders town,
   At yonders place of tavern,
   I gave a treat to the ladies 'round
   But my heart to Barbara Allen."

8. He turned his pale face to the wall,
   He turned his back upon them:
   "Adieu, adieu, fair friends to all,
   Be good to Barbara Allen."

9. Slowly, slowly she got up,
   And slowly she went from him.
   She had not gone but a mile in town,
   Till she heard his death-bell tolling.

10. As she was riding towards her home
    She heard the birds a-singing.
    They sang so loud and whistled so clear:
    "Hard-hearted Barbara Allen."

11. She looked to the east, she looked to the west,
    She saw the corpse a-coming--
    "Lay down, lay down that deathly frame
    And let me look upon it."

12. The more she looked, the more she wept,
    Until she burst out crying:
    "I might have saved one young man's life
    If I'd a done my duty.

13. "Oh, mother, dear mother, go make my bed,
    And make it soft and easy;
    Sweet William died for me today;
    I'll die for him tomorrow."

14. Sweet William died on Saturday eve,
    And Barbara died on Sunday;
    Her mother died for love of both--
    She died on Easter's Monday.

Maurice Matteson and Mellinger Edward Henry, eds. Beech Mountain Folk-Songs and Ballads. N.Y.: Schirmer, 1936, p. 12. Rpt. in Bertrand Harris Bronson. The Traditional Tunes of the Child Ballads. Princeton, N.J.: Princeton University Press, 1962, II, 350-51 (variant No. 81).

CHRISTINE A. CARTWRIGHT

"BARBARA ALLEN":
Love and Death in an Anglo-American Narrative Folksong

A purpose central to folklore scholarship is understanding the folk: using the expressive materials shared by cultural groups to illuminate the shared values, attitudes, anxieties, aesthetics, and modes of thought which make those materials meaningful and satisfying. Not only can this approach provide invaluable help to outsiders attempting to understand another cultural group, but it can also increase self-understanding within the culture itself. The ability to explain why Anglo-American folksong repeatedly conjoins love and death would be no mere academic feather in the cap of folkloristics, but a source of insight into practical and urgent social problems. The ballads are narratives of human crises. Their content, their processes of variation and performance, and the comments of singers and audience members upon them speak directly to the dynamics of crisis in Anglo-American culture: to the nature of depression and grief, to the causes of suicide, and to the cultural ways of responding to death.

Bertrand Bronson pointed out some years ago that of all the British ballads found in oral tradition in North America, the greatest favorites are songs in which love is "a disease from which no one recovers."[1] Charles Joyner in South Carolina and Colin Quigley in Newfoundland both discovered that the Child ballads found in greatest abundance in these regions almost all involve the death of one or both of a pair of lovers.[2] Roger Abrahams, comparing American versions with their British precursors, felt that New World developments often increased their fatalism, making romantic love even more hopeless and deadly than it was in the older British texts.[3] He and George Foss later devoted an entire chapter to the role of love and death as a central thematic pair in Anglo-American folksong.[4]

There is some evidence that the pair's centrality can be apparent to singers as well as to scholars--an important epistemological point in this era of concern with etic and emic perspectives in the interpretation of cultural materials.[5] Collectors in the Appalachians have learned that they must ask for "love songs" if they want Child ballads, a fact which suggests that love (if not death) is a definitive characteristic of the genre in regional thought.[6] A more complete blending of the two, in effect and in imagery, is suggested by two kinds of responses I have heard Americans make to the topic of ballads. A young New Englander recently commented: "The ballads pierce me; they do something to me I can't describe. They're so beautiful and so horrible."[7] More than one American has responded to my description of Child ballads by saying, "Oh, like the red rose and the briar: that kind of song." These spontaneous, immediate associations of the concept "ballad" with the wrenching qualities of beauty and horror in the first case, and with the emblem of dead true lovers in the second, raises the possibility that the twisting of love and death together in narrative song may help to define the ballad as an ethnic genre.

If love and death indeed form what Levi-Strauss might call a binary opposition, a pair of irreconcilable inseparables whose juxtaposition in art arouses strong, ambivalent emotions and gives depth and power to a large number of different folksongs, then a large number of folksong motifs, descriptive conventions, and general plotlines should serve to express the basic, unstated opposition. Images culturally associated with love and with death should appear in pairs, balanced one against the other in descriptions of characters, events, and scenes; they should also appear as single images with alternate or bipolar meanings. As in Chomsky's transformational grammar, a range of different plot types and individual versions should explore different aspects of the basic opposition, placing primary focus upon love or upon death, expressing a range of emotional responses to it, and using various kinds of mediation or resolution--saying the same thing, as it were, in different ways, each of which lends its own particular cast to the deep, unifying structure. In addition, if the opposition is truly cultural and truly between love and death (rather than, for instance, between love and hate or life and death), the imagery of folksong should recur in other cultural contexts in which love and death are central, such as Valentine's Day, weddings, and funerals.

Roger deV. Renwick has recently analyzed the imagery used and the attitudes expressed in English traditional songs dealing with sexual liaisons--songs in which romantic love is either absent or unrequited. He concluded that one group of these songs, the symbolic (as opposed to the euphemistic and the metaphorical), possesses a binary structure which contrasts homogeneity (qualities and states which are safe but barren) with heterogeneity (qualities and states which are fertile but threatening).[8] For example, the song may open with green fields and a May morning, which provide the context for the sexual encounter, and close with dark rooms and cold nights in which the abandoned girl must nurse her child.[9] The capacity to fall in love and the capacity to conceive are both presented as vulnerabilities: characters who possess one or both frequently suffer victimization or murder, or commit suicide.

I would argue that there is a close and significant relationship between what Renwick has termed the homogeneity-heterogeneity opposition and the love-death juxtaposition found in the romantic and tragic ballads. A key difference between the two sets of categories is that in the liason songs, love and human fertility are frequently grouped with images of cold, darkness, and death, rather than with the warmth, light, and natural fertility present in the setting for the sexual encounter. Outside of this crucial transposition, the traditional descriptive tendencies for romantic love and for heterogeneity are much the same. The resultant similarities between songs of true love and songs of sexual liasons highlight the reason for the transposition: the results of deep love and of childbirth, being potentially permanent, lead to a tragic ending <u>when they occur within the context of a temporary relationship</u>. (It is an interesting reflection of our cultural world view that pregnancy without love is not necessarily viewed as tragic, but unrequited love, with or without pregnancy, is.)

Space does not here allow for a structural-semiotic analysis of the full romantic and tragic group of ballads to complement Renwick's "The Semiotics of Sexual Liaisons." I here offer a detailed examination of only one, but a favorite: "Barbara Allen." The sources of the texts used in this study are listed at the end of the notes.

B. H. Bronson said of this most ubiquitious of British ballads in North America:

> Its popularity from the days of Pepys onward to the present, in the face of its undistinguished and unexciting content, its portrayal of unresisting surrender to untoward fortune, is, if we take the song as a fundamental expression of the spirit of the English-speaking people, a phenomenon so strange and mysterious as to deserve prolonged meditation. No love-triangle; no struggle; no complications; no hope; no courage; nothing but passive acceptance; result, the universal favourite![10]

"Barbara Allen"'s simplicity in comparison with other romantic and tragic British ballads is much like the simplicity which Mrs. Brown of Falkland's versions often possess in comparison with other versions: it is romantic tragedy pared to the essence.[11] There are no characters other than the lovers; their love does nothing but kill them both; and there is neither motive nor agent of death other than love itself.

Formally, the narrative has the abab symmetry which often shapes its stanzas: it consists of a solitary walk to the first sickbed; a procession to the graveyard; a solitary walk to the second sickbed; and a final scene after the second funeral procession. Structurally, however, "Barbara Allen" is built like a wedding. The lover initiates the action by sending his servants or friends to fetch his beloved; she follows "slowly" (a detail singers never seem to omit), as the bride's measured walk to the altar is always slow. When she reaches the place where he waits for her, he gives her a declaration, and often a token, of his love. This token is either something gold and circular, such as his watch and rings or gold coins, or it is the "outpouring" of his heart in blood or tears. (His blood is sometimes given in a white napkin, forming a powerful use of the traditional Valentine colors.) Church bells ring as she departs. The groom's friends (and in some cases the bride's also) escort him to the "home" which they will share. The bride's mother makes her daughter's bed, the two are laid side by side, and the ballad closes with the image of the lovers permanently entwined in a "true love knot" of inseparable romantic union.

It is clear that English speakers find "Barbara Allen" thoroughly satisfying without a love-triangle, without struggle, without complications. Nor is this a cultural anomaly: as Henry Glassie notes, British traditional drama can also be enjoyed for reasons which have little to do with plot development. The appeal of the Derby Tup is an especially clear example.[12] The reason in both cases may be that their art consists not so much of story as of ceremony.[13] The ballad perhaps holds love up to death as to a mirror, reflecting in detailed reversal the cultural norms for the accomplishment of permanent romantic unions. This union is brought about through the cold rejection of one lover by the other. The swelling buds and twining roses, gold rings and church bells which beautify and solemnize many traditional Anglo-American weddings here usher a young man and woman out of the community of the living rather than uniting them to bring new children into it. True love here is proven by the lovers' immediate deaths for one another rather than by their devoting their lives to one another. The ballad perhaps stands without developmental complexity because it possesses great affective density: its power to move lies less in its melody than in its chords.

The possibility that reversal is the principle from which "Barbara Allen" draws much of its cultural power is strengthened by a number of constituent reversals which appear in a high number of versions. Barbara is usually placed in the role of rejector, a role which is primarily a masculine one in Renwick's songs of sexual liaisons. Her lover, in his passive and helpless death of true love, resembles the murdered and suicidal maidens of the liaison songs. The ballad even includes a scene in which the lovers meet in the fields on what might well be a May morning, since the green buds are usually swelling as the ballad opens. Here it is the man rather than the woman who is "laid down" by his pallbearers, so that he lies on his back amid the grass and flowers while the woman bends over him. As in the liaison songs, this scene results in the woman's becoming deeply and permanently bonded to the man, but through death rather than through pregnancy. Even the usual assignation of the rose to the woman's grave and the briar to the man's is reversed in the majority of North American texts I have examined.

The reversal of ceremonies and relationships which are in themselves both metaphorically rich and structurally important is not uncommon in festivity and ritual. The medieval Feast of Fools, for example, included a mock Mass celebrated by a young boy dressed in the Bishop's robes, while the Bishop himself, along with the rest of the clergy and the upper classes, received all sorts of embarrassing treatment.[14] The feminine hero and masculine heroine of "Barbara Allen," joined in death through the ceremonial structure which is supposed to join couples in love, inverts cultural norms as central and powerful as those of the medieval Mass. Like the ethnographer's strategy of breaking cultural rules in order to clarify them, the ballad throws the normal course of courtship and marriage into sharp relief.[15]

One further structural contributor to the popularity of "Barbara Allen" should be noted. Textual variation in North America occurs primarily at two points in the narrative: the bedside scene, in which rejection is stated and accepted, and the bier-side scene, in which Barbara is confronted with her responsibility for the young man's death. Thus the emotional sequence which takes place within the central character, leading from rejection through recognition to remorse intense enough to kill her, seems to be an organizing structure used by many singers in the recreative or mnemonic process. This sequence suggests that what

singers <u>consciously</u> build when performing "Barbara Allen" is
a tale of two deaths told in three parts. Henry Glassie has
demonstrated the importance of bilateral tripartite symmetry
in the design of American folk objects such as houses and
gravestones;[16] it is logical that Americans should find the
same kinds of symmetry satisfying in ballads as they do in
other cultural creative forms.[17] The role of reversal in
contributing to the ballad's effect is likely to be less
conscious: it simply makes the ballad fascinating and
disturbing.

Fascinating and disturbing it certainly is. The New
Englander's comment on ballads in general--that they are
beautiful and horrible--is echoed in the specific responses
of two Appalachian singers to "Barbara Allen." Mrs. Rena
Hicks of Beech Mountain, North Carolina, in discussing the
ballad with folklorist Thomas Burton, applauded the depth of
love which Barbara must have had for the young man in order
to die for him while condemning the "hard-hearted" behavior
which caused her to reject him and brought about his death.
She felt that while both were real true lovers, and as such
were worthy of admiration and perhaps a bit of envy, the
sadness and irony of their fate was certainly not exemplary
or even desirable. Attracted and repelled, Mrs. Hicks felt
that the song was true to life: full of real human
ambivalencies and ambiguities.[18] Her neighbour, Lena Harmon,
summed up the ballad in this way:

> She caused a lot of this by her pride and stubborn-
> ness. She didn't think that she loved this boy;
> and, seems like, she was a little bit spiteful; a
> little bit stubborn. She did a lot of this, it
> seems, to hurt him. And then when he worried until
> he was taken sick . . . and he sent for her, and
> she was still stubborn, rejected him and all this
> until he died from grief. Then later on, you know,
> she'd seen what she'd done and started grieving
> over it, and she ended up the same way--just
> grieved herself to death; that's the way it seems
> to me. . . . I think it shows that love is
> stronger than death.[19]

The juxtaposition of love and anger or coldness in Barbara
before her lover's death, and love and grief or guilt after
it, seems to form a sort of affective tangle within the
ballad plot, one which produces a corresponding tangle in
both singers' reactions to it. A similar ambivalence is
voiced by American novelist Sterling North, whose child
character Jeremiah listens to his grandmother sing the
ballad as she weaves:

> Jeremiah could not understand the strange comfort
> old folks seemed to derive from the sorrowful story
> of the dead lovers. In his own heart it caused a
> wistful unrest. . . .[20]

Admiration and envy for true lovers, frustration at the
folly of human pride and stubbornness, strange comfort and a
wistful unrest--all probably mingle for a great many North
Americans in hearing or singing the ballad. In addition to
these explicit comments, however, we have the patterns of
textual variation and stability to use in clarifying the
relationship between the folksong and the folk.

First, the slight which Barbara fails to forgive in
time to save her young man's life, though it is left
unexplained in some texts, is always the same when it is
stated: he has toasted, bought drinks for, or flirted with
other women at a tavern or a dance. (This feature may help
to explain why the ballad could double as a dance or play-
party song in the southeastern United States and in
Newfoundland: it may have been considered an appropriate
comment on the context, and the very hyperbole of the deaths
as the consequence of improper behavior may have made it
amusing.)[21] The young man never denies that he performed the
actions of which she accuses him; his defense, when he makes
one, is that his doing so was a social and trivial gesture,
while his love for her is romantic and serious. In no
version is she ever convinced by this.

Of all the causes for which Anglo-American women
actually become cold toward their menfolk, drinking and
flirtation are probably at the top of the list. However, to
go so far as to withdraw one's love completely brings one
into conflict with the cultural premise which states that
these masculine behaviors (within certain fairly generous
limits) can and should be forgiven. Although women seem to
feel less obliged to forgive than they used to, the
stability of the Anglo-American marriage traditionally owed
much to the existence of this cultural premise. Tammy
Wynette's "Stand By Your Man," to take an explicit and
extreme example, could not have attained the popularity it
did if the premise were not there.[22] That Country and
Western music and romantic and tragic ballads are both
popular in the same areas (notably the southeastern United
States and Newfoundland) may indicate that the premise
varies in strength from one region to another. The ballad's
presentation of a woman who breaks the premise and thus
kills her lover and ultimately herself may perhaps reinforce
the idea that the lives of both men and women depend largely
upon women's capacity to forgive even when to do so is
difficult and painful.

For Lena Harmon, the theme of forgiveness in "Barbara Allen" applies to people and situations in general and not only to the classic issues requiring forgiveness from women for men. She commented in her discussion of the ballad:

> A lot of this, like in our own lives, our stubbornness, our pride maybe, when we should be layin' our pride aside and make a decision for some reason that we might be a-tryin' to get back at somebody or we'd been hurt and wanted to hurt back over some trivial something, like that when he drank this to the ladies round and slighted her.[23]

This comment raises two important points for the understanding of the cultural function of love songs in general and of this ballad in particular. First, the romantic and tragic ballads are centrally concerned with strong emotions and close relationships rather than with young love alone. Responses and interpretations such as Harmon's help to explain why "Barbara Allen" has been sung for collectors by people of all ages. If the ballad can be felt to be about the importance of giving up and giving in so that life and love may continue, it can probably be felt to be about the struggle to live with guilt or with romantic rejection. For North's Jeremiah, the ballad was about his parents' deaths: his father went into a burning stable to rescue the horse his mother loved, his mother went in after him, and they were buried side by side. In the coverlet his grandmother wove to tell him the story, a rose and briar twined above their graves.[24] Second, Harmon's response shows that in addition to seeing themes and concerns other than the romantic in "Barbara Allen," individuals may use romantic themes and concerns as associative images for other issues.

"Barbara Allen" seems to belong equally to men and women: certainly it has been collected from many men. The male has a smaller role and a less stable identity in the ballad. While he may be called Lord John Graham, Jimmy or Jemmy Groves, Sweet William, or any one of several other names, his quiet death is nonetheless the ballad's pivotal event: it changes Barbara's heart, causes her death, and in fact gets the young man what he wanted. To cope with romantic rejection by dying may seem both irrational and improbable, but in eight years of lay counseling I have yet to see any American, male or female, undergo it without fantasizing this solution. I suspect that some people find the young man rather enviable in that he does not have to commit suicide but simply dies, and also in that Barbara reacts appropriately: "Then he/she will be sorry" is a common strand of the suicidal fantasy.

If the popularity of the Blues (with Anglo- as well as black Americans) is any indication, the sense of passive helplessness in the face of romantic rejection may perhaps be more common, or deeper, among American men than among women, and this may explain why men have not altered the plot of "Barbara Allen" to include a longer defense or a more active rejoinder. The young man frequently gives Barbara a bowl of blood or tears he has shed for her or a napkin containing blood or his gold watch and chain, any of which could serve as images for a deep and sacrificial love given at great personal cost. He also sometimes asks for a kiss to cure him, which she inevitably refuses; one or both of these traits appear in a high number of the versions collected from male singers both in Britain and in North America.[25] For some men, the ballad may be about a loving man who is at the end of his rope, having given all a human being can give, whose beloved still rejects him either for a fault she has blown out of proportion or for one which she refuses to explain at all. This interpretation would bring the ballad into the center of the Blues paradigm. In one of the Blues-related songs to attain great popularity in the United States, the suicidal solution to this dilemma is chosen. The man is unnamed, but Irene, his beloved, is the cause of his temptation to jump in the river and drown, or to take morphine and die. The persona of "Goodnight Irene," bidding farewell to his love and hoping to see (or "get") her in his dreams is not too distant from the young man bidding farewell to Barbara Allen; he in fact does get her in his death.[26]

"Barbara Allen" consistently and exclusively uses the four most heavily symbolic colors in English folklore: red, white, green, and gold. Red in the ballads describes the beauty of maidens' cheeks and lips and the streaming blood of the dying; white describes the beauty of maidens' skin and hands and the pallour of the dying, of corpses, and of revenants. Green buds swelling, green grass growing evoke the verdant settings of lovers' "sport and play," but green clothing generally marks ballad characters as nonhuman and/or deadly; and the riddle "What is greener than the grass?" in "The Elfin Knight" brings the answer, "Death."[27] Gold is sometimes the enticement which induces one lover to break the other's heart, as in "Fair Annie" and "Lord Thomas and Fair Eleanor." Gold rings make frequent love tokens, but lovers may also wish for a coffin-like "golden box to keep my true love in."[28] All four colors are used in the ballads in ways which make explicit the juxtaposition of love and death: deep structure it may be, but theoretical it is not. Green buds open the ballad and a red rose closes it; white, red, and gold gifts are given both as love tokens and as part of the young man's verbal will, for he often asks friends to deliver them just before turning "his pale face to the wall." Some versions use only one or two colors to describe the love tokens while many omit them altogether, but no other color appears anywhere in the texts I have examined. This density and clarity of bipolar significance makes the color imagery coherent in its ambivalence and forms a powerful contribution to the thematic and structural juxtapositions of love and death.

The rose and briar may well have struck North Americans as a satisfying ending for "Barbara Allen" because it twists love and death together. The ending is not present in the broadside versions reprinted numerous times in the United States and in Britain[29] but was apparently added by American singers who had encountered it in "Fair Margaret and Sweet William," "The Lass of Roch Royal," "Lord Lovel," "Lord Thomas and Fair Annet," or "Lady Alice." This addition indicates that the ballad was widely felt to belong to a definite semantic group: the ending is only given to ballads about true, not-yet-wed lovers who inadvertently cause each other's deaths. Had so many singers not associated "Barbara Allen" with these ballads through the addition of the rose and briar, one might wonder if Barbara was considered a lover at all. Some texts (notably those in which she "made every man cry 'Well away'" and in which the deathbed conversation is rather brief and formal)[30] make it sound as if the young man was only one of many who were in love with her, or as if his love had always been unrequited. The twining of the two plants together acts somewhat like the posthumous miracles associated with saints' graves: it settles all doubts about the actual qualities of the persons buried there and identifies Barbara as a true lover rather than an attractive young woman who unfortunately was saddled with the death of a sickly and unwanted suitor.

The emotional impact of the rose and briar, in North America and elsewhere, springs from deep and complex sources. First, from Greece to Newfoundland the red rose itself is the most common plant to be placed on graves and has been for centuries.[31] It is also a standard ingredient in potions to kindle or reawaken love. Robert W. Gordon maintains:

> . . . the rose was never associated with black magic, or witchcraft, but there was never a love philter . . . that did not contain rose-water or rose oil, or some part of this . . . flower. . . .[32]

Thus traditional usage, as well as traditional song, give the rose bipolar significance. Second, it forms one of the areas in which there is marked cultural continuity between customs and narratives of sacred love-death and romantic love-death. Gordon cites two legends which explain the origin of the "briar rose" as follows:

> According to one, Judas hung himself on a thorn tree which later burst into bloom as a sign that the blood of Christ was shed even for sinners. The other version has the briar rose emerge from the crown of thorns, . . . the roses forming from his blood.[33]

That the Easter Passion may bear traditional imagistic relation to the love-death ballads in general is suggested by the use of white, red, and thorns in the traditional carol, "The Holly and the Ivy," to describe the purity, love, and pain of the Incarnation, and by the numerous occurrences of rose imagery in references to Christ and Mary, as in the meditations of the Rosary, and as in the carol "Lo, How a Rose E'er Blooming."[34] That it may have particularly conscious relevance to "Barbara Allen" for some American singers is strongly suggested by the presence in America of versions in which the young man dies on Holy Saturday and Barbara on Easter Sunday. Bronson alone prints fifteen variants.[35]

On a more secular level, there is also some similarity between the thorn-wrapped red rose and the arrow-pierced red heart, the simplest, most widespread of all love tokens used by English speakers. This emblem itself, innocuous as it has become, joins love and death: the effect of a real arrow through the heart is obvious. In a cultural setting which takes such a sign for romantic love for granted, is it any wonder that our ballads portray love as "a disease from which no one recovers"? The association between the rose and the Valentine heart is made through contiguity as well as visual and affective similarity: the red rose, with a long stem and sharp thorns, is the most common serious love token given by North American men to women at Valentine's Day and at other times of personal rather than cultural romantic importance. The importance of the thorns in the overall appropriateness of the rose may not often be consciously recognized; yet a florist told me once that a thornless rose had been bred, but people would not buy it. The thorns are as necessary to complete the sign as the arrow.

The use of the words "rose" and "briar" to designate two different plants is by no means universal in the English-speaking world: "briar rose" is a fairly common name, in Newfoundland and elsewhere, for the roses planted on graves.[36] Their separation and recombining through the true love knot perhaps intensifies the effect already present in the fact that roses and thorns co-occur in nature. By making their combination <u>deliberate</u>, the ballad image perhaps makes a virtue out of a necessity: it may convey the idea that true lovers embrace pain with joy, choosing to love deeply although this choice means great suffering. One of the cultural tests of a true heart, expressed in this and other love-death ballads, is that it truly can be broken.

The shape of the loveknot also may have traditional meaning. As it appears on the insignia of the Royal Household Cavalry of England, it is made by intertwining two separate strands, each made into two loops forming a heart shape. The "hearts" are placed side by side and interpenetrate, as shown below.[37]

The Loveknot

While this may not be the only knot referred to as a "loveknot," for singers familiar with it, its shape clearly could add to the effect of the rose and the briar.

In view of its shape, its colors, its contexts of occurrence, and the reactions of members of a culture to it,

it seems more than likely that the rose and briar acts as
what Sherry Ortner has termed a summarizing symbol: one of
the types of symbols which, when understood, take one a long
way into the cognitive and emotional dynamics of cultural
attitudes and behavior. This particular type of symbol
"summarizes" complex cultural experiences, ideas,
narratives, and orientations; it does not so much aid or
provoke the sorting out of experience as invoke it in a
strong, unified form:

> Summarizing symbols . . . are those which are seen
> as summing up, expressing, representing for the
> participants in an emotionally powerful and
> relatively undifferentiated way, what the system
> means to them. This category is essentially the
> category of sacred symbols in the broadest sense,
> and includes all those items which are objects of
> reverence or catalysts of emotion: the flag, the
> cross, the churinga, . . . etc. The American flag,
> for example, for certain Americans, stands for
> something called "the American way," a conglomerate
> of ideas and feelings including (theoretically)
> democracy, free enterprise, hard work, competition,
> progress, national superiority, freedom, etc. And
> it stands for them all at once. It does not
> encourage reflection on the logical relations among
> these ideas, nor on the logical consequences of
> them as they are played out in social actuality,
> over time and history. On the contrary, the flag
> encourages a sort of all-or-nothing allegiance
> . . . . And this is the point about summarizing
> symbols in general--they operate to compound and
> synthesize a complex system of ideas, to
> "summarize" them in a unitary form which . . .
> "stands for" the system as a whole.[38]

Summarizing symbols also imply that certain attitudes and
courses of action are sensible and appropriate; they address
attitudes toward that which they summarize. What does the
rose and briar summarize, and what attitudes and courses of
action does it encourage?

First, it summarizes contradictory emotions and ironic
experiences. The contexts of courtship in which red roses
are frequently given are often fraught with hope and fear,
since falling in love brings an awareness of terrific
vulnerability to many people. Romantic love itself
frequently is described by English speakers as both more
beautiful and more painful--piercingly painful--than any
other experience. The contexts of death in which the rose
appears, planted on graves and carved on gravestones, are

contexts in which complicated grieving takes place. People
in this culture feel at least four strong emotions at the
graveside of a loved one recently dead: love, sorrow, anger
at the dead one for having abandoned them or at God or fate
for having taken him, and fear of the unknown, the forces
larger than those culture can order or control. Gerald L.
Pocius has suggested that this last emotion is one of the
factors which causes people to "culturize" the grave and
graveyard as much as possible--with paint, fences, straight
rows of graves, cultivated flowers, and even gravel and
asphalt.[39] Certainly it is one of the emotions which
contributes to the creation of balanced, distanced,
structured ballads in which personal tragedies and ironies
receive cultural expression.

Next, the rose and briar summarizes a complex of
cultural attitudes toward "true love," one which can be seen
in the Irish tale of Deirdre, in the Arthurian legends, in
Tristan and Iseult, in Romeo and Juliet, and in many of the
films of Greta Garbo and James Dean. True love, in these and
other narratives, is a passion both fatal and exalted which
spurs people both to self-sacrifice and to self-destruction.
The Greek linguistic differentiation between exalted and
sacrifical love (agape) and passionate, potentially
destructive love (eros) is not present in English, nor is it
stressed in the cultural worldview. Consequently, love is
often somewhat paradoxically defined, and narratives which
heighten its inherent paradox possess notable cultural power
to move the emotions in strong and ambivalent ways. If the
rose and the briar can sum up the wrenching emotions evoked
by falling in love and by the death of loved ones, it can
perhaps also sum up the definition of true love as that
which impells people to live or to die for one another.[40]

Living with rose-and-briar ballads can thus encourage
both life-affirming and death-affirming courses of action.
On the one hand, this choice can strengthen in individuals
the faith that love is worth suffering for and hence help to
keep marriages and families together. (Lena Harmon, with no
doubts about which were the stronger and better values to
live by, contrasted the values of the ballads with the "easy
come, easy go" relationships of the current society.)[41] It
can also strengthen individuals in the faith that crisis and
irony are common to humans--culturally expressible, if not
fully comprehensible. On the other hand, it may well
encourage self-destructive behavior in the name of love,
making it seem almost "hard-hearted" to survive romantic
rejection or the death of a loved one. It may be no
coincidence that the traditional culture of the Southern
Mountains, which gives a cherished place to ballads, once
allowed the avenging of deaths in long family feuds. Its

folk religion still centers emotionally upon the personal realization that one has been died for, upon personal repentant grief, and upon personal burial with Christ in baptism.

Within the context of ballad "signifiers" of love and death, the rose and briar emerges as a uniquely resolving symbol. Balladry is rich in bipolar images, but in no other image is their coexistence so explicit or their relationship so balanced. The riddle images of "Captain Wedderburn's Courtship" (particularly in its most common North American form, "I Gave My Love a Cherry") pose impossible separations between love and death: cherries without stones, birds without gall or bone, endless rings, and babies with no crying. The answers to the riddles, however, offer only temporary separations: they focus upon the early stages of development in each image. The blossom, the egg, the ring "in melting" or "rolling," and the baby "when it's making," "sleeping," or "in the belly" will all eventually develop the stones, bones, endings, and tears which are necessary for their completion. The recognition that they must come if the gifts--and the love that goes with them--are accepted is not overt, however, but covert. The alternative answers are not sung:

> If the cherry-blossom's frozen,
>   there'll be no stone;
>
> And if the egg is broken,
>   there'll be no bone;
>
> A ring left unfinished,
>   it has no end;
>
> A baby that is stillborn
>   has no crying.

In the same way, the young widow of "The Lowlands of Holland" sings:

> There shall nae mantle cross my back,
> Nor comb gae in my hair;
> Neither shall coal nor candle light
> Shine in my bower mair;
> Nor shall I hae anither love
> Until the day I dee;
> I never lo'ed a lad but ane
> And he's drowned in the sea.[42]

Here, too, the warmth and light and hope associated with love are present only as absences. Only in the rose and

briar do love-imagery and death-imagery come face to face--
and embrace.

If the business of folkloristics is to use traditional
artistry to learn about the dynamics of culture, "Barbara
Allen" more than repays the effort of inquiry. Its
structural balances and cultural reversals illuminate the
aesthetics and the social values from which they spring and
to which they speak. Its imagery illuminates both other
ballads and other cultural contexts in which it occurs,
suggesting possible connecting elements of thought and
emotion between them. Its themes, revealed through the
patterns of continuation and elaboration worked upon the
ballad by countless singers, not only clarify the grounds of
its appeal, but point to deep and usually unarticulated
attitudes in cultural world view.

If the texts can tell us much about the reasons for the
ballad's popularity, the fact of its popularity can also
tell us something about the ballad. Its popularity indicates
that the beauty and horror of this particular narrative, its
particular kind of confrontation with love and death, is
appealing and valuable to a significant number of English-
speaking people. Its long, thriving life in oral culture in
several regions shows that people found it worth
remembering. (It has been suggested that "Barbara Allen" is
widespread because it was often printed in songsters. I
suspect that, on the contrary, it was printed in songsters
because it was popular.)[43] The very lack of struggle which
Bronson noted may have contributed to its appeal and its
value.

"Barbara Allen" is a story of unreasonable and tragic
deaths--the sort of deaths it can take people years to get
over. It is a story of deep suffering, first of the man and
then of the woman, an ironic story of events which should
never have happened. The only relief offered by the ballad
from the intense and reasonless human sadness which fills it
is natural beauty--green buds, red roses--and perhaps its
imagistic alliance of that sadness with the Easter Passion.
Yet it is told, in many versions, with a quietness that is
clearly more than emotional control; it is told with
emotional acceptance of life as the ballad pictures it. The
springing of the rose and briar from the graves does
suggest, as Lena Harmon pointed out, that love is stronger
than death. Their twining, in its balanced shape, its
pressing together of beauty and pain, suggests the kind of
unity and sense to life which is only achieved after the
irreconcilable inseparables of human experience have been
embraced. It takes time to feel about life's horrors that
they are joined with its love and joy in a true love knot

that meets, as often as not, over a church top. Perhaps this
is one reason why the rose and briar ballads, ostensibly
about the young, are often loved and sung most by the old.
William Blake called this achievement the innocence of the
lion: the loving sanity which comes after the full horror of
hard hearts and tragic deaths has been experienced.[44]
"Barbara Allen" may perhaps be loved because it helps people
achieve that high perspective.[45]

> They climbed and climbed to the old church top,
>   Till they could climb no higher,
> And there they twined in a true love knot,
>   The red rose and the briar.

SOURCES

With "Barbara Allen," one must attempt a representative rather than exhaustive survey unless one has several years to spend. For the purposes of this study, therefore, I have limited myself to a temporally and geographically varied sample containing 112 full narrative versions. The sources used (in addition to Child's three texts) were as follows:

Beard, Anne Winsmore. "The Personal Folksong Collection of Bascom Lumar Lunsford: A Thesis." Master's thesis, Miami University, 1959, pp. 73-76. One version.

Bronson, Bertrand Harris. The Traditional Tunes of the Child Ballads, II. Princeton, N.J.: Princeton University Press, 1962, pp. 321-91. Eighty-seven versions.

Burton, Thomas G. Some Ballad Folks. N.p.: East Tennessee State University Research Development Committee, 1978, pp. 91, 102. Two versions.

Coldwell, Joyce Ione Harrington. The Joyce Ione Harrington Coldwell Folklore Collection, Memorial University of Newfoundland Folklore and Language Archive, Accession No. 81-029. Six versions, transcribed from tape-recorded interviews by Helen Creighton, and the submissions of contributors to Creighton's MSS.

Creighton, Helen, and Doreen Senior, eds. Traditional Songs from Nova Scotia. Toronto: Ryerson Press, 1950, pp. 49-58. Seven versions.

Greenleaf, Elisabeth Bristol, and Grace Yarrow Mansfield, eds. Ballads and Sea Songs of Newfoundland. 1933; rpt. Hatboro, Pa.: Folklore Associates, 1968, pp. 26-27. One version.

Joyner, Charles W. Folk Song in South Carolina. Tricentennial Booklet No. 9. Columbia: University of South Carolina Press, 1971, pp. 21-22. One version.

Peacock, Kenneth, ed. Songs of the Newfoundland Outports, National Museum Bulletin No. 197, Anthropological Series No. 65. Ottawa: National Museum of Man, 1965, III, 649-51. One version.

NOTES

With this title, I certainly don't mean to imply that "Barbara Allen" is only an American ballad. Rather, I call attention to the limited application of my findings. Instead of offering a universal cross-cultural study of "Barbara Allen"'s meaning and function, I simply try to suggest some of the reasons why it might appeal to some people, in some places, particularly in North America during the last thirty to fifty years.

[1] Bertrand Harris Bronson, "About the Most Favorite British Ballads," in his The Ballad as Song (Berkeley: University of California Press, 1969), p. 167.

[2] Charles W. Joyner, Folk Song in South Carolina, Tricentennial Booklet No. 9 (Columbia: University of South Carolina Press, 1971), p. 10. Colin Quigley, "The Child Ballad as Found in Newfoundland," Culture & Tradition, 5 (1980), 25.

[3] Roger D. Abrahams, "Patterns of Structure and Role Relationships in the Child Ballad in the United States," Journal of American Folklore, 79 (1966), 452.

[4] Roger D. Abrahams and George Foss, "The Content of the Songs: Love and Death," in Anglo-American Folksong Style (Englewood Cliffs, N.J.: Prentice-Hall, 1968), pp. 92-131.

[5] For a full discussion of these distinctions and their implications for cultural interpretation see Kenneth L. Pike, "A Stereoscopic Window on the World," Bibliotheca Sacra, 114:454 (1957), 141-56. Rpt. in his Language and Life (Glendale, Ca.: Summer Institute of Linguistics, n.d.), pp. 141-56.

[6] See Cecil J. Sharp, Introduction, English Folk Songs from the Southern Appalachians, ed. Maud Karpeles (London: Oxford University Press, 1932), I, xxvi. For singers' comments on the "love songs," see Thomas G. Burton, Some Ballad Folks (n.p.: East Tennessee State University Research Development Committee, 1978), pp. 11-12, 30.

[7]Personal interview with Stephanie Toise, St. John's, Newfoundland, 17 September 1982.

[8]Roger deV. Renwick, "The Semiotics of Sexual Liaisons," in his English Folk Poetry: Structure and Meaning (Philadelphia: University of Pennsylvania Press, 1980), p. 58.

[9]See, for example, "Jamie Douglas" ("Waly, Waly"), Child 204; "Died of Love," in James Reeves, The Everlasting Circle: English Traditional Verse (London: Heinemann, 1960), pp. 96-97; "The Seeds of Love," in Reeves, pp. 229-38.

[10]Bronson, "Favorite British Ballads," p. 163.

[11]See Bronson, "Mrs. Brown and the Ballad," in his The Ballad as Song, pp. 64-78; David D. Buchan, "The Oral Ballads of Mrs. Brown," in The Ballad and the Folk (London: Routledge & Kegan Paul, 1972), pp. 62-73.

[12]I am indebted to Ms. M. Georgina Smith for this insight into the grounds (and non-grounds) for the Tup's popularity. For a thorough study of the play as it is performed in South Yorkshire and Derbyshire today, see Ian Russell, "'Here Comes Me and Our Old Lass, Short of Money and Short of Brass': A Survey of Traditional Drama in North East Derbyshire 1970-8," Folk Music Journal, 5 (1979), 399-478.

[13]For a discussion of the nature of mumming as an art form see Henry Glassie, All Silver and No Brass: An Irish Christmas Mumming (Bloomington: Indiana University Press, 1975), pp. 53-61.

[14]Harvey Cox, The Feast of Fools: A Theological Essay on Festivity (New York: Harper & Row, 1970), pp. 1-20.

[15]On cultural reversal, see Barbara A. Babcock, ed. The Reversible World: Symbolic Inversion in Art and Society, Proc. of the Forms of Symbolic Inversion Symposium, Toronto, 1972 (Ithaca: Cornell University Press, 1978).

[16]Henry Glassie, Pattern in the Material Folk Culture of the Eastern United States (Philadelphia: University of Pennsylvania Press, 1969).

[17]On qualitative, cross-generic coherence in Cultural aesthetic productions, see Robert Plant Armstrong, The Affecting Presence: An Essay in Humanistic Anthropology (Urbana: University of Illinois Press, 1971); A. L. Kroeber, Style and Civilizations (Ithaca: Cornell University Press, 1957).

[18]Burton, p. 11.

[19]Ibid., pp. 38-39.

[20]Sterling North, So Dear to My Heart (Garden City, N.Y.: Doubleday, 1947), p. 65.

[21]Citations for such uses appear in the following sources. For New Brunswick, Louise Manny, Letter to Joyce Harrington Coldwell, 16 August 1954, in the Joyce Ione Harrington Coldwell Folklore Collection, Memorial University of Newfoundland Folklore and Language Archive, Accession No. 82-109. Also in William Wells Newell, Games and Songs of American Children (New York: Harper & Brothers, 1823), p. 78. For Nebraska, Louise Pound, "Traditional Ballads in Nebraska," Journal of American Folklore, 26 (1913), 353. For England, Sharp, English Folksongs from the Southern Mountains, p. xiv. For Kentucky, Mary Wheeler, Kentucky Mountain Folk-Songs (Boston: the Boston Music Company, 1937), p. 39. For Job's Cove, Conception Bay, Newfoundland, c. 1920-30, personal interview with Mrs. Anastasia Ryall, St. John's, Nfld., 11 September 1982.

[22]Tammy Wynette, "Stand by your Man," Greatest Hits, Epic BN-26486, 12" LP.

[23]Burton, pp. 38-39.

[24]North, p. 169.

[25]See, for example, Bronson's texts nos. 3, 12, 27, 32, 35, 36, 44, 45, 67, 82, 85, 97, 133, 138, 156, 169, in The Traditional Tunes of the Child Ballads, II (Princeton, N. J.: Princeton University Press, 1962), 321-91. A total of sixty of Bronson's 198 versions were identified as having been sung by male informants. (Not all versions are accompanied by the singer's name.) Of these sixty, fourteen give the tune only; another seventeen give only one or two verses. Of the twenty-nine full narratives collected from

male singers, thirteen lack these features and sixteen possess them. The young man does, however, weep in four of the thirteen which lack the request for a kiss or embrace and lack the gifts. Only four versions collected from women bear either of these features, however, and one of these had been learned by the singer from her father. A total of 111 versions are specified as having been sung by women: twenty-two give only the tune; forty-one give only one or two verses; and forty-three full narratives lack the request for the kiss and the love-gifts. In seven of these, however, the young man weeps, and in three he attempts to touch her. Only one male singer (James Horsby of Lincolnshire, version 27) includes the attempt at touch, and here he merely "stretched out his lily-white arms," and Barbara's immediate leap backward, present in the three versions collected from women, is absent.

[26]"Irene," by Huddie Ledbetter. In John Lomax, Negro Folk Songs as Sung by Leadbelly (New York: Macmillan, 1936), p. 235. Also in Alan Lomax, The Folk Songs of North America in the English Language (Garden City, N. Y.: Doubleday, 1960), p. 593.

[27]See Lowry Charles Wimberly, Folklore in the English and Scottish Ballads (Chicago: University of Chicago Press, 1928), pp. 178, 241-42; J. Barre Toelken, "'Riddles Wisely Expounded,'" Western Folklore, 25 (1966), 1-16; James L. Boren, "Color Symbolism in Sir Gawain and the Green Knight," English 518, University of Oregon, 13 February 1979, author's cassette tape no. SGGK1.

[28]This image occurs in a lyric song known to the author from oral tradition, Colorado Rocky Mountains, July 1964. It's also in "The Red Rosy Bush," The Belafonte Folk Singers, on Belafonte Returns to Carnegie Hall, Harry Belafonte with Odetta, the Chad Mitchell Trio, Miriam Makeba, and the Belafonte Folk Singers, RCA Victor LOC/LSO 6007, 1960, 12" LP.

[29]See Child's texts A, B; Bronson's texts 14, 40. For a full discussion of the ballad's history in print see Ed Cray, "Barbara Allen: Cheap Print and Reprint," in Folklore International: A Festschrift for Wayland Debs Hand, ed. D. K. Wilgus (Hatboro, Pa.: Folklore Associates, 1967), 41-50.

[30]See, for example, Bronson's text no. 14 (a common broadside and songster version); 15, 16, which are close to it; 62, 63, 73, 89.

[31]See Robert W. Gordon, Folk Songs of America, National Service Bureau Publication (Washington, D. C., 1938), pp. 12-17, 63, 96, here taken from the "rose and briar motif" section of the card file, Coldwell Folklore Collection, Memorial University Folklore and Language Archive. Information about the tradition in Newfoundland was kindly provided by Ms. Margaret Fitzpatrick, an undergraduate major in the Department of Folklore, Memorial University of Newfoundland (personal conversation, 14 September 1982).

[32]Gordon, p. 17.

[33]Ibid., p. 11.

[34]"The Holly and the Ivy" (trad.), in William Henry Husk, ed., Songs of the Nativity: Being Christmas Carols Ancient and Modern (London, /1868/), pp. 85-86; "Lo, How a Rose E'er Blooming" ("Es ist ein' Ros," German, fifteenth century), Speierschen Gesangbüch (Cologne, 1600), trans. Theodore Baker, 1894.

[35]See Bronson's texts 65, 66, 68, 71, 73, 76, 81, 86, 101, 116, 136, 148, 159, 169, 179.

[36]One evidence for the familiarity of this term on a more-than-regional basis among English speakers is that it was chosen as the translation for Sleeping Beauty's name, "Dornröschen" ("Little Thornrose"), Margaret Hunt, trans., The Complete Grimm's Fairy Tales (New York: Pantheon, 1944), pp. 237-40. Gordon uses the phrase several times. The "double briar rose" or cultivated rose (as opposed to the wild rose, which has only a single circle of petals) is favored for the decoration of graves and gardens in some Newfoundland communities (M. Fitzpatrick, 14 September 1982).

[37]After a photograph in Herman A. Gombrich, The Sense of Order: A Study in the Psychology of Decorative Art (Ithaca, N. Y.: Cornell University Press, 1979), p. 250. Illustrations of harvest knots in shapes resembling the loveknot appear in Kevin Danaher, The Year in Ireland (Cork: The Mercier Press, 1972), pp. 193, 196, 198. An actual harvest knot in the single heart shape is in the MUNFLA collection.

[38]Sherry B. Ortner, "On Key Symbols," American Anthropologist, 75 (1973), 1339-40.

[39]Gerald L. Pocius, "The Place of Burial: Spatial Focus of Contact of the Living and the Dead in Eastern Areas of the Avalon Peninsula of Newfoundland," Master's thesis, Memorial University of Newfoundland, 1976, pp. 175-215. See also Kenneth L. Ames, "Ideologies in Stone: Meanings in Victorian Gravestones," Journal of Popular Culture, 14 (1981), 641-56; Charles O. Jackson, "Death Shall Have no Dominion: The Passing of the World of the Dead in America," in Death and Dying: Views from Many Cultures, ed. Richard A. Kalsh (Farmingdale, N. Y.: Baywood, 1972), pp. 47-55.

[40]The fullest discussion of the Western definition of "true love" is to be found in Denis de Rougemont, Love in the Western World, trans. Montgomery Belgion, rev. ed. (New York: Harper Colophon, 1940).

[41]Burton, p. 39.

[42]"The Lowlands o' Holland," in Gavin Greig, Folk-Song in Buchan and Folk-Song of the North-East (1907-1911; rpt. Hatboro, Pa.: Folklore Associates, 1963), article no. 135, n.p. Also see Sharp, I, p. 200.

[43]Tristram P. Coffin, The British Traditional Ballad in North America, rev. ed., supplement by Roger deV. Renwick (Austin: University of Texas Press, 1977), p. 84.

[44]William Blake, "Night," in Songs of Innocence and of Experience, Shewing the Two Contrary States of the Human Soul, 1789-94, ed. Geoffrey Keynes (London: Oxford University Press, 1977), plates 21-22.

[45]I am indebted to Mr. Martin Lovelace of the Department of Folklore, Memorial University of Newfoundland, for valuable critical suggestions during the preparation of this paper.

Memorial University of Newfoundland
St. John's

PREACHING FOR BACON

London: H. P. Suce, Machine Printer and
Publisher, 177, Union Street, Boro'.

1. A Methodist parson whose name it was George,
   A jolly dun Tinker who knew how to forge;
   A good honest woman who was George's friend,
   He often went to her, her soul for to mend.

   > Derry down, down, I derry down.

2. This good woman's husband, no methodist he,
   He was a true Churchman so jovial and free,
   He loved his brown jug with his glass in his hand,
   And his house was hung round with Bacon and Ham.

3. George loved this man's wife and often went to her,
   And out of a great slice of Bacon would do her,
   Which made her old husband to vow and protest,
   For he plainly perceived that his Bacon grew less.

4. He went out one morning pretending to work
   But the cunning old sly-boots went for nought but to lurk,
   He came into the house and he found them at prayer,
   They seemed very serious, devout and sincere.

5. He came into the house and he looked very sly,
   And into George's pocket he cast a quick eye,
   He saw something in it tied up in a rag.
   Quoth he, "honest friend, what hast thou in thy bag?"

6. "Oh," then replied George, "it is God's Holy Word.
   The Sacred Scriptures I've had from the Lord,
   And when I'm alone I cannot be idle,
   For I take great delight in reading the Bible."

7. "Then pull out thy Bible," this good man replied,
   "Or else by the devil I'll Bible thy hide,
   I'll Bible thy hide as it ne'er was in thy life,
   For this Bible is Bacon thou'st got from my wife!"

8. Then shivering and shaking George quick pull'd it out,
   'Twas a great piece of Bacon tied up in a clout!
   Away then he ran, for he durst not be idle,
   And ever since then he has preached without Bible.

266

9.   Come all you young fellows who lead jovial lives,
     I'd have you take care of your Bacon and wives;
     These methodist parsons I believe they're all shaken,
     For they'll preach like the Devil where there's plenty
          of Bacon.

Broadside Text British Library: Crampton Collection, Shelf
Mark: 11621.h.11, vol. III, fol. 95.   Undated /1845-1917.

RAINER WEHSE

CRITICISM IN HUMOROUS NARRATIVE BROADSIDE SONGS

Either the term <u>criticism</u> as such has undergone a change, or the borderline between the two distinct concepts of <u>representation</u> on the one hand and <u>critical evaluation</u> on the other has been confused in the more recent scholarly literature. This borderline may have been erased consciously for the sake of ideological indoctrination, or, more likely, it may have been subconsciously neglected, demonstrating the incapability of logical thinking. According to this confused concept, humorous narrative songs (schwank songs) are frequently regarded as a genre concerned with social criticism. Whether this new vantage point is justified will be shown by the following discussion.

We shall first look at criteria <u>immanent</u> in a given song text. In treating a subject, the text can either give a mere neutral representation of reality or it can achieve a critical evaluation, these being the two extreme view points. To illustrate this point theoretically I will refer to an example from economy: a map in an economic atlas shows the different gross national products of various countries, encompassing several with high standards of living and several with low standard of living. This information is a mere representation of facts. Nobody would attribute critical intentions to such a fact-oriented compilation of data. But this does not exclude the possibility that the users of the atlas will come to different conclusions: some may wish more affluence for the poorer countries because for them wealth is a positive human value; others will be happy that poorer countries exist because they regard a high standard of living as decadent. But those deductions happen in the mind of the <u>reader</u>; they have nothing to do with the <u>text</u> as such.

A sequence of examples shall now depict the individual steps leading from the one extreme position (mere factual representation) to the other (critical evaluation):

(1) A and B earn $2.000. per month. A gives 20% of his wages to the poor, B only 1%.

This is a mere factual representation.

(2) B gives only 1% to the poor because he can't be bothered with grievances.

Here a new dimension has been added: the explanation for the nature of a certain phenomenon. This explanation is again a neutral statement, even if according to _our_ ethical standards (not for B's who might have given this explanation without any prick of conscience) B might be rated an inferior human being. This evaluation, however, is not expressed by the text which by no means can be called critical.

(3) B gives only 1% to the poor because he can't be bothered by grievances. Therefore he is an egotist who has no regard for social justice.

This stage gives a fact-oriented evaluation which even now is not yet a critical evaluation. These two concepts are by no means synonymous.

(4) B gives only 1% to the poor because he can't be bothered by grievances. Therefore he is an egotist who has no regard for social justice. Since he is a member of a humanitarian society, it should be his duty to show sympathy and help the poor.

This, finally, is _criticism_. The concept is derived from the Greek _kritike_ meaning "the art of judgment." It is defined as the exposure of the virtues and weaknesses of objects or proceedings and the analysis of their causes. But criticism also has an important additional function for the recipients: it deliberately points out the quality of facts and objects by accepting or refusing them, thus provoking individual judgment. These responses are an intentional means of provoking a critical attitute towards certain aspects of reality. Applied to folkloric material it follows that criticism requires a message, a direct address to the recipients by the (fictitious) author of a text. The new and decisive criteria of example no. 4, which alone gives genuine critical advice is exactly this: a statement by the author with the direct purpose of provoking a critical decision by his readers, singers, or listeners. Only if both of these elements are given can we accept a text as bearing critical implications.

The challenge is intentional and has to be perceptible in the text itself, speaking of a strictly text-immanent interpretation. The agents for a critical message can be of a verbal nature (as in the example above) or they can, for example, also be an ironical estrangement by saying the opposite of what is actually meant, as is the case in the genre of satire. Let us recapitulate: provided a text-immanent interpretation is applied, then criticism means an evaluation of objects or facts _and_ the intended challenge for the recipient to make his own moral decision. For this same purpose fables, examples, and other genres use a moral. The biblical parable ends with an additional line commenting on the aforesaid, and thereby induces an opinion from the reader. Without those additional comments none of the genres mentioned could be called critical.

Apart from criticism immanent in a text or commentary affixed to it we also have to deal with criticism implied by a given connotation or situation. Let us take a neutral verbal statement concerning a certain grievance, rendered in a closely related group of people. The group is defined by the fact that all members of it agree that the grievance is highly deplorable and that its causes should, by all means, be altered. In that case the presentation need not be critical because criticism is already implied by the context. The text of the presentation as such if read to an outsider, however, would not necessarily show or provoke any critical attitudes. Here text-immanent research is insufficient for recognizing the true implications. Only knowledge of the context can lead to actual results.

For historical humorous narratives and songs this knowledge is severely limited. Findings concerning the reception of British and American street literature are very rare. In the case of schwank ballads in particular there are practically no facts hinting at the possible critical function of the genre. The protest songs of the impoverished masses of the nineteenth century--to quote only one possible example of a situation favoring social criticism--have never been the humorous ballads. If this type of song had been perceived as critical, then the wide distribution and moderate price of broadside ballads would have been an excellent opportunity for propagating criticism. But that was not the case--a further proof that schwank songs were thought unfit for distributing ideological messages. Elfriede Moser-Rath warns us not to overrate realistic tendencies and social implications of humorous narratives.[1] Too many important historical or actual facts and events are not even touched upon by this genre, while conversely, certain genre specific peculiarities have no counterpart in real life. This statement, although derived from a profound knowledge of German material, can be transferred to folk literature in the English language without being modified.

After having nicely anticipated the results of this article, we now shall look for some examples of humorous ballads from broadsides and chapbooks which might contain social criticism, or which at least come close to such criticism and thus could lead to the erroneous idea of schwank songs as vehicles for criticism. Social criticism has to be directed against aspects or members of the society. According to the ballad plots there exist the following possible targets:

(1) Nations and ethnic groups

(2) Organizations (The Church, religious communities, and so forth.)

(3) Occupations and professions

(4) Individual people

(5) The order of society

(6) Human nature (vices, peculiarities, and so forth.)

Formal possibilities:

(1) The entire ballad is critical

(2) The ballad is used for critical purposes through an attached moral

(3) The ballad contains critical interpolations or other such additions

According to the above definition of criticism there is not a single broadside ballad meeting the requirements of formal possibility no. 1, with one exception: in the middle of the seventeenth century "King John and the Bishop" (Child 45) was turned into a critical parody directed against the Puritans. For that purpose, however, the text had to be completely rewritten. The new version, "King Henry and a Bishop" ends with the following moral: "Unlearned men hard matters out can find / When learned bishops princes' eyes do blind."[2] The rewriting as such is significant. If the original, already somewhat anti-clerical text, had served its purpose then a critical parody would not have been necessary.

Formal possibility no. 2, the moral at the end of a ballad, is typical for the seventeenth century. Towards the end of the nineteenth century, which likewise is the end of the broadside era, the moral gradually disappeared or took on parodistic elements. Throughout the centuries approximately 20-30% of the texts have had a moral affixed.

An integrated moral rarely occurs. In that particular case one of the characters from the story teaches somebody else a lesson, referring to the events which have happened before. This is the case in "The Farmer's Blunder," a broadside printed around 1800.[3] The last verses read:

> 'Tis owing to you I am now in disgrace,
> You should never put people out of their place,
> To the Country I soon will be jogging amain,
> And I hope I shall never zee London again.

This quasi-moral is directed against landlords in the function of leaseholders and also against arrogant members of the upper classes.

In all other cases, however, the moral appears grafted upon an unsuitable stem (the text). It seems to be the personal concern of a narrator, who here speaks for the first time, drawing his private conclusions which occasionally seem to lack all relation to the preceeding text.[4] In this case one can hardly speak of means immanent in a text. Text-immanent criticism would render a moral unnecessary. Why, then, a moral? When it comes to erotic texts a moral possibly has an apologetic function: the singer has a chance to add some moralistic ornaments and thus reconciles listeners appalled by the otherwise unsavory story. In order not to be blamed for bluntly enjoying sexual themes the whole thing is--at its very end--turned into something highly reputable: "Look at those obscene things our schwank characters have been doing. Fie upon them! Let's learn from their wicked deeds, dear brethren, not to do such abominable things." According to this hypothesis the moral produces an alibi for a story otherwise unprintable in some centuries. The actual intention of the text is thus camouflaged and legalized because it now seems to serve a higher purpose. The schwank text as such represents the opposite attitude: an open-hearted display of unrestricted love play and intrigue, a frank and candid interest in the more earthly joys of copulation. At no point in the narrative is the reader in doubt about the real center of activity and interest. Thus in many cases the moral appears utterly hypocritical. Sometimes, however, one can find real ethical concern on the side of the person behind it.

On the whole it may be plausible to call the moral a petrified convention without much of a function and without a connection to the preceding text. It is perhaps this emptiness which has led to parody in younger schwank songs. Such petrification is reminiscent of formulas. An opening formula like "Come all ye, . . ." "Come listen to my story," or "It's of a, . . ." is set against a finishing formula: the moral. Thus the ribald fullbloodedness of the Schwank is wedged into a solid frame of surrounding formulas.

Following are presented samples from three centuries. The moral is not always limited to one stanza only. In a broadside from 1681, "The Fanatick's Barber," it covers three stanzas:

> Therefore I pray you listen well
> To what ye have heard this daie,
> First of all cause by such fould deeds
> You will your selves bewry.
>
> Secondlie for that you offend
> The Brethren that are weak;
> Thirdlie and lastlie for your own
> And this poor Parsons sake.
>
> Therefore I tell ye once again
> Take notice of my rime
> Write it' th' tables of your hearts;
> And so much for the time.[5]

This extremely outspoken curtain lecture cannot be adjudged merely a formulaic convention, particularly because a thematic introduction, modelled so as to be taken up by the moral, shows a similar genuine concern with the issue. Rather, this case has to do with a hybrid of example and Schwank comparable to those sermons (Predigtmärlein) of the Baroque period which use traditional folk narratives. Here the main purpose is a moral effect illustrated by a story supposedly taken from real life. The actual Schwank serves as a vehicle for a different and predominant concern.

The opposite of the above-mentioned longest moral found in schwank songs appears at the end of "Yea-and-Nay the Hypocrite" (1672-94): "This comes when innocent Lambs they do play."[6] Here the moral has shrunk to just one line, unintelligible for somebody who does not know the preceding song. The "innocent lambs," as they are called ironically, turn out to be a Quaker and his sister who have incestuously begotten twins. "The Crafty Country Woman" (circa 1697) has a moral which can be understood without knowledge of the text which it follows:

> Now, now, you lusty Bakers,
> that hears my song this day,
> Be warned by your Brother,
> and do not run astray.
> Least in a trap they catch you,
> when you have had your will;
> For they will have satisfaction,
> for grinding in their Mill.[7]

The style and diction of the moral does not change in the eighteenth century, as is demonstrated by "The Saint Turned Sinner" (before 1720):

> And thus we see how Preachers
> That should be Gospel-Teachers,
> How they are strangely blinded,
> And are so feebly minded,
> Like Carnal Men inclined
> To lie with any Whore.[8]

In the schwank songs of the nineteenth century there is a definite change. The moral loses its zeal; it is told with a twinkling eye:

> Come all you young fellows who lead jovial lives,
> I'd have you take care of your Bacon and wives,
> These Methodist Parsons I believe they're all shaken,
> For they'll preach like the Devil where ther's plenty
> of Bacon.

("Preaching for Bacon" 1837 /circa 1852_7)[9]

> For he loves food and liquor, as every one knows
> The one fattens his sides, t'other reddens his nose,
> But fat sides and red noses will never teach wit,
> As you see by the priest whom the swine herd had Bit.

("The Parson and Hodge's Son," nineteenth century)[10]

The circle closes with the final stanza of "The Monkey Turned Barber" (1813-38).[11] Here it is again a character from the Schwank itself who passes a judgment upon one of the other people involved in the plot. Yet the lesson taught is so little abstracted from the ballad events that the effect demanded by criticism hardly challenges the listener to follow suit:

> Why sure man alive you must have been mad,
> To sit while he cut your nose and chin so bad,
> But come to a grog shop the story to tell,
> We'll try if good whiskey won't make your face well.

The latter example, especially, only can be understood if the entire text is known. It is thus more closely related to the actual Schwank than the usual concluding moral. The development follows an immanent necessity because it is imperative for the moral as an integrated textual device of the uncritical genre of Schwank to lose its original function. It can only survive as a kind of rudimentary organ.

The moral as such must be ranked as a highly critical device. But if, in the mind of the recipient, it is only understood as a mere formula comparable to the opening and closing formulas of a Märchen, then the moral can probably be regarded as a blind motif (a motif without a function) or at least as a blunted motif (a motif with restricted effectiveness). The moral is rarely integrated into the actual ballad plot. Likewise it has not, as could be expected, any relationship of content with the punchline. This lack of relationship also is indicated by typographical devices; larger indentions and lead, as well as a different kind of type, set it apart from the actual text. As has been demonstrated above, different variants have different morals. It follows again that the moral thus is not an integrated part of a tale type. The critical effect is enacted by a statement commenting on the depicted events and also frequently by a direct address to the listeners. They are thus motivated to reflect upon their own opinions, thoughts, and actions. From a didactic point of view the positioning of the moral behind the punchline is a favorable one. The action of a Schwank progresses quite slowly until its climax. At the climax all of a sudden there is a concentration of action, a time-lapse picture which captures all possible attention. The mind of the reader is wide awake at that point; he is ready to lend a willing ear to the stimulus of the moral.

On the other hand, in spite of its formulaic character and its standing apart from the actual text, the moral shows a close relationship to the preceding narrative. As mentioned above, the Schwank treats the same basic human situations as proverbs. The latter genre, however, summarizes and analyzes the situation more pointedly. We know hardly any schwank plot which does not exist in the form of a proverb or which does not challenge a proverbial quintessence. This challenge is met perfectly by a concluding and summarizing moral. Hermann Bausinger was the first to emphasize the Schwank's popular and didactic character.[12] And in fact, proverbs do appear instead of a moral. In "The Young-man and Maiden's Fore-Cast," a seventeenth-century broadside variant of AT 1430, the last line of the moral is formed by a proverb:

All you Yound Men live vertuous Lives,
And think to get Portions now by our Wives;
Take Warning by me before you are Matcht,
Pray count not your chickens before they are Hatcht.[13]

We shall now turn to the last formal possibility of criticism in Schwank: insertions of elements not strictly belonging to the text itself. The title and subtitle of some songs already hint at criticism:

"The Saint Turned Sinner: Or, The Dissenting Parson's Text Under the Quaker's Petticoats"; "The Fanatics Barber. Or, A New Cut for Non-Conformists"; "'Yea-and-Nay the Hypocrite, or, A Brief Relation of a pretended Quaker near Yarmouth, who having lain with his own Sister, got her with Child, so that she brought him Two Sons at a Birth for a New-years-Gift.'

To the Tune of THE TOUCH OF THE TIMES."

But one must keep in mind the four steps leading from the neutral presentation of facts to their critical evaluation:

1 Presentation
  of the facts

2   "   & reasons
             for them

3   "   "   & evaluation

4   "   "   "   & judgment and challenge
                                  to the recipient to
                                  follow the advice.

Which of those elements do the title and pre-title sequences contain? A brief <u>presentation</u> is achieved by the title or the pre-title sequence. The <u>reason</u> why things happen is not mentioned, but it is obvious that in the Quaker story it can only be human weakness. An <u>evaluation</u> is indicated by the word 'hypocrite' ("Yea-and-Nay" is a nickname for Quakers because according to the rules of their denomination a member is only allowed to answer with a straight "yes" or "no"). The most important element of criticism though, no. 4, is completely missing. The title thus remains below the level of genuine criticism. The tune "The Touch of the Times," however, reinforces the near-critical tendency a little by alluding to fashionable behaviour. A similar contrivance is used by another ballad for which the tune of "All the Town Shan't Save Thee" has been chosen.

Choruses only rarely are used for criticism although their regular repetition offers an excellent means for passing on messages. In "The Protestant Cuckold" the refrain ironically warns: "Oh ye Tories look big, and rejoice at this News, / For Benjamin's Wife is made free of the Stews."[14] But the ballad itself is an exception among all the other

broadside Schwank texts. The characters in it are not the
normal stereotypes with ficticious names but well-known
people from public life: the Tories Benjamin and Ruth H.,
Timothy Dash, and others. The song is abundant with
allusions to contemporary political matters. A quotation
from Horace is unconventionally placed in front of the text:
"Deprendi miserum est." Without a doubt the Schwank was
intended as an invective addressing itself to an educated
stratum of the population, which is not very often the case
with broadsides. For its derisive purposes the text uses a
humorous adultery story. But invective and social criticism
are not exactly on the same level. The latter wants to alter
things, the former only satisfies a craving for malicious
joy, for hurting people and for delighting in the suffering
caused by the attack. By doing this an invective may
function as a social corrective but it does not criticize.

Apart from the examples mentioned there may be critical
interpolations in the frame of a story (the concluding part
of the frame being the moral):

> O Women, you that can so well
> Beweile your own misfortunes
> Come cry with me, for man undone,
> For acting 'tween the Curtaines,
>
> They say the Saracens are cruel,
> And Tartars they are grim;
> But fie upon Christian English man
> They never did like him.
>
> Now that I may your longing Save
> And set your tongues a gabling,
> My song concerns a Parson: Lord!
> Will men of God be dabling?
>
> Yea verily even so it is,
> For mortal flesh is frail.
> And men of God like other men
> Bear lecherie in tayle.

("The Fanaticks Barber")[15]

The example above is one of the rare cases of real social
criticism in schwank songs. But again it is not part of the
action as such but of the introduction preceding it. In some
other songs there are quasi-critical insertions which in a
favorable context could well be attributed a critical
effect. But, interpreted by the references we have which are
limited to the bare printed text, they are preliminaries of
criticism, not the real thing:

In the year '98, when our troubles were great,
And it was treason to be a Milesian,
That black-whiskered set we will never forget,
Though history tells us they were Hessians . . .

(The beginning of "The Cow That Ate the Piper")[16]

But Bob the deceiver he took us all in,
For he married a Papish called Brigid McGinn,
Turned Popish himself and forsook the old cause
That gave us our freedom, religion, and laws.

("The Old Orange Flute")[17]

If so far I have given the impression that street literature
in general does not contain genuine criticism this certainly
was not my intention. On the contrary, social charges
against virtually almost everything are one of the most
predominant characteristics of broadside balladry. And just
a comparison of the abundant examples of critical songs with
schwanks, excellently illustrates the utterly uncritical
attitude of the latter. Three protest songs from the last
two centuries may suffice to make this point clear:

THE DEBTOR

Now I'm getting every day still deeper into debt,
There's no one left to credit me they're such a shabby set
But I'll not forget my creditors whereever I may go,
Tho' I feel now I cannot pay what little debts I owe;
When my little debts are read I feel very much afraid,
They'll find that I forgot all the promise I made,
With a dun close by my shoulder & a bailiff by my side
They'll be taking me to Bellevue goal & lock me up inside.

When I'm there the lawyers will be madly rushing on,
To get me through the court at once before my money's gone
They'll say that from prison they can quickly set me free
I wish I was a law-maker like Cottenham or Brougham,
I'd have all sheriffs sent abroad & bailiffs locked at home
And these who'd form the prisons should always be in dread
For I'd turn out all the debtors and lock them up instead.[18]

The DEVIL of a Marriage; OR A HUE and CRY

After my Lord -xxxx----'s Lady, a beautiful young
Girl of Fifteen, whom his Lordship trepann'd,
after Marriage to go to France on a Party of
Pleasure, and there left her confin'd in a Convent.

WHEN great Men take it into their Heads to be guilty of
Vices of this Sort, it cannot be thought Extraordinary that
those of a meaner Class readily follow their Steps. The
Case of this young Lady is as follows: She being young and
beautiful, the Nobleman was charmed with her, nor could he
asswage his raging Lust till he had enjoyed her, and which
he could not accomplish till after Marriage, so consented.
Soon after the Nuptials were celebrated . . .[19]

YELLOW, WHITE, AND BROWN

Fellow men, my song attend, and you will plainly see,
That talent's but a worthless name, if pennyless you be,
Although you all be clever men, possessed of common sense,
The world demands at your commands, pounds, shillings and
  the pence.

The Queen and Prince of Wales, lords, dukes and barons bold
Would sink below our level low, if they possessed no gold.
So to gain the world's esteem, and with it wide renown
You must to heap, and then to keep, the yellow, white and
  brown.

The greatest cheat and knave on earth, for sterling worth
  must pass,
If he can show the golden group, the silver, and the brass,
He may get drunk, and curse and swear, and fall in pools
  of sin,
The world laughs at his wickedness, because he's lots of tin,
With a gold chain round his neck, and gold watch by his
  side,
And a sovereign shining through his purse, the secret knell
  must glide;
With lords and nobles he can dine, with wealth, and his
  renown,
There's magic in those words, so rich are yellow, white and
  brown.[20]

Despite the above examples it was difficult to find
even isolated schwank ballads offering criticism, or at
least coming close to it. Without exception, criticism in
humorous narrative songs never belonged to the actual
schwank story itself. Instead, such criticism is restricted
to titles, subtitles, preliminaries, introductions, frames
narrated in the first person, choruses, and the moral. In
addition, all examples quoted in this paper which show a
genuine critical attitude are marginal cases of the genre of
Schwank: cante fables, invective songs, rewritten versions
of traditional ballads, or types which don't really belong
to either the folk or the broadside tradition (as is the

case with the numbers 467 and 522 "The Old Orange Flute"). In the later ballad a flute takes the part of the protagonist. The only element of social criticism which bears some importance in a considerable number of schwank ballads or broadsides is the moral. But again, this is a secondary addition which only changes the emphasis of the ballad itself. Grievances treated by Schwanks are never the object of theoretical comments. They are always embodied in stereotyped characters like adulterers, misers, usurers, or members of occupational groups who symbolically stand for certain human qualities (tailors: lechery and physical weakness; millers: thieving and virility; advocates: dishonesty; and so forth). While there are no known cases of Schwank songs having been prohibited for political reasons, this would have necessarily been the case, if they had been used as a weapon of social criticism. Protest songs, however, have quite a history of being prohibited.

We know little about the possible critical function of the Schwank in context. But we can suppose that this task was generally fulfilled by the protest song--a genre flourishing beside the Schwank throughout the centuries. Why should Schwank have been abused for critical issues if, at the same time, another genre more apt to fulfill the requirements was at everybody's disposal? One doesn't hammer in a nail with a screwdriver if a hammer is at hand. Already under Henry VIII (1491-1547) broadside literature was abundant with protest songs directed against taxation, monopolies, exaggerated rents, the competition of foreign workers, storage of agricultural goods, the Papacy, vices, and many other issues. Protest songs also have a much longer broadside tradition than folksongs. Why then should the older broadside protest song have passed on its function as a critical agent to the less suitable genre of Schwank? My assumption is supported by the fact that protest songs did not disappear when schwank songs increasingly dominated the broadside scene. There are, however, singular incidents of humorous ballads fulfilling a contextual critical function: under Henry VIII Robin Hood ballads were ranked as protest songs because of their anticlerical tendencies.

As far as protest songs are concerned there was no change from the sixteenth to the seventeenth century. "The Old and New Courtier" passes a satirical sentence on the nouveau riche; "The Map of Mock Begger Hall" indulges in polemics against the unpartriarchal and snobbish demeanour of the new landed proprietors. The civil wars and their consequences under Charles II, James II, and William II again reap a great harvest of social criticism through broadsides.[21] The situation remains the same throughout the eighteenth and nineteenth centuries. Rarely or never does the title of a Schwank appear listed among protest songs. For the Schwank does not reflect reality; it is too untopical in its nature to serve as a pointed weapon for attacking something. Criticism, however, builds upon reality. If this principle is dropped, its basis has been lost. If the Schwank actually mirrored reality, then every tailor would weigh forty pounds and every parson need be called a lecher.

At its best, the laughter generated by the Schwank lashes out at abnormalities in a subtle way, at the abnormal which dares to counteract social conventions. But such laughter has to be interpreted as a social gesture which at the same time neutralizes its own criticism by humor.[22] We do side with characters from schwank comedy or repudiate their actions. We stand up for something every day throughout our lives. But this cannot be qualified as criticism. Criticism means really to look through facts; it means to analyze, to evaluate, and to accept or to reject them. Animals, for example, are not able to criticize because they lack the intellectual qualities necessary. But just those qualities are a condition sine qua non. Taking sides may be just an unconscious feeling of sympathy or antipathy of which even an animal is capable. Life is a continuous process of making decisions, of accepting, rejecting, or ignoring choices: these acts, however, cannot a priori be called critical because then all products of literature and art, in fact all human moral, aesthetic, or religious objectifications could be regarded as criticism.

NOTES

[1]Elfriede Moser-Rath, _Schwank, Witz, Anekdote: Entwurf einer Katalogisierung nach Typen und Motiven_ (Göttingen: Enzyclopaedie des Märchens, 1969).

[2]J. Woodfall Ebsworth and William Chappell ed., _The Roxburghe Ballads_ (Hertford: S. Austin, 1889), VI, 750.

[3]Rainer Wehse, _Schwanklied und Flugblatt in Grossbritannien_ /Humorous Narrative Ballads on British Broadsides/ (Frankfurt: Lang, 1979), no. 507.

[4]The discussion concerning the discrepancy between text and moral is rather old. See Jürgen Beyer, _Schwank und Moral: Untersuchungen zum altfranzösischen Fabliau und verwandten Formen_ (Heidelberg: C. Winter, 1969).

[5]Wehse, no. 344.

[6]Wehse, no. 95.

[7]Wehse, no. 364.

[8]Wehse, no. 74.

[9]Wehse, no. 476.

[10]Wehse, no. 473.

[11]Wehse, no. 508.

[12]Hermann Bausinger, "Bemerkungen zum Schwank und seinen Formtypen," _Fabula_, 9 (1967), 119.

[13]Wehse, no. 455.

[14]Wehse, no. 336.

[15]Wehse, no. 344.

[16]Wehse, no. 467.

[17]Wehse, no. 522.

[18]Broadside printed and sold by John O. Bebbington, 22 Goulden Street, Oldham Road, Manchester /‾circa 183⁊/‾; also by J. Beaumont, 176, York Street, Leeds. /no./ 84, /‾circa 185₂/. Harvard College Library, shelf-mark 25242.17*, vol. 9, 80.

[19]Broadside printed 1749. Chetham's Library, Manchester, Halliwell-Phillips Collection of Broadsides, no. 127.

[20]Broadside printed by W. S. Fortey, 2 & 3 Monmouth Court, Seven Dials, /London 1860-1885/. British Library, London, A Collection of Ballads / . . . / Collected by Sabine Baring-Gould, Shelf-mark L.R.271.a.2, vol. 2, 19.

[21]Cf. Sir Charles Harding Firth, "The Ballad History of the Reigns of Henry VII and Henry VIII," Transactions of the Royal Historical Society, 3rd Ser., 2 (1908), 33; Louis B. Wright, "Ephemeral Reading," in Louis B. Wright, Middle Class Culture in Elizabethan England (Chapel Hill: University of North Carolina Press, 1935), p. 423; Vivian de Sola Pinto, "Broadsheets," in Chamber's Encyclopaedia, II (1955), 595. Vivian de Sola Pinto, and A. E. Rodway, The Common Muse (London: Chatto & Windus, 1957), pp. 21, 23; Leslie Shepard, The History of Street Literature (Newton Abbot: Gale, 1973), pp. 35, 122.

[22]Cf. Henri Bergson, Das Lachen /‾Le rire _/ (Meisenheim: Westkulturverlag, 1948), pp. 15, 106.

Göttingen, Germany

MARGJIT OG TARGJEI RISVOLLO

Oppskrift 1857 av Sophus Bugge etter Anne Skalen,
Mo, Telemark.

1. Margjit gjæter i lio nor
   ho blæs i forgylte pipe
   dæ høyrer en Jon i Vaddelio
   dæ aukar en stor sorg å kvie.
      --Dæ va mi å alli di som jalar uppunde lio

2. /Margjit gjæter i lio nor
   ho blæs i forgylte7 honn
   /dæ høyrer en Jon i Vaddelio
   dæn aukar en7 store sorgjir.

3. Så låg dei ihop den notti så lang
   mæ kvorannas sie
   notti lei å soli kom
   dei skjuldest mæ sorg a kvie.

4. Så låg /dei ihop den notti så lang7
   på /kvorannas7 arm
   /notti lei å soli kom
   dei skjuldest mæ sorg å7 harm.

5. Dæ va no ho Margjit fruva
   klappar på durakinn
   statt upp Kristi terna mi
   du slepper meg fulle inn.

6. Dæ va no ho Kristi terna
   fyr dei ori så bleiv ho vrei
   dæ sømer ingje skjøne jomfruve
   på skogjen å gange ei.

7. Eg for vilt på viddan hei
   ikringum en dvergestein
   rår no Gud fyr minne færen
   eg ha' snær 'kji hitta heim.

8. /Eg for vilt på viddan hei
   ikringum en dverge7runni
   /rar no Gud fyr minne færen
   eg ha'snær 'kji7 heimi funni.

9. For du vilt pa viddan hei
   ikringum en dvergestein
   rår /no Gud fyr7 dinne /færen7
   tru Here Jon vå 'kje ein.

10. For du /vilt pa viddan hei
    ikringum en dverge7runni
    /rår no Gud fyr7 dinne /færen7
    du hev en vist Here Jon funni.

11. Ja høyrer du de du Kristi terna
    du tar kje mine sorginne binde
    du heve sett din føesdagjen
    sveipt uti heljelinde.

12. /Ja høyrer du de du Kristi terna
    du tar kje mine sorginne7 auke
    du heve sett din føesdagjen
    /sveipt uti helje7laukjen.

13. Høyr du de du Margit fruva
    eg sko 'kje din nøi føre
    eg sko fyr'o Targjei stande
    som du sjov de være.

14. Hev eg noko førtala meg
    så gjer eg de no så gjønni
    eg sko eta upp ori mine
    som søte natakjønner.

15. No høyrer me dei brumennar koma
    inkje hev luen låti
    bruri sit i bastogunne
    våte liksom ei kråke.

16. No /høyrer me dei brumennar7 koma
    inkje hava me luen høyrt
    inkje heve me lefsunne baka
    å inkje æ stumpen steikt.

17. De va no han unge Targjei
    kom seg riandes i går
    uti stende Kristi terna
    ho va væl sveipt i mår.

18. De va no han unge Targjei
    studde seg på sit svær
    hori æ no Margjit fruva
    som skrøyte sko minne fær.

19. Høyrer du de du unge Targjei
    hot eg seia deg vi'
    du æ' kje lagje du unge Targjei
    mæ 'a Margit rie.

20. Ho æ kveisa undi bryst
    å ho inna svier
    du æ' kje /lagje du unge Targjei
    mæ 'a Margit̅7 rie.

21. Ho æ /k̅veisa undi bryst
    å ho inna̅7 verkjer
    /d̅u æ' kje lagje du unge Targjei̅7
    t̅i stinge dine hendar i hennes s̅erkjen.

22. Høyr de adde brumennar
    gakk inn å drikk mjø å vin av skal
    eg vi' upp i høielofti
    å høyre pa Margjits mål.

23. De va no han unge Targjei
    sette sitt svær i stetti
    no førby eg mine mennar
    dær sko ingjen koma etti.

24. Dæ va no han unge Targjei
    inn igjenom dynnanne gjenge
    så helsar han gudmoren
    så gjere adde nyte drengjir.

25. Dæ va no han unge Targjei
    breidde av blomstranne gule å blå
    så bleiv en vari tvo deilige sønner
    på kvore armen lag.

26. Targjei læte seg kvende klæ
    mæ bån unde kvore hende
    men dæ va' Margits støste glei
    at ingjen 'en Targjei kjende.

27. /T̅argjei læte seg kvende klæ
    mæ bån unde kvore̅7 hand
    Margjit sit i løy̅nde lofti
    mæ stor sut å sorg.

28. Targjei stend unde kyrkjevegg
    å drenginne molli bore
    de va' Targjei unna klæe
    som egginne holli skore.

29. Targjei /stend unde kyrkjevegg
    å drenginne/ bore moll
    /de va' Targjei unna klæe
    som egginne/ skore holl.

30. Dæ va' no han unge Targjei
    inn igjenom dynnanne gjenge
    de va ho stolts Margjit
    ho spurde ette bonni sine.

31. Presten i løyndom kristna dei
    dei sova i molli vigde.

32. Vene va no hesten den
    en sjave Targjei rei
    enda venare va' no den
    'en akta sinne møy.

33. De va no han unge Targjei
    han reiste mæ sorg a sut
    lause løype brurehesten
    etter svoddo ut.

Reprinted in Adel Gjøstein Blom and Olav Bø. Norske balladar
i oppskrifter fra 1800-talet. Oslo: Samlaget, 1973.

MARGIT AND TARGJEI RISVOLLO

1. Margit is herding the cattle north;
    She blows her gilded whistle pipe.
    Jon i Vaddelio hears it well,
    Becomes sorrowful and sad:
    "That was mine and never thine, that called from the
        hillside."

2. repeats stanza 1.

3. They slept together the long long night,
    Side by side they lay;
    When night ended and the sun came up,
    They parted in sorrow and pain.

4. repeats stanza 3.

5. There was fair Margit coming home,
    Knocking lightly on the door:
    "Stand up, Kristi, my faithful maid
    You certainly let me in."

6. There was Kristi, the maid of hers,
    Showed anger with these words:
    "It ill befits a young virgin
    To go to the forest alone."

7. "I lost the way in the hillside wild,
    A dwarf caused me to do so;
    But for the help of the merciful God
    I would never have found my home."

8. repeats stanza 7.

9. "You lost the way in the hillside wild,
    A dwarf caused you to do so;
    May the merciful God help you then,
    For I think you found Master Jon."

10. repeats stanza 9.

11. "Listen to me, Kristi, my maid,
    Don't you increase my sorrows.
    You have not* seen your days of life
    when wrapped in clothes of death."

12. repeats stanza 11.

13. "Listen to me, my fair Margit,
    I don't wish you any harm;
    I shall stand before young Targjei
    Just as you were to do."

14. "If I have already said too much,
    I would gladly swallow my words.
    I would do that just as easily
    As were they sweet kernels of nuts."

15. Now we hear the bridegroom's men,
    The horn has not yet been blown;
    The bride still takes her bath,
    Sits wet just like a bird.

16. Now we hear the bridegroom's men,
    But we have not blown the horn;
    The cakes have not been baked,
    Nor have we made the bread.

17. There he was, young Targjei,
    Riding into the yard;
    Out comes the maiden, Kristi,
    All wrapped in marten fur.

18. There he was, young Targjei,
    Takes out his shining sword;
    Says, "Where is my fair bride Margjit,
    Who should welcome my ride?"

19. "Listen to me, young Targjei,
    I want to say this to you:
    It was not meant for you, young Targjei
    To ride at Margjit's side."

20. "She has pain below her chest,
    And is suffering inside;
    It was not meant for you, young Targjei
    To ride at Margjit's side."

21. "She has pain and suffering,
    Inside her she aches;
    You, young Targjei, were not meant
    To put your hand under her skirts."

22. "Listen", he said to his wedding men
    "Go in--drink beer and wine,
    And I will go to the high loft
    And hear the voice of my bride."

23. There he was, young Targjei,
    He sticks his sword in the stairs:
    "I forbid any of my men
    To follow me past this spot."

24. There he was, young Targjei,
    He goes into the room;
    There he bids her good morning
    As does a courteous man.

25. There he was, young Targjei,
    Took aside the heavy quilt;
    He saw two beautiful sons
    That lay within her arms.

26. Targjei put on a woman's dress,
    Took both the sons in his arms;
    Margit's greatest happiness was
    That nobody knew Targjei.

27. Targjei put on a woman's dress,
    Took both the sons in his arms;
    Margjit she lies in the loft alone
    With suffering and pain.

28. "Targjei stands by the church alone,
    His servants covered the graves;
    Targjei felt the pain as hard
    As knives cutting living flesh.

29. repeats stanza 28

30. There he was, young Targjei,
    He slowly goes through the door;
    There she was, proud Margjit,
    She asked where the children were.

31. The minister secretly christened them;
    They sleep in blessed soil.

32. A beautiful horse it truly was
    That Targjei was riding alone;
    Even better was the one
    He intended for his bride.

33.   There he was, young Targjei,
      He left in sorrow and pain;
      After him runs the bride's horse,
      Runs lightly without the bride.

      Translated from the Norwegian by Olav Bø.

*Some variants have this negative form which clarifies the
meaning.

/Stanzas 14, 15 and 16 are obviously not original to the
ballad, but inserted from stefs.7

OLAV BØ

"MARGJIT OG TARGJEI RISVOLLO":
The Classic Triangle in a Norwegian Medieval Ballad

Listed as A 57 in <u>The Types of the Scandinavian Ballad</u>, is the Norwegian ballad about Margjit and Targjei Risvollo. The narrative is summarized as follows:

> Margjit has been seduced by a gnome. When her bridegroom comes to take her to the wedding he finds her with two newborn sons. He dresses up as a woman and takes the babies to the priest. When he returns to Margjit he tells her that he has had the children baptized and buried. Then mournfully he leaves her.[1]

In my opinion this summary concentrates too much on one particular side of the narrative and is therefore incomplete, with the result that the drama of the triangle relationship is robbed of much of its inner tension. At the same time the background which the ballad has in folk beliefs and attitudes becomes less easy to appreciate.

There are five relatively comprehensive or complete versions of the ballad, as well as some fragments. Those versions that are fairly complete are all from the central ballad area in Telemark and are dated between 1856 and 1912. The collectors are all ranked among our best-known and reliable: three of the versions were recorded by Sophus Bugge. Most of the informants, too, are well known.

The ballad has in fact received very little attention, but Anne Swang has recently contributed a thorough discussion of the contents based on one of the fuller versions obtained from an informant who was looked down upon by her neighbours but who is a source of many of our ballads.[2] Anne Swang disagrees with the view expressed in an older article by Rikard Berge where he tried to prove that the ballad had a historical basis and that the seducer was a priest.[3] As a Catholic priest he could not marry, and the ballad was the story of an unhappy love affair. I do not think this can be the correct interpretation, and in taking this as a starting point I am in full agreement with Anne Swang. The same view has been expressed earlier in the restored popular edition of Norwegian ballads by Knut Liestøl and Moltke Moe (first published in Oslo 1920-24).[4] Characteristically enough, this view is supported by information given by the first collector, Sophus Bugge, who cites his two women informants thus: "the women who sang for me were both of the definite opinion that Jon of Vaddelio was a tusse or bergmann," that is, one of the hillfolk.

We must, then, be fairly safe in assuming that the ballad is about a triangle where a woman is betrothed to a man but at the same time is bound to a supernatural being. Such a bondage is familiar from a large number of folktales, and is in full accordance with folklore, which time and again tells of the compelling power that a vette can exert over a mortal. It is a misleading simplification to talk about seduction in this connection, since the ballad only has sympathy for the difficult position that Margjit finds herself in when the wedding with her betrothed approaches and she knows that she is carrying the vette's child.

A more complete rendering of the narrative can be formulated as follows:

For some time there has been a close relationship between the woman and the bergmann or tusse. He has given her a pipe or horn to blow should she need his help. Already in the first stanza she goes out into the forest and sends the agreed signal. The vette understands the cause and is filled with sorrow. They meet, and in one version he tries to persuade the woman to come away and live with him, in two beautiful stanzas of love poetry:

Eg sill' gjeva ut hest og sal'e,
venast i lunden gjeng,
var du Margjit så glad i meg
som lauvet i logjen brenn.

/I would give you horse and saddle, / Fairest to step through the fern /orig., wood or grove7 / If you loved me so dear Margjit / As the leaves in the bright flame burn.7

Eg sill' gjeva ut hest og sal'e,
venast du ville ride,
var du Margjit kjærasten min
og eg sov innmed di side.

/I would give you horse and saddle, / Fairest of all you would ride, / If you were my own love, Margjit / And I slept by your side.7

She replies that she is not free to make her own choice, since she has been betrothed (by others--her parents or close relatives) to Tarjei Risvollo. In other words, we have a situation which is characteristic of the old Norwegian farming society: a woman did not usually have a free choice of husband. It was her family who decided for her.

The subsequent verses, occurring in all the best versions, tell how Margjit spends the whole night with Jon the vette and how the two part sorrowfully at sunrise. The struggle inside Margjit is made clearly apparent in these verses. She could have chosen a life in the mountain, the vette-home, but the ties binding her to her own kind and her betrothed were stronger.

Similarly, the different versions all include, in detail, the meeting between Margjit and her maidservant when Margjit comes home. She is forced to lie, saying that she was lost in the forest and has only just managed to find her way home again. But the servant guesses what has happened and says that she must have met herre Jon. This word herre is used by Rikard Berge as one of the arguments supporting his contention that a priest is involved, since the word was used as the title for a priest. At the same time it was also used for men of comparatively high social rank, as we see frequently in the ballads.

In the next two stanzas, Margjit tries to explain her plight, not directly, but by getting the servant to imagine herself in trouble: "She did not know what her own position would be. . . ." These stanzas have two difficult words which none of the informants understood: heljelauk and heljelinde. The first part of these words is probably identical with hel, "death," and the meaning seems clear, despite the misunderstanding to which the words could give rise.

The servant offers to receive Margjit's betrothed when he comes to fetch her, for she sees that Margjit must take to her bed. This fetching of the bride plays an important role in the ballad, and each detail in the narrative is in full accord with ancient Norwegian wedding customs. The bridegroom has to take the bride home. He brings a horse for her to ride, and is accompanied by groomsmen. The bride is expected to be finely dressed and to meet the bridegroom and his company with words of welcome and give them something to drink. All this the servant has to do. The bridegroom, Targjei, guesses from her words that something is wrong with Margjit and goes to speak to her alone. He finds that she has given birth to twins. It is implicitly understood that they must be baptized immediately. Because of this urgency, Targjei undertakes the task. To conceal the truth, he puts on woman's clothes and goes to the priest. It seems that the children must have died immediately after the baptism, for one verse tells of Targjei looking on while they are buried, thinking of his own difficult positon. It is, says the ballad with a strong expression of sorrow, "Som eggjine skåre hold" (as if sharp blades are carving into his living flesh).

Juding from the different versions, what happens later is not quite clear, but it is reasonable to assume from some of them that Tarjei has returned to Margjit and told her about the baptism, thus consoling her. Then Margjit has died, and the ballad ends with an arresting stanza where Tarjei is riding homeward followed by the bride's horse with its empty saddle. This verse is one of the best constructed and most full of feeling in ballad literature.

We must not forget the refrain: "Det var mi og alli di / som hjala her unde lio" (that was mine and never thine that called from the hillside). Who is being referred to here, Tarjei or Jon? Much of the triangle problem is present in this formulation, to which it is impossible to give a clear answer.

In the Scandinavian ballad catalogue this ballad is included among the ballads of the supernatural, and this classification is completely justifiable. Knut Liestøl and Moltke Moe had earlier listed the ballad of Margjit and Tarjei and Jon as a ballad of chivalry, presumably because they felt that this was indicated by certain words and titles such as herre Jon, fruva Margjit, or by the fact that Margjit had a terne (maidservant). I believe that this vocabulary has a much more obvious and simpler explanation, that of the linguistic influence of the many ballads of chivalry which flourished in the same social environment and were sung and recited by the same informants. All the expressions belong naturally to the so-called language of the ballads of chivalry.

If we ignore such external elements, it is clear that the social environment depicted in the ballads is that of a Norwegian farming community. While Rikard Berge is correct here, I think that he is mistaken when he tries to make the ballad historical and linked to particular localities, especially on the basis of place names in the texts. Place names in ballads are not in themselves a decisive criterion for localization, since in many cases they have crept into the texts at a late stage, after transmission has affected the contents.

The environment depicted in this ballad is altogether so completely Norwegian that we are not surprised that there are no corresponding ballads in the other Nordic countries or elsewhere. It is true that there is a certain resemblance of motif with the Danish ballad "Brud i Vaande" (DgF 277) and with the English "Little Musgrave and Lady Barnard" (Child 81), and some place names resemble Icelandic and Færoese names, but there can be no question of any direct parallel.

The characters in the ballad, then, with the exception of the bergmann, Jon, must be recognised as members of a Norwegian farming community. The customs that are described are the same ones that we know from hundreds of descriptions of farming community traditions. This supposition is also true of one of the main points affecting our interpretation of the ballad, that is, whether or not the third main character is a supernatural being.

Here it should suffice to cite generally accepted folklore where there is almost no end to accounts of human beings carried away as captives to another world under the mountains, of rescuers, and of conflicts with supernatural beings, but also of peaceful coexistence. Neither Margjit's servant nor her betrothed accuses her of unfaithfulness, a serious crime; both accept the situation and even show understanding. This response has its roots in the attitude that the forces of nature--and these include all that comes from under the earth--in many ways were stronger than mortals, and thus through their arts could exert power over such mortals. Whoever fell into the hands of these supernatural forces could not stand up against such forces on equal terms, but was at a disadvantage from the start. Very strong forces would be needed to help those who clashed with the supernatural (rescue was usually associated with the ringing of church bells).

This set of beliefs has many facets, but the ballad's tone always is fateful, hinting of lurking dangers. Whoever finds himself or herself in such a situation has no real control over the course of events, but is at the mercy of stronger powers. This explains why neither the betrothed nor the maidservant thinks of accusing Margjit of unfaithfulness. In "Brud i Vaande" we have a completely different situation, one where the husband knows that his wife has been seduced, but nevertheless forgives her and tries to help her as best he can. Targjei does the same, but for different reasons.

The natural setting, the conceptions of supernatural beings, and the customs which are described are all, then,

at decisive points, in accord with a Norwegian folk
environment. These factors are not, perhaps, by themselves
enough to prove without a doubt that this is a Norwegian
ballad that has sprung from a Norwegian farming environment
and that is founded on its common beliefs and customs. An
examination of the words and expressions that occur in the
texts can therefore be illuminating.

We have already, in passing, mentioned place names in
the ballad. While these place names are all found in a
somewhat larger geographical area than where the ballad was
recorded, they are not, therefore, proof of its provenance
and even less of its historicity. It is, of course, possible
that the ballad could have originated in Telemark, but the
personal names give only a weak basis for linking it with
particular individuals.

The woman's name, Margjit (Margit), is one of the most
frequently occurring in the Norwegian ballad tradition,
while the man's name, Targjei (a dialect form of Torgeir),
was common throughout the whole medieval period and later
both in Telemark and in surrounding communities.[5] The name
given to the bergmann, Jon, has, it is true, a Christian
origin (a more common form of Johannes), but it is hardly
proof that only humans could have such a name. We find it
used several times in the tradition about the folk from
inside the mountains. The explanations must be that the name
was so common that it could be used in all sorts of
connections. The fourth name, of the maidservant Kristi, has
similarly long been in common use. It is more noteworthy,
however, that the word terne is used for a servant girl.
This word is today used only in one place in the country,
far from Telemark, but it belonged to the old ballad
vocabulary and to romantic literary poetry.

Two of the best versions say that Margjit was attending
cattle on the hillsides to the north. While it is not
completely unthinkable that a grown woman would be doing so,
usually it was older children who were given this job. In
folk tradition it is sometimes very young, unmarried women
tending animals who fall prey to a bergmann or tusse and his
wiles.

That this incident happened to the north is perhaps not
merely accidental. Instead, this motif indicates that folk
beliefs are involved, because the folk constantly talk of
evil coming from the north, where danger always threatens.
There the jotuns of mythology were to be found, and in folk
belief danger always came from that direction. It must,
therefore, be more than a coincidence that the north is
mentioned in these versions. Tending cattle is also a sure

sign that this is a farm-woman. Of course this detail can also be a later addition, an attempt to provide a good reason for Margjit going out alone. Other versions merely say that she is walking, not that she is tending cattle.

When the servant Kristi reproves Margjit and says that it is not seemly for an unmarried girl to walk alone in the forest this statement must be regarded as general advice. We can compare it with what we find in other ballads, for example the ballad of the spell cast over Margjit Hjukse (TSB A54). This Margjit was stolen away precisely because she insisted on taking a short-cut when riding to church.

In the ballad there are also inserted two gamlestev to the effect that preparations for receiving guests were incomplete. It is not unusual that such independent single verses or series of single verses should be included in the epic ballad when the occasion occurred. The gamlestev, with the same formal structure as the four-line ballad stanza, was for a long time considered common property, and easily could be used to fill in a space in the narrative. In our ballad it is true that we do not have a farm wedding but the fetching of the bride to the bridegroom's farm, where the wedding was usually held. Also, while the fetching of the bride was an occasion which had to be marked by ceremony, the preparations for this ceremony had not been properly carried out. The tradition has used gamlestev to mark this omission.

The most important point in the ballad, apart from the fatal capitulation to the bergmann Jon, is the meeting between the betrothed and his appointed bride. Here we must, I feel, assume that the tradition has failed to make clear, or, more correctly, to retain, what originally appears to have transpired in their conversation and what subsequently took place. This scene treats unusual happenings in the epic ballad: it depicts human emotions stripped of all external drama and concentration of action. Yet the transcriptions agree relatively well and all have Targjei in woman's clothes taking the children to be baptised. This touch of the woman's clothes is characteristic of what tradition can retain. Targjei obviously does it to hide the identity of those concerned. But in any case, at such an emergency baptism there was no real formal question of establishing who the children's parents were. According to folk belief and practice the most important matter was that the children should be baptised; otherwise they had no claim to the bliss of heaven.

As I have already mentioned, part of the ballad motif offers a certain resemblance to other ballads and to folktales. In "Brud i Vaande" we are told of a knight who is betrothed to, and takes home, a wife who gives birth to two children on the bridal journey itself. She only can think of burying the newborn babies alive, but the knight manages to find them foster-parents. Then he escorts his bride home and tries to shield her as well as he can during the wedding itself. He himself spends the wedding night on a bed of straw and tells his mother that the custom in his bride's country is for the bride to sleep alone for six weeks after the wedding. The bridegroom does not lose his love for the bride. In "Little Musgrave and Lady Barnard" we have infidelity and clandestine meetings, a betrothed who comes home unexpectedly, a horn blown, and, as the chief feature, the woman dying. The end, then, is tragic, but in a completely different way than in our ballad.

The humane attitude of the knight in "Brud i Vaande" has a parallel in the actions of Targjei Risvollo. He too, helps Margjit in her difficulties in every way he can, and does not reject her as he might well have done. One could say that this behaviour is a demonstration of the humane religious viewpoint which humans represent in contrast with the non-human. But here it must be added that neither is Margjit forced to stay with the vette. This could have happened in the folk tradition. It seems as if the author (and the tradition) have concentrated on a different aspect of the tragedy. Some Icelandic folktales show a similar tendency, for example "Kötludraumar."[6] In this tale the man concerned is gripped by a heavy sorrow, but forgives the woman because there were powers that none could resist.

And here we also can see the framework of the epic action in the ballad of Margjit, Targjei and Jon that the author and the tradition have taken pains to emphasize, one side of the dangerous relationship between humans and non-humans. The supernatural provides a background for the fateful events, but human knowledge and deep sympathy with the victims raise the theme from the trivial to the tragic. It becomes an illustration of how difficult life can be. Without such a background of belief the theme could not achieve such a tragic treatment. Forgiveness is taken for granted precisely because of the firm belief in the realities inherent in such contact with the supernatural.

This ballad also illustrates that ballad composers could take up complicated psychological themes. We can, with a certain amount of justification, compare it with the most famous of all love poems of the Middle Ages, the story of Tristram and Isolde. There we recognize the same theme, but without the supernatural beings. The fatal love in the story of Tristram and Isolde is explained by the use of a love potion, in our ballad by the presence of non-mortals.

From the point of view of composition we must be aware that the ballad holds something back until the final stanzas. In this way the introduction takes on a character which is premonitory and which creates the necessary mood. The author only allows illumination to come gradually as the action unfolds, until eventually characters and events stand revealed. This gives the ballad a special artistic value. If the tradition has succeeded in retaining its hold on the feelings of the ballad's audience, it must be the result of the continuing vitality of folk beliefs right up to the time when the ballad was transcribed in the middle of the nineteenth century.

Finally, let me add a few words on the informants' choice of repertoire and the role of the informant in the transmission process. In my view it is quite satisfying that informants have attracted more attention in recent years from researchers in folklore. They had long been a neglected group in whom few took interest. It can, however, be of doubtful value to attach too much weight to what one can infer from each individual informant's repertoire, and, still more, from the life story of the person concerned. Of course there can be a connection, but other factors play their part, too. Nor must we forget that much is purely accidental. We know little or nothing about the many people who transmitted these traditions in previous generations, or what aroused their interest. Nor can it be right to delve too deeply into the private life of individuals. Such probing seldom leads to scientifically valuable evidence.

NOTES

[1] Bengt R. Jonsson, Svale Solheim, and Eva Danielson, eds., with Mortan Nolsøe and W. Edson Richmond, The Types of the Scandinavian Medieval Ballad: A Descriptive Catalogue (Oslo: Universitetsforlaget, 1978), p. 41.

[2] Anne Swang, "Tankar kring visa om Margit og Targjei Risvollo," Norveg, 21 (1978), 167-82 /English summary7.

[3] Rikard Berge, "Margit og Targjeir paa Risvoddom," Norsk Folkekultur, 2 (1916), 185-210.

[4] Knut Liestøl and Moltke Moe, eds., Norske Folkevisor, 3 vols. (Kristiania: J. Dybwad, 1920-24).

[5] Eyvind Fjeld Halvorsen, "Personnavn i Setesdal i middelalderen," Norveg, 21 (1978), 5-24 /English summary7.

[6] Jon Arnason, Islanzkar Þjoosogur og ævintyri (Reykjavik: Bokautgafn, 1954), I, 59.

Oslo University
Oslo, Norway

PERFORMANCE THEORY AND BALLAD PERFORMERS

THE BERRYFIELDS O' BLAIR

by Belle Stewart

1. Oh when berrytime comes roond each year, Blair's
      population's swellin',
   There's every kind o' picker there an' every kind o'
      dwellin',
   There's tents an' huts an' caravans, there's bothies and
      there's bivvies,* /*bivouacs7
   And shelters made wi' tattie-bags* an' dugoots made wi'
      divvies*. /*potato sacks,*divots7

2. Noo there's corner-boys frae Glescae*, kettle-boilers fae
      Lochee, /*Glasgow7
   An' miners fae the pits o' Fife, mill-workers fae Dundee,
   An' fisher-folk fae Peterheid an' tramps fae everywhere
   Aa lookin' for a livin' aff the berryfields o' Blair.

3. Noo there's Traivellers fae the Western Isles, fae
      Arran, Mull an' Skye,
   Fae Harris, Lewis an' Kyles o' Bute they come their luck
      tae try;
   Fae Inverness and Aiberdeen, fae Stornoway and Wick,
   Aa flock tae Blair at the berrytime the straws and rasps
      tae pick.

4. Noo there's some who earn a pound or twa, some cannae
      earn their keep,
   And some wad pick fae morn tae nicht, an' some wad
      raither sleep;
   But there's some wha has tae pick or stairve, and some
      wha dinnae care,
   And there's some wha bless, an' some wha curse, the
      berryfields o' Blair.

5. Noo there's families pickin' for one purse an' some wha
      pick alane,
   And there's men wha share an' share alike wi' wives
      that's no' their ain,
   There's gladness and there's sadness tae, there's happy
      hairts an' sair*, /*sore7
   For there's comedy an' tragedy played on the fields o'
      Blair.

303

6. But afore I put my pen awa' it's this I wad like to say:
   Ye'll traivel far before you'll meet a kinder lot than
   they;
   For I've mixed wi' them in field an' pub, and while I've
   breath to spare,
   I'll bless the hand that led me tae the berryfields o'
   Blair.

JAMES PORTER

PARODY AND SATIRE AS MEDIATORS OF CHANGE IN THE
TRADITIONAL SONGS OF BELLE STEWART

Explaining the nature of human traditions, general or
particular, has been a continuous challenge to scholarship.
Commenting on the paradoxical aspect of "tradition" as an
abstraction, Bertrand Bronson observes that, human nature
being what it is, "always at the heels of tradition lurks an
ironic negative."[1] Thus the canons and norms of a
traditional art form, for instance, are accompanied by an
urge to contradict or invert these canons and norms. Often
this occurs at the distance of a generation: ". . . the
high seriousness of the parents is the children's favorite
joke. . . . The passing generations do not see things in
quite the same way, or with the same eyes. History itself
is continually subject to reinterpretation."[2] One could
argue that this trait is also perceptible, synchronically as
it were, in the artistry of the individual performer, who
juggles ambivalence towards his or her tradition in
accordance with the dualisms of personality.

The much-cited tendencies of conservatism and
innovation are clearly embedded in this ambivalence. If one
accepts the notion, grounded in Piaget's view of language as
"whole, capable of transformation, self-regulating,
autonomous and internally coherent,"[3] that the creation and
performance of traditional genres involve the emergence of
styles that revolt against the old, not as their antithesis
but as a recasting of permanent elements, then parody and
satire in particular assume a significant role.[4] In folklore
performance these last two especially serve a mediating
function between the poles of conservatism and innovation.
As devices in both literary and oral genres, satire and
parody actively reshape traditions by drawing attention to
their outmoded parameters of style, making them
"perceptible" again.[5] This is notably the case with parody,
which is associated as much with the manipulation of
conventional form as it is with social lampoon. Satire, on
the other hand, is generally considered to carry a more
direct social function by means of its content.[6]

The creative personality in a traditional society will
often recast familiar material in a contrastive mold. For the
sake of situational effect this may mean the metamorphosis

305

of venerable ballad, say, into satire or the turning of a
sentimental lyric into bawdry. Refacimentos of a parodic
character, even when they appear to embody "the ironic
negative," are nevertheless traditional since satire and
parody are related on the one hand to the need for social
change (their contextual function) aand on the other to the
exigencies of style change (their generic function).[7] Parody
and satire, therefore, fulfill essential transformational
roles as mediators between the canons and norms of
traditional expressive structures and the constant need, on
the part of the creative individual, to reassess and renew
these "rules" of composition. Since in folk traditions such
roles and functions mean performance, parody and satire
serve as contextual and generic mediators.[8] Satirical songs,
it should be emphasized, are not mere passive agents of
change but forms that catalyze, and reconstruct, the
conventions of art and society.

"Tradition" and "traditional society" as used here
deserve brief clarification. "Traditionality" has been
attacked as a criterion for defining folklore,[9] but it has
also been defended for its conveying a sense of the
persistence and pervasiveness that underlie human modes of
communication and expression.[10] One may allow, at least,
that the more concrete entity of "traditional society" draws
on "tradition" as the basic criterion for social activity.
Eisenstadt, for example, has stressed that traditional
societies share in the acceptance of tradition, "the
givenness of some actual or symbolic past event, order or
figure as the major focus of their collective identity;
traditionality not only serves as a symbol of continuity, it
delineates the legitimate limits of creativity and
innovation and is the major criterion of their
legitimacy."[11] Put more concisely, traditionality is a
valuative means of structuring collective experience.

Determining where the limits of a "local tradition" lie
is also problematic and has been the subject of some
dispute: Redfield's "folk-urban continuum" is one of the
best-known, and controversial, formulations.[12] Even if one
were to accept a certain amount of homogeneity in a small-
scale society such as that postulated by the more utopian
anthropologists, the question of "local boundaries" in a
complex society still has to be answered: do these lie at
the edge of a village or small town community, or on the
periphery of the urban ghetto? Are they delimited by
language or dialect; are they bound by ethnicity or by a
larger abstraction such as state or nation? A constituent
member of a subgroup in a complex society may feel attached
to more than one, or indeed all of these communities, to
some degree at various times. Psychologically, people

possess a number of identities that they manipulate according to a given situation.[13]

In small-scale societies, as Max Gluckman has argued, a person plays a multiplicity of roles with the same set of people in the same locale and is unable to segregate his different roles by locating them in different groups and places; he therefore relies on rituals, taboos and elaborate etiquette to signal his movement from one role to another.[14] In an urbanized community, where the varied roles of the individual are divided among separate groups and locales, elaborate ritual is not required to separate them.[15] Debatable though it may be, this hypothesis of the "multiplexity" of relationships in a bounded community has some significance in studying the evolution of subgroups in more complex societies, especially in the matter of ritual behavior.[16] On could suggest, in applying Gluckman's notion to such subgroups in a complex society as, for instance, Travelling People in Northern Europe, that the gradual assimilation through which they are currently passing involves some learning by the individual of separate kinds of role behavior that were neither necessary nor useful in the relatively homogeneous community of a generation ago.

As noted above, small-scale societies have been somewhat idealized in scholarly formulations.[17] But in observing life in a traditional society it is useful to bear in mind not only Durkheim's notion of ritual as contributing to social solidarity but also the Gemeinschaft of Tonnies and Mauss's idea of reciprocity as the basis of social life.[18] Victor Turner's more recent concept of communitas has similar associations, though stripped of romantic idealism. A community of this kind operates by means of informal contracts and a reciprocity that is realized through a restricted network of kin and acquaintances as well as within an oicotypal system of social and cultural values. "Local tradition," then, refers to a nexus of traditional life circumscribed by cultural, economic, and valuative boundaries that, following Malinowski's famous injunction, are recognized, drawn, and articulated by those who belong to that tradition.[19]

A further problem in assessing the mechanisms of a local tradition, and of conservatism and innovation in relation to artistic activity, is the tension between the individual and society. As Jakobson and Bogatyrev have remarked, the weight of conservatism in attitudes and values within traditional groups imposes firm and usually formalized constraints on individual creativity: the creative personality in a folk society is bound by tradition and has to face a prohibition against overcoming

censorship.[20] While such strict censoriousness was perhaps
truer of the Eastern European peasant communities Jakobson
and Bogatyrev had in mind than their small-scale rural
counterparts in Western Europe, where the historical
development was more rapid and the social structure more
diversified, the principle of limitations on creativity that
are informally imposed by the community is plausible enough
for the present discussion. The traditional artist may seek,
however, for personal or social reasons, to accelerate the
rate of change governing his local community's assumptions
or world view. But he can often only accomplish this,
paradoxically, by adapting traditional styles of expression.
The innovative artist is forced to enliven the "ironic
negative" of tradition by cultivating forms such as parody
and satire so that organic movement is given an active,
stimulating impulse. At the same time, these poetic and
musical structures act as socially sanctioned mediators
between conservatism and innovation; their content may be
original, but their form tends to remain stable.[21]

The text of a song, for instance, may carry a message
that is satirically explicit, or parodically implicit, while
its musical and poetic design follows established norms. It
must be stressed here, though, that the singer's mode of
performance can be of crucial importance, for the degree of
emphasis or shading of a sung line in concrete enactments
can transform the surface meaning, just as in prose or
spoken verse. As several commentators have noted, the
contextual factor therefore must be considered in
conjunction with the linguistic code and meaning, so that
these are seen as different aspects of a single event.[22]
Context influences the mediating function of parody and
satire as these are cast in specific forms of prose, song,
or verse and performed for particular audiences in bounded
situations. The gentler style or accommodating tone of the
enactor may modify the effect, for instance, of the language
in a verse lampoon.[23]

The social and expressive world of performance for the
traditional artist, in western societies, nurtured before
World War II has been transformed during the past few
generations. Rapid change has disturbed the intimacy and
reciprocity characteristic of traditional communities but
has also offered adaptive strategies such that numerous folk
performers have contrived to adjust their traditional skills
to an extension of boundaries and new audiences. Yet the
experience of some who began to concertize during the 1950s
and 1960s has suggested that the further the performer moves
from the locus of creativity (kin, restricted network of
acquaintances, domestic and local concerns, standards and
values) the harder the sanctions on communication and

meaning tend to become, while concurrently the demand for relevance on a more universal plane increases. In such cases the relative flexibility of tradition in local contexts, where the artist and audience know with some exactitude how constraints may be extended or when communicative and interpretive codes may be switched, is exchanged for an apparently broader structure of repertoire and wider frame of reference, though these are actually more constricted because the social base of tradition has been transformed. The "unified expressive system" of poetic forms believed by Jakobson and Bogatyrev to be typical of the traditional folk society has been modified by a new set of aesthetic norms governing performance, namely those of mass entertainment.[24]

The singer who moves out of the circumscribed, traditional community into a populous, mobile and highly commercial world has often been misunderstood, or typecast as naive, primitive or quaint. Not surprisingly in such contexts, singers have tended to drift into "art" on the one hand (namely, idiosyncratic treatment of traditional material) or "folksiness" on the other (that is, self-parody induced by the exchange of traditional for non-traditional contexts of performance). Without local referents and interpreters the symbolic meaning, or meanings, of the individual song invite distortion through misinterpretation of the code.[25]

There is evidence, certainly, that this has occurred in some cases: singers from small, rural or self-contained communities have found it difficult or impossible to adjust to the anonymity, fads, pace and stress of urban life and mass media pressures. Yet the human personality is resilient: moreover, it is frequently those performers who have been at odds in some way with their community who have adjusted most confidently to the wider contexts of club circuit and concert stage. Such artists have generally encountered and mastered, in their experience, three types of context in the performance of traditional songs: first, the domestic, small-scale and familiar kind that corresponds to the norms of traditional society; second, the milieu of informal ceilidhs and folk festivals, where the audience is composed mainly though not exclusively of local persons; and third, the full-blown concert tour, which involves audiences of strangers at staged performances in unfamiliar locations. However the individual singer may react to these last two contexts in particular, it is nevertheless valid to admit the less stable and controllable nature of these contexts for the performance of traditional material. This naturally carries important implications for the understanding, by a non-local audience, of satirical songs whose essential function and purpose lie in local, traditional circumstances.

Considerations of this kind are a necessary prelude to the study of traditional performers who have experienced the move from their traditional society to the wider world of mass entertainment. In the case of Belle Stewart, whose family has played a significant part in the Scottish and American Folksong Revival of the 1950s and 1960s, such factors are germane to any discussion of culture change or individual strategies of adaptation. Belle, with her late husband Alex and her daughters Cathie and Sheila, are well enough known even to casual observers of the Revival that centered on the Lowland Travellers of Scotland, first made known to the "outside" world through recordings and stage appearances in the 1960s. The Stewart family has recorded traditional songs and music for major companies such as Topic (London) and has performed widely in folk clubs and at festivals throughout Britain and North America.[26] An extended study of the family is currently being prepared, and Belle herself is the subject of a dissertation.[27]

With their immediate relatives in Blairgowrie, the little Perthshire town where Belle and her daughters still live, and with Jeannie Robertson and her family from Aberdeen in the Northeast, the Stewarts have formed the nucleus of the Revival since the mid-1950s, when folklorists such as Hamish Henderson and anthropologists such as Frank Vallee and Farnham Rehfisch began to study the traditional life of Travellers around Blairgowrie in the heart of the Strathmore fruit fields.[28] At that time (1954) the Stewarts, who had settled in the area, owned a berryfield on a hill slope at Wester Essendy, overlooking Marlee Loch. Later they also had a fruit field at The Cleaves beside the circle of Standing Stones through which the road passes on its way from Blairgowrie to Essendy.[29] Maurice Fleming, a native of Blairgowrie, was the first to draw attention to the talents of the Stewart family as traditional musicians and singers. Hamish Henderson, during fieldwork, had heard a singer from Elgin in the Northeast, John MacDonald, perform a song he called "The Berryfields o' Blair" and had asked Fleming to track down the composer of this satirical song, who turned out to be Belle: "the paradoxical truth is, therefore," wrote Henderson later, "that the Stewarts became known mainly because one of their songs had become 'anonymous,' i.e., had proved itself a folk song."[30]

As Henderson has also observed, the berrypicking season that formed the topic of Belle's song was the occasion for socializing and music-making among the Travellers, many of whom relied on seasonal labor, and for the creative mingling of traditional expressive genres:

> Unlike most of the rich berryfield owners in the area, the then proprietors of the "Standing Stones" /berryfield7 were of traveller stock--Alex and Belle Stewart, themselves notable folk performers --and they were naturally on intimate friendly terms with the gaberlunzie families, still "on the road," who camped on their land and helped to harvest their crop of berries. This gave the Standing Stones the feel almost of a little traveller principality of its own, a joyful snook cocked at orthodox law and order, like Garcia Lorca's "City of the Gypsies." . . . After the day's picking was over, and the evening feed cooked and eaten, there was a bit of moving to and fro between the camp-fires. Two or three folk from one "camp" would join their neighbours, and a ceilidh would get under way. . . . By this time, four or five similar ceilidhs might well be going on in the one berryfield, and the excited collector would have to decide whether to stay on at the first camp-fire of his choice, or move to another . . . from which, maybe, he could hear tantalizing fragments of a rare Child ballad, or the high flamenco-like cadences of a Gaelic tinker love-lament. Recording in the berryfields, in fact, was--and is--like holding a tin-can under the Niagara Falls; in a single session you can hear everything from ancient Ossianic hero-tales, whose content reflects the life of primitive hunter-tribesmen, to the caustic pop-song parodies thought up by Clydeside teenagers the same afternoon.[31]

The speculative origins of the Travellers (the term they themselves insist on in preference to the pejorative "tinker") need not be recounted again here.[32] It is perhaps enough to note their proud adherence to surnames like Macgregor, Robertson, or Stewart; their uncomfortable relationship with the settled population, which tends to regard them as parasitical; their cultivation of traditional trades and crafts (tin-smithing, horse-trading and, more recently, car-dealing), and their lively and variegated repertoire of oral expressive forms.[33] The traditional life and social organization of Scottish Travellers, both Highland and Lowland, have parallels among travelling groups in Ireland and other parts of northern Europe.[34] As a subgroup in complex society, bound by ties of kinship, reciprocity and ritual, the Lowland Travellers conform very nearly to the concept of a small-scale, traditional society

of the type formulated by folklorists and social
anthropologists. Change, however, in the form of
legislation on settlement and education and intermarriage
with non-Travellers, has begun to overtake them and to
affect the patterns of interaction with the wider society.[35]

It was into the pre-integration society of Travellers
that Belle Macgregor was born on July 18, 1907 in the
township of Alyth, four and a half miles northeast of
Blairgowrie. Her mother, Martha Stewart, came from Caputh,
another village five miles on the way to the ancient Celtic
site of Dunkeld as one travels west into the wooded glens of
central Perthshire. Her father, Donald Macgregor, was a
native of Blair Atholl, a village a dozen or so miles to the
north. Belle's family were travelling tinsmiths who
traversed the Perthshire highlands buying and selling goods
and working on the farms at harvest time. Her grandfather,
she has related, was brutally murdered as the result of
differences with another travelling clan.[36]

Belle's mother and mother-in-law were first cousins, a
link that typifies the complex chain of kin structure among
Travellers. These blood relationships account in large part
for their close-knit traditional life, at least until
recently.[37] Alex's mother, moreover, was renowned among her
people as a singer and narrator: Belle heard her first sing
the lyric that later became famous in the Folksong Revival,
"The Mountain Streams Where the Moorcock Crows."[38] Reared in
the eastern seaboard city of Montrose, she also taught
Belle's daughters some of her tale repertoire. Like many
Lowland Travellers, Belle's mother-in-law and her husband
were familiar with Highland ways (she was a Campbell from
Argyll in the West Highlands), and they farmed a small
property for a while at Milton of Tullymet, near Ballinluig
in the Perthshire upcountry. Old John Stewart lived with
Alex and Belle in 1954, and was honored as a champion piper
in his own right, having won every major pibroch award in
Scotland. He is reputed to have composed the tune familiar
to a generation of bagpipers, "The Braes o' Tullymet," as
well as "The Top of Craig Vinean," "Dunkeld Bridge," and
others.[39]

The practice of making songs and composing tunes after
traditional models pervades Traveller culture and is central
to the study of Belle and her family, since it was their
habit to create songs about themselves or acquaintances,
especially at New Year's time. Sheila and Belle, commenting
on their composition entitled "My Father's Name Is Alex,"
described the process:

> We always make it wir business tae. . . . Every
> Hogmanay /New Year's Eve7 night we make something
> up. . . . When we go to wir brithers' hooses an' rin
> aboot to the rest o' them, ye know? Sing it to
> them. . . . Everybody has to make something up.[40]

This competitiveness, involving texts of compositional
ability within the immediate kin group, and the frequent use
of parody and satire, tends to suggest a hypothesis of the
family's collective orientation towards active change within
a traditional framework. Competition, organized in terms of
an annual ritual, served as a device to encourage individual
competence in developing fresh linguistic and symbolic
shapes from the conjunction of parody or satire and
traditional form.

Belle was the youngest in her family and the only girl.
Because her father died when she was only seven months old,
her two brothers were especially protective. Donald, the
elder, taught Belle most of the traditional versions of
songs he had learned from their father, and the two became
so attached that she would sometimes refer to Donald, when
she was still quite young, as her father. This
psychological dependence may account in part for Belle's
preference for certain types of song, specifically those
that impressed themselves on her in listening to and
imitating Donald (her surrogate father) as she developed
musical and verbal competences. The younger brother, Andy,
was likewise musical and fond of songs but because he was
more reserved he did not practice singing in public.

Belle's brothers died within a week of each other:
Donald first, from complications brought on by bronchitis
and asthma, according to Belle. At exactly 5:15 the
following Sunday, Andy passed away although there was
apparently nothing amiss. Because the brothers had been
inseparable while alive, Belle remarked how the Traveller
community believed that Donald "came back for Andy," and she
herself still feels an acute sense of loss as the Christmas
period approaches (her brothers died December 20 and 27).

Belle knew Alex Stewart, her husband-to-be, when she
was growing up in Blairgowrie, but he migrated to Ireland in
the fashion of many Lowland Travellers, remaining there
eighteen years. Thus Belle only met him again later; they
were married in Ireland and Cathie was born there. The
family encountered many friendly folk in their Irish travels
but also ran into trouble on occasion from local Travellers
who felt they were untrustworthy.[41] Belle picked up songs
during this period although most of her repertoire in her
formative years came from her brother Donald, who was "so

fond of singing it was almost a habit." Like Jeannie Robertson her cousin in her own family circle, Belle felt her imagination gripped by the magic of the older ballads and ballad-singing. "The Twa Brothers" (Child 49) quickly became one of her favorites as a song known widely among the Macgregor and Stewart clans.[42]

Donald could not write but Belle, who on the whole did not regard herself as "a good scholar," developed the practice of writing out the words of this and other songs for her daughters Cathie and Sheila. She would give them the text in this way and the tune by demonstration, transmitting the songs not in the purely oral fashion as she had learned them but by supplementing direct oral transmission with written words, a common practice among Lowland Travellers in the past few generations.[43] As in the case of Jeannie Robertson again, Belle was fascinated by the older songs and tales as performed items, as enactments that contained both "truth" in an experiential sense and resonant symbols of identity for Travellers. The content and style, combined with the communication of feeling, were for her the central appeal of traditional singing, and these affective modes of expression she has imparted to her daughters.

Several issues emerge from this outline of traditional singing and composing within the Stewart family. These may be shortly defined as (1) the process of learning and transmitting a cultural code and system of symbols (2) the meaning of these symbols as they appear in songs and singing, and (3) the creation of original songs within a traditional framework.

In discussing the first issue, one can note that the acquisition of various competences such as language is attributed by some, notably Noam Chomsky, in large part to a genetically determined process; others believe that competence rather can be attributed to learning, as in behaviorist models; still others favor a fundamentally interactive approach, such as that of Piaget and most developmental psychologists.[44] Critical of the view that the mind consists of deep, generalized operational structures that undergo broad, stage-like development, Howard Gardner has recently outlined seven kinds of competence that humans appear to acquire: linguistic, spatial, logical-mathematical, bodily kinesthetic, musical, interpersonal (interaction with "significant others," cooperation), and intrapersonal (self-knowledge); these are cross-cut by three realms of knowledge (the physical and social worlds, the world of artifacts) and by two forms of knowledge (propositional and intuitive).[45] Intellectual change in these various competences may undergo separate, independent courses of development. More importantly, some cultures may choose to highlight certain types of intelligence while minimizing or even negating other types: logical-mathematical intelligence, for instance, may be assigned primacy in western societies but may be of relatively little value elsewhere, whereas interpersonal musical or intelligences may be held in greater esteem in more traditional cultural settings.[46]

It could reasonably be proposed that Traveller society, in which Belle Stewart's family participated as constituent members, has ordered these competences in a hierarchy distinct from that of the settled population. The collectively bound nature of Traveller culture and Traveller's consciousness of being a despised minority has meant the powerful development of competences other than the logical-mathematical sort: in spatial orientation, for example, the semi-mobile world of the Travellers and their compulsive need to merge, as the Stewarts were wont to do in the summer months, with the natural world of the open road has been visually processed by them and integrated into a world view that values freedom as the primary condition of existence. Bodily kinesthetic skills, among Travellers, would include all manner of crafts as well as such roles as "the athlete, the actor, the hunter, and the dancer," while the musical faculty involves sensitivity to pitch, tonal relations and rhythmic structures and presupposes a functioning--and, one might add, discriminating--auditory system.[47] The Traveller, moreover, has traditionally viewed himself as more intelligent and versatile than his settled counterpart because he is not limited to one kind of competence or skill.[48] Other areas of development that lie outside the notion of cognition in the strict sense and that deserve examination in a more complete study of Traveller cultural modalities, include moral, social and ego development.[49]

The intelligences acquired by Belle Stewart in her Traveller childhood and transmitted by her to her daughters, notably in the performance of traditional singing, are of course primarily musical and linguistic, although to a lesser extent kinesthetic competence is involved in the paralinguistic codes accompanying a singing style: stance, gesture, facial expression.[50] These skills absorbed through face-to-face interaction may be supplemented by another relatively restricted locus of transmission for linguistic and musical competence, namely radio and recordings of traditional songs (the communication channel of written texts has already been noted). Competence in other domains, such as in the interpersonal skills of ritual and etiquette that constitute significant aspects of Traveller behavior, are transmitted in a more generalized and informal way through contact with relatives and the Traveller community at large.

Learning by imitation or observation is of course the basic kind for the novice: it is adopted spontaneously by children the world over. For many types of learning, in fact, observation alone seems sufficient to produce a competent performance, though this is often supplemented by more focussed forms of instruction such as written material and paralinguistic cues that include gesture and pantomime.[51] When information reaches a level of complexity where demonstration alone, or learning a list of rules, is unlikely to lead to mastery, other forms of information processing evolve cross-culturally: perhaps the most important and relevant of these here is the master-apprentice relationship, which exists to teach complex techniques in the arts to younger members of the society. The progress towards mastery of a form of artistic expression such as traditional singing has been compared to steps through several domains, from novice through apprentice, journeyman, craftsman, expert, master and so on, the ultimate goal being the achievement of individuality.[52] It seems clear that if these could be identified as separate stages through which Belle, and later Cathie and Sheila Stewart progressed as traditional singers, they reached the stage of mastery relatively early in the maturation process, being skilled public singers by adolescence. This suggests not only a natural aptitude for traditionally approved modes of artistic communication but also an inculcated tendency to emulate and surpass family members in competitive, ritualized situations.[53] The adaptation by the family to the formal "competitions" that have become part of many folk music festivals represents a further stage in the development of this aptitude.

The second issue that concerns us here is that of symbols and their meaning. Symbols, of course, are employed in the cognitive construction of the human world; they perform a unique function, that of representation.[54] The expressive symbols that appear in Traveller cultural forms are part of a wider system of symbols that represent Traveller identity, values, and worldview, though it should be noted that these symbols occasionally overlap with those of the settled culture. In general, however, they render dramatically what is important to the Traveller view of the world: freedom from legislation and imposed material values, union with nature, the triumph of love over adversity, the inevitability of fate. These are often expressed as themes rather than in specific images, and the difficulty of using the term "symbol" has been suggested by some scholars, who prefer such formulations as "meaning system" in order to avoid confusion between internal meanings and external signs.[55] Even here, the location of meaning offers a familiar problem: Douglas Hofstadter has reiterated the question as to whether meaning is inherent in a message or whether it is manufactured by the interaction of a mind or a mechanism with a message. In the latter case, meaning could not be said to be located in any single place nor to have any universal or objective meaning since each observer might bring its own meaning to each message; but in the former case, meaning would have both location and universality. As a result of the interaction between what is contained in cultural messages and what is contained in the interpretive system of the mind, "as a general rule, one cannot locate cultural meanings in the message."[56] Thus, an important distinction must be made between message and meaning.

Discussion of meaning inevitably involves a consideration of the mediating power of symbols, or "meaning sets," primarily as instruments of cognition and secondarily of communication. While linguistics has made some progress towards explaining the structures and functions of language, a theory of nonlinguistic signs, such as music or gesture, is still tentative despite the work of Bogatyrev, Jakobson, and Mukarovsky.[57] Jakobson has made the useful suggestion, however, in relation to music and other nonrepresentational arts, that their "imputed similarity" is the basis of an "introversive semiosis," a message that signifies itself, or where the referential component is absent or minimal. According to Jakobson, the emotive connotation remains important in those arts in which the referential or conceptual component is scanty.[58] This emphasis on the heightening of the emotive function and weakening of the referential one in such structures has broad implications for cultural behavior in general.

All cultural behavior is, by definition, based on learning and is supported by an essential aesthetic component.[59] It seems to be the case, moreover, that any human system of meaning is also likely to involve an emotional reaction: symbolic forms such as poetry and music arouse strong and well-organized responses.[60] Emotion and cognition, again, should not be seen as in opposition. following Suzanne Langer's insistence on the distinctiveness of "a vast and special evolution of <u>feeling</u> in the hominid stock," especially regarding aspects of meaningful symbolic form,[61] some have argued for a concentrated focus on the cognitive features of emotion.[62] Observing, for instance, that the making and experiencing of art is a process in which cognition and emotion are inextricably intertwined, Mihaly Csikszentmihalyi has pointed out that the conflicts art attempts to master cannot be encoded by the unambiguous symbols that reason relies on.[63]   Like any other form of knowledge, art is an adaptive tool by which we master forces in the environment in order to survive in it.   Artistic cognition models experiences that are ambiguous, and therefore it must use codes that are multivalent, changeable, and holistic but highly specific.[64]   Thus the artistic process learned, adapted and modelled by a traditional artist such as Belle Stewart involves mastery of a symbol system, or set of meanings, in which both her own and Traveller experience were embedded.   These learned representations reside, though, not just in the texts or music of her songs, but also in the style of performance that overarches them, since it encompasses a range of intelligences and behaviors that lie outside the "text" or "product" alone.   For this reason, the study of repertoire cannot afford to neglect the interpretation of performance.

Personal associations have frequently been identified as a central aesthetic factor in determining whether an artistic item will become prominent in a traditional singer's repertoire, just as "Son David" (Edward, Child 13) did in the case of Jeannie Robertson or as "Andrew Lammie" (Child 233) did for Jane Turriff, two other comparable singers of note in the Lowland Traveller tradition.[65]   "The Twa Brothers" (Child 49) was symbolically part of Belle Stewart's family experience, and her close relationship with her brothers suggests that she would inevitably attach deep personal significance to the song.   The theme of "accidental" fratricide in the text of "The Twa Brothers," however, is an oblique symbol of human failings and passions and inarticulated family conflicts. The violence that often surfaces in Traveller relationships is masked here, as in other Traveller variant texts, by a context of ostensible sport and competition between the two brothers.   In some non-Traveller variant texts the conflict is more open, revolving around the rivalry for a young woman.[66]   It is this latter, explicit reason for the conflict that has led some scholars to posit "The Two Brothers" as the parent ballad to "Son David," although these two songs, with their variant texts and tunes, are distinct and separate in Traveller tradition.[67]

The conflict here is disguised, as it is in other recorded Traveller versions, by the suggestion that the deadly blow is accidental, a parsing of the act not only to lend intensified poignance to the story but also, symbolically, to reinforce Traveller solidarity and blood ties. William's knife slips from his pocket to wound John mortally, but the former tenderly binds the wound and volunteers answers that will explain John's absence to

family members (sister, brother, sweetheart, father, step-
mother). Why William should offer two separate explanations,
however, one false, one true, to his sister and brother on
the one hand and to the sweetheart, father and stepmother on
the other is not entirely clear. But what is apparent is
that the first explanation ("You can tell her I'm away tae a
London school") may suggest a preoccupation among Lowland
Travellers with formal education and its desirability, and
the second a fixation on death as the ultimate, unifying
force with nature ("You can tell him I'm dead and in graves
laid / And the grass is growin' green").[68]

It is worth noting that Sheila, Belle's younger
daughter, who sings this ballad on a recently-issued disc,
performs a ten-stanza variant that can be instructively
compared to Belle's eight-stanza one.[69] The final sequence
of "What will you tell to your father (sweetheart, step-
mother) dear?" in Belle's text is amplified by Sheila to
"What will you tell to your brother (sister, sweetheart,
father, stepmother) dear?" These two texts were recorded in
the same year, 1955, and it appears likely that Sheila's
text was the original one taught to her by Belle, a version
that Belle subsequently shortened from five-fold to three-
fold repetition. This process is paralleled in Jeannie
Robertson's truncating of the mare, hound, hawk, brother
John sequence in "Son David" to a three-fold structure,
omitting the hawk stanza; although originally this was done
because of time restrictions in a broadcast performance,
Jeannie's "Son David" thereafter was limited to three-fold
repetition.[70] In a comparable fashion, Belle has begun in
her later years to distill her focus on songs in her
repertoire that are both essential to her personal system of
preferences and that will please her audiences. It could
also be proposed that, as singers grow older, the urge to
conserve energy results in conciseness, and this occurs at
the level of repertoire as well as within the individual
song.

Belle's repertoire in fact includes few of the older
ballads since her taste leans more towards a lyric
sensibility. The only ballads of this type sung by her on
file in the Archives of the School of Scottish Studies, or
performed by her on commercial disc, are "The Dowie Dens o'
Yarrow" (Child 214) and "The Bonnie Hoose o' Airlie" (Child
199), songs in the repertoire of Traveller singers that
often deal with family strife or heroic, quasi-historical
events. In "The Bonnie Hoose o' Airlie," for instance,
Belle's text is firmly set in the period of the Jacobite
Rising (1745-6) although the historical siege of Airlie took
place a century earlier.[71] In popular conceptions, the
original battle of Harlaw in 1411 has become entangled with

the more recent trauma of Culloden (1746), a battle that sealed the fate of the social system in the Highlands, and more searchingly, the nature of the two cultures in Scotland, Highland and Lowland.[73]

Belle learned "The Bonnie Hoose o' Airlie" from a cousin, Jimmie Whyte of Brechin in the county of Angus, when she was seven or eight, and it is one of the few songs in which, in over twenty-five years of recorded performances by her, any slackening of the tempo is perceptible. Generally, her style of singing in these and broadside ballads such as "In London's Fair City" (The Oxford Tragedy, Laws P35), "Caroline of Edinburgh Town" (Laws P27), or "transitional" lyrics (e.g., "Huntingtower") is consistent over the years, veering towards the gently pathetic rather than the grand or heroic.[74] Belle's voice is lighter in weight and texture than that of either Sheila or Cathie, who are also more vocal and outspoken that their mother, at least in the presence of outsiders. Her personality, which is warm, cheerful, and confidently assertive rather than imposing or hieratic, inclines more naturally to domestic, humorous, parodic and satirical themes in traditional singing.

These themes, as conveyed through symbols or meaning sets that represent Traveller modes of perception, behavior, and values are found in other song types: lyrics that express desire ("Here's a Health to All True Lovers") or lament lost passion ("The Banks o' Red Roses"), and comic chansons d'aventure of urban provenance such as "The Overgate," a popular Dundee song that tells of a rustic losing his money to a streetwise hussy.[75] Songs of this sort and others that deal with country life are not of course necessarily of Traveller composition, but they have been adapted by individual Traveller singers into their repertoire and retained there as the pace of urban, industrialized life in Scotland finds other means of expression. A bothy ballad such as "Bogie's Bonnie Belle," for instance, merges easily in Belle's repertoire, for reasons of association by name, with ditties such as "My Name is Betsy Bell," a saga of a search for a husband that has been traced to the days of the Victorian music-hall.[76] Belle discovered this song as a penny broadsheet in a Dundee store known as The Poet's Box when she was twelve, and put a tune she knew to the words.[77] The song is rarely sung in Revival circles but Belle has preserved the text, seeing in it, probably, the plight of women during World War I. What may also be suggested is that Belle's view of herself, and of her name as representing her persona, supplies a reason for giving these two songs a prominent place in her repertoire. Jeannie Robertson manifested the same tendency with songs enclosing her name: "O Jeannie My Dear Would Ye

Marry Me?" or "Cruel Fate" (Burns's words in the latter
song refer to his wife, Jean Armour).[78]

Belle also sings a number of Irish songs, picked up in
Ireland from Travellers or in Scotland from itinerant
laborers. Among these are "The Galway Shawl," "She Moved
Through the Fair," "The Maid of Kilmore," "The Mountain Dew"
(a song about poteen), "The Irish Soldier Boy," and what the
family calls "The Bold Colin /or Cailin/ Donn," a song
learned from a Gaelic-speaking friend who lived nearby,
Flora Beaton, originally from the Isle of Lewis.[79] Cathie
sings "One Morning Early As I Roved Out," a version of "The
Dawning of the Day," which was printed by the Scottish
editor John Ord in his Bothy Songs and Ballads (1930), with
a note on its inclusion in P. W. Joyce's Ancient Irish Music
(1912).[80] The precise locus of written or published sources
for songs known to Lowland Travellers has still to be
investigated on a systematic basis, however, and it is quite
possible that Ord's printing repopularized the ballad, at
least among certain of the Lowland Travellers, after its
published appearance. The magnet that Ireland and Irish
culture holds for Scottish Lowland Travellers has never been
adequately explained, although it could be inferred that the
informal, spirited, nonmaterialistic coloration of Irish
rural life greatly appealed to them. The directness and
spontaneity that Belle and her family encountered, as well
as the much-valued propensity among the rural Irish for
music-making, provided a context for the participation in,
and acquisition of, songs whose content and style symbolize
this perception of Irish life.[81]

While her husband Alex was alive, Belle would sometimes
sing to the accompaniment of his droneless bagpipe, the
"goose."[82] Tying the meaning of a song to the character of
Highland culture, Alex's playing could bring into affective
focus the kinship of feeling that joins Lowland Travellers
to their Highland cousins. While Lowland Travellers of
Belle's generation now no longer, or rarely, speak Gaelic,
blood ties still exist between the two groups, and their
oral repertoire, especially in musical genres, overlaps to
some extent. Whereas the Highland Travellers hold a
conservative preference for the great Highland bagpipe,
Alex's cultivation of the droneless instrument may be
conceived of as a counterpart to the domestic Irish
instrument since both are intended for indoor use. Its
chamber-like personality emphasizes the domestic element in
the musical repertoire of the Stewarts; on the other hand
its organological form is related to the Highland pipe, not
the bellows-blown Irish instrument, whose origin lies in
continental models of the seventeenth and eighteenth
centuries.[83]

In treating the third and final aspect of Belle Stewart's songs one must consider those songs composed by Belle herself or on which she has collaborated: among them are "Loch Duie," "The Hielan' Chief," "Frank and Ruby," and "The Berryfields o' Blair." Her creativity has also extended to adding stanzas to songs, as for instance in the ditty she first heard over thirty years ago from an old ploughman who was "tattie-howking" (potato-lifting) near Blairgowrie:

> For when Micky comes home I get battered
> He batters me all black and blue,
> And if I say a word I get scattered
> From the kitchen right ben* to the room. /*through_/
>
> So I'll go an' I'll get blue bleezin' blind drunk,
> Just to give Micky a warnin',
> And just for spite I will stay out all night
> And come rollin' home drunk in the mornin'.
>
> Oh but whisky I ne'er was a lover,
> But what can a puir woman do?
> I'll go and I'll drown all me sorrows
> But, I wish I could drown Micky too.
>
> So I'll go an' I'll get blue bleezin' blind drunk,
> Just to give Micky a warnin',
> And just for spite I will stay out all night
> And come rollin' home drunk in the mornin'.

To this song, which is apparently Irish in origin, Belle added an introductory stanza, partly as an opening to the song and partly to provide a reason for the man's treatment of his wife, namely that she had married him for his money:

> Oh friends I have a sad story,
> A very sad story tae tell:
> I married a man for his money
> But he's worse than the devil himsel'.[84]

Belle's preference for comic or satirical songs grounded in domestic life emerges in such numbers. During her concert or stage appearances she would occasionally substitute "Alex" for "Micky" in the above song, thereby endeavoring to uncover the real referent, namely her husband, although local audiences could recognize that the original version was, in fact, a symbolic tribute to him. The community audience, whether Travellers or not, realized the implications of the song as she sang it, and to decode its meaning accordingly. In a contrasting situation in the

United States, the audience took the words literally when Belle made the substitution; the result was that audience members, embarrassed, avoided Belle at the interval. Alex's comment to her was, "You've made a blunder, Belle!"[85] The coding of songs for local contexts, where the audience can process intimate meanings and esoteric allusions, was replaced by the harder sanctions on meaning demanded by the third type of context, that of the concert stage.

"The Berryfields o' Blair" is undoubtedly Belle's best-known composition. It was written about 1930 with Alex's help; he chose the tune of the Northeast bothy song, "Nicky Tams," to match the text. The family tradition of songmaking normally involved coining the text first and later finding a suitable melody, though the rhythmic pattern of a song tune, or tunes, may have lingered in the background during the process of composition. The practice of making songs in general within the family may have arisen from the example of a cousin, Tommy Stewart of Aberdeen, who was reputed to have composed a number of songs; but the competitive way in which this process developed with the Stewart family hinges on the incentive that satire in particular provides. It has functioned as the essential spur to creative response, and "The Berryfields o' Blair" is perhaps the most artistically successful product to emerge from the family tradition of songmaking.

Conceived in the seasonal framework of the berrypicking in midsummer, when subgroups of diverse origin converge on the country around Blairgowrie, the song evokes a scene in which pickers of every description are sketched with a pungent but never malicious eye. As Henderson's earlier description makes plain, songs and music would arise as a matter of course after the day's work was over, either in the field or by the campfires of the bivouacked Travellers. The nature of these annual convergences led to their being viewed as the direct ancestor of the Folk Music Revival and "the first unofficial folk festival in Scotland."[86] When in 1966 the first Festival of Traditional Music was held in Blairgworie, as the climax of the Revival's first energetic phase that began in the 1950s, it seemed a natural consequence and continuation of a phenomenon that had existed for many years, possibly since the turn of the century or even earlier. The need for seasonal labor stems at least from the economic transformations of the late eighteenth and early nineteenth centuries.[87] As several commentators have remarked, it is all the more fitting that Belle Stewart, who had lived all her life in the area and had participated in the oral tradition of the Travellers should have created a song, and more specifically a song text, that is now a hallmark of the Revival.[88]

The song is cast in the bothy ballad structure that the
Northeast tune reasonantly reinforces; it also embodies a
variant form of the "Come-All-Ye" type of song that began to
proliferate in Scotland and Ireland during the nineteenth
century. This is not to suggest, however, that it is in
some sense a downgraded ballad or ersatz narrative song, for
its topic is purely descriptive and satirical. It fits the
character of the typical song that forms part of the social
conditions from which the "bothy ballad" sprang.[89] Embedded
in the text, for instance, is an entire world of native
ethnographic observation that is more significant than the
conventional reference to written poetry in the final stanza
would imply. It has a great deal in common with those bothy
ballads that treat a humorous incident from daily life, or
indeed with the almost purely oral tradition of bawdy
ballads like "The Ball o' Kirriemuir." The native collector
of Northeast folksong at the turn of the century, Gavin
Greig, asserted that ". . . these ditties of farm life . . .
may not amount to much as poetry: but there is an air of
sincerity and conviction about them that makes for force and
vitality. Further, they illustrate local life and language
better than any other kind of song or ballad which we
have."[90]

In this respect, songs modelled on the bothy type offer
a contrast in content and style to the older ballads, as
David Buchan has shown.[91] The Travellers, however, lie
outside the general development of economic and social
conditions in Scotland, including the situation that
generated the bothy songs of the late nineteenth and early
twentieth centuries, and their dependence on the new mode of
literacy and rote memorization of textual and melodic
material came late, when it came at all. Their preferred
medium of expression was oral and experiential rather than
literate and memorial, at least until recently. It is for
this reason that the older oral style of balladry lived on
among them when it had begun to give way to the bothy style
among the settled population. That is not to say that song
texts and tunes were not memorized on occasion or in
principle by Travellers who had received formal schooling,
nor that literary or written sources were not available and
drawn upon. But these were transformed through the
reflexive modalities of Traveller creative behavior, which
in turn is associated with a value system with clearly-
defined limits. Herein lies the significance of the song
compositions of the Stewart family for these, like others by
Traveller singers in recent years, are modelled on the
realism and structural conventions of the bothy type rather
than on those of the classic ballad.[92] David Buchan traces
the emergence of the bothy ballad to the transitional period
between the oral and literary stages of ballad evolution in

Lowland Scotland, when the oral ballad became increasingly localized.93

The language of "The Berryfields," with its mixture of dialect and literary conventions, betrays a close affinity with the bothy song, as do its patterns of assonance and rhyme, especially in the opening stanza. The imagery and characterization likewise portray a convergence of free social groupings of the kind peculiar to Travellers, with their idiosyncratic views on property and social structure ("there's men wha share an' share alike / Wi' wives that's no' their ain"). Characterization is laid out in terms of opposite types: the industrious and the lazy, the desperate and the apathetic, the individualistic and the more communally-minded. As variant types they are eventually subsumed under the idealized, optimistic description of pickers as "a kind lot" who make the journey to the berryfields into a valued annual experience.

On the commercial disc, Festival At Blairgowrie (recorded in 1967 and issued in 1968), Belle sings a parody, or what might be termed a continuing instalment of "The Berryfields," entitled "The Festival o' Blair." Encouraged by the success of her first satirical song she has addressed the formal social consequence of "The Berryfields":

THE FESTIVAL O' BLAIR

(to the same tune as "The Berryfields")

1. When berrytime comes roond each year, Blair's population's swellin',
   But it's no' aboot the berrytime this tale that I am tellin',
   It's aa aboot anither event that's goin' tae tak' place there:
   It's that wonderful achievement caa'd the Festival o' Blair.

2. We'll hae singers fae the Sooth Countree and some fae owre the sea,
   An' we have our local talent an' some experts fae Dundee;
   An' then we have musicians wha'll come fae everywhere,
   Tae mak' this time a great success at the Festival o' Blair.

3. Noo the Cooncil were upset last year wi' things that
    happened here,
    But it's awfy hard tae hae control if ye've drank a lot
    o' beer;
    But I'm sure it winnae happen here wi' the folk that
    will be there,
    For I think they've learned tae hae respect for the
    Festival o' Blair.

4. But afore I put ma pen awa' it's this I would like tae
    say:
    It'll be the best and happiest time ye've had for
    mony's a day;
    So jist pack up an' tak' the road, forget aa worries
    an' care,
    An' remember for the years tae come the Festival o'
    Blair.

In a satirical tradition stretching back to William Dunbar's
castigation of Edinburgh City Council (circa 1500), the
third stanza lampoons civic starchiness. The song closes,
in contrast, with the sentiment that the ensuing festival
will be the best in many years.[94]

The song also betrays more obvious marks of Traveller
acculturation. Because the Stewarts have been more or less
permanently settled, as have the majority of Lowland
Travellers since World War II, it is not surprising that
they have begun to acquire the values of the surrounding
population. Theirs is a culture is in transition, having
experienced the powerful twin influences of intermarriage
and legal strictures on education and housing.[95] These
pressures had already forced Belle's generation into
accommodation with the settled culture.

Yet it is an optimistic sign in social relations that
Belle and her family are generally respected in the
locality, more particularly because of their fame as
musicians and tradition-bearers. Whether this accommodation
has taken a heavy toll on the fundamental mechanisms of
Traveller culture remains to be seen, but it is clear that a
provisional transformation has occurred in the last two
generations: intermarriage and education appear to be vital
factors for culture change.[96] The Stewarts themselves,
however, have weathered this process of change with relative
skill and, as has been suggested here, this may result from
their orientation towards parody and satire as strategies
for social and artistic change.

Belle's taste for parody, on a level of personal
artistry, mirrors her need not to take herself too

seriously. But this inclination also provides a symbolic means of handling attachments or emotions too compelling to be dealt with or communicated in any other way. When feeling outruns reason parody offers an escape valve, though miscalculation could occur with a change of context, as in "When Micky Comes Home." Parody and satire, in traditional communities tightly bound to local referents and shared codes of meaning, do not transpose well across regional or cultural frontiers, even when the language itself is comprehensible to the audience.

Her repertoire, in terms of size, is comparable to those of Jeannie Robertson, Jane Turriff, and other Traveller singers of the older generation. Unlike the cast and proportions of Jeannie's songs, however, which tend towards weighty ballads, serious lyrics, or dance-like numbers, or those of Jeannie's daughter Lizzie with her preference for lyrics set to pipe tunes, Belle's songs are closest in style to the affectionate, domestic, and parodic items found in Jane Turriff's songs.[97]

Like Jeannie, nevertheless, Belle sees herself as possessing the conniach, the knowledge and power of the Highland bard to move all who listen, whether native to the tradition or not, and this is clear from the recordings made in concert. Here, one might propose a feature of style that transcends the harder sanctions on meaning and relevance when the local context is exchanged for the exoteric: Belle's personality, with that of Jeannie, Jane, or Lizzie, has the ability to charm an audience and to convey a sense of the tradition and its essence through sheer affection for the songs. This powerful and confident feeling for stylistic integrity, rooted equally in talent and learning, modifies loss of the local referents embedded in song texts, tunes, and the affective modes of a particular singing tradition, namely that of the Perthshire Travellers and specifically the Stewart family.

A stylistic aptitude of this kind forms a substantial explanation of the family's success in adapting to the change of context they have encountered through a move to the concert stage as "performers." To some extent the experience of having to ingratiate themselves with a hostile or indifferent population in their everyday life may account for this ability: in common with Romanies, Travellers have been forced to read social situations and attitudes swiftly and unerringly.[98] Yet Belle's singing also contains a direct appeal that bypasses the awkwardnesses of a dialectal text or idiosyncracies of a local aesthetic: her singing style, in other words, succeeds because she is able to adjust both the role that is expected of her and her response to different contexts. Her analysis of audiences and situations draws on her wider perception of social attitudes among non-Travellers.

To a marked degree, then, Belle and her family have succeeded in negotiating the transfer of their traditional style to extralocal contexts, often through the mediating device of parody or satire. This transfer has been achieved even when esoteric allusion was a factor in a repertoire item, or when self-parody might threaten to surface in the adjustment process.[99] The proficient passage from one context to another can be attributed, as noted above, to a dominant sense of artistic identity and affective focus that Belle brings to her public performances. Her majestic presence so impressed the anthropologist Frank Vallee in 1955 that he compared her to Scott's description of Helen Macgregor, Rob Roy's wife, who declared, "My foot is on my native heath, and my name is Macgregor."[100] This assertion of identity, and territorial claim, may be easily transferred in Belle's case to the authority of local context in matters of traditional art and creativity: to have a foot on one's native heath is a symbolic way of affirming both artistic persona and the wellspring of sources for song composition.

More remarkable is the way in which Belle's need for creative change has applied the generic strategy of satire as "the ironic negative" of tradition. Behind Belle's humorous, effective parodies, one might infer, lies an awareness of how satire functions as a device for accelerating social and artistic change yet, paradoxically, provides a mechanism for the renewal of traditional forms and styles. Her creativity demonstrates, moreover, how the limits of a local tradition are shaped as much by the ambivalence of the performer towards his or her art as by the stabilizing, conservative effect of the community with its rules of conduct and prescriptions for aesthetic practice.[101]

Parody and satire function, then, not only as mediators between tradition and innovation: they also dissolve the conceptual boundaries between the song text derived from a "subliterary" style (e.g., "The Berryfields o' Blair") and a dominantly oral tradition whose means of transmission were, and still are to some extent, based on an ordering of learned intelligences that is distinct from that of the surrounding population. The songs composed by Belle and her family, however, while employing images, symbols, or meaning sets that represent aspects of Traveller life and relationships (heroic or familial conflict, experience of Irish culture, seasonal labor and communal celebration), have adapted a style and versification that betray a merging of theme and image with the more recent popular verse traditions of Scotland. Parody and satire there, too, provide as they have always done a socially acceptable way of reassessing values, both social and artistic, through amicable criticism. If, as Aldous Huxley has remarked, parodies and caricatures are the most penetrating of criticisms, then Belle Stewart's satirical songs may be interpreted as telling indicators of, and agents for, culture change and the renewal of traditional, expressive forms.

[1]See Bertrand H. Bronson, "'Let's Make It a Tradition'," Yearbook of the International Folk Music Council 1979, 11 (1980), 27-39.

[2]Ibid., p. 33.

[3]Cf. Terence Hawkes, Structuralism and Semiotics (Berkeley: University of California Press, 1977), p. 71.

[4]Ibid., pp. 71-72.

[5]Victor Ehrlich, Russian Formalism: History-Doctrine, rev. ed. (The Hague: Mouton, 1965), p. 258; quoted in Hawkes, p. 72.

[6]These terms are not used interchangeably here, although the critical difference between them is not stressed for the purposes of this paper. The "formal" connotations of parody and the "social" implications of satire shade into each other imperceptibly.

[7]Cf. Hawkes, pp. 71-72.

[8]See Dan Ben-Amos and Kenneth S. Goldstein eds., Folklore: Performance and Communication (The Hague: Mouton, 1975).

[9]Dan Ben-Amos, "Towards a Definition of Folklore in Context," Journal of American Folklore, 84 (1971), 8.

[10]Robert A. Georges, "Towards a Resolution of the Text/Context Controversy," Western Folklore, 39 (1980), 36-37.

[11]S. N. Eisenstadt, "Some Observations on the Dynamics of Traditions," Comparative Studies in Society and History, 11 (1969), 453-54.

[12]See esp. Robert Redfield, The Primitive World and Its Transformations (Ithaca, NY: Cornell University Press, /1953/).

[13]Fredrik Barth, ed., Ethnic Groups and Boundaries: The Social Organization of Cultural Difference (Boston: Little, Brown, 1969), pp. 33-34.

[14]Max Gluckman, "Les rites de passage," in Essays on the Ritual of Social Relations, ed. Max Gluckman (Manchester: Manchester University Press, 1962), p. 27.

[15]Ibid., p. 27.

[16]Ibid., p. 27. See also James L. Peacock, Consciousness and Change: Symbolic Anthropology in Evolutionary Perspective (Oxford: Basil Blackwell, 1975), pp. 18-21.

[17]Roger Abrahams, "Personal Power and Social Restraint in the Definition of Folklore," Journal of American Folklore, 84 (1971), 24 ff.

[18]Cf. Émile Durkheim, The Elementary Forms of the Religious Life (1915); Ferdinand Tönnies, Gemeinschaft und Gesellschaft (1887; trans. Charles P. Loomis, Community and Society, 1957); Marcel Mauss, Essai sur le don (1925; trans. as The Gift, 1954); Victor Turner, The Ritual Process: Structure and Antistructure (London: Routledge & Kegan Paul, 1969).

[19]Bronislaw Malinowski, A Diary In the Strict Sense of the Term (New York: Harcourt, Brace, 1967).

[20]Roman Jakobson and Petr Bogatyrev, "On the Boundary Between Studies of Folklore and Literature," in Readings in Russian Poetics: Formalist and Structuralist Views, ed. Ladislav Matejka and Krystyna Pomorska (Cambridge, Mass.: MIT Press, 1971), p. 92.

[21]Cf. Alan Dundes, The Study of Folklore (Englewood Cliffs, N. J.: Prentice-Hall, 1965), p. 127.

[22]Roman Jakobson, "Closing Statement: Linguistics and Poetics," in Thomas A. Sebeok ed., Style in Language (Cambridge, Mass.: MIT Press, 1960), p. 353; also Edward T. Hall, Beyond Culture (Garden City, N.Y.: Doubleday, 1976), p. 79.

[23]Donald Ward, "The Satirical Song: Text Versus Context," Western Folklore, 36 (1977), 347-54.

[24]Jakobson and Bogatyrev, p. 93.

[25]This is also true of the relationship between custom and kinship in traditional societies; see Mihai Pop, "The Relationship Between the System of Kinship Relations and the System of Customs," personal communication.

[26]For a biographical sketch of the family, see Maurice Fleming, "The Stewarts of Blair," Tocher (Edinburgh), 21 (1976), 164 ff.; also Hamish Henderson, liner notes to The Stewarts of Blair, Topic 12T138 (1965): "By general consent the Stewarts rank high among the singing 'folk' families of Europe and the world. . . ." Cf. further the disc Folksongs and Music From the Berryfields of Blair, Prestige International 25016 (n.d.), The Travelling Stewarts, Topic 12T179 (1968), The Back o' Benachie, Topic 12T180 (1968), Festival at Blairgowrie, Topic 12T181 (1986), A Prospect of Scotland. Topic TPS 169 (n.d.), and Belle Stewart: Queen Among the Heather, Topic 12TS307 (1977). The Stewarts also appear as the subjects of a documentary film, The Summer Walkers (1980), by Timothy Neat.

[27]I have not seen either of these works-in-progress, but I should acknowledge here various helpful communications from Sheila Douglas, author of the forthcoming dissertation on Belle. Several of the family's songs have been published, including both traditional and composed items: Belle's "The Overgate" and Sheila's "Bogie's Bonny Belle" are in A Collection of Scots Songs (Edinburgh: School of Scottish Studies, 1972), pp. 15, 27-28; also Belle's "The Twa Brithers" in B. H. Bronson, The Traditional Tunes of the Child Ballads (1972) IV 464, and her "The Bonnie Hoose o' Airlie" in Tocher, 21 (1976), 174. Other versions of songs sung by Belle and Sheila are in Ailie Munro, The Folk Music Revival in Scotland (London: Kahn & Averill, 1984): Sheila sings "My Bold Chailin Donn" (pp. 104-6) and "When Micky Comes Home I Get Battered" (pp. 119-20); Belle's recorded versions include "Oh Ma Name Is Betsy Bell" (pp. 120-22), "The Berryfields o' Blair" (pp. 159-61), "Here's a Health To All True Lovers" (pp. 169-70). See also the short description of Belle and her repertoire in Mary Ellen Brown and Sheila Douglas, "Some Approaches to Scottish Ballad Study," Lore and Language, 3 (1981), 101-07.

[28]See Hamish Henderson, "Scots Folk-Song Discography, Part 5," Tocher, 32 (1979-80), 132-33.

[29]Fleming, p. 166. See also Peter Sheapherd, liner notes to Festival at Blairgowrie, Topic 12T181 (1968).

[30]Hamish Henderson, liner notes to The Stewarts of Blair, Topic 12T138 (1965).

[31]Hamish Henderson, liner notes to Folksongs & Music from the Berryfields of Blair, Prestige International 25016 (n.d.).

[32]See my discussion in "The Turriff Family of Fetterangus: Society Learning, Creation and Recreation of Traditional Song," Folk Life (Cardiff), 16 (1978), 5-26 and the sources cited therein.

[33]Henderson, The Stewarts of Blair.

[34]See Farnham Rehfisch ed., Gypsies, Tinkers and Other Travellers (London: Academic Press, 1975); A. and F. Rehfisch, "Scottish Travellers or Tinkers," pp. 271-83. Other relevant essays of interest in this anthology are Bettina Barnes, "Irish Travelling People," pp. 231-56 and Fredrik Barth, "The Social Organization of a Pariah Group in Norway," pp. 285-99.

[35]Cf. Farnham Rehfisch, "Marriage and the Elementary Family Among the Scottish Tinkers," Scottish Studies, 5 (1961), 121-48; also Hugh Gentleman and Susan Swift, Scotland's Travelling People: Problems and Solutions (Edinburgh: HM Government, 1971). The situation in Ireland is treated in George Gmelch, "The Effects of Economic Change on Irish Traveller Sex Roles and Marriage Patterns," in F. Rehfisch ed., op. cit., pp. 257-69. "Traveller" is capitalized here by analogy with "Gypsy," even though the histories of the two groups differ and their inter-relationship is unclear.

[36]Information from interview with Belle Stewart and James Porter, School of Scottish Studies Archive, SA 1972/243-5.

[37]Rehfisch, "Marriage and the Elementary Family."

[38]Interview, SA 1972/243-5.

[39]Fleming, pp. 167-08.

[40] Ibid., p. 181.

[41] Interview, SA 1972/243-5.

[42] Hamish Henderson, liner notes to The Muckle Sangs: Classic Scots Ballads, Tangent TGNM 119/D (1975), p. 8.

[43] Interview, SA 1972/243-5.

[44] See Howard Gardner, "The Development of Competence in Culturally Defined Domains: "A Preliminary Framework," in Richard A. Shweder and Robert A. LeVine eds., Culture Theory: Essays on Mind, Self, and Emotion (Cambridge: Cambridge University Press, 1984), p. 259.

[45] Ibid., pp. 257-75.

[46] Ibid., p. 266.

[47] Ibid., pp. 263-64.

[48] A. and F. Rehfisch, "Scottish Travellers or Tinkers," pp. 275-76.

[49] Gardner, p. 272.

[50] Cf. Alan Lomax, Folk Song Style and Culture (Washington: American Association for the Advancement of Science, 1968).

[51] Gardner, p. 268.

[52] See David Feldman, "A Response to Csikszentmihalyi: Discussion of 'Phylogenetic and Ontogenetic Functions of Artistic Cognition'," Stanley S. Madeja ed., The Arts, Cognition, and Basic Skills (St. Louis, Missouri: CEMREL, 1978), p. 131.

[53] Especially, of course, the ritual of New Year's songmaking; see note 40 above.

[54] See the discussion in Heinz Werner and Bernard Kaplan, Symbol Formation: An Organismic-Developmental Approach to Language and the Expression of Thought (New York: John Wiley, 1963), 12 ff.

[55] Roy G. D'Andrade, "Cultural Meaning Systems," in Shweder and LeVine eds., Culture Theory, p. 101.

[56] Douglas Hofstadter, Godel, Escher, Bach: An Eternal Golden Braid (New York: Random House, 1979), p. 158.

[57] See Irene Portis Winner, "The Semiotic Character of the Aesthetic Function as Defined by the Prague Linguistic Circle," William C. MacCormack, Stephen A. Wurm eds., Language and Thought: Anthropological Issues (The Hague, Paris, 1977), pp. 407-40.

[58] Winner, p. 426.

[59] Ibid., p. 426.

[60] D'Andrade, p. 99.

[61] See Robert I. Levy, "Emotion, Knowing, and Culture," in Culture Theory, ed. Richard A. Shweder and Robert A. Levine, p. 217.

[62] Mihaly Csikszentmihalyi, "Phylogenetic and Onto-genetic Functions of Artistic Cognition," in The Arts, Cognition, and Basic

David': A Conceptual P
Folklore, 89 (1976), 5-26; also "The Turriff Family of Fetterangus," cited above, note 32.

[66] See those listed, for example, in B. H. Bronson, The Traditional Tunes of the Child Ballads, I (1959), 384-402.

[67] William Motherwell seems to have been the first to suggest the connection (Minstrelsy: Ancient and Modern /Glasgow: J. Wylie, 1827/). It was taken up by Phillips Barry in "British Ballads," Bulletin of the Folksong Society of the Northeast, no. 5 (1933), p. 6 where he includes "Lizie Wan" as a close relative of "Edward" and "The Two

Brothers." Archer Taylor further proposed that "Edward" had come into contact with "The King's Dochter Lady Jean" or some similar ballad dealing with incest; see "A Contamination in 'Lord Randall,'" Modern Philology, 29 (1931), 105-07. See also the discussion in Tristram P. Coffin, "The Murder Motive in 'Edward,'" Western Folklore, 8 (1949), 314-19.

[68] These preoccupations are ones that can be found in Scottish cultural attitudes as well as in Traveller values. See, for example, the remarks in Ewan MacColl and Peggy Seeger, Travellers' Songs From England and Scotland (Knoxville: University of Tennessee Press, 1977), pp. 1-16.

[69] The Muckle Sangs; see note 42. Sheila's version of "The Twa Brithers" is on Side 1, 5. A great proportion of the ballads on this disc are in variants sung by Travellers.

[70] Porter, "Jeannie Robertson's 'My Son David.'"

[71] A transcription of text and tune is in Fleming, "The Stewarts of Blair," pp. 174-75.

[72] See David Buchan, "History and Harlaw," Journal of the Folklore Institute, 5 (1968), 58-67.

[73] See David Daiches, The Paradox of Scottish Culture: The Eighteenth Century Experience (London: Oxford University Press, 1964).

[74] Belle learned "In London's Fair City" from her sister-in-law Bella Higgins of Blairgowrie, who has herself recorded many songs and tales for the School of Scottish Studies (her version begins, "In Belfast's Fair City"). "Caroline of Edinburgh Town" was first encountered by Belle in Ireland, where she heard a singer called Mary Douglas sing it. Belle's cousin Donald Macgregor, who died in 1926, was the first native she heard sing the song. See Henderson, liner notes to The Stewarts of Blair.

[75] An Aberdeen version, "The Overgate," with a different tune and verse refrain, is also popular; Jeannie Robertson knew and recorded both (Jazz Selection JES 4, Prestige International 13006, Prestige International 13075, Riverside RLP 12-633, and Folktracks FSA 067).

[76] Munro, The Folk Music Revival, p. 49.

[77]Ibid., p. 49.

[78]See Herschel Gower and James Porter, "Jeannie Robertson: The Lyric Songs," Scottish Studies, 21 (1977), 55-103.

[79]The Gaelic words of the title are not Scottish, however, but Irish Gaelic: "bold Colin Donn" is probably a transformation of "buachailin donn," meaning "fair young man."

[80]John Ord, Bothy Songs and Ballads (Paisley: Alexander Gardner, 1930), p. 163. Joyce notes that the song used to be performed as a street ballad in Ireland and "was still well-known in the southern counties." It also appeared in Edward Walsh's Popular Irish Songs (1847).

[81]See also the portrayal of Irish Travellers in Bettina Barnes.

[82]No one has yet suggested, to my knowledge, that "goose" may be a transformation of the medieval word for the instrument, namely chorus. See Grove's Dictionary of Music & Musicians, 6th ed. (1980), IV, 357-58.

[83]Cf. Grove's Dictionary, IV, 357-58.

[84]Transcribed in Munro, pp. 45-46.

[85]Ibid., p. 47.

[86]Ibid., p. 91.

[87]See David Buchan, The Ballad and the Folk (London: Routledge & Kegan Paul, 1972), pp. 190-201.

[88]Belle has recorded the song on Festival at Blairgowrie (Side 2, 7).

[89]Buchan, pp. 255-70.

[90]Ibid., p. 266.

[91]Ibid., p. 260.

[92]Ibid., see esp. pp. 262-70.

[93]Ibid., p. 260.

[94]The song is also included on Festival at Blairgowrie (Side 1, 1).

[95]See Gentleman and Swift, and A. and R. Rehfisch, "Scottish Tinkers."

[96]Ibid.

[97]See Porter, "The Turriff Family of Fetterangus."

[98]Cf. MacColl and Seeger.

[99]See the treatment of stylistic exaggeration in Ruth Katz, "Mannerism and Culture Change: An Ethnomusicological Example," Current Anthropology, 11 (1970), 465-75.

[100]See Henderson, liner notes to the disc The Stewarts of Blair.

[101]Cf. Jakobson and Bogatyrev. For another study of a family singing tradition see Edward Kerr Miller, "An Ethnography of Singing: The Use and Meaning of Song Within a Scottish Family," Diss. University of Texas at Austin, 1982.

University of California
Los Angeles

PESEN ZA STEFAN I DONKA

by Marin Ivanov Nikolov

Stefan si spomen ostavi
če kojto gšte se zaženi
da gleda i da izbira
če tova ne e hubavo

5   žena neštastna da ostavi
s tri drebni dečica.
Stefan v Hisare otiva
tam da se Stefan lekuva
žena i deca zabravi.

10   s edna moma se zapozna
na ime Donka Koleva
cjal mesec v Hisare sjadali
trăgvat da si otivat
Stefan na Donka dumaše

15   nemoga Donke bez tebe
bulkata šte si napusna
ti šte mi bădeš stopanka
kato si v kăšti otiva
i si ženata tormozi

20   vednaga toj si rešava
zavede delo za razvod
lăžlivi drugari namira
i si deloto nasroči
te se v săda zakleha

25   kato na bani otišel
negovata bulka hubava
s čuždi maže obštuvala
taka se săda proiznasja
Stefan deloto spečeli.

30   I taka Anka v tjach trăgnala
i na decata kazala
maštecha majka šte dojde
ako vi vazi rugae
elate vie pri mene.

35 a Stefan togava rešava
   v drugo selo otiva
   momata Donka prebira
   malko sa vreme živjali
   Stefan na krăčma izliza

40 kăsno se ot krăčma zavrăšta
   taman v dvora šte vliza
   nasrešta čovek izliza
   zapali puška ubi go
   na drugija den go pogrebvat

45 žena mu kat se nauči
   pravo si v tjach otiva
   momata Donka izgoni
   i tăj si deca prebira
   da vzeme da gi otgleda

50 kat vsjaka majka roždenna
   a Stefan v groba da gnie.

THE SONG ABOUT STEFAN AND DONKA

Stefan left a reminder
That he who is going to marry
Should look out and choose well,
Because it is not good

5   To leave behind an unhappy wife
With three little children.
Stefan went to Hisarya
There to be cured.
He forgot his wife and children.

10   A girl he got to know
Whose name was Donka Koleva.
A whole month they spent in Hisarya
And when they prepared to go home
Stefan said to Donka:

15   "I cannot be without you, Donka,
I will forsake my wife
And you will be my housewife."
And when he came home,
He began to torment his wife

20   And immediately decided
To file a petition for divorce.
Lying friends he found
And set a date for the hearing.
And they swore an oath in the court,

25   That while he was gone to the spa
His pretty wife was
Having relations with other men.
Thus the court pronounced
That Stefan won the suit.

30   And thus Anka went back to her own
And said to her children:
"A step-mother will come to you as a mother
And if she abuses you,
Then you come to me."

35   Then Stefan decided
To move to another village.
The girl Donka he took with him.
For a short time they lived together,
Stefan went to the pub

40   And late he returned from the pub,
       And just as he entered the yard,
       A man moved up to him,
       Fired a gun and killed him.
       The next day they buried him.

45   When his wife learnt of this
       Straight to them she went
       And chased the girl Donka away.
       And then she took her children,
       She took them to raise them

50   Like every real mother.
       And may Stefan rot in his grave.

Parva cast na Marin Ivanov Nikolov--Naroden Pevec, roden v s. Karas--Vracansko, zivust Sofija, ul. Pernik No. 30. PESNOPOJKA s hubavi narodni pesni. /First part of Marin Ivanov Nikolov--Folk Singer, born in the village of Karash, district of Vraca, living in Sofia, 30 Pernik Street. SONGSTER with beautiful folk songs._7 Sofia 1982, 8 p., price 20 stotinki.

KLAUS ROTH AND JULIANA ROTH

A BULGARIAN PROFESSIONAL STREET SINGER AND HIS SONGS

Professional street singers used to be a familiar sight in most European cities and towns well into our century. With the appearance of modern mass media and a shift in popular attitudes and interests they gradually lost their functions and their audiences. In some countries, like Britain, they disappeared in the first decades of our century, in others, like Germany, Czechoslovakia, or Belgium they continued to sing their topical songs and to sell their song chapbooks for a few more decades; in Italy, street singers of a somewhat modernized kind performed their songs until recently.[1] One of the very few European countries that still has a living tradition of professional street singing is Bulgaria.

Like the other southeastern European countries, Bulgaria has had a long and strong tradition of professional singing.[2] The first extant reports of travelers, dating from the sixteenth century, mention blind beggars who traveled the country individually or in groups and sang mostly epic songs, accompanying themselves on the knee fiddle (gădulka) or some other traditional instrument.[3] The length and complexity of epic songs led relatively early to the development of a class of professionalists, and according to several reports these singers often obtained their professional training in special "singers' schools" until the beginning of our century.[4] The singers were almost exclusively men who sang and begged predominantly in the rural parts of the country, but also ventured into the towns and cities.[5]

It is most probably from this group of rural epic singers that, towards the end of the nineteenth century, there developed another kind of professional singer that closely resembles those singers from central or western Europe known as "market-place singers," "mountabanks," or "Bänkelsänger." In his outfit, his appearance, and his song repertoire this Bulgarian urban "market-place singer" (panairdžijski pevec) differed considerably from his rural colleague.[6] While the latter played a traditional instrument, moved around from street to street and from village to village, and often had an animal (bear, monkey)

343

with him to attract attention, the modern urban singer played a small portable but yet heavy harmonium (fisharmonika) that was usually imported from France or Italy.[7] For hours or whole days he sat in one place, usually a busy street, a market-place, a fairground or the site of some festival, in an elevated position on some kind of bench or scaffolding to be visible to his audience; his typical outfit was a huge black umbrella (čadăr) that protected him from sunshine or rain, and a formal suit and a hat. The rural singer begged for money or kind as a reward for his performance; the urban market-place singer never begged for money. His economic basis was the sale of small song chapbooks[8] or songsters (pesnopojki)[9] that contained the songs he sang to his audience. And while the rural singer sang mostly traditional songs, the urban singer composed and sang topical narrative songs or street ballads on sensational and extraordinary events like murders and suicides, accidents and catastrophies, battles and heroic feats, tragic love stories and happy reunions, soldiers' fates and haiduks' good and evil deeds, but he also sang traditional ballads, lyrical songs, modern music-hall songs, and hits. From the beginning, the Bulgarian urban singer was strongly influenced by the central European street singing and music-hall tradition. Unlike most European street singers, however, he never used the large painted pictures showing the crucial episodes of the songs. The Bulgarian market-place singer soon became one of the prominent performers and bearers of the new urban popular culture;[10] the rural singers, on the other hand, remained active performers and bearers of the traditional folk culture.

Both types of professional singers still exist in Bulgaria. The rural singers are no longer blind beggars, though; as a rule they are gypsies who play the fiddle or some other traditional instrument and sing traditional and modern songs in the villages and in the cities.[11] But while the begging gypsy singers are thriving, the urban market-place singers have ceased to be a relevant factor of urban popular culture. A few of them still practice their profession, but they are old and have no successors. Before we present one of the last of his kind we will give a brief outline of the historical development of the profession.

The date of the first appearance of the new type of professional singer in Bulgaria has not yet been determined with sufficient exactness. N. Raškova links his origin closely to the later very famous singer Marin Parušev Kovačev, whom she believes to have created this specific variety of street singing as an individual and to have made his first public appearance on the Plovdiv Fair in 1982.[12] The evidence of the songsters in the National Library in

Sofia, however, points to an earlier beginning. There exist at least eight songsters of 8 to 32 pages from the time before 1890 that were most probably produced for public sale by street singers. Bearing in mind that other popular genres appeared at the same time, we may surmise that market-place singing as a genre was developed in Bulgaria shortly after the liberation of the country from Ottoman rule in 1878. Whatever its initial stages and the exact year of its creation, the new art very soon found its own specific style and image which it kept fairly unaltered up to the present day. The first literary descriptions date from the period before World War I and depict the performance in a way which is still valid:

> In the middle of this market-place on market days one of these traveling folk singers settled with his harmonium and sang to the crowd gathered around him old folk songs or songs which he himself had composed. He offered for sale little song chapbooks printed at his order that contained songs which he himself performed, and when he had finished his endless tune he descended from his unique portable stage and offered his chapbooks to his listeners.[13]

This description from Sofia is supported by a contemporary report of the singing of the famous Parušev in Plovdiv:

> On Thursday, too, there was no lack of entertainment. Among the folk-singers, Parušev had the greatest charm. The villagers knew his voice, and when they heard a song, walked straight in that direction. He accompanied himself on the harmonium, chanted his tunes one after the other, knew when to close his eyes, when to lower or raise his voice. The simple villagers stood straight around him with open mouths and listened to him spell-bound. Parušev would sing one or two of his sad ones, then hit the keyboard forcefully, move in position on his stool, smile to show that he had chased away grief and sorrow, and begin to sing some joyful dancing tune. And when he sang, he would suddenly stop. Time had come to offer his songsters for sale! The villagers would buy them; they felt that they were obliged to do so. After all they had listened for so long a time to the singer.[14]

Soon after its appearance market-place singing became a popular and well-known public entertainment which attracted large crowds. It reached its peak in the period between 1920 and 1940 when scores of singers roamed the country and sang in the larger cities as well as the smaller towns and even villages and sold the songsters by the thousands. The National Library in Sofia has more than 900 different songsters from over 200 singers.[15] Marin Parušev Kovačev (1915) and his son Paruš M. Parušev (1936) were popular celebrities and to the present day the name "Parušev" is synonymous with "market-place singer" to many Bulgarians. P. M. Parušev (see fig. 1), who received a formal musical training at the Odessa Conservatory, even produced several popular records.[16]

The great majority of the singers were born in the villages, and since they advertized that fact on the title-pages of their songsters we must assume that their audience considered this an asset. The reason probably was that because of the rapid economic and social changes in that period the majority of the urban population were themselves villagers who had only recently moved into the suburbs of the cities. To them, to the peasants visiting the city, and later also to those living in the villages, the singers offered both a thrilling entertainment and a representation of the alien urban world that was traditional in tune and style, but yet "European" in its appearance, and this may have helped them to accept the rapid modernization of their traditional life style. The songsters were printed and distributed in very large quantities and it is thus very likely that at least since the beginning of our century they had a lasting impact on traditional folk singing.[17] As our informant, the singer M. Iv. Nikolov says, "our songsters were the most important literature in the peasant households."

Marin Ivanov Nikolov is one of the last active performers of urban market-place singing in Bulgaria. When he began his career as a singer in 1936, this type of street singing had already reached and passed its climax. He may thus be studied as a singer who in his personal development represents the decline and the final phase of a popular art that grew and bloomed in Bulgaria for almost a century and that deeply influenced the popular imagination and culture.

M. Iv. Mikolov considers himself and his companion R. A. Rusev the last active professional street singers in Bulgaria. He was born in 1911 to a peasant family in the village of Karaš, district of Vraca, some 40 miles north of the capital. While still a child, he lost his father in the First World War; after the war, he attended school for only four years. His mother and his sister were good singers. Unfortunately, his sister died of nephritis, an illness that affected many in his village, and which later caused the village to be abandoned because of its unhealthy

environment. When his mother died, a neighboring family
took him in, keeping him on as a farm hand. His foster
parent's strict, puritanical attitudes, as well as their
musical interests, strongly influenced his attitude toward
life, an influence that dominates in his songs and opinions
to the present day. The late twenties and early thirties, a
time of economic crisis in Bulgaria, were an extremely hard
period of his life. An unskilled laborer, without education
or professional training, he worked as a handyman at various
places, and was frequently unemployed. When he realized that
he had no chance of getting a job, and that instead he could
make his living with street singing, he decided to become a
professional street singer:

> I saw that the others who could sing and play just
> like me were earning . . . money. I just kept
> watching them, and since I had no education and a
> musical talent, the music just drove me forward, so
> what else could I do? Even with an education, you
> couldn't get a job in those days.[18]

In the same year, 1936, he moved to the city of Vraca,
marrying soon after. While Nikolov had never received any
formal musical training, he taught himself to play the
harmonium and the mouth organ in a short time. "I can play
any instrument," he insists, "but I decided to take the
harmonium because the harmonies just enticed me." For his
first harmonium, which was put together for him from the
remnants of old and used instruments, he paid 2500 Leva, a
sum of money for which he had to work an entire summer.
With this harmonium he began performing in the villages and
towns of his native district of Vraca. In 1937 he
successfully passed a state examination as an approved "folk
singer" (naroden pevec) at the Bulgarian State Music Academy
and obtained a work permit that enabled him to sing all over
Bulgaria. The most important facts of his life are
summarized on the title-pages of his first songsters; the
practice of giving autobiographical information on the
songster was very common at that time. The title-page of an
early songster is quoted here as an illustrative example:

NAJ-NOVA NARODNA PESNOPOJKA "KAVAL SVIRI NA
POLJANA" ot 1939 god. ot izvestnija naroden pevec
MARIN IV. NIKOLOV, majstor na ustna harmonika . . .
NEWEST POPULAR SONGSTER "A FLUTE PLAYS IN THE
MEADOW," of the year 1939, of the famous folk
singer MARIN IV. NIKOLOV, master on the mouth
organ. Marin Iv. Nikolov, village of Karaš,
district of Vraca, who is a lover of this
profession from childhood and a self-taught man. He
began in 1936 and he appeared for examinations on

July 4, 5, 6, 7, and 8, 1937, in the Bulgarian
State Music Academy and in Radio Sofia, and he
passed his exams with very good success, and from
the Ministry of Popular Education under No. 589023
was granted the right and is free to sing all over
Bulgaria.

I play and I sing - laments I diffuse,
I sing and accompany myself in the market-places,
I gather people around me / I sell my songsters,
My voice I do not give away.

Come here to me all of you / And buy my songster.[19]

Like most songsters of that period, this one also has a
photograph of the singer on the title-page (see fig. 2).

Since Nikolov had joined the Union of Young Workers
before the war, and during it had helped to hide partisans,
after the war he was awarded the title of "Active Fighter
Against Fascism." This fact became crucial to his further
career, most probably helping him to survive the political
changes to come. In 1950 he and his family moved to Sofia
where he built a small house in which he still lives.

The year 1952, it seems, was another turning-point in
the development of professional street singing in Bulgaria.
In that year the Ministry of Culture and Popular Education
requested all active street singers to take an examination;
the majority of them failed and had to give up singing,
while the others were allowed to continue but had to seek
the Ministry's permission for each songster to be published.
Since then, all songsters bear the Ministry's imprimatur. In
addition, all street singers were obliged to carry a work
permit which identifies them as approved "folk singers."

Nikolov's view of life was molded by his foster parents
and, to a certain extent, by the great street singer P. M.
Parušev. He feels very strongly about such modern vices as
drinking, smoking, wearing make-up, and dressing too
fashionably; his views are shared by his wife. Some of his
songsters contain warnings (in prose) to parents to keep
their children away from alcohol, "that fearful
enemy . . . which killed more people than water /did/,
destroyed thousands of talents and took the bread from many
a child." Some of P. M. Parušev's songsters also contain
such warnings. On the other hand he fervently preaches the
learning of Esperanto, "the language which will unite the
youth of the whole planet." He himself does not speak
Esperanto, but Bulgaria is a stronghold of that language in
Europe. It must be added that he admires Stalin as "the
greatest strategist of all times who dealt fascism a deadly

blow," and loves to sing Stalin's favorite song ("Suliko") in public. The song is printed in part VI of his present series of songsters.

The singer's songs and songsters are strongly tied to his life history and personal experience, as is demonstrated by his change of attitude toward one of his early favorite slogans. Most of his early songsters, like those of P. M. Parušev and other singers of that time, have the proverb "He who sings thinks no evil" (Kojto pee, zlo ne misli) printed in bold face on the title-page. As Nikolov pointed out in the interviews, a famous and able fellow street singer led a bad and vicious life, thus proving to him that the proverb must not always be true. As a consequence he dropped the proverb from all his songsters. After a steady drop in attendance at his public singing he now feels that the interest in his art is rising again. He has more listeners, he has been filmed for television and movies, and visitors tape record his singing. But since he has no successor, he feels that the art will die with him.

Nikolov is a tall and impressive man who was seventy-one in 1982. His professional outfit and appearance correspond to the descriptions and photographs of earlier singers; his clothing, however, is less formal and dignified today than it used to be. On his simple jacket he always wears the badge of an "Active Fighter Against Fascism." Because of his old age he now plays a harmonium that weighs only 18 kgs. (40 lbs.); it has a range of almost three octaves and a powerful sound. The air pressure is generated by two bellows which have to be pedaled constantly; the air flows through the legs into a chamber underneath the piano keyboard. The legs of the harmonium fold together and the instrument sinks into a solid wooden box. Another wooden box contains the parts of a scaffolding which he assembles in a few minutes. On this one-half foot high platform he places his harmonium and the box which he uses as a seat. The obligatory black umbrella, fastened on top of the harmonium, and a small box filled with packs of songsters complete his outfit, which weighs a total of 32 kgs., or 70 lbs. (see fig. 3).

Nikolov's performance is a lively mixture of singing, playing, and talking. When he begins singing after he has mounted his stage he draws a fresh crowd by first playing a fast dance tune, a horo. When he has gathered enough people he sings songs of his own choice or by request, usually alternating longer and shorter pieces, and accompanying his singing and recitation on the harmonium. Often, though, he talks to his listeners between songs or even stanzas, explaining his narratives, telling stories about important

historical events, particularly the fight against Ottoman
rule and fascism, warning against alcohol and tobacco,
encouraging the study of Esperanto, and advertising and
selling his songsters. While talking he usually continues
playing tunes on the harmonium. From time to time he chats
with acquaintances or market women, passers-by or listeners.
His public performance is thus a rather complex and varied
communicative event. Because of his long experience as a
professional performer he has become, in his words,
"somewhat of a psychologist"; in fact, he reacts very
sensitively to the moods and desires of his listeners.

His singing attracts varying crowds, from only a few
people up to some forty or fifty listeners, depending on the
songs he sings, the weather conditions, the time of the day,
and the number of people shopping at the market. His
listeners belong to all age groups, although older people
seem to be in the majority. While many shoppers just stop
and listen for a short while, others stay on for several
songs and listen attentively to his singing. According to
informants who often visit the market, some women even start
to cry when he occasionally sings one of his gruesome street
ballads. The majority of the listeners appear to be workers,
blue-collar employees or peasants, but other social groups
are also represented in the audience (see fig. 4). The
songsters, which sell for 20 stotinki each, are bought quite
frequently, usually one or two at a time, but sometimes the
entire series of six. Nikolov lives on the sale of his
songsters and can afford a modest living standard for his
family.

From fall to springtime he regularly sings at his usual
place in the "Women's Market" (ženski pazar) in Sofia, the
capital. In the summer, however, he joins his companion,
Rusi Angelov Rusev from the village of Kardam, district of
Popovo, and together they travel by train or by bus, singing
at market-places and fairs, at festivals and săbors (village
festivals), in towns and cities, in holiday resorts and
spas. In August 1982, for example, he covered thirteen towns
in eighteen days. His itenerary, which took him from Sofia
to Karlovo, Hisarja (a spa), Plovdiv, Dimitrovgrad, Burgas,
Sliven, Šumen, Gorna Orjahovica, Pleven, Bjala Slatina,
Mihajlovgrad, Văršec (a spa), Mezdra, and back to Sofia,
shows that he and his colleague visit almost all parts of
the country.

Like those of the other street singers, Nikolov's songs
can be grouped into four rather distinct categories:
Traditional narrative songs (type A), modern street ballads
(type B), traditional lyrical songs (type C), and finally
modern popular songs of various kinds and origins (type

Fig. 1. P. M. Parusěv, the famous Bulgarian street singer (1911). (from a 1922 songster)

Fig. 2. Title page of an early songster of Marin Iv. Nikolov (*circa* 1944)

Fig. 4. M. Iv. Nikolov singing in the Women's Market in Sofia in 1982. (Photograph by the authors).

Fig. 3. M. Iv. Nikolov singing in his customary place in Sofia in 1982.

D).[20] The four categories of form and content can be described as follows:

Type A: The traditional ballads are long (50 to 270 lines, with an average of 132 lines) and consist exclusively of unrhymed verses of one line length, a form that is characteristic of Bulgarian traditional ballads. The songs deal with love and family affairs, fatal events, haiduks' and soldiers' feats, and with the Turkish occupation; more than half of them involve murders or suicides. In comparison with the oral versions, the street singer's versions tend to be more sentimental and often moralistic.

Type B: In length and poetic form, the composed street ballads do not differ from the traditional ballads; their themes, too, are similar to those of traditional ballads, but they favor the horrible, the macabre, and the fatal event. While the traditional ballads are vague and general, the street ballads give the exact date and the full names of the people and places involved in the sensational deeds and events depicted. The titles of these songs are often quite descriptive, similar to newspaper headlines, as the following examples show:

Song about Petko Iv. Grănčarski, age 22, from the village of Strupec, district of Vraca, who died as a result of Miss Laca Laškova's amorous character on May 24, 1936.

Song about Ivančo Vasilov from the village of Jablenica, district of Teteven, who was slain by thunder on June 13, 1936.

Song about Kalojan Dragnev from the village of Kumanci, who drowned his wife in his own well.

Newest song about Stefan Dimitrov from the village of Manastirište, a prisoner of war who returned on January 25, 1942.

Type C: The traditional lyrical songs are much shorter than the narrative songs (12 to 45 lines), but they have the same poetic form. They are songs of happy or unhappy love, songs about haiduks and soldiers, dialogues or jocular songs of various kinds; often they are printed on the front or back cover pages or between long narrative songs to fill gaps.

Type D: The last group consists of a medley of all kinds of modern ditties, urban street songs, Bulgarian and foreign hits, literary poems (e.g., by Christo Botev),[21] marching and drinking songs, political and contemporary songs, new love songs, translations of foreign folk songs and the like. Three out of four songs in this group are written in rhyming stanzas, usually quatrains, and are very short, from 6 to 40 lines.

Nikolov presently sells a series of six songsters or "parts" of eight pages each; their title-pages read:

Part ONE (two, three . . .) of MARIN IVANOV NIKOLOV --FOLK SINGER, born in the village of Karaš, district of Vraca, living in Sofia, No. 30, Pernik Street, SONGSTER with beautiful folk songs. Price 20 stotinki. /At the bottom of the page, below the title song:/ Letter of the Ministry of Education and Culture No. 7728.

This series of songsters has been sold by him more or less unaltered for more than a decade and thus fairly well represents his present active repertoire. The series contains 72 songs, two of which appear twice. The songs are distributed unevenly: Parts I to IV contain only 7, 5, 7 and 3 (longer) songs, whereas parts V and VI contain 20 and 28 šlageri, short hits of type D, and a few traditional songs (type C). These two songsters also include warnings to beware of alcohol and tobacco.

Since Nikolov began his career as a street singer some forty-five years ago, it would be of great importance to learn how his repertoire developed in that period of time and where he obtained or learned his songs. Fortunately we are in a position to answer these questions; because of his proclaimed interest in history the singer has kept an archive of his own songsters and of those of other singers. This archive--although a rather unordered bunch of paper with many torn and defective songsters--turned out to be an invaluable source that reveals the development of a typical Bulgarian street singer's art in the final phase of urban street singing in the country.

The collection comprises 47 songsters, seventeen of which are incomplete in varying degrees. These songsters can be divided into three groups:

(1) Ten of Nikolov's earlier songsters; the National Library in Sofia has three more of his early songsters (Balgarski knigi Nos. 31819f).

(2) 26 songsters from the time before September 1944 from twelve different street singers; six songsters are from P. M. Parušev and six more from A. St. Ivanov ("The Priest") who appears to have

been very popular in the late 1930's. Both singers had a strong impact on Nikolov as a young singer.

(3) Eleven songsters are from the time after the war, eight of them from his companion R. A. Rusev; his songs are mostly identical with Nikolov's. The remaining three songsters are from other post-war singers (M. Iv. Močev, K. T. Bajraktarov, and D. Iv. Pečev) whom Nikolov must have known well or even cooperated with, since many of their songs are identical with his.

Comparison of the earlier songsters with the recent ones is quite revealing. To judge by the songsters, the end of the war appears to have been a sharp dividing line. Those songsters before and after that caesura differ in many respects, a difference that indicates deeper changes. Nikolov's few songsters of the early post-war period belong to an intermediate stage. His oldest extant songster (1937) and those of the following seven years closely resemble those of numerous other street singers of that time. Their format (16°) and number of pages (16-18), their elaborate title-page (with a photograph of the singer and verses portraying him), their price as well as their songs, clearly indicate that Nikolov was an integral part of a thriving tradition. His early repertoire, too, is equivalent to that of his contemporaries. His eight early songsters contain 58 songs, but since he reprinted a few songs several times, there are only 46 song-types.

The distribution of these songs into the four song categories differs considerably from the distribution of the post-war period, as the following table shows:

Period:	1937-1944		1945-1982	
	song-types	songs	song-types	songs
Type A (Traditional ballads)	10 (22%)	17 (29%)	9 (11%)	20 (19%)
Type B (Street ballads)	18 (39%)	23 (40%)	5 (6%)	11 (10%)
Type C (Traditional songs)	6 (13%)	6 (10%)	15 (18%)	16 (15%)
Type D (Modern songs)	12 (26%)	12 (21%)	54 (65%)	59 (56%)
sum total	46	58	83	106

The older songsters show a predominance of narrative songs (61%) which is even higher when the repeated songs are included (69%); after the war the narrative songs account for only 17% (resp. 29%). Among the narrative songs of the early period, the street ballads prevail significantly, so that these topical songs can be said to have been the bread-and-butter of Nikolov's trade. His first extant songster contains only such ballads, others consist almost exclusively of them. After the war, however, the traditional ballads outnumber the street ballads, but both are by far outnumbered by a mass of short modern songs. It is certainly significant that in both periods almost only narrative songs, particularly traditional ballads, are reprinted again and again. Altogether 23 songs appear more than once in Nikolov's songsters, seventeen of them narrative songs. The following seven ballads seem to have been Nikolov's most popular ballads, his Evergreens, as they occur more than twice:

Type A:

Ivančo Čobančeto
(Ivan the Shepherd)   5 times (1943-1982)

Dvamata bratja bliznaci
(The Two Twin Brothers)   4 times (1942-1982)

Lazar i Petkana
(Lazar and Petkana: "Lenore")   3 times (1939-1943)

Hitrata snaha
(The Clever Daughter-in-law)   3 times (1942-1944)

Stojan i Pašata
(Stojan and the Pasha)   3 times (1952-1982)

Type B:

Plennici v Gărcija
(Prisoners in Greece)   5 times (1942-1982)

Laca Laškova
(Laca Laskova)   3 times (1937-1944)

Nikolov reprinted fewer street ballads than traditional ballads, probably because the precise information they give soon rendered them out-of-date. If he decided to reprint them, he consequently had to work these songs over either by re-dating them or by dropping this information and by making other necessary changes. In this process, his more popular street ballads show a marked tendency toward gradually losing their topicality and realism, adopting instead the vagueness and timelessness of traditional ballads. After the war, his street ballads lack any precise information: The dates are left out, and the names are vague or ubiquitous. For moral or political reasons he gave up writing new street ballads and only reprinted some of his own or those of other singers. In doing so, he usually shortened the ballads by stripping them of details and motifs which he felt to be unimportant or inadequate. He thus abandoned the specific style of the street ballad in a relatively short period after the war, while those street ballads that survived gradually became traditional ballads. The songsters of other post-war singers (M. Iv. Močev and R. A. Rusev) show that they continued to write new street ballads only until the early 1950s.

Nikolov's post-war repertoire thus has very little in common with that of his early period. Only five narrative songs survived the year 1944; three of them are in his present repertoire: <u>Ivančo Čobančeto</u>, <u>Dvamata bratja bliznaci</u>, <u>Plennici v Gărcija</u>. This fundamental change of repertoire and of style points to more general changes. Nikolov started out as a typical urban street singer who, like his colleagues, held the attention of his audience by singing primarily his own street ballads and traditional ballads, whereas today he earns his money by singing almost exclusively traditional ballads and various short popular songs. Although they are not in his printed repertoire, he still knows the old street ballads by heart and sings them on special request, reluctantly and disapproving, though, because he feels that only the deeds of positive heroes are worth being sung about. That recently the protagonist of one of his early popular murder ballads, Laca Laškova, after many years in prison came by to hear him sing "her" song, however, deeply moved him. To him the topical street ballad is extinct, because, as he puts it, this kind of song does not fit into the "present circumstances."

As yet we have left aside the question of the origin and sources of Nikolov's songs. Both his songsters and the interviews--in which he is rather evasive on that matter--offer little information. In all his songsters he signed only 15 street ballads and two modern songs with his name ("made by the singer M. Iv. Nikolov, village of Karaš," or a similar comment). Three more songs were "improved," "worked over," or "corrected" by him, and in only four cases does he give the name of another author, in one case P. M. Parušev. His recent songsters contain no information whatsoever about authorship.

Although the signing of his street ballads is inconsistent and sometimes dubious (the same song is signed in one songster, but not in the next one), there can be no doubt that he wrote most of his street ballads himself. Several others, however, were copied verbatim or in a worked-over form from the songsters of colleagues; in the songsters in Nikolov's archive, some of the songs are marked in his handwriting da se pecati (to be printed). At least five narrative songs and four modern songs are taken from P. M. Parušev, J. Vasilev, and above all from A. St. Ivanov, without quoting their names. A few more songs are poems by Bulgarian poets. The majority of his songs, though, must have been taken from other sources. In the interviews, Nikolov often referred to his musical family and the rich song tradition of his native village. "The folk tradition is a trove," he states emphatically, and he obviously borrowed from it. On the other hand, he often mentioned the records of popular street singers like P. M. Parušev which he heard as a young man being played again and again in the coffee-houses. From oral tradition and from these records, but very likely also from printed sources, he gleaned all the other songs in his songsters and the many others he knows by heart.

Compared with the street singers of his early period, Nikolov was a moderately talented song-writer; his language is fairly simple and often formulaic, sentences and phrases keep recurring frequently, and his diction is altogether close to that of traditional songs. Like other singers, he sentimentalizes his songs, but not as strongly as A. St. Ivanov; and like his model P. K. Parusev he tends to work out the moral aspects of his songs and to bring his message home to his listeners. Apart from the necessary changes in his street ballads, he varies his songs very little; his reprints are usually verbatim. Nikolov can thus be categorized as a "rationalizing singer."[22]

The analysis of the singer's career and his published song repertoire leads to the conclusion that after a relatively short creative period (1936-1944) in which he composed topical ballads, Nikolov carried on his profession for almost four decades, but in a very different manner: he wrote or composed almost no more songs. Instead, he continued to perform a few of his and other singers' evergreen ballads, their mainstays, which gradually acquired all characteristics of traditional balladry. For this lack of creativity he compensated by taking more and more traditional ballads and songs and--above all--numerous modern popular songs into his repertoire. As yet, we can only conjecture about the reasons for this basic changes. Besides the singer's personal reasons, such as his change of attitude towards certain categories of songs and subjects, there are definitely societal, social, and political developments that account for this change, among them secular changes in social patterns and attitudes, the regulating influence of the state, and the growing influence of modern mass media. These questions, however, will have to be studied in more detail.

Since Nikolov's development as a professional singer seems to be typical of professional street singing in Bulgaria, it leads us to assume that the functions of street singing must have changed considerably. The early songs and ballads indicate that professional street singing then must have had entertaining, informative, didactic, social, psychological, and other functions, particularly for a less educated peasant population that had recently moved into the cities; in the post-war period, however, it appears to have been reduced more and more to fulfilling only the need for public entertainment. The recent rise in interest in the art may to some extent be genuine, but there are indications that the "bard from the capital" has come to be viewed as representing the olden days, as a remainder and symbol of a lost urban popular culture. This nostalgic interest--from which he now profits--may have a lasting impact on the art by encouraging younger singers to continue it. Whatever its future, though, urban professional street singing in Bulgaria will certainly never again be that lively and colorful topical performing art it once used to be.

NOTES

[1]For a description of British street singing and song chapbooks see Leslie Shepard, The Broadside Ballad: A Study of Origins and Meaning (East Ardsley, Eng., 1962; rpt. Hatboro, Penn.: Legacy, 1978) and The History of Street Literature, (Newton Abbot, Eng.: David & Charles, 1973); and Klaus Roth, "Chapbook," Enzyklopädie des Märchens, II (Berlin: Walter De Gruyter, 1979), and the literature quoted there. German Bänkelsang has been treated comprehensively by Karl Veit Riedel, Der Bänkelsang: Wesen und Funktion einer volkstümlichen Kunst (Hamburg: Museum für Hamburgische Geschichte, 1963), and Leander Petzoldt, Bänkelsang (Stuttgart: Metzler, 1974). In "Der Niedergang eines Fahrenden Gewerbes," Schweizer Archiv für Volkskunde, 68-69 (1972-73), 521-533, Petzoldt presents one of the last German singers. For Czechoslovakia, see, for example, Bohuslav Beneš, "Die Bänkelballade in Mitteleuropa," Jahrbuch für Volksliedforschung, 16 (1971), 9-41. For a historical study of Belgian street singers, see Stefaan Top, "Det Marktzanger en zijn lied in de literatuur en de invloed ervan op het volksverhaal," Volkskunde, 82 (1981), 192-211. The volume he edited is devoted mainly to European Street singing: 12. Arbeitstagung über Probleme der europäischen Balladen in Alden Biesen-Belgium, 1981 (Brussels: CVV-Studies, 1982 /forthcoming/). Italian street singers sing topical songs to the guitar, and use modern electronic equipment. See Rudolf Schenda, "Der italienische Bänkelsang heute," Zeitschrift für Volkskunde, 63 (1967), 17-39.

[2]Professional epic singers have been studied intensively by Albert B. Lord, The Singer of Tales (Cambridge: Harvard University Press, 1960), and many other scholars. On the epic tradition in Bulgaria, see Stefana Stojkova, "Nositeli i razprostraniteli na bălgarskija junaški epos," in Bălgarski junaški epos, ed. Cvetana Romanska (Sofia: Balgarska akademia na aukite, 1971), pp. 42-61.

[3]Josef Konstantin Jireček, Knjažestvo Bălgarija, "Part I: Bălgarska dăržava" (Plovdiv, 1899), p. 101.

[4]Petăr Dinekov, Bălgarski folklor (Sofia: Bălgarski pisatel, 1972), pp. 227-31; Stojkova, "Nositeli," pp. 49 ff.; Christo Vakarelski, "Schöpfer des bulgarischen Volksliedes," in Serta slavica in memoriam Aloisii Schmaus, ed. Wolfgang Gesemann (Munich: Trofenik, 1971), pp. 726-732.

[5]Jirecek, p. 101.

[6]For a fuller treatment of the rural professional singer in comparison to the urban market-place singer, see Klaus Roth and Juliana Roth, "Zum Problem des Bänkelsangs in Bulgarien," in 12.Arbeitstagung, 60-74.

[7]Apparently most of these instruments were imported, but there is evidence that at least one Bulgarian factory, in Teteven, produced them.

[8]The Bulgarian song chapbooks or songsters have been treated by us in more detail. See our "Naj-nova pesnopojka s narodni pesni: . . . Populare Liederbücher und Liederheftchen in Bulgarien," Jahrbuch für Volksliedforschung, 27-28 (1982-83), 242-57.

[9]"Pesnopojka," pl., "pesnopojki," originally meant "female singer of songs," but since the middle of the nineteenth century, it has denoted "popular songster," or "songbook." See Roth and Roth, "Populare Liederbücher," pp. 242 ff.

[10]See Peter Burke, Popular Culture in Early Modern Europe (London: Harper & Row, 1978).

[11]In 1980 we recorded one of these rural professional singers in a small village in the Balkan mountains, a gypsy who played the knee fiddle, sang both traditional and composed ballads, had a little monkey with him, and begged for money. See "Zum Problem des Bänkelsangs."

[12]Natalja Raškova, "Panairdžijskite pevci Parusevi," Balgarski folklor, 7, No. 2 (1981), 29-37.

[13]Rajna Kostenceva, Mojat roden grad Sofija: Predi 75 godini i posle (Sofia: OF, 1979), p. 102.

[14]Nikola Alvadžiev, Plovdivska chronika (Plovdiv: Danov, 1971), p. 232.

[15]The songsters are indexed alphabetically by the authors' or editors' name in Bălgarski knigi, 1878-1944: Bibliografskiukazatel. Vols. I-VI (Sofia: Narodna Biblioteka, 1978-1983).

[16]The records are archived in the Institut za muzikoznanie in Sofia.

[17]Cf. Gerhard Gesemann, "Zur Erforschung der bulgarischen Volksepik," in Sbornik v čest na Professor L. Miletič (Sofia: Macedonian Academy, 1933), p. 493; Stefana Stojkova, "Botevite pesni v bălgarskija folklor," Bălgarski Folklor 2, Nos. 3-4 (1976), pp. 5 ff.; Raškova, "Panaidzijs-kite," p. 29.

[18]In August, 1982, we interviewed M. Iv. Nikolov several times in his home. For his willingness to tell us his life history, to talk about his songs and his singing, to sing for us, and to give us access to his personal archive of songsters, we owe him many thanks.

[19]Vraca, 1939, 16 p., 16°, 5 Leva. National Library, Sofia, No. I 21558.

[20]Klaus Roth and Juliana Roth, "Naj-nova pesnopojka s narodni pesni," pp. 252-53.

[21]See Stojkova, "Botevite pesni v bălgarskija folklor."

[22]Eleanor R. Long, "Ballad Singers, Ballad Makers, and Ballad Etiology," Western Folklore, 32 (1973), 233.

Munich University
Munich, Germany

THE COVERING BLUE

1. "My father he locks the doors at nicht,
      My mither the keys carries ben, ben;
    There's naebody dare gae out, /_"_7 she says,
      /_"_7 And as few dare come in, in,
    And as few dare come in."

2. "I will mak a lang ladder,
      Wi' fifty steps and three, three,
    I will mak a lang ladder,
      And lichtly come doun to thee, thee,
      And lichtly come doun to thee."

3. He has made a lang ladder,
      Wi' fifty steps and three, three,
    And he has made a lang ladder,
      And lichtly come doun the lum, lum,
      And /_lichtly*_7 come doun the lum.

4. They had na kiss'd, nor lang clappit,
      (As lovers do whan they meet, meet)
    Till the auld wife says to the auld man,--
      "I hear some body speak, speak,
      I hear some body speak.

5. I dreamed a dream sin late yestreen,
      And I'm fear'd my dream be true, true;
    I dream'd that the rattens cam thro' the wa'
      And cuttit the covering blue, blue,
      And cuttit the covering blue.

6. Ye'll rise, ye'll rise, my auld gudeman,
      And see gin this be true, true,"--
    "If ye're wanting rising, rise yoursel,
      For I wish the auld chiel had you, you,
      For I wish the auld chiel had you,"

7. "I dream'd a dream sin late yestreen,
      And I'm fear'd my dream be true, true;
    I dream'd that the clerk, and our ae dother,
      War rowed in the covering blue, blue,
      War rowed in the covering blue.

8. Ye'll rise, ye'll rise, my auld gudeman,
   And see gin this be true, true,"--
"If ye're wanting rising, rise yoursel,
   For I wish the auld chiel had you, you,
   For I wish the auld chiel had you."

9. But up she raise, and but she gaes,
   And she fell into a gin, gin;
He gied the tow a clever tit,
   That brocht her out at the lum, lum,
   That brocht her out at the lum.

10. "Ye'll, rise, ye'll rise, my auld gudeman,
   Ye'll rise and come to me now, now;
For him that ye've gien me sae lang til,
   I fear he has gotten me now, now,
   I fear he has gotten me now."

11. "The grip that he's gotten, I wish he may haud,
   And never lat it gae, gae;
For atween you and your ae dother,
   I rest neither nicht nor day, day,
   I rest neither nicht nor day."

Child 281-D from George Ritchie Kinloch's The Ballad Book
(Edinburgh, 1827), presumably a version sold by Charles
Leslie.

*ms. lihtly

MARY ELLEN BROWN

THE STREET LAUREATE OF ABERDEEN:
Charles Leslie, alias Musle Mou'd Charlie, 1677-1782

The text-centered approach has dominated ballad and folksong scholarship, to some extent because of the early interest in balladry by literary scholars and the availability of multiple texts for scrutiny. The paucity of data on early creators and singers of ballad and song also encouraged the textual approach. Recent scholarship, however, has amply affirmed that there is information on creators, singers--even performance--for historical and, of course, contemporary times, allowing study beyond the textual. An encounter with a book I'd long wanted to read, W. W. Walker's The Bards of Bon Accord,[1] in the National Library of Scotland one summer day in 1978 sent me on the trail of an early singer, hawker, and creator of ballad and song material: Charles Leslie, popularly known as Musle Mou'd Charlie (?1677-1782). This paper will seek to describe the bibliographical material, to present the known or presumed facts, and to create a hypothetical repertoire for this individual whose death was chronicled in two of the periodical publications of the day--the Aberdeen Journal and The North British Weekly Magazine, or, Caledonian Miscellany, of Knowledge, Instruction, and Entertainment:

> Lately died in Oldrain, aged 105, Charles Leslie, a
> hawker or ballad singer, well known in this country
> by the name of Musle-mou'd Charlie. He followed his
> occupation till within a few weeks of his death.

His life and activities are also recorded in a biographical song which exists in two related versions:

> AIR,--"Highland Laddie"
> O dolefu' rings the bell o' Raine!
>   Bonny Laddie, Highland Laddie,
> For Charlie ne'er will sing again,
>   My bonnie Highland Laddie.
>
> Grim Death has clos'd his mussel mou',
>   Bonny Laddie, Highland Laddie,
> Be this a warning bell to you,
>   My bonny Highland Laddie.

He's dead and shortly will be rotten,
  Bonnie Laddie, Highland Laddie,
But he must never be forgotten,
  My bonnie Highland Laddie.

He danc'd and sang years five score and five,
  Bonnie Laddie, Highland Laddie,
Few men like him are now alive,
  My bonnie Highland Laddie.

Gae lads and lasses to the fair,
  Bonnie Laddie, Highland Laddie,
For Charlie ne'er will meet you there,
  My bonnie Highland Laddie.

Nor in the streets of Aberdeen,
  Bonnie Laddie, Highland Laddie,
Will his lang spindle shanks be seen,
  My bonny Highland Laddie.

The hardest heart would surely melt,
  Bonnie Laddie, Highland Laddie,
To see his wig, hat, coat, and belt,
  My bonny Highland Laddie.

To see them by a broomstick borne,
  Bonny Laddie, Highland Laddie,
To scare the rooks frae early corn,
  My bonny Highland Laddie.

His bag where ballad books have been,
  Bonny Laddie, Highland Laddie,
In rags hang wagging on a pin,
  My bonny Highland Laddie.

And his lang staff, which lang he wore,
  Bonny Laddie, Highland Laddie,
Drive off the dogs frae the kirk door,
  My bonny Highland Laddie.

Had I the powers of Parson Wesley,
  Bonny Laddie, Highland Laddie,
I'd preach in praise of Charlie Lesly,
  My bonny Highland Laddie.

For, troth, he was a canty carle, and
  Bonny Laddie, Highland Laddie,
Many a brave ballad made, and garland,
  My bonny Highland Laddie.

And all his garlands, all his ballads,
  Bonny Laddie, Highland Laddie,
All bonny lasses pleased, and all lads,
  My bonny Highland Laddie.

The fame of Charlie wander'd far,
  Bonny Laddie, Highland Laddie,
Through Angus, Buchan, Mearns, and Mar,
  My bonny Highland Laddie.

Strathbogie can, and Garioch, tell,
  Bonny Laddie, Highland Laddie,
That oft he sent the Whigs to hell,
  My bonny Highland Laddie.

And how he went to Crookieden,
  Bonny Laddie, Highland Laddie,
To see Prince Charlie's Highlandmen,
  My bonny Highland Laddie.

And how, for comfort of his life,
  Bonny Laddie, Highland Laddie,
In Edinburgh he bought a wife,
  My bonny Highland Laddie.

Each Ballad a bawbee him brought,
  Bonny Laddie, Highland Laddie,
And for that sum his wife he bought,
  My bonny Highland Laddie.

Her tocher was not quite worth a plack O,
  Bonny Laddie, Highland Laddie,
A farthing's worth of cut tobacco,
  My bonny Highland Laddie.

The songs he sang and many more,
  Bonnie Laddie, Highland Laddie,
And deep and hollow was his roar,
  My bonny Highland Laddie.

Those songs in the lang nights of winter,
  Bonnie Laddie, Highland Laddie,
He made, and Chalmers was the printer,
  My bonny Highland Laddie.

Oh mourn, good master Chalmers, mourn,
  Bonnie Laddie, Highland Laddie,
For Charlie will no more return,
  My bonny Highland Laddie.

Blind Jamie now, and Ross, they say,
  Bonny Laddie, Highland Laddie,
Maun sing your books when he's away,
  My bonny Highland Laddie.

And so farewell, good people all,
  Bonny Laddie, Highland Laddie,
Both old and young, both great and small,
  My bonny Highland Laddie.

Good luck betide you, late and early,
  Bonny Laddie, Highland Laddie,
And may you live as long as Charlie,
  My bonny Highland Laddie.

Leslie attracted interest, primarily from regional enthusiasts, in the nineteenth century but only the obituary notice of 1782 records his existence in print in the eighteenth century. George Ritchie Kinloch in The Ballad Book[2] and James Maidment in Scotish Ballads and Songs[3] refer to a collection printed for Charles Lesly (an accepted alternate spelling for Leslie) in 1746:

Three excellent New Songs: 1. A New Song, called The Jacobite Lamentation: 2. The True Briton's Thought: 3. John Armstrong's Last Goodnight, declaring how he and his eight score men fought a bloody Battle at Edinburgh: Edinburgh. Printed for Charles Lesly, Flying Stationer, the Author, 1746.

As yet, however, I have not been able to locate a copy of this work. A song attributed to Charlie describes a battle which took place in 1746 as well--"MacLeod's Defeat at Inverury." Information on and interest in Charles Leslie, however, appeared after his death, primarily in the nineteenth century, and offers an interesting example of how buried and elusive, but available, information on early singers and creators of balladry and song can be.

Charles Leslie is the focus of an undated chapbook Garioch Garland[4] (GG), (Garioch refers to the area from which Charlie came), one copy of which exists at the Bodleian. The title page accurately describes the content:

GARIOCH GARLAND

On the LIFE and DEATH of the famous
Charles Leslie, Ballad-Singer,
Commonly called musle-mow'd Charlie.

                    Who died at Old Rayne, aged Five Score and Five.
                            To which is added,
                    Two excellent new SONGS,
                            Entitled and called
                    JOHNY LAD, and the Old Way of the
                            HIGHLAND LADDIE,
                            By the foresaid Author,
                    With the right and true Effigies of the said
                            CHARLES LESLIE.
                    Licensed and entered according to order.

The life and death story is found, not in a prose account,
but in a version of the song quoted above. The Garland
itself is bound with twenty-five other items titled Scots
Poetry; the material which is dated comes from the last
quarter of the eighteenth century. Since the volume itself
bears the crest of Reverend Johnathan Boucher (1738-1804),
presumably the Garland dates from shortly after Leslie's
death in 1782 and was intended to capitalize on his
popularity.

James Hogg picked up on Leslie in the second volume of
The Jacobite Relics[5] (JR) no doubt because he shared
Charlie's Jacobite sentiments. Hogg attributes portions of a
song "Geordie sits in Charlie's Chair" to Leslie, but
suggests that Charlie was more singer than creator. A letter
dated 1825, however, makes clear that Leslie was a "makar"
as well. The letter, written by James Troup of Lochead Skene
to Alexander Irvine of Drum[6] (NLS), contains an eye-witness
account of Leslie and includes a song at least partially by
him--"MacLeod's Defeat at Inverury." Troup calls Leslie "the
last of the Shennachies or old Scots Bards," and says he was
the natural son of Leslie of Pitcaple in the Garioch. He
describes Leslie as tall--about 5'10"--and thin, with a long
chin, red hair, and small red eyes, and says he customarily
carried a long staff taller than himself and a large bag
over his shoulder filled with his ballads and a Bible. Troup
says he was a welcome guest, particularly for his news,
about the time of Culloden (1745) and that he frequently
travelled to Edinburgh to record the "last speech and dying
words" of anyone about to be hanged. No doubt such accounts
of hangings were "news" too and may well have been later
incorporated into songs.

Charlie's singing--especially of Jacobite songs--often
so offended the Magistrates of Aberdeen that he was jailed.
When questioned why he couldn't sing other songs, Charlie is
reported to have replied, "They winna buy them." When asked
why he sang at all, he replied that he sang "for a bit of
bread." When asked where he bought the songs he sang and
sold in printed copies, he told them he purchased copies

where they were cheapest, perhaps at the forerunner of 46 Castle Street, an Aberdeen wholesale distributor mentioned by Helen Beaton in At the Back o' Benachie.[7] Clearly, Charlie had a good business mind and was aware of his audience's preferences. Once while he was in jail, word was received of Macleod's defeat at Inverury, thus giving momentary political power to the Jacobite adherents: Charlie and others were released to make room for the newly captured individuals. By the time he reached the center of the town-- his customary place of business--he is said to have composed a song recounting that defeat. His visits to jail intensified his Jacobite leanings, leading to such inflamatory verses as the following:

> The Whiggs are gaen to hell
> Bonny Laddie highland Laddie
> Horn'd Geordie is there himsell
> My Bonny highland Laddie.

Troup further says that Charlie would sing all day to "plenty of Company" and that a "Mr. Turner of Turner hall" regularly sent him food. The last time Troup saw him, he was being led by a woman, suggesting that he was blind in his last years.

Although Troup's account has provided the basis for most later discussions of Leslie, the fullest treatment of Charles Leslie was published two years after the Troup letter was written--in 1827--by the antiquary George Kinloch in a slim volume issued in forty copies, called The Ballad Book (BB). The Dictionary of National Biography describes Kinloch as a native of Stonehaven, Kincardineshire (fifteen miles from Leslie's center of operation, Aberdeen), a lawyer, register of deeds at the Register House in Edinburgh, philanthropist, adviser to Jamieson's Scottish Dictionary, and editor of Ancient Scottish Ballads, praised by Walter Scott in the Minstrelsy. The Ballad Book, published in the same year as Ancient Scottish Ballads, is dismissed as a "miscellaneous 'Ballad Book' of little value." This book, however, contains on the title page an engraving of "Mussel Mou'd Charlie" and a detailed six page "Biographia Leslyana" which provides additional information about Leslie. Kinloch says he was nicknamed Musle Mou'd Charlie because of a protrusion of the nether or lower lip and that he was so popular in Aberdeen that he was allowed to have a virtual monopoly, singing his songs--often with Jacobite content such as "Will ye go to Crookieden" and "A New Song, called The Jacobite's Lamentation"--in a "deep hollow roar." Tradition, Kinloch avers, says he activated his Jacobite sentiments and was "out" in the rebellions of 1715 and 1745. In an interesting personal touch, Kinloch says that Leslie purchased a wife whose tocher, or dowry, was so small it only enabled him to purchase a farthing's worth of tobacco.

Following the "Biographia," Kinloch prints a version of the biographical song. Interestingly, in one copy of The Ballad Book at the National Library of Scotland, the original owner, Charles Kirkpatrick Sharpe, has penned an alternate version of the song preceded by the line: "This from a MSs I think better than the song printed." The book proper consists of the texts of twenty-nine items, presumed later by Walter Scott and William Walker--respected cognoscenti--to be items of Leslie's stock-in-trade. Since Kinloch nowhere states the relationship of the items to the prefatory biography, the matter remains open to speculation. Examination of Kinloch's manuscripts (those copied by MacMath which are now housed at the Hornel Library, Kirkcudbright as well as the originals at the Houghton Library, Harvard University) does not settle the question. Twenty-three of the items found in The Ballad Book do appear in the manuscripts, but some represent different versions from those in the printed copy. At least fourteen of the items were recorded in the hand of James Beattie; one song each is attributed to the singing or recitation of Beattie's Aunt Elizabeth, Mary Barr, Kinloch's nephew Kinnear, a Mr. Weir, and a Mr. Chambers. There is nothing here to prove, to disprove, or to explain the relationship of these items to Charles Leslie--but the existence of his picture and biography does suggest that the items represent his "budget" or "pack." No doubt the existence of the slim volume (which may have been the one referred to by Kinloch in a letter to Scott as a limited edition of poetry of indelicate character, to be printed for its antiquarian interest and value as indicator of the nature of early poetry) in forty copies only has contributed to its neglect and to the neglect of Leslie as well.

The book, together with three comparably slim volumes, was reprinted privately in 1868 by T. G. Stevenson as Four Books of Choice Old Scottish Ballads in an edition of one hundred and fifty-five copies.[6] Stevenson adds an additional portrait of Leslie but in no way suggests the relationship of Leslie to the items contained in The Ballad Book, thus shedding no light on the matter. When Edmund Goldsmid reprinted the book in his Bibliotheca Curiosa in three hundred and fifty copies later in the nineteenth century, the biography was deleted. Goldmid's edition has been the most available one and here the absence of the biography and picture has, of course, contributed to the neglect of Leslie, whatever his relationship to the items.

Another book also implicitly links Charles Leslie to a number of texts but in no way asserts the relationship: Peter Buchan's An Interesting and Faithful Narrative of the Wanderings of Prince Charles Stuart and Miss Flora MacDonald (IFN).[9] Buchan was quite interested in Leslie and mentions him in several letters, especially those to the antiquaries C. K. Sharpe and Hugh Irvine, inheritor of James Troup's important biographical letter. In An Interesting and Faithful Narrative, Buchan refers to Leslie as "the last and most singular of the followers and professors of the craft of Old Homer, he, like his great prototype, not only composed, but sung his own compositions for his daily bread."

Buchan prints an additional engraving of Leslie opposite the title page (used later by Stevenson in Four Books of Choice Old Scottish Ballads), summarizes and quotes material about him utilizing Troup's letter, includes the biographical song which he calls "Elegy on the Death of Mussel-Mou'd Charlie," and then prints five Jacobite songs: "MacLeod's Defeat at Inverury," "The Duke of Cumberland," "For A' That and A' Ahat," "Flora and Charlie," "The White Cockade." The next item in the book is a discussion of Castle Campbell, followed by fifteen additional Jacobite songs. The framing of the above five songs by the two discussions, those about Leslie and Castle Campbell, suggests an implicit attribution of those songs to Leslie, especially since they begin with an item--"MacLeod's Defeat at Inverury"--definitely linked to Leslie in the Troup letter.

Walter Scott, in his "Introductory Remarks on Popular Poetry," mentions Leslie fleetingly when discussing Kinloch's The Ballad Book.[10] He assumes that Kinloch's work contains Leslie's "budget or stock-in-trade." James Maidment in Scotish Ballads and Songs (SBS) mentions a chap collection, described above, said to have been printed for Leslie in 1746. Maidment accepts "A New Song, called The Jacobite Lamentation" as Charlie's, but disavows him as the author of "The True Briton's Thought" and "John Armstrong's Last Goodnight." Nonetheless, the latter two were certainly items he sold and sang since they appeared in a chapbook bearing Leslie's name. (According to Kinloch, Maidment had a copy of the chapbook.)

The last extended reference to Charles Leslie was made in William Walker's The Bards of Bon Accord (BBA) the work which initially introduced me to this peripatetic figure whom Walker calls a "Jacobite Homer." Walker is, of course, well-known to cognoscenti as a correspondent of Francis James Child and as a figure of note in regional antiquarian circles. (Less well-known is the fact that he was by profession a pawn-broker.) The Bards of Bon Accord is a regional anthology of local, often minor poets, arranged in chronological order. Little new information is added in Walker's eleven-page discussion, which is derived principally from the Kinloch and Buchan works described earlier. Walker expands and fleshes out, however, the earlier accounts:

> He took early in life to hawking and singing ballads through the country--a Jacobite Homer singing his own compositions--and was ever a welcome presence in the hamlets of the shire in those days, when news travelled slowly, and gossips were less numerous than now. He was a most devoted Jacobite--sang everywhere their bitterest satires, and very probably was the "impious wretch" whom the author of "Scotland's Glory and her Shame" heard at Laurence Fair, singing that abominable song, "Whirry Whigs awa, man," to the delight of the "profane rabble."

He includes the biographical song and provides comment on some of the items contained in Kinloch's slim volume, presumed to be all that remains of Leslie's "stock-in-trade." Sporadic questions and responses in Scottish Notes and Queries towards the end of the nineteenth century and brief references in local newspapers and regional publications add no new information on Aberdeen's own minstrel.[11]

The weight of the evidence certainly affirms that there was a Charles Leslie. As an illegitimate offspring, he seems to have been excluded from family histories though his is a name oft-used in the family.[12] As a character, he was well-known and special enough to have two likenesses made in addition to the biographical song or elegy. His longevity must have contributed to his uniqueness, as undoubtedly did his peculiar lower lip, not to mention his extreme and public Jacobite views. Charlie was a professional singer, seller, and creator and as such could not have survived if there had not been an audience to buy, to listen, to affirm. While he did pass on news (gossip?) as he travelled and sometimes recounted the genealogies of local Aberdeen families, Leslie was principally involved with song, performing at fairs and in the streets of towns from Rattray Head to the Firth of Forth, but particularly in the northeast. In Aberdeen, his main place of business, he sang and sold throughout the day to lots of company--in a deep, hollow voice, needed to attract attention. The audience clearly liked him and appreciated what he sang, or else they would not have assured him of a lifetime monopoly.

Since the key to understanding Musle Mou'd Charlie's popularity may lie in an analysis of his songs and their content, I have created a hypothetical corpus of songs in Leslie's repertoire, based on the circumstantial evidence contained in the works already discussed. The repertoire, or stock-in-trade, contains a mixture of items: some attributed to him, others perhaps edited or redacted, but more certainly sold by him. Available information suggests that there are forty-one texts associated with his name; the titles are listed below with the sources of the actual texts (or parts thereof) underlined and sources of attribution or relationship to Leslie given without underlining. The abbreviations provided in the initial discussion of works mentioning Leslie will be used in giving the sources rather than the complete titles.

Items directly attributed to Leslie:

Will ye go to Crookieden or Old Way of the Highland Laddie GG, BB, IFN, BBA
A new song called the Jacobite's Lamentation BB, SBS, BBA
Geordie Sits in Charlie's Chair JR, NLS, IFN, BBA
MacLeod's Defeat at Inverury NLS, IFN, BBA
Johny Lad GG, BB, BBA

Items associated with Leslie's name:

The Duke of Cumberland IFN
For A' That And A' Ahat IFN
Flora and Charlie IFN
The White Cockade IFN, BBA
The Widow o' Westmoreland BB, BBA
The Sleepy Merchant BB, BBA
The Magdalene's Lament BB, BBA
(Awa wi' your slavery hiremen) BB, BBA
Jock Sheep BB, BBA
(The lassie and the laddie) BB, BBA
The Friar BB, BBA
(The beef, and the bacon) BB, BBA
Earl of Errol BB, BBA
The Astrologer BB, BBA
Kempy Kaye BB, BBA
Hey the Mantle BB, BBA
(Four-and-twenty cripple tailors, riding on a snail) BB, BBA
The Man in the Moon BB, BBA
The Shoemaker BB, BBA
The Maiden's Dream BB, BBA

```
The Covering Blue  BB, BBA
The Muir Hen  BB, BBA
(Widows are sour, and widows are dour)  BB, BBA
Bonnie Buchairn  BB, BBA
(It fell on a morning, a morning in May)  BB, BBA
(First there cam whipmen, and that not a few)  BB, BBA
Laird o Leys  BB, BBA
Tam Barrow  BB, BBA
(Johnie cam to our town)  BB, BBA
The Ram of Diram  BB, BBA
The Knave  BB, BBA
(There was a little wee bridelie)  BB, BBA
The Mautman  BB, BBA
The True Briton's Thought  BB, SBS
John Armstrong's Last Goodnight  BB, SBS
```

Whirry Whigs awa', man BBA

Of the forty-one titles, there are texts or parts of texts for thirty-eight. The subject matter of the corpus is at first glance a curious blend: there are a number of items containing Jacobite sentiments and even more which William Walker characterized as containing "dirt." Walker's description refers specifically to the twenty-nine texts printed in The Ballad Book. Earlier I mentioned a letter written by Kinloch, that book's editor, to Walter Scott (National Library of Scotland, MS. 3904) describing his plan to publish a limited edition of material of "indelicate character" in response to Scott's encouraging him "to persevere in rescuing from oblivion the remains of our ancient traditionary poetry." The majority of the texts in The Ballad Book deal with various aspects of interpersonal relationships (Walker's "dirt" and immorality; Kinloch's "indelicate character"): impotency, seduction, suspicion of extra-marital relations, adultery. The theme of seduction dominates as, for example, in "The Knave":

> I gaed to the market,
>   As an honest woman shou'd,
> The knave followed me,
>   As ye ken a knave wou'd.
>
> And a knave has his knave tricks,
>   Aye where'er he be,
> And I'll tell ye bye and bye,
>   How the knave guided me.
>
> I boucht a pint ale,
>   As an honest woman shou'd;
> The knave drank it a',
>   As ye ken a knave wou'd.

I cam my ways hame,
  As an honest woman shou'd,
The knave follow'd me,
  As ye ken a knave wou'd.

I gied him cheese and bread,
  As an honest woman shou'd;
The knave ate it a',
  As ye ken a knave wou'd.

I gaed to my bed,
  As an honest woman shou'd;
The knave follow'd me,
  As ye ken a knave wou'd.

I happen'd to be wi' bairn,
  As an honest woman shou'd;
The knave ran awa,
  As ye ken a knave wou'd.

I paid the nourice fee,
  As an honest woman wou'd;
The knave got the widdie,
  As ye ken a knave shou'd.

And a knave has his knave tricks,
  Aye where e'er he be,
And I've tamed / sic / you now
  How the knave guided me.

Charles Leslie's repertoire, in general terms, deals with two familiar topics--politics and sex; those subjects may well explain Leslie's popularity. And, of course, similar material in mass circulated newspapers certainly re-affirms the contention that chap literature was indeed the fore-runner of the newspaper.

Information suggests that Charlie was born around 1677 and died in 1782. There are references to printed texts as early as 1746, the year before Mrs. Brown of Falkland was born. Where then do Charlie and his printed texts fit into David Buchan's formulations: oral (1550-1750), chap (1750-1830), and modern (1830 to the present)?[13] On the basis of preliminary analysis of four of Leslie's texts which appear in Francis James Child's The English and Scottish Popular Ballads (Child 33B, "Kempy Kaye," Child 231D, "Earl of Errol," Child 241B, "The Laird o' Leys," and Child 281D, "The Covering Blue"), I suggest that Leslie's texts should probably be considered transition texts: while the familiar structuring in binary, trinary, and annular patterns remains--especially in stanzaic, and to some extent in character, structure--the texts contain a high proportion of narrative over dialogue and utilize a variety of rhyming sounds, in addition to the predominant ee sound of Mrs. Brown's texts. Interestingly then, Anna Gordon's acquisition of the recreative technique, the basis for discussion of the oral ballad, and certainly her redaction of texts using that method, came during or after the time Charles Leslie was actively selling, singing, printing, and creating texts which reflect the movement towards literacy, an altered cultural milieu. And Charlie sang in the streets of the very town Anna Gordon must herself have known well as a child. She, however, learned her ballad stories, not in the urban area already infected with literacy and other forms of improvement but in the country, still unselfconsciously maintaining the oral ballad and possibly its attendant means of recreation.

The information on Charles Leslie, as incomplete as it is, does provide a glimpse of a ballad and song singer, creator, and seller which pushes our concrete knowledge of the ballad milieu in Scotland back into the first half of the eighteenth century. The data also offer a picture of Musle Mou'd Charlie, an active participant in the folksong tradition and in life, singing--largely in urban contexts-- songs about current politics and human relationships. Such subject matter surely suggests a continuity in topics of human interest and concern. Further, the references to chapbooks of songs printed for Charlie as early as 1746 suggest that print and literacy, at least in urban Aberdeen, must have come earlier and been more widespread than has been maintained. And my preliminary designation of Charlie's texts as transitional texts suggests that in actuality, all kinds of balladry and song--oral and chap, even modern--may potentially exist simultaneously, as Mrs. Brown's oral texts may have with Leslie's "transition" texts; neat, definitive lines cannot be drawn. Finally, examination of the Charles Leslie material gives life and resonance to a body of texts, affirming not only the availability but also the importance of information beyond the textual. As the biographical song admonishes the hearers and readers:

He's dead and shortly will be rotten,
    Bonnie Laddie, Highland Laddie,
But he must never be forgotten,
    My bonnie Highland Laddie.

NOTES

[1] W. W. Walker, The Bards of Bon Accord: 1375-1860 (Aberdeen: J. & J. P. Edmond & Spark, 1887).

[2] George Ritchie Kinloch, The Ballad Book (Edinburgh: n. p., 1827).

[3] James Maidment, Scotish Ballads and Songs (Edinburgh: Thomas George Stevenson, 1859).

[4] Garioch Garland (n. p.: n. p., n. d.), Douce S370 (6), Bodlein Library, Oxford.

[5] James Hogg, The Jacobite Relics (Edinburgh: n. p., 1821).

[6] Letter to Alexander Irvine of Drum, 1825, MS 912, ff 277-80, National Library of Scotland, Edinburgh.

[7] Helen Beaton, At the Back o' Benachie; or, Life in the Garioch in the Nineteenth Century (Aberdeen: The Central Press, 1923).

[8] T. G. Stevenson, Four Books of Choice Old Scottish Ballads was republished in 1976 by EP Publishing Limited, East Ardsley, Wakefield, West Yorkshire, England.

[9] Peter Buchan, An Interesting and Faithful Narrative of the Wanderings of Prince Charles Stuart and Miss Flora MacDonald (London: W. S. Orr, 1839).

[10] Walter Scott, "Introductory Remarks on Popular Poetry, and on the Various Collections of Ballads of Britain, particularly those of Scotland," in The Poetical Works of Sir Walter Scott, Bart. (Edinburgh: Adam and Charles Black, 1851), pp. 537-55.

[11] See, for example, Alexander McConnochie, Bennachie (Aberdeen: D. Wylie & Son, 1890).

377

[12]See Colonel Leslie, <u>Historical Records of Leslie from 1067 to 1868-9</u> (Edinburgh: Edmonston and Douglas, 1969).

[13]David Buchan, <u>The Ballad and the Folk</u> (London: Routledge & Kegan Paul, 1972).

<u>Indiana University</u>
<u>Bloomington</u>

STRUCTURALISM AND SEMIOTICS

THE DEIL'S COURTING

From the recitation of John McWhinnie, collier, Newton Green, Ayr; Motherwell MS.

1. A lady wonned on yonder hill,
     Hee ba and balou ba
   And she had musick at her will.
     And the wind has blown my plaid awa

2. Up and cam an auld, auld man,
   Wi his blue bonnet in his han.

3. "I will ask ye questions three;
   Resolve them, or ye'll gang wi me.

4. "Ye maun mak to me a sark,
   It maun be free o woman's wark.

5. "Ye maun shape it knife-sheerless,
   And ye maun sew it needle-threedless.

6. "Ye maun wash it in yonder well,
   Whare rain nor dew has ever fell.

7. "Ye maun dry it on yonder thorn,
   Where leaf neer grew since man was born."

8. "I will ask ye questions three;
   Resolve them, or ye'll neer get me.

9. "I hae a rig o bonnie land
   Atween the saut sea and the sand.

10. "Ye maun plow it wi ae horse bane,
    And harrow it wi ae harrow pin.

11. "Ye maun shear 't wi a whang o leather,
    And ye maun bind 't bot strap or tether.

12. "Ye maun stack it in the sea,
    And bring the stale hame dry to me.

13. "Ye maun mak a cart o stane,
    And yoke the wren and bring it hame.

14. "Ye maun thresh 't atween your lufes,
    And ye maun sack 't atween your thies."

15. "My curse on those wha learnèd thee;
    This night I weend ye'd gane wi me."

DAVID BUCHAN

THE WIT-COMBAT BALLADS

The subject of this essay is that group of types in classical balladry which I have called the "wit-combat ballads." These are conventionally called the riddling ballads, but since riddles proper appear in only some of the types while wit combats occur in them all, it would seem more logical and apposite to term them the wit-combat ballads.[1] The analytic approach to this small sub-genre enlists the services of Propp's concept of tale role, a concept which has not been exploited by anglophone scholarship. The basic cause of this ignoring lies with the English translation of Propp's Morphology, a translation which renders indiscriminately with three English terms the two Russian terms used by Propp to indicate on the one hand the abstract concept of tale role and on the other the concrete fact of character. A recent paper that tested against one ballad repertoire Propp's percept as a means of analysis and classification found it of considerable usefulness. It provided insight into the essential nature of the ballad genre itself and of the constituent sub-genres as well as insight into the relationships of individual types; it also illuminated some cultural concerns and messages intrinsic to the genre. Its usefulness there suggested quite forcibly that its general utility be tested across the spectrum of balladry.[2] Here, then, a start is made with the wit-combat ballads.

On the basis of the riddle tales in folk narrative, Child describes three classes of riddling ballad: one where riddles have to be guessed or a heavy penalty such as death has to be paid; one where a male suitor gains a partner by solving enigmas; and one where "The Clever Lass" gains a partner (or, as Child should have added, evades an unwanted suitor) by successfully matching wits with him.[3] Wimberly, however, points to the existence of a fourth class, one where a mortal confronts an Otherworld being.[4] This in fact is the important class, for only one type of the wit-combat ballads has no versions including such a confrontation. Consequently the wit-combat ballads can be perceived most practically in just two groupings: group A, the supernatural group with the Otherworld beings and group B, the secular group without the Otherworld beings. Some types have versions in both groups, as can be seen from the Appendix, where an asterisk denotes the less characteristic versions. Four types (1, 2, 3, 47) belong primarily to group A, and two (46, 78) secondarily; conversely two types (45, 46) belong primarily to group B, and two (1, 2) secondarily.

In the wit-combat ballads taken as a whole there is a central relationship between two characters, one of whom poses problems in cleverness which the other has to solve or match. There are just two tale roles: Poser and Matcher. These two tale roles are set in firm juxtaposition, for this sub-genre deals with direct confrontations. These confrontations take the form of a battle of wits, a fact which makes the sub-genre a highly verbal one, one where the main interest resides in the words and the minds of the combatants rather than on narrative action or even lyric emotion. There exists, in short, a somewhat cerebral quality to this sub-genre that distinguishes it from the others. For most of the types a dramatic dialogue stands at the heart of the story, presented either as a series of interactions or as one comprehensive interaction. The verbal material that makes up these interactions, the actual stuff of the wit-combats, merits some attention.

The material usually lumped together as "riddlings" consists diversely of questions, commands, and assertions. The questions often involve superlatives--"What is the fairest flower, tell me, / That grows in mire or dale?" (47B:13)--or "firsts," a kind of superlative--"Now what is the flower, the ae first flower, / Springs either on moor or dale?" (47A:7)--or comparatives implying superlatives--"What is greener than the grass, what's higher than the tree?" (46A:12). The interrogation may include straightforwardly mundane questions leading up to a trick question, as in type 3:

> "Wha's aucht they sheep?"
> "They are mine and my mither's."
>
> "How monie o them are mine?"
> "A' they that hae blue tails."   (3A:4, 5)

Atypically, the questions may appear unanswerable because of their subjectivity, as in type 45: "Lett me know within one pennye. What I am worth . . . How soone I may goe the whole world about . . . And thirdly . . . What is the thing, bishopp, that I doe thinke" (45A:7,8). The first-person subjectivity of this type, which is also a novella, stands in contrast to the relative objectivity of the askings in the other types. The commands call for the performance of impossible tasks, whether downright impossibles--"Go fetch me . . . water from a stone" (78F:7)--or fantastical impossibles--"Ye maun make me a fine Holland sark, / Without ony stitching or needle wark" (2D:5)--or apparent impossibles that require quick thinking--"You maun get to my supper a cherry but a stane" (46A:9)--or that require the production of a ferlie--"You man get to me a plumb that does in winter grow" (46A:15) (an asking that reminds one of the requests made to Marlowe's Dr. Faustus in a play built on another confrontation of mortal and unmortal). The assertions, with their counter-assertions, occur only in type 3:

> "I wiss ye were on yon tree:"
> "And a gude ladder under me."
>
> "And the ladder for to break:"
> "And you for to fa down."   (3A:6, 7)

The verbal combats take somewhat different forms in the individual types. Type 1 has questions (comparatives), type 47 questions that are mainly superlatives, and type 3 the simple and trick questions together with the assertions. Type 2, ubiquitously, and type 78, in just some of its versions, have commands involving the various kinds of tasks. Of the two basically secular types, 45 has the subjective questions and 46 has, unusually, both questions (firsts, comparatives, and straight superlatives) and commands (tasks requiring not only quick thinking but also the production of ferlies). The loosely-used term "riddle" comprehends, it can be seen, a diversity of referents in these types.

What precisely it is that makes up the dynamics of the "riddling," that constitutes the "wit" in the wit combats, bears some investigation. First of all the combatants have to demonstrate their ability to think; and the kinds of thinking required are those that inform traditional riddling practices. They include the metaphorical thinking that answers the "sparrow's horn" question--"there's ane in every tae" (46A:16)--the trickster-like cunning that answers the "tell to me truly what I do think" question (45B:6), and the perception of process that answers the well-known command:

> You maun get to my supper a cherry but a stane,
> And you man get to my supper a capon but a bane.
> . . . .
> A cherry whan in blossom is a cherry but a stane;
> a capon when he's in the egg canna hae a bane.
>   (46A:9¹,², 10¹,²)

Here the responder has to be aware of the natural processes of creation and growth, of the evolutionary unity within diversity. The combatants, then, have to display their competence in the patterns of thinking intrinsic to the traditional intellectual genre of riddling. They also have to demonstrate their ability to act, that is, to think on their feet and interact verbally with an adversary in a specific situation. In order to do this they must possess a knowledge of procedures, the rules of the game for these joustings; he that would sup with the Devil "maun hae a lang-shankit speen": one has to know how the Devil is to be, and is not to be, spoken to. Just as their ability to act effectively depends on a knowledge of procedures, their ability to think depends to a great extent on their possession of knowledge.

This knowledge may be traditional wisdom as contained in its generic forms--"Honger ys scharpper than /ys/ þe thorne"[5]--or knowledge of a special kind--"Tell me some o that wondrous lied / Ye've learnt in Archerdale" (47D:5)--or general knowledge of a quite comprehensive range. Consider, from versions IC, ID (both Scottish, early nineteenth century), IE (English, late nineteenth century), and IA* (English, circa 1450),[6] the ideas that fill the slots in the question and answer:

O what is _____er than the _____? O _____ is _____ er...

Version C:

heigher	tree	heaven	(Also in D,A*)
deeper	sea	hell	(D,A*)
heavier	lead	sin	
better	breid	blessing	
		Godys flesse	(A*)
whiter	milk	snaw	(D)
safter	silk	down	
		love	(D)
	melting wax	love	(E)
	flex	selke	(A*)
sharper	thorn	hunger	(D,E,A*)
/strenger	dede	payne	(A*)
louder	horn	shame	
		thunder	(D,A*)
		rumour	(E)

greener	grass	pies are	
		peas are	(Cb)
		poison	(D)
		envy	(E)
grenner	wode	grass	(A*)
waur	woman	Clootie	
	was	the Devil	(D)
	a woman's wuss /̄curs_e_7̄	the Fiend	(Cb)

Version D:

longer	way	wind	
		loukynge /̄expectatio_n_7̄	(A*)
colder	clay	death	

Version E:

smoother	crystal glass	flattery
brighter	light	truth
darker	night	falsehood
keener	axe	revenge
rounder	ring	the world

Version A*

ra_d_er /̄quicke_r_7̄	day	syn
swetter	note	loue
swifter	wynd	þowt
recher	kynge	Ihesus
zeluer	wex	safer /̄saffro_n_7̄7

The answers demand of the combatant knowledge of the abstract and the concrete, the eschatological and the social, the cosmic and the natural, the intellectual and the emotional, the moral and the sensory, and of good and evil. The responses needed, in short, require a succinct but pregnant formulation of wide-ranging information about nature, man, and his place in the cosmos.

In a number of versions of the wit-combat types there occur overt indications of the importance of possessing knowledge or "wyssedom." When, in an Ayrshire coalminer's version of type 2, the woman verbally vanquishes "the auld, auld man," he pays an indirect compliment to her acquisition of knowledge:

> My curse on those wha learnĕd thee;
> This night I weend ye'd gane wi me.   (2 I 15)[8]

In type 45 the moral of the story is encapsulated, unusually for the ballads, in the proverb "a fool may learn a wiseman wit" (B13). And in IA* the "fovle fende" makes this offer,

> Mayd, mote y thi leman be,
> Wyssedom y wolle teche the:
>
> All þe wyssedom off the world,
> Hyf þou wolt be true and forward holde.   (3,4)

to which the maid responds:

> Ihesu, for þy myld myzth,
> As thu art kynge and knyzt,
>
> Lene me wisdome to answere here ryzth,
> And schylde me fram the fovle wyzth! (13, 14)

Here the diabolic offer parallels Satan's temptation of Christ, and the maid wisely invokes Jesus' aid that she may answer "right," both correctly and with moral force. Wisdom in this type overtly, and in other types implicitly, seems to be strongly associated with moral knowledge. IA* presents very powerfully the situation of the mortal who must herself battle the threatening unmortal but who can draw on the help of Christ.[9] In most versions of the Group A types, however, the mortals are starkly alone, fortified only by their knowledge and their interactional wits. In this sub-genre that has links with the traditional intellectual genre of riddling and, to a lesser extent, the wisdom genre of the proverb, the main concern does not reside in narrative action or emotion but in the dramatic interplay of intellect between two characters. The general dynamics of the ballad-types derive from the abilities of the characters to think and to interact effectively, abilities predicated on their possession of "knowledges"; and the persistent equation of wisdom and moral knowledge would suggest that implicit in the working out of these dynamics, embodied in the action, is at least one particular cultural value.

Individual types of course may contain other elements, additional to those common through the sub-genre, within the dynamics of their specific verbal combat, as in Child 2.[10] In this type the Poser commands the woman to fashion him a shirt, an asking that occurs in some ballads as part of the courtship process and which reflects a customary practice whereby "a man's asking a maid to sew him a shirt is equivalent to asking for her love, and her consent to sew the shirt to an acceptance of the suitor."[11] The Poser commands that she perform a typifying action of woman's work, detailing the creation of the shirt through the shaping, the sewing, the washing, and the drying:

Ye maun shape it knife-sheerless,
And ye maun sew it needle-threedless.

Ye maun wash it in yonder well,
Whare rain nor dew has ever fell.

Ye maun dry it on yonder thorn,
Where leaf neer grew since man was born. (2 I 5-7)

The commands have clearly a fantastical air to them, but they also, looked at from a slightly different angle, have a series of negations whereby each order carries with it a disabling injunction: shape it with a knife, but without cutting; sew it with a needle, but without thread; wash it in a well, but one without dew or rainwater; dry it on a thornbush, but one that has never had leaves. In this sinewy version recorded by Motherwell from an Ayrshire coalminer, the element of negation is given pointed expression in the Poser's initial command:

Ye maun mak to me a sark,
It maun be free o woman's wark. (2 I 4)

The unmortal, it would seem, is demanding that she prove her domestic capabilities as a woman while at the same time denying her the means to demonstrate these capabilities. The inbuilt negation indicates that while he is ostensibly testing her as a woman through the performance of domestic tasks, on a more fundamental level he is testing her by setting an intellectual task which requires that she demonstrate the womanly powers of intelligence necessary to combat an unmortal.

The woman responds to his orders with a comparable set of commands requiring that he perform the typifying activities of man's work, those relating to the harvesting of the earth and constituting the central processes of the farming year. She demands that for her "rig o bonnie land / Atween the saut sea and the sand":

> Ye maun plow it wi ae horse bane,
> And harrow it wi ae harrow pin.
>
> Ye maun shear't wi a whang o leather
> And ye maun bind't bot strap or tether.
>
> Ye maun stack it in the sea,
> And bring the stale* hame dry to me. /‾*the foundation
>   of a stack_/
> Ye maun mak a cart o stane,
> And yoke the wren and bring it hame.
>
> Ye maun thresh't atween your lufes,
> And ye maun sack't atween your thies. (2 I 10-14)

Her responses have the obvious fantastic component--perhaps even more pronouncedly--but also do not lack the negation, expressed most directly in "ye maun saw it without a seed" (2 C 13[1]).

Some additional light may be cast on the combat by the deposition of a seventeenth-century witch in Moray, Isobel Goudie:

> The Devill held the plewgh, and Johne Yonge
> in Mebestowne, our officer, did drywe the plewgh.
> Toads did draw the pleugh, as oxen; qwickens
> /couch-grass/ were sowmes /draught-chain/, a riglen's
> horne /gelded animal's horn/ was a cowter,
> and ane piece of ane riglen's horne was
> ane sok /ploughshare/. We went seuerall
> tymes abowt; and all we of the Coven went
> still up and downe with the plewghe
> prayeing to the Devill for the fruit of that land,
> and that thistles and brieries might grow ther.[12]

Here plough-parts connote barrenness, and the purpose of the exercise is clearly to induce sterility. A pair of correspondences relate the witch's account and the Matcher's commands. First there is the smallness of scale (corresponding to the couch-grass as draught-chain, the toads as plough-team) that conditions many of her commands ("sack it in your gluve," "winno't in your leuve /fist/" (2 D 14), and shows especially in those involving small creatures ("Ye'll big a cart o stane and lime, / Gar Robin Redbreast trail it syne" /D16, cfA13/; "Ye maun mak a cart o stane, / And yoke the wren and bring it hame" /I 13/; "And ye maun barn't in yon mouse hole" /D 13/[1]). Second, there is the appearance of the animal horn in both, though rarely is it specified in the ballad versions as a gelded animal's horn. In those texts, however, where the Poser is introduced as an elfin knight, she asks him quite assertively to plough it with "your (blawing, touting) horn," as if she were intent on turning against him, or nullifying, the potentialities of this Otherworldly instrument. Certainly it would be unwise to make too much of the individual associations, but in general terms the deposition does help bring into focus the element of sterile negation that occurs both in the witches' cursing and in the wit combatants' commands-with-provisos. This is not, of course, to ignore the element of extravagant fantasy that permeates many of the commands but simply to point to a darker constituent strand. It is perhaps worth observing that the further the story moves in its versions from an interaction of mortal and unmortal, the more the element of sterility declines and the more the fantasy tends to the whimsical.

Within the story of type 2 the verbal interaction involves a symbolic part of the courtship process, typifying activities of male and female gender roles; it also involves a governing strain of sterile negation. That this thematic strain pervades the exchange is entirely appropriate since it reflects a central fact about this courting combat: the sterility for the woman (in terms of a full life in a human context) of any possible union between mortal and unmortal. Behind the raillery of apparent courtship lies a much darker struggle for domination. In this, I would suggest, is the genesis of the sex-death bipolarity in the Ozarks version discussed by Toelken. Beyond the elements common to the dynamics of the sub-genre, then, there may exist elements particular to the dynamics of the individual types.

The discussion of the interactional features of the sub-genre as a whole now allows a return to the two constituent groupings of types and to the tale roles. In the types of group A, those involving supernatural characters, there is a central relationship between a human being and an Otherworld being; the mortal must match wits and win a riddling combat in order to avoid submission to the unmortal (a term I am using for brevity's sake, instead of the cumbersome "Otherworld being"). The mortal can do this by answering testing questions or by countering enigmatic statements (the questions, assertions, and commands). In a unique version of 46 from Newfoundland the mortal escapes by posing problems the unmortal cannot solve: here the woman is the Poser and the diabolic interlocutor the failed Matcher, failed because he cannot fetch "the priest unborn."[13] Only in one type, 47, does the mortal initiate the combat, and this is the sole type where the mortal succumbs to the greater wit-powers, the greater intellect, of the unmortal (and here of course the submission is "for her own good" since the unmortal humbles her excessive pride). Apart from that version and that type, all Poser roles are occupied by unmortals, and all Matcher roles by mortals. And the Matcher, except for the maverick Newfoundland version, always wins.

The unmortal is the Devil or a diabolic character in three types (1, 3, 46), a revenant in two (47, 78), and variously elf, Devil, or revenant in one (2).[14] The mortal is a woman in five of the types and a child in the sixth (3); in the two revenant ballads the woman is respectively sister and true-love to the ghost. In one very unusual version of 46, again from Newfoundland and Labrador, the two roles are filled by the Devil and the Blessed Virgin Mary.[15] Clearly the ballads in this group belong by conventional classification to both the wit-combat category and the magical and marvellous category, except for that last, unusual, version which might fall among the religious ballads.

Except for 47 the unmortal is the verbal aggressor, the one who instigates the match; the mortal responds. When we look at the mortal characters filling the tale roles we discover five women and one child: the weaker and consequently more vulnerable members of a community. The wit-combat, therefore, pits weaker members of the community against various denizens of the Otherworld. In general terms the wit-combat serves to dramatize the clash that can occur at the interface between the Otherworld and this world. In specific terms, it shows in types 1, 2, 3, and 46 how a mortal can repulse the unwelcome attentions of an unmortal, and avoid falling into his power; it shows in type 78 how a mortal can redeem a troth-plight from a revenant and thereby escape having to follow him to the grave.[16] In type 47, where the woman initiates the verbal exchange--which underlines her sin of pride--she loses the combat to the revenant who uses his position of vantage to strike home with a homily on his sister's sin. The wit-combats serve not only as battles of wits but also as tests of "knowledges." To cope with the unmortal the mortal must have a range of informational knowledge for answering the various kinds of question posed and must also have a knowledge of procedures, of the rules governing these interactions between human and Otherworld beings. The mortal must know not only what but how to respond. If, like Proud Lady Margaret, the mortal reverses the customary roles and initiates the exchange, then the upshot may be not to her liking. Once the unmortal has instigated an interaction, however, then the mortal must counter, or "flyte," with him and must continue demonstrating her skill in repartee--always getting her word in until she has the last word;[17] climactically she can dispel a diabolic character by naming him:

> As sune as she the fiend did name,
> He flew awa in a blazing flame. (IC:19)

These ballad types constitute a kind of pocket Goffman: they provide rules for the interactional rituals between mortal and unmortal. When, then, one analyzes the types of group A in the light of the tale roles and the characters occupying the tale roles, one can perceive something of the group's cultural functioning. The primary concern of the group is the interaction of human and Otherworld beings, and the main cultural messages those relating to the knowledges and skills required by the more vulnerable members of the community to prevail in these interactions. The wit-combat ballads of group A present models for behaviour towards unchancy unmortals: strategies for survival.

The secular types and versions of group B also have as tale roles Poser and Matcher. In three types (1, 2, 46) the relationship is between male and female, where one character wins the wit combat to avoid an unwanted suitor or to gain a partner; and in the fourth the central relationship is between king and subject, where the loss of the wit combat would entail the loss of the subject's head. This type, 45, stands out from the other wit-combat ballads for a number of reasons. First, in this story where the king poses three riddles to a churchman but has them answered by an ordinary man, the second tale role contains two characters, the unsuccessful and the successful Matcher: the only occurrence in the wit-combat ballads of three characters filling the two tale role slots. Second, it is the only type which contains no unmortal character in any version (though its riddles sometimes have an eschatological or cosmic cast). Third, it is the only type with marked changes in the scene-settings, and consequently the only one without concentration on one sustained interaction. Fourth, it is the only "death penalty" type. And fifth, it is the only type to have an Aarne-Thompson listing: AT922. Its dissimilarities would certainly reinforce the view that this story existed as a novella before it was recreated in ballad form. Type 46 ("Captain Wedderburn's Courtship") is the other predominantly secular type of group B. In it a suitor proves his worth for a woman, though, as we have seen, three versions from Newfoundland have the Devil being repulsed by the Woman. The other two types belong primarily to group A but have some secular versions where the unmortal has metamorphosed into a human being. At one time Child thought the human being was the original figure and the unmortal an intruder, but by volume V and the turning up of the 1450 text of "Inter Diabolus et Virgo" he had changed his mind.[18] Although Child titled type 2 "The Elfin Knight" and his five primary versions (A-E) all have an elfin knight, he rather paradoxically insisted that the stanzas with the elfin knight belonged to a different type. Wimberly, however, declares that the elf "is probably the original character," which certainly seems the more logical viewpoint.[19] In the type 2 secular versions the woman repels her human suitor as she had the unmortal, but in the type 1 secular versions the woman's display of wit leads to her marriage with the ordinary knight who has supplanted the "unco knicht."

The type-versions of group B involve wit-combats between mortals. Those types with versions containing male-female interaction have tests of cleverness dominating the action and the viewpoint of the woman, whether pleased Poser or happy Matcher, conditioning the tone of the ballad's ending. In type 1, H, the male protagonist tests S's, the heronie's, cleverness and S, by showing her intelligence, gains a desirable partner; in type 2, H tests S's cleverness and S, in demonstrating her intelligence, avoids an undesirable partner; and in type 46, S tests H's cleverness and H, by showing his intelligence, demonstrates both that he is a desirable partner for S and that S has herself no lack of wit to design the test in the first place. Again, then, one can see, intrinsic to the types in this group, a cultural concern with cleverness and with women. If these can be taken as models, then the cultural declaration seems fairly clear: that women, to do well in their courting relationships with men, must develop and exercise their powers of intelligence.

By and large Child tends to view the supernatural elements in the wit-combat ballads as later insertions, but Wimberly, in redressing the balance, states that "in all our riddle ballads, except two (45, 46), a preternatural being of some kind is made to play a role (1, 2, 47, 78). And it would not be too great a hazard, perhaps, to venture a guess that one of these exceptions, Captain Wedderburn's Courtship (46), has supernatural affiliations by virtue of some as yet undiscovered text in which the maid or the hero is an Otherworld personage."[20] Not just one but three texts of this kind, having unmortals for either or both characters, have in fact been recorded, all in Newfoundland.[21] In the light of the evidence that has been accumulating over the past hundred years (Child's Part I of Volume I was published in 1882) we can now reverse Child's perspective: the wit-combat ballad types more often than not involve a supernatural character. The conservatism of Child's viewpoint has, however, something to be said for it, since we should beware seeing the traditional process as one-way, as a process whereby the supernatural is only rationalized and secularized. One of the more arresting features of anglophone ballad tradition to come to light in recent years has been that the process works the other way too in traditional dynamics: secular ballad material can be "supernaturalized." Hugh Shields, for example, discusses this phenomenon in his studies of "The Dead Lover's Return" and "The Grey Cock."[22] The evidence for this phenomenon in North America derives largely from the Atlantic provinces of Canada--often, it would seem, from an Irish tradition.[23] The wit-combat ballad-types illustrate the way the dynamic processes of tradition operate in both directions, developing supernatural into secular and secular into supernatural.

Since individual types contain both secular and supernatural versions, any attempt to classify by a rigidly monolithic conception of type would lead to confusion. As folktale scholars found some time back, one should utilize the concept of type for its manifold benefits but should not be restrictively bound by it. What is needed for classification purposes is a method that affords in simple fashion a means of showing clearly constants and variables in key features of the material. The ordering by tale role and character can supply that means, at least in the material discussed here, for the tale roles have the major constants (the roles of Poser and Matcher) and the character listings show the major variables. This ordering also provides a means of perceiving the nature of the relationship between the wit-combat sub-genre and other sub-genres--most notably the large magical and marvellous category (type 78, for example, is a revenant ballad type that has wit-combat versions)--as well as the relationships within the wit-combat ballad types themselves (such as, for example, those linking 1, 2, 3, and 46).[24] From these relationships we can deduce how developments within types may occur: how, given the basic molds, types 1 and 46 have come to interact--to take one instance. It would seem that wit-combats will tend to attract supernatural characters, and that supernatural characters in a two-tale-role inter-action will tend to attract wit combats.[25]

The essential nature of the sub-genre itself is revealed by the tale-role pattern and the relationships of the characters. With these clear, one can observe that such a piece as "Harpkin"[26] (which has analogues in Types of the Scandinavian Medieval Ballad Type F70)[27] conforms to the norms of the sub-genre, and that type 45 by its anomalies advertises its provenance in the novella form. The tale-role and character patterning indicate the main cultural concerns of the sub-genre. It has a stark apposition of two tale roles, in contrast to the three-tale-role pattern in Anna Brown's repertoire, and deals in its character patterning with just three sets of relationships: most frequently, that between unmortal and mortal; less frequently, that between male and female; and, in one type only, that between king and subject. These three kinds of relationship constitute central concerns of other sub-genres as well, but this sub-genre differs from others (on the evidence of the Anna Brown repertoire) in typically lacking the three-character interaction, the familial complexities attendant on the man-woman relationship, and indeed the usual range of characters determined by family role. (Here there is only the revenant brother of type 47). The features absent as well as the features present help define the focus on the sub-genre's main cultural concern: woman, and her adversarial relations with men, in group B, and with unmortals, in group A. In the versions of the latter group, children appear as well as women, a fact which serves to underline that the general concern is with the weaker and more vulnerable members of a community who must use their wits rather than physical prowess to counter certain problems or dangers in their environment.

The cultural concerns lead on to the suggestion that certain cultural values inform the sub-genre. The types and their versions emphasize the importance of cleverness and its particular utility in certain kinds of adversarial interaction; they emphasize the importance of knowing, knowing both kinds of information and kinds of behavior; and they emphasize how a superior intellect, one both clever and knowing, can not only defeat certain dangers but also ensure a richer life. This sub-genre, in short, constitutes a celebration of cunning, where "cunning" subsumes both its modern meaning of cleverness and its original acceptation of knowing.

APPENDIX

Wit-combat Ballads

Tale Role:		POSER	MATCHER	
Group A:				
Character:	1	UD	S	("Riddles Wisely Expounded")
	2	U(D,F,Rev)	S	("The Elfin Knight")
	3	UD	Ch	("The Fause Knight Upon The Road")
	46*	S	UDu	("Captain Wedderburn's Courtship")
	46*	UD	S	
	46*	UD	BV	
	47	S	SBRev	("Proud Lady Margaret")
	78*	HRev	S	("The Unquiet Grave")
Group B:				
	1*	H	S	
	2*	H	S	
	45	K	H	("King John and the Bishop")
			Clu	
	46	S	H	

*denotes some (or just one), less characteristic versions

The Abbreviations:

```
     H:  He, Hero, Leading Male Character
     S:  She, Heroine, Leading Female Character
    SB:  S's Brother
    Ch:  Child
     K:  King
    Cl:  Clergyman
    BV:  Blessed Virgin
     U:  Unmortal
    UD:  Unmortal: Devil
    UF:  Unmortal: Fairy
   Rev:  Revenant
(& e.g. HRev:  H as Revenant)
u(as in UDu):  unsuccessful (Matcher)
```

[1]This is an expanded version of a paper given at the 13. Arbeitstagung of the Kommission für Volksdichtung (Sheffield, 1982); I would like to thank my colleagues there who responded with stimulating comments: Rolf Brednich, Mary Ellen Brown, Sheila Douglas, Bill Nicolaisen, Hugh Shields, Stefaan Top, and Natascha Würzbach.

[2]"Propp's Tale Role and a Ballad Repertoire," Journal of American Folklore, 95 (1982), 159-72. Vladimir Propp's Morphology of The Folktale was first published in Russian in 1928 and translated into English in 1958 in an edition which was revised in 1968 (Austin: University of Texas Press). I am grateful to my colleague, Emeritus Professor Herbert Halpert, who, with his customary fecundity of reference, directed me to two German-language writings where the relationship between stable role and variable character is discussed, empirically by Matti Kuusi in Regen Bei Sonnenschein, Folklore Fellows Communications, No. 171, (Helsinki: Suomalainen Tiedeakatemia, 1957), pp. 13-16, and more generally by Wayland D. Hand in "Stabile Funktion und Variable Dramatis Personae in der Volkssage," Acta Ethnographica, 13 (1964), 49-54.

[3]Francis J. Child, The English and Scottish Popular Ballads, 5 vols. (Boston: Houghton Mifflin, 1882-98), I, 1.

[4]Lowry C. Wimberly, Folklore in the English and Scottish Popular Ballads (Chicago, 1928; rpt. New York: Dover, 1965), pp. 309-10.

[5]Child, V, 283: 1A*16 (A* being the designation given this version by Kittredge). See William G. Smith, ed., The Oxford Dictionary of English Proverbs, 3rd ed., ed. F. P. Wilson (Oxford: Oxford University Press, 1970), p. 392, where the earliest occurrence is listed as 1550.

[6]For 1A* see preceding note. Cb refers to the version of Mrs. Storie that is printed in E. B. Lyle, ed., Andrew Crawfurd's Collection of Ballads and Songs, I (Edinburgh: Scottish Text Society, 1975), 113-14; it has one or two minor differences from her Motherwell MS text (Child's C).

[7]B. J. Whiting, in "Proverbial Material in the Popular Ballad," Journal of American Folklore, 47 (1934), 22-44,

lists just twelve lines from type 1, ten of the "What is _____ er than the _____?" construction but only two of the "_____ is _____er than the _____" construction ("Gras ys grenner þan ys þe wode"; þowt ys swifter þan ys the wynde"). He lists as a comparison "What ys scharpper þan ys þe þorne?" but fails to note the response "Hongyr ys scharpper than /ys/ þe thorne" as a proverb proper. A detailed investigation of the traditional wisdom genres in the wit-combat ballads would repay the efforts of a proverb scholar; it could throw light on proverb studies (particularly through the material in the _circa_ 1450 text) and also provide an interesting foray into ways of traditional thinking and the interrelationship of traditional genres.

[8]See also Bertrand H. Bronson, The Traditional Tunes of the Child Ballads, the Child Ballads, I (Princeton, N. J.: Princeton University Press, 1959), 38, for a version of type 3 learned in Ireland and recorded in Vermont in 1932:

"Who taught you so well?"
Said the false, false knight to the child on the road.
"My teachers and my mamma,"
Said the pretty boy seven years old.

"What did they teach you so well for?"
Said the false, false knight to the child on the road.
"To keep me from you and from your wicked Hell,"
And he bowed seven times on the road.

"Bad luck to the teacher that taught you so well,"
Said the false, false knight to the child on the road.
"Good luck to the teacher that kept me from you
And from your wicked Hell,"
Said the pretty boy seven years old. (5-7)

[9]Bronson prints two versions of type 1 from Virginia, one from Giles County (1922) and one from Salem (1941) but both entitled "The Devil's Nine Questions" (1,7-8), which contain a reflection of this idea. The Devil declares at the outset "Oh, you must answer my questions nine, / Or you're not God's, you're one of mine." and concludes "O you have answered my questions nine, / And you are God's, you're none of mine."

[10]J. Barre Toelken, for example, has shown that in a secular version of type 2 from the Ozarks ambiguous overtones of death and sex pervade the lover's commands and the woman's counter-commands: "Riddles Wisely Expounded," Western Folklore, 25 (1966), 7-16.

[11]Child, V, 284.

[12]Robert Pitcairn, Criminal Trails in Scotland, 3 vols. (Edinburgh: William Tait, 1833). I have been unable to consult the original and must give the passage as cited (with no page reference to Pitcairn) in F. Marian McNeill, The Silver Bough (Glasgow: W. Maclellan, 1957), I, 146.

[13]Maud Karpeles, ed., Folk Songs from Newfoundland (London: Faber and Faber, 1971), pp. 40-41.

[14]See Roger deV. Renwick, in Tristram Potter Coffin, The British Traditional Ballad in North America, rev. ed., supplement by Roger deV. Renwick (Austin: University of Texas Press, 1977), p. 224, for the argument that the Devil is the interlocutor in certain versions of type 46.

[15]MacEdward Leach, Folk Ballads and Songs of the Lower Labrador Coast (Ottawa: National Museum of Canada, Bulletin no. 201, 1965), pp. 26-29.

[16]Wimberly, pp. 306-07; Ruth Harvey, "The Unquiet Grave," Journal of the English Folk Dance and Song Society, 4 (1940-45), 54-55; both follow the troth-plight interpretation advanced by Sabine Baring-Gould in S. Baring-Gould, H. Fleetwood Sheppard, and F. W. Bussell, Songs of the West: Folk Songs of Devon & Cornwall collected from the mouths of the people, 7th ed. in 1 vol. (London: Metheun, 1928), pp. 12-13, and pp. 3 and 14-16 of the "Notes on the Songs," where (p. 15 of the Notes) he prints a significant stanza overlooked by Child. Even if the troth-plight idea makes good sense of much of the action, certain peculiarities remain; as Wimberly says: "it must be that motives are mixed in our ballad or that the logic of ghostdom is other than that of mortals" (p. 307). A study of all the versions of "The Unquiet Grave" could prove a beneficial undertaking.

[17]See Child, I, 21n and 485, for his dismissal and then his retraction of the dismissal of Mrs. Jessie Saxby's comment that "The only safeguard against witches is 'to flight wi dem,' that is, draw them into a controversy and scold them roundly."

[18]Child, V, 283-84.

[19]Wimberly, p. 305.

[20]Wimberly, p. 309.

[21]Karpeles, pp. 39-40, 40-41; Leach, pp. 26-29.

[22]"The Dead Lover's Return in Modern English Ballad Tradition," Jahrbuch für Volksliedforschung, 17 (1972), 98-114; "'The Grey Cock': Dawn Song or Revenant Ballad?" Ballad Studies, ed. E. B. Lyle (Cambridge: D. S. Brewer, 1976), pp. 67-92.

[23]Coffin/Renwick, p. 200.

[24]Coffin/Renwick, pp. 209-11, 223-24.

[25]The form of the wit-combat ballads invites their comparison with other dialogue songs. For a measured survey of dialogue songs and the classical ballad's place within their wide range, see B. H. Bronson, "The Dialogue Song; or Proteus Observed," Philological Quarterly, 54 (1975), 117-36.

[26]Child, 1, 21; Robert Chambers, Popular Rhymes of Scotland 4th ed. (Edinburgh, 1870; rpt. Detroit: Singing Tree, 1969), p. 66.

[27]The Types of the Scandinavian Medieval Ballad, eds. Bengt R. Jonsson, Svale Solheim and Eva Danielson, in collaboration with Mortan Nolsøe and W. Edson Richmond (Stockholm and Oslo: Universitetsforlaget, 1978), p. 289.

Memorial University of Newfoundland
St. John's

GUY REED

by Joe Scott

Sung by Phil Walsh, Northwest Bridge, New Brunswick.

1. How well do I remember
     One dark and stormy night,
   The rain it fell in torrents,
     The lightning flashed so bright.
   The moon and stars above me
     Did not their light reveal,
   For dark clouds so gloomy
     Did their welcome light conceal.

2. The post brought me a letter,
     I hastened to peruse,
   T'was written by a friend of mine,
     But bore me startling news.
   For one I knew, a fine young man
     As you would wish to see,
   In an instant he was hurled
     Into eternity.

3. He and his companions,
     Where the waters they do roar,
   Were breaking in the landing
     On the Androscoggin shore;
   They had picked a face on one of them
     From bottom to the top,
   Fully thirty feet this landing had
     A perpendicular drop.

4. To work the face much longer
       Would be a foolish part,
    A jar so slight, you see, it might
       This lofty landing start.
    There were a few among them
       Did volunteer to go
    To roll a log from off the top
       To start the logs below.

5. This young man he among them
       With heart so stout and brave,
    Not thinking he e'er night would be
       All straightened for the grave,
    Not thinking that death's cruel hand
       So soon would lay him low,
    To leave those ones he loved behind,
       In sorrow, grief and woe.

6. This log they quickly started,
       The landing creaked below,
    And on it sped unto the verge
       But would no further go.
    This young man now approaches
       The verge of landing high,
    While all the crew with pallid cheeks
       And trembling limb stood by.

7. Up went a shout of warning
       To warn him of his fate,
    And just an instant he did pause,
       He seemed to hesitate.
    He rolled the log just half way o'er,
       The landing broke like glass,
    And quick as thought he disappeared
       Into the rolling mass.

8. Those logs they rolled carefully
       From off his mangled form,
    The birds were singing sweetly,
       The sun shone bright and warm.
    Strong men knelt down beside him
       Who could not their grief command,
    Unbidden tears burst from their eyes
       And fell into the sand.

9. Tenderly they bore him,
       Gently laid him on the green
    Beneath a shady tree that grew
       Near by a purling stream.

The bubbling, sparkling waters
  Stealing o'er its sandy bed,
Seemed to murmer /sic/, sweetly, softly,
  A farewell unto the dead.

10. His remains were buried
      By the order of K. P.,
    A funeral more attended
      You would seldom ever see.
    The church and yard were crowded
      With people young and old,
    Once more to see that face once fair,
      In death now pale and cold.

11. His casket was decorated
      With roses sweet and fair,
    His pillow, too, with every hue
      Of flowers bright and rare;
    His brothers of the Order,
      As they marched two by two,
    On the casket a spray let fall,
      A token of adieu.

12. His mother she died early
      When he was but a child,
    They laid her down to slumber
      Near a forest fair and wild;
    His brother and his sister
      Are sleeping by her side
    In a quiet country churchyard
      Near the river's dancing tide.

13. This young man's name was Guy Reed,
      His age was twenty-three,
    On September the eighth was killed
      In a town known as Riley.
    In the little town of Byron
      Was laid beneath the earth,
    He sleeps beside his kindred
      Near the spot that gave him birth.

14. His poor feeble father
      Is stricken now with grief,
    The joy of earthly pleasures
      Will bring him no relief.
    For untold gold or silver,
      Position, wealth in store,
    Sunny skies or music sweet
      Will not the dead restore.

15. The robin and the swallow,
   The sunshine and the rain,
The cuckoo and the sparrow
   With the spring will come again.
The blackbird and the thrushes
   From foreign lands will soar,
But loved ones that in death doeth sleep,
   Will come again no more.

16. Kind friends and loving kindred
   Of him who's dead and gone
To a better land in heaven,
   Far away beyond the sun,
The one you loved so dearly,
   You will ne'er again see more,
Till you pass through death's dark valley
   To that bright celestial shore.

Edward D. Ives. Joe Scott: The Woodsman-Songmaker. Urbana: University of Illinois Press, 1978, pp. 143-47.

ROGER deV. RENWICK

ON THE INTERPRETATION OF FOLK POETRY

Over ten years ago John F. Szwed paid homage to the depth and breadth of folksong analysts' textual scholarship but added an important qualification to his words of praise: while outstanding in so many ways, wrote Szwed, our work had not much to say about what song texts meant to their native singers and audiences.[1] Since then we've seen, certainly, an increase in interpretive studies of folksong, yet I doubt anyone would claim that we've evolved very far in our endeavors, whereas scholars of other folklore genres, particularly myth and ritual, have made enormous advances.

In my opinion, our weakness is chiefly a function of the ad hoc nature of many of our interpretations. This ad hoc quality manifests itself in two contrasting ways, one overly denotative in its perceptions of folk poetry, the other overly connotative. The first--I'll call it the literal approach--looks for meaning in either historical facts, which is to say in the empirical setting of a song's composition or popularity, or in the equally real cultural facts--for instance, in the conventions of "the tradition." The second--let's call it the thematic approach--makes an inductive leap from text to meaning in ascribing to folk poetry fairly abstract ideas like "sacrifice," "regeneration," and so forth. Literalism is ad hoc in the sense that meaning is so dependent on what's unique in both text and context that, in extreme cases, the interpretation is just about redundant with the text itself. Thematicism is ad hoc in the relationship not between text and context but between text and analyst, since the interpretation seems too dependent on his or her own degree and kind of sensitivity, insightfulness, or imagination.

There is nothing reprehensible or even faulty about either of these approaches. Most notably, literal interpretations are credible; thematic interpretations, interesting. But because of their shared ad hoc quality neither seems to have resulted in a sustained analytical movement among contemporary folk poetry scholars, as have, say, approaches to studying texts' narrative form or evolutionary histories. It is my hope that we will find an approach which stimulates more widespread and concerted searches for meaning. I'd also hope that such an approach will emulate both the empirical spirit of the literal temperament, grounding analyzed texts in their relevant contexts, as well as the imaginative spirit of the thematic,

405

recognizing that folk poetry does not simply retell commonly accessible facts, knowledge, and attitudes but selects their significant aspects, combines them into a coherent design, and relates them to more general systems of meaning-- "recodes" experience, so to speak, through a socially conscious and communicable <u>poetic</u> conception.

The interpretive approach I've found that best satisfies the requirements I think we need is an ersatz blend of many ideas, but the majority come from structuralism, semiology, and systems theory. The first has contributed the idea of coherence, the second a sensitivity to degrees and kinds of denotativeness and connotativeness, and the third a disposition to think in terms of dynamic interrelationships among phenomena. For actual techniques, however, I am indebted most to Levi-Straussian structuralism. Whatever its influences, the approach makes use of an analytical apparatus, a necessity if we wish to indulge in comparative studies of meaning and to downplay the ad hoc in analysis, for while not denying the worth of either the literal or the thematic spirit, the structuralist approach is not, I think, as dependent as either of these approaches on the uniqueness of the material analyzed or on the personally perceptive and imaginative skills of the analyst. Moreover, a structuralist apparatus allows us to see more clearly not just <u>what</u> a meaning might be but also <u>how</u> that meaning is articulated.

It is probably this last quality, if any--a quality emerging from the assumption, in contrast with literal interpretations, that there is a "gap" between text and meaning, and from the ability, in contrast with thematic interpretations, to fill that gap with greater clarity of detail--that would be most amenable to folk poetry scholars, I suspect. A structuralist procedure has this quality because its operational constructs are not just component parts but, more critically, <u>relationships</u> among parts, even <u>relationships among relationships</u>. Indeed, the molecular unit of meaning is defined in relational terms: "a difference which makes a difference."[2] That is to say, first, that an image does not "mean" intrinsically (say, according to some property it may possess autonomously) but in its relationship of difference to some other image or images; and second, that although all images--signs--are "differences," only some "make a difference"--that is, refer to ideas and to values rather than to "things" and thus have an important, truly meaningful effect on the environment in which they appear. In short, such images connote.

This fundamental unit of poetic meaning, a sign that "makes a difference," is called a <u>signifier</u>; its basic relational quality is called an <u>opposition</u>. The concept is especially germane for an analytical instrument designed to study creative products like folklore, which, many people seem to agree, addresses the problematic in human life-- complications, rifts, conflicts, disjunctions, paradoxes. Indeed, frequently folk literature goes to some lengths to put explicitly into its texts both members of an opposed pair, whereas in practical discourse more commonly one side of the opposition is tacitly taken for granted. No folklorist, of course, would either advance or countenance a claim that a folksong's text alone carries all the information one needs to understand its meaning.[3] No matter how self-contained a text might seem, there will always be signifiers whose semantic opposites are not given but are assumed to lie in "tacit knowledge." Obviously, the more one knows of the culture's pragmatic world view ("the ethnography") and poetic world view ("the tradition"), the more meaning one will see in the text. It does seem likely, though, that a folksong which appeals to a fairly heterogeneous audience (as measured, for instance, in its popularity over time and space) will either contain in its text the most significant oppositions or will take for granted a fairly widespread, even quasi-universal world view, thus making an interpretive endeavor more accessible to non-specialists in the culture.

The analytical apparatus of a structuralist procedure is built up systematically. At a text's most concrete level an oppositional relationship will exist between <u>signifiers</u> (for instance, a church and a tavern, Sunday and Saturday), which belong to more abstract <u>domains</u> (the domains of time and place, for instance), themselves categories of the yet more abstract <u>paradigms</u> (like sacred and profane), which are categories of the even more general <u>province of meaning</u> (for example, man's celebratory activities). Running throughout this structure may be associated values (+ or -), also in opposition. Meaningful relationships that may obtain throughout are not just the fundamental one, opposition, but also analogy, homology, inversion, mediation, dialectic, transformation, and--two terms I've borrowed from system theory's cybernetic persuasion--negative feedback and positive feedback. There is no rule of absolutism to this apparatus other than the logical rules all tree structures follow of progressive inclusion on the vertical dimension, exclusion on the horizontal. Moreover, for texts of folk poetry whose world view is relatively simple, concrete, and narrowly bounded, only two or three analytical levels may be sufficient for explication. Texts which are more complex, abstract, and expansive may require more levels than the four I've identified, in which case we might simply incorporate <u>sub-domains</u>, even <u>sub-paradigms</u>, as needed, so long as we maintain the logic of relationships between concrete and abstract.

I won't describe here all these diverse parts of a structuralist apparatus, since only some will be applicable to the textual analysis I shall shortly conduct and since the interested reader may easily find such elaboration elsewhere.[4] Moreover--and more importantly--the purpose of the present essay is not just to illustrate this kind of interpretive analysis, nor to increase our understanding of the meaning of the particular texts I'm going to analyze, nor even to argue for the wider adoption of this particular apparatus, which after all is only one version of similar structuralist instruments that others have applied with varying degrees of success to other folklore genres.[5] Rather, my purpose is more general than any of the above: to stimulate folk poetry scholars to search for analytical apparati, whatever their content, that will lay bare lineaments of meaning that are complete, integrated, credible, and interesting, and will employ techniques that are systematic, that are replicable, and that allow comparative study.

The material onto which I shall attempt to map a structuralist model comes to us through the pioneering, extraordinarily diligent, thorough, and sensitive work of Edward D. Ives, whose twenty-odd years of folklore research in the northeastern United States and maritime Canada is nothing short of astounding. His first full-length publication, on songmaker Larry Gorman, has become a classic, a status that his more recent volume on songmaker Joe Scott will also surely attain. It is from this book, <u>Joe Scott: The Woodsman-Songmaker</u>, that I draw the material for my main exposition.[6]

The third of five sons in a family of nine children, Scott was born in the farming community of Lower Woodstock, Prince Edward Island, in 1867. At nineteen or so he left for the Maine lumberwoods, where, with some exceptions, he worked as a lumberman up to the time of a progressively incapacitating illness and, in 1918, his death. Engaged to Lizzie Morse of Maine's Rumford Falls in 1893, Scott was much affected emotionally when Lizzie broke off the engagement in 1894. He did marry another woman in 1899, but the couple separated--permanently--in 1901. Perhaps as early as 1894 but certainly by 1897 the lumberman had become an accomplished maker of songs on local events that were disseminated both orally and in print throughout the region. As time went by, Scott added to (in fact, there is evidence that he <u>substituted</u> for) his songmaking talents those associated with the somewhat more eccentric roles of amateur magician, ventriloquist, fortune teller, and dabbler in the occult, eventually becoming in later years a local prankster, even buffoon. His brief, more conventional occupations included selling sewing machines door-to-door, farm labor, and a two-year stint homesteading a hundred acres in northern Quebec.

Ives has found full versions (in some cases, many full versions) of thirteen songs which Joe Scott most likely made. One measure of the composer's skill in appealing to popular taste is that four of his songs have been collected often enough by different folksong collectors to gain admittance to G. Malcolm Laws's inventory of Native American Balladry; not coincidentally, these four--"Howard Carey" (Laws E23), "Guy Reed" (Laws C9), "The Plain Golden Band" (Laws H17), and "Benjamin Deane" (Laws F32)--were probably among the first five songs Joe Scott composed. All four treat verifiably historical events of local occurrence, and except perhaps for "Plain Golden Band," probably all were made within a twelve-month period, from mid-1897 to mid-1898. Even though, because of their content, Laws classified each in a different category, the fact that they all come from the same composer and were written within a very short time period allows the assumption that they share a common world view and ethos.

Ives suggests that "Howard Carey" was probably Scott's earliest song, at least of those songs which survive. The event which stimulated Scott's urge to poetic composition was the protagonist's suicide: "according to the death record in the Rumford city clerk's office, Howard Carrick, age thirty-two, laborer, single, was a 'suicide by hanging' on May 5, 1897. Place of birth was given simply as New Brunswick. . . ."[7] The ballad, whose formal model seems to have been chiefly the "last goodnight," tells in the first person of the narrator's leaving his New Brunswick home as a youth for the transient life of a lumberman. Despite his mother's strictures, he falls into a fast world of "bad company"--including "bad whiskey," "bad women," and probably gambling--until, sick, poor, and disgraced, he hangs himself in a Rumford Falls, Maine, boarding-house room. He is buried next to his mother, who had died while her son was away on his rambling career. The text I use comes from a more or less contemporary broadside.[8]

On his first reading, an analyst is likely to be struck most forcibly by an opposition in the fifth stanza. Pointing to the profusion of natural growth covering the "yonder hillside" that lies beyond the farm's borders, Mrs. Carey says to Howard:

> Those flowers are magnificent
> And attractive to the eye,
> But still remember that the snake
> Beneath their colors lie.

The significance of this image is manifest: safe, attractive, visible exteriors (let's call this "appearance") and dangerous, repulsive, hidden interiors ("essence") are meaningful in their difference from each other. After extending this principle from the natural example to phenomena in general--"Each pleasure has its poison, too, / And every sweet its snare"--Mrs. Carey becomes once more specific, but this time with an application to cultural rather than natural objects:

> And don't forget that old proverb,
> One that's true and old:
> All are not gems that sparkle,
> All that glitters is not gold.

This idea that a bivalent quality of safe appearance-cum-dangerous essence is shared by both the natural and the cultural is further suggested in two analogies: the first is Mrs. Carey's assertion that the beautiful dewdrops "sparkle in the sun / Like diamonds rich and rare," the second is Howard's description of his later life, during which he either forgets or ignores his mother's warning and, traveling in the fast lane, gets "tangled in a silky web" just "like the silly fly."

Another quite explicit opposition we find in the domain of, not materiality this time but temporality: the signified opposition is between relative permanence and relative impermanence. As was the case with appearance/essence, nature displays both impermanence (the dewdrops disappear from the rose as morning progresses) and permanence: in Howard's words,

> . . . this world will roll on
> Just the same as e'er,
> The fawn will play and birds will sing
> In shady woodlands fair,
> The grass will grow on just as green,
> The flowers will bloom as gay. . . .

In culture we find impermanence in Howard's ramblings ("I've traveled in the East, / And in the South also, / I've traveled in the western lands") and in the money, friends, and even life he so quickly loses. Its opposite, permanence, is available in culture even though Howard does not, unfortunately, take advantage of it: as Mrs. Carey reveals, it consists of the moral strength and courage to resist appearance's temptation.

Yet a third domain opposes signifiers of superfluity and, an inseparable characteristic, interaction-among-parts on the one hand to signifiers of dearth and disjunction-between-parts on the other. In nature, these ideas are connoted by the profusion of "fragrant flowers numberless" (superfluity) and by the dewdrops dampening the flowers and sparkling in the sun (interaction) in the first case, and by the dewdrops disappearing "beneath the sun's bright rays" in the second. As for culture, superfluity and interaction are suggested by Howard's giddy life in "bad company," its opposite by his lonely death in the solitude of his boarding house room.

A first reading will probably elicit at least this much. Let me recapitulate. The text's repertoire of signifiers suggests two dominant categories--I'll call them paradigms--of the natural, whose locus is chiefly the "woodlands," and the cultural, whose main milieu is the town. The two paradigms are analogous in the sense that each possesses the same three characteristics--I've called these domains--of the material, the temporal, and the systemic, as well as homologous in that each exhibits similar internal oppositions between appearance (attractive, supposedly safe, beneficent, bright and shining, visible) and essence (repulsive, actually dangerous, maleficent, "dark"--this will become more evident--and invisible); between permanence and impermanence; and between superfluity of interacting parts on the one hand, dearth of parts and general fragmentation on the other.

Having something to work with, we can now give the text a second reading, which will probably lead us to conclude that the song's world view suggests the following: true to our first reading, natural phenomena and cultural phenomena are indeed substantively alike in that each displays contrasting states in their common features, but when the two are brought together to form an ecosystem then they contrast in that natural signifiers exhibit revealing brightness, permanence, superfluity, and so forth, which are opposed to cultural signifiers' hidden darkness, impermanence, dearth, and so on. The image which most clearly brings the two paradigms together comes in Howard's final contemplation, part of which I've already quoted to illustrate nature's permanent quality, all of which I'll give now:

And when I'm dead this world will roll on
Just the same as e'er,
The fawn will play and birds will sing
In shady woodlands fair,
The grass will grow on just as green,
The flowers will bloom as gay,
What signifies a mortal man
When slumbering in the clay.

A diagram conveniently summarizes what we've discovered so far about Joe Scott's poetic world view as articulated in one song (the arrows denote relationships) (see fig. 1). Even after our two readings, there is still quite a bit of "Howard Carey" that we've not recognized as signifying, but so far we do have an integrated structure, even though perhaps incomplete. Let me go on to another song and save a third reading until we've looked at our other examples of Joe Scott's songmaking skills. I'll look at "Benjamin Deane" next, then "The Plain Golden Band," and finally "Guy Reed."

Even more than "Howard Carey," "Benjamin Deane" is set squarely in the cultural realm that we've suggested is a paradigm, one whose most objectified, physical representation is the town. The two songs share much in common, most overtly the conventional form of the "last goodnight" story-type. Once again, I use a broadside text.[9] Told from the first person point of view, the song first describes Deane's birthplace in New Brunswick, then recounts his move to Maine's Berlin Falls, which is experiencing a boom in industry and associated population growth. Energetically, Deane takes advantage of the economic opportunities boom times offer: he becomes an entrepreneur, keeping a small store and restaurant, and soon has made many acquaintances as well as accumulated much personal wealth. He marries a lovely, well-bred woman. As time passes his actions become more and more illegal, and his wealth increases correspondingly. Despite his wife's entreaties that he change his ways and despite his gradual loss of friends, he continues on his scurrilous path; eventually, he loses both his wealth and his family, his wife leaving him for another man. Hoping he'll persuade her to return, Deane goes to the house of her new protector, finds her in an upstairs room with her head on the lover's shoulder, and shoots her. His wife dies, and Deane, about to die himself, warns other young men against his errors.

Since the song's setting is almost entirely the town, meaning in "Benjamin Deane" is generated primarily by oppositions within the cultural paradigm. As in "Howard Carey," the appearance/essence opposition is perhaps the

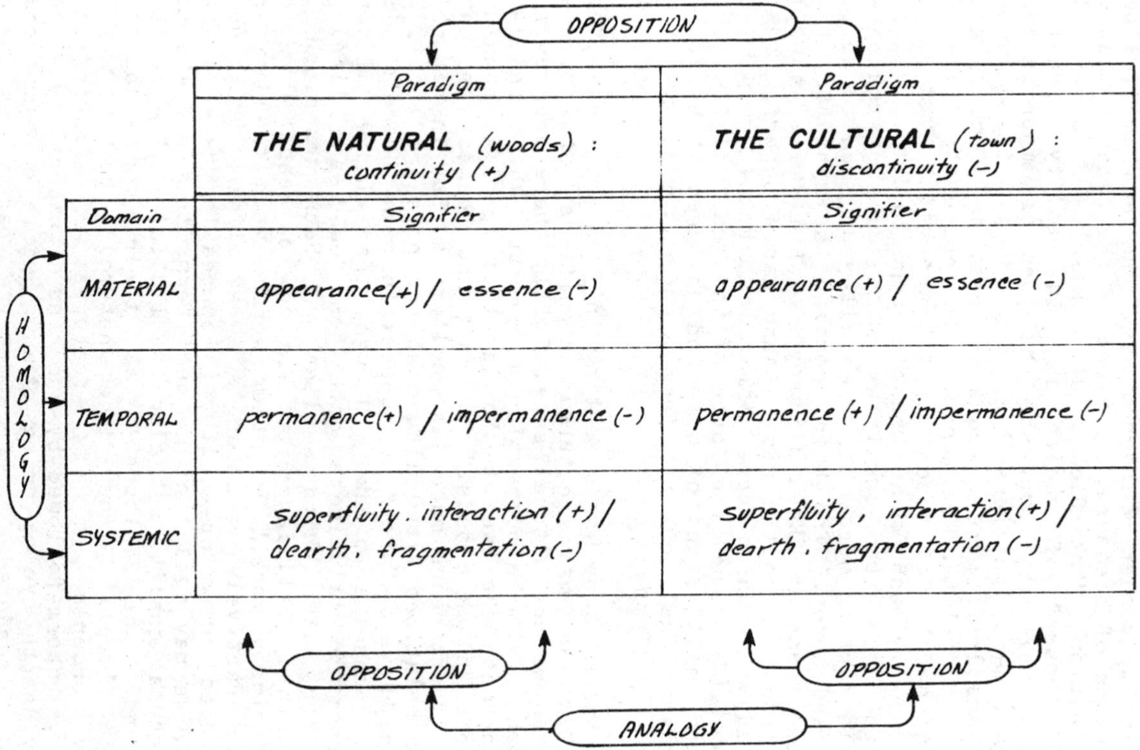

Paradigm   OPPOSITION   Paradigm

Domain	THE NATURAL (woods): continuity (+) — Signifier	THE CULTURAL (town): discontinuity (-) — Signifier
MATERIAL	appearance(+) / essence (-)	appearance(+) / essence (-)
TEMPORAL	permanence(+) / impermanence (-)	permanence (+) / impermanence (-)
SYSTEMIC	superfluity, interaction (+) / dearth, fragmentation (-)	superfluity, interaction(+) / dearth, fragmentation (-)

HOMOLOGY

OPPOSITION   ANALOGY   OPPOSITION

Figure 1

most striking. Deane is seduced by the bright, visible
exterior of "gold" to the point that "By its glitter I was
blinded / And my danger could not see." He sees and follows
only "the paths of pleasure," unaware of the essence that is
their destination, "the fields of crime." His apparently
substantial "house" of wealth is, in reality, fragile.
Clearly this image also suggests the idea of impermanence,
as do many other signifiers like the speed with which he
both makes and loses money, acquaintances, and family, and,
of course, his life. Permanence in culture's town is
signified by people "of decent grade" who stick fast to an
ethos of honesty and shun Deane's opportunistic values.
According to Deane, the qualities of cultural permanence,
which in his closing words he urges all young men to adopt,
are "truth and honor." The third domain, the systemic, that
we found prominent in "Howard Carey" we find here as well:
when his fortune is on the rise, Deane has a superfluity of
gold and silver, which come "flowing like a brook"; of
acquaintances ("I gained the favor of the great, / The rich,
the poor and small"); and of wife and children at home, but
soon becomes a lonely outcast from such networks, as he is
deserted by all of them.

Since there is no woods setting in "Benjamin Deane," we
do not find as many natural signifiers of internal
opposition as we do cultural ones. Still, there are several
images, such as the aforementioned "brook," which indicate
analogies between the two at the level of specific domains.
Thus nature's "black clouds," "storm," and "sands" indicate
a temporal impermanence much like culture's. But in nature's
ecosystemic relations with culture at the paradigm level, we
find as in "Howard Carey" an opposition: as Deane's wife
lies dead, sunshine breaks through the window of the
darkened room to illuminate both her "cold and lifeless
face" and her hair, which earlier had been described in
terms of shining brilliance but is now darkened with the
stain of "crimson gore." In other words, when the two are
linked interactively, nature's revealing brightness
opposes--indeed, shows up--culture's concealing darkness. At
this point, we may feel that we need terms to designate not
only the general quality but also the implicit value of "the
natural" and "the cultural" at their more abstract
paradigmatic level. Since "the natural" seems to be
predictably ordered in its features of flower/snake
materiality, storm-followed-by-sunshine temporality, and
superfluity/dearth cycle, among others, while culture seems
random and disordered, I'll summarize nature as being
"continuous," culture as "discontinuous."

So "Benjamin Deane" is informed by a world view similar
to that of "Howard Carey," a world view less fully portrayed

in some aspects, more fully so in others, particularly in cultural conceptions. Once again, we'll pass over a fair portion of the text which treats a milieu that seems different enough from both woods and town to warrant further investigation--I'm referring to the opening four stanzas that describe Deane's birthplace in New Brunswick; but, as for similar parts of "Howard Carey," we'll come back to these. For now let me move on to "The Plain Golden Band," the most unusual song of this group of four.

The relative uniqueness of "Plain Golden Band" rests in its formal models. Like the first two songs, it is told in the first person, but its narrative quality is weak; the story is advanced chiefly through dialogue between sweethearts in the process of breaking off their engagement. Its model is more the sentimental, "refined" songbook poetry than it is the "vulgar," street-ballad type of poetry which popularized the "last goodnight." The song begins with the male narrator recalling first the natural surroundings of those happier times of the lovers' engagement and then the scene of the breakup itself. The woman initiates the parting, asking that he take back the ring, since she's been unfaithful to him. He protests, but she is adamant that they cannot now wed. She does ask forgiveness and express the wish to be buried with both his love letters and engagement ring, which she evidently decides to keep, agreeing at least to his injunction that she retain it, if not to his plea that they remain engaged. The song ends by returning to the present: the narrator, his memorial musings over, can be found alone in the forest.[10]

"Plain Golden Band" does not display significant internal oppositions (as "Benjamin Deane" does); instead, the signifiers are cast at that higher level of meaning, the paradigms, where nature contrasts with culture. The world view is the same, though (the forest is mentioned in passing as exhibiting internal contrasts of "wild and grand"), just pitched at a more abstract level appropriate to the topic. Thus the first two stanzas are full of nature's superfluity and interactional quality: the sun clambers over the mountain, the dewdrops kiss the rose, the wild roses bloom on the banks, and so forth. Similarly, the closing stanza returns to a nature--this time, explicitly the woods--"where the deer loves to roam and the child loves to play, / Where all nature is gay" (I do not hesitate to see this child as a "natural" rather than "cultural" creature). Contrasts with the cultural paradigm are clear: not only are the couple breaking up, but the narrator's fate, social isolation, is highlighted. We also find contrast in the material domain's appearance versus essence: nature reveals with its brightness; civilization conceals with its "darkness." Most germane in this regard is Lizzie's encounter with the stranger she meets the night she roams from the safety of her cottage to walk on the shore: in contrast with nature's moonlight which diffuses over the surroundings "her pale mellow light," the stranger conceals the truth ("He told me false stories, false stories of you, / He vowed that he loved me and offered his hand"). The third domain that we have found prominent in the other two songs, temporality and its permanence/impermanence contrast, may also be communicated here--nature being permanent, culture impermanent--but we'll pass it by, since the song is not as explicit about this as was "Howard Carey" or even "Benjamin Deane." In sum, then, "The Plain Golden Band" contains the same underlying world view: the continuity of a nature which changes, but in a consistent, cyclical process, is opposed to the discontinuity of culture which breaks apart. Noteworthy, though, is the relatively muted quality of the oppositions in this song, certainly when compared with "Howard Carey" and "Benjamin Deane." The tone is mournful, to be sure, but it hardly suggests the tragic, fatalistic tone of the first two. The semantic structure is reflective of this tone--witness the paucity of oppositions and their lack of complex interrelationships. Indeed, there is even a suggestion of dialectic rather than just opposition in the nature-cum-culture ecosystem--a hint that the "cool shady forest" in some small measure soothes and protects the betrayed protagonist with its relative darkness. This is but a hint, however; more clearly signified is the contrast--the gay abundance of the forest, the sad loneliness of the quondam lover.

Let's look now at the fourth song, "Guy Reed." While the progenitors of this song's model are ancient and widespread, "Guy Reed" is most immediately influenced by an ubiquitous genre of woods song, the death-on-the-job. Like many makers of local song, Scott apparently was very attracted to the device of first person narrator, and so we find one here as we have in his other songs, even though by critical literary standards the device seems uncalled for. One night, the narrator receives a letter bearing news of a friend's death. The rest of the ballad, told entirely in the third person, recounts the details of the accident. The young lumberman, Guy Reed, attempts to break a log jam on the landing at which his crew is working; the jam breaks much more quickly than expected, and the whole landing collapses into the river, taking Guy with it. He is crushed to death. The rest of the song is non-narrative, describing his funeral and burial, giving a few facts of his life, telling of his father's grief, and offering some animadversions on the implications of death.[11]

I have left "Guy Reed" for last because it not only fleshes out some so-far hazy as well as ignored aspects of meaning in Joe Scott's songs, but also extends those conceptions somewhat beyond the boundaries of the ecosystem we've recognized so far: the nature-cum-culture connection. "Guy Reed" is a mirror image of "Benjamin Deane" in that it's set primarily in nature's most representative locale, the woods, whereas "Benjamin Deane" was set primarily in the town. Consequently, the concrete level of oppositional signifiers are chiefly of the woods sort. The song opens with images that signify those negative aspects of nature's dualism--impermanence; an underlying essence that is dark, dangerous, and concealing; and discordance among its parts. Indeed, we may recognize all these in the opening stanza:

> How well do I remember
> One dark and stormy night,
> The rain it fell in torrents,
> The lightning flashed so bright.
> The moon and stars above me
> Did not their light reveal,
> For dark clouds so gloomy
> Did their welcome light conceal.

Similarly, it seem likely that natural impermanence is suggested by the fragility of the landing, which, though in a strict sense manmade, consists of logs dumped on the riverbank "in whatever form gravity and shape of the bank allowed."[12] The same image could also signify nature's appearance/essence contradiction--at least, from Guy's viewpoint. In any event, whether in multiple images or in just one, the bivalent "fair and wild" quality of nature (a phrase reminiscent of the forest's "wild but grand" characterization in "Plain Golden Band") is suggested when the sun shines brightly to reveal the scene of Guy Reed's fatal accident, contrasting with the earlier concealing storm.

This last image is extremely important in "Guy Reed," carrying a heavy semantic load, so to speak. Its placement is critical:

> Those logs they rolled carefully
> From off his mangled form,
> The birds were singing sweetly,
> The sun shone bright and warm.

This juxtaposition, a bit startling at first reading, becomes more understandable when we remember that at the more abstract level of paradigms, nature's continuity is opposed to people's discontinuity. Thus as in "Benjamin

Deane," where the sun suddenly shines through the window to illuminate the wife's dead form, here the animated birds and sun contrast sharply with man's mortality. A few stanzas later the nature/culture contrast is made more apparent in words reminiscent of a stanza in "Howard Carey," though here the cyclical aspect of nature (its predictable movement from superfluity to dearth and back again) is more explicit, truly supporting the designation "continuity":

> The robin and the swallow,
> The sunshine and the rain,
> The cuckoo and the sparrow
> With the spring will come again.
> The blackbird and the thrushes
> From foreign lands will soar,
> But loved ones that in death doeth sleep,
> Will come again no more.

Let us once more recapitulate what we've discovered so far about the world view that informs Joe Scott's earliest and most popular songs. While some songs emphasize one paradigm, other songs another, all four share the concrete view that nature, whose most common, objectified context is the woods, is similar to culture, whose clearest, most representative context is the town. Each possesses innately, states of widely contrasting appearance (bright, warm, attractive, revealing) and essence (dark, cold, repulsive, concealing); permanence and impermanence; and superfluity and interdependence among parts on the one hand, dearth and separation of parts on the other. When nature and culture are linked into a more inclusive ecosystem, however, what were fairly independent similarities turn out to be contrasts of a more abstract sort: nature's cyclical, determinate qualities constitute what I have called continuity, while culture's disordered, indeterminate qualities constitute discontinuity. Thus whether he chooses the woods or the town as a habitat, or even if he spends his time alternating between them, presumably man's lot is going to be an internally contradictory, difficult one.

Is there, in this world view, any environmental option for people other than those disjointed ones of town, or woods, or town-and-woods? Yes there is, though it's by no means a perfect solution. This possibility is manifested in a third paradigm that is not so much natural or even cultural as pastoral, its reified milieu a farm or even village. To discover its significant properties, I must now go back to those parts of the four songs I set aside in earlier readings.

First, let's consider the openings of "Howard Carey" and "Benjamin Deane," which describe the pastoral homesteads of each protagonist. In Carey's birthplace, for instance, the systemic domain's interactional quality applies to both nature and culture. The cultural cottage sits pleasingly on the banks of the river:

> Where small birds chant their notes so true,
> Where the trembling waters roar,
> The ivy vine doth thickly twine
> Round that cottage on the shore.

Similarly, Benjamin Deane's homeland on the Atlantic seaboard, even though in "the city of St. John," is depicted in the serene, ordered, uncluttered, harmonizing imagery of pastoral conventions: seagulls rock on the surface of the "silvery tide," graceful willow trees "bow before the breeze," and winds speed on "sails as white as snow."[13] Also similar are the endings of both "Howard Carey" and "Guy Reed," when the bodies of both are returned to a pastoral locale. Guy, for instance, is buried alongside his mother, brother, and sister in "a quiet country churchyard," the casket "decorated / With roses sweet and fair." In sum, the pastoral's systemic domain represents neither superfluity, whether that superfluity be Howard Carey's "company," or Benjamin Dean's "the great, / the rich, the poor and small," nor its opposite, dearth--the dearth of the eventually isolated protagonists--but something in between: the relative fewness, relatedness, privacy, and comfortableness-with-nature that characterizes the nuclear family in its rural mileau.

To repeat, however, the solution is hardly perfect. The structural relationship between this pastoral paradigm and the natural and cultural paradigms is not dialectical--in which case the pastoral would synthesize the other two--but mediational. The pastoral paradigm only <u>reduces</u> the degree of opposition; it does not eliminate it. For instance, in the burial example just given, the systemic domain's "parts," while not fragmented from each other, are certainly not interactional either; Howard Carey and Guy Reed may be buried next to their kin but they're all, of course, dead, all simply <u>contiguous</u> with each other. Even when the inhabitants of this pastoral locus are alive on the farm all is not perfect, as Howard Carey makes clear: he had to leave home, he says, because "our little farm was small" and "Could not sustain us all." (And indeed, despite his departure, the parents eventually sell the farm and move across the border.)

We find the same less than perfect mediation in the way the pastoral paradigm portrays the other domains, the temporal and the material. In life, while the boys have to leave the farm, they're only relatively impermanent, for they're expected not to forget the homestead and eventually to return (as "Howard Carey" suggests). Similarly, in death they're only relatively permanent, for their bodies slowly "moulder" ("Howard Carey," "Benjamin Deane"). As for the material domain with its appearance/essence opposition, here too the differences are only somewhat collapsed. The bodies are hidden, concealed, cannot be "seen" ("Guy Reed"), and "sleep" in the "dark," but they are in marked graves whose exterior appearance indicates with some degree of accuracy the essence six feet below (I'm assuming that these significations are implicit in the song).

It is in the material domain, too, the domain of essences and appearances, that Scott's most ingenious signifier, the plain golden band itself, is most relevant. Recall that both nature and culture exhibited bright, shining appearances, primarily from sunshine in the former's case, the sparkle of monetary gold in the latter's. But when the two were directly contrasted, nature's gold, sunshine, itself able to make the darkness light, revealed the essence of culture's gold: its disguising, dark, and dangerous nature. The plain golden band seems to mediate between these two, neither revealing nor concealing but simply standing for, representing the ideas of love, interdependence, and longevity of relationship. There is, of course, no explicit rural locale in "Plain Golden Band," as there is in the other songs; even so, the ring doesn't have to bear the entire burden of mediation, since the pastoral conception clearly informs the two stanzas:

> She threw her arms round me and cried in despair,
> While a gentle breeze ruffled her dark wavy hair,
> And the moonlight of heaven fell on her fair hand,
> The fair light shone bright on the plain golden band.
>
> "Forgive, oh forgive me, my darling I crave,
> E'er they lay me to sleep in a cold silent grave,
> With those fond cherished letters penned by your own
>   hand
> And on my cold bosom that plain golden band."

Still, the band is only a token; it is not itself "true love." The opposition has not been overcome.

We have, therefore, a fuller picture of Joe Scott's poetic world view during his early period of songmaking. The closest thing Scott could conceive of as at least mitigating the antithetical properties of nature and culture was a third paradigm, the pastoral, objectified in a rural homestead. But even here matters were imperfect, for farms were too small to support large families: children had to leave, people couldn't make enough money, owners had to sell and move away, kin could reunite only in death. At the paradigmatic level, it appears, the pastoral had not the cyclical quality of nature's continuity nor the unstable quality of culture's discontinuity, but a quality somewhere between the two, exhibiting a sort of slow-changing but progressive dissolution. A suitable designation, I think, would be entropy (see fig. 2). Was this the extent of Scott's poetic word view, then, this flawed best-of-a-bad-lot picture of and attitude toward life? In two of his songs, "Howard Carey" and "Benjamin Deane," the answer is yes, in "The Plain Golden Band," a qualified yes. "Guy Reed," however, exhibits a fuller world view which suggests that Joe's philosophy actually dreamt of a further possibility that did admit a purer resolution, though to achieve it Scott had to envisage the structural relationship among signifiers that I've called "transformation" (here, of a particular kind, "transcendence"). The key stanza is the song's final one:

> Kind friends and loving kindred
> Of him who's dead and gone
> To a better land in heaven,
> Far away beyond the sun,
> The one you loved so dearly,
> You will ne'er again see more
> Till you pass through death's dark valley
> To that bright celestial shore.

Here, Scott transcends the province of meaning that is "the world" by projecting it, so to speak, into a province of meaning that contains the natural, the cultural, and the pastoral but that is different enough to be a system in its own right--that is, a distinct province of meaning, "the cosmos." In the cosmological frame of reference, all those properties of the natural, the cultural, and the pastoral are synthesized into a superordinate paradigm of "earthly pleasures," whose shared feature is that they have, in essence, no true value.

This more inclusive paradigm of negatively valued "earthly pleasures" can now be contrasted with an opposing superordinate paradigm (+) in which pure resolution--organic wholeness--can be found: let's call it "eternal truths" (true" is a favorite word in Joe's songs). The negatively valued paradigm is depicted in the following stanza:

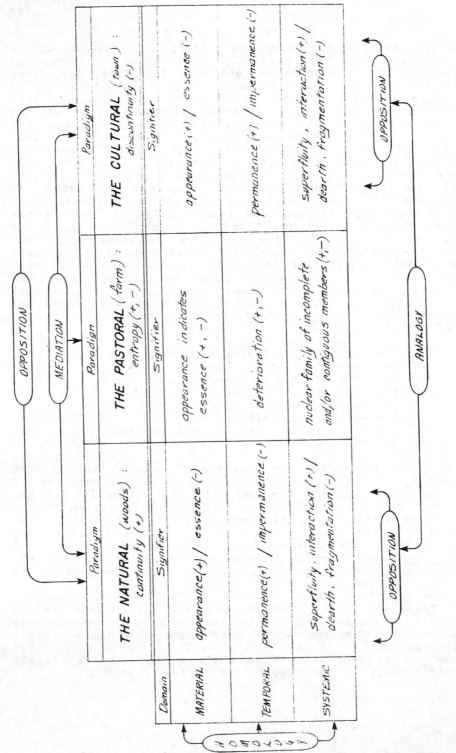

Figure 2

His poor feeble father
Is sticken now with grief,
The joy of earthly pleasures
Will bring him no relief.
For untold gold or silver,
Position, wealth in store,
Sunny skies or music sweet
Will not the dead restore.

The locus of the paradigm of eternal truths far transcends the world of woods, town, and farm: it is the "bright celestial shore." Here, finally, oppositions from even the most concrete level of signifiers are finally overcome. On the bright celestial shore all one's "kindred" as well as "kind friends" interact (systemic domain), everlastingly (temporal domain), in continual brightness beyond the sun (certainly far beyond its cultural analogue, gold), where there is no difference between appearance and essence, simply presence (material domain), and where the whole notion of things that possess "exchange value" becomes irrelevant; there is only, one suspects, sharing (see fig. 3).

Looking back, we can see hints of at least a disposition to such transcendence in the three other songs, although they're set squarely in the worldly province of meaning. For instance, there's a concern with man's essential meaninglessness, a function of his mortality: "What signifies a mortal man / When slumbering in the clay?" asks Howard Carey. The narrator of "Plain Golden Band" proclaims that "my love it is true and will never grow cold." And the plain golden band itself has touches of a multivocal symbolism much greater than I've given it credit for: Lizzie wishes to be buried with the ring on her bosom. (Indeed, someone with more semiological sensibility than I possess might elicit much from the goldness of sun, money, and ring.)

Still, the philosophical solution "Guy Reed" proposes to the fundamental problems of existence evidently could not provide peace of mind to one who was apparently of as secular and impractical (poetic?) a temperament as was Joe Scott. Consequently, his career seems to have been unusually picaresque, even for that time and place. His songs suggest why: he found quite unfulfilling the life of a "pure" woodsman, of a "pure" townsman, or even of one whose schizophrenic routine consisted of a spartan season earning money in the woods, followed by a bacchanalian off-season spending it in town. The potential for most fulfillment lay in a farm, and Scott did emigrate back to the family's New Brunswick homestead apparently intending to settle down on

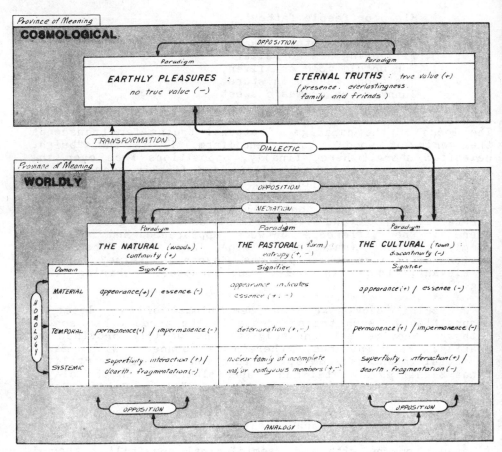

Figure 3

at least one, perhaps two, occasions, later sticking out a
two-year residence on his Quebec claim. In between, he did
the occasional stint on various farms in Maine. But
predictably none of his attempts to stay with the pastoral
life lasted for long. His only consistent response to all
those bad Gestalten was to increasingly embrace one side of
the world's inherent dualisms, becoming more and more
impermanent, more and more a loner who strove in his diverse
and bizarre roles to be different from his fellows, more and
more a devotee of illusionary appearances--conjuror,
prankster, occultist.

So: the meanings we've uncovered don't seem to
contradict what we know about Joe's life or about
lumberman's culture in general. I must especially emphasize
that they don't contradict Ives's more literal or thematic
interpretations either, but simply help to fill in the gap
between the two. My interpretations are quite consistent
with the view that Scott's songs reported events pretty much
the way they were thought to have happened;[14] or that fatal
accidents on the job, shattered love affairs, illness and
premature death from incontinent living, and shady schemes
of get-rich-quick entrepreneurs were not uncommon kinds of
events in that time and place;[15] or that Joe's depicting of
such matters in a popular song may have dramatized and
served as cautionary tale or even stimulated cathartic
identification for those engaged in lumbering.[16] These are,
of course, fairly literal interpretations of the songs'
meanings. But even Ives's thematic interpretations--for
instance, that the songs contain "paradise lost" and "return
to mother" themes[17]--are in no way contradicted, simply
fleshed out and made more specific. Moreover, my
interpretations may allow even more clarification of some
slightly problematic contents of Joe's songs--the question
of why, for instance, nature imagery seems so
disproportionately stressed for stories that are apparently
about a tragic accident on a drive or about a young man
committing suicide in a boarding house room; the question of
why Lizzie is not depicted as the "false love" in "Plain
Golden Band" and properly excoriated, as conventional
folksong models would do; and even why the engagement ring
is a plain golden one rather than, more empirically
probable, a silver one.

Let's now look at some quite distinct material: a song
which, while also native Anglo-North American, with a real-
life topic, and of fairly localized relevance and
distribution, bears no special similarities or differences
to Joe Scott's songs in any other than an obvious and
superficial sense. "The Bachelor's Song," by Newfoundlander
Paul E. Hall, was brought to our attention by John F. Szwed

in his short but most perceptive 1970 essay. For the most part, I'm not going to analyze this song myself, but accept Szwed's analysis and interpretation. However, since I'm trying to illustrate my suggestion that an interpretive apparatus permits clearer comparison of meaning, I will have to translate his analysis, so to speak, to fit the terminology and general make-up of the apparatus I used with Joe Scott's songs (a fairly simple task, since Szwed's analysis is itself informed by general structuralist principles). Briefly, the song is Hall's attempt to address an issue responsible for tension within his community: Hall was unmarried and living by himself in a society where married adults and close-knit family networks were normative. "Bachelor's Hall" catalogues the narrator's professed descriptions of his unmarried lifestyle; the song's purpose, one deduces, was to allay the community's uneasiness.

The dominant category of paradims-in-opposition is married men, with a general thematic quality of "safe" and an associated positive value, and unmarried men, generally unsafe and negatively valued. Hall chooses at least five characteristics--domains in my terminology--of these paradigms to address. In no particular order, these are as follows. First, we find a domain of signifying oppositions between having closely related kin (safe), especially wife and children, and having none (unsafe, implying a certain selfishness, a break in the stability and continuity of family line and its associated landownership and use, an inability to lend extra hands to neighbors needing help in domestic or field tasks, among others). Second, there's the opposition between lack of surplus money (no "discretionary income," the safe norm in subsistence economies and associated with such positively-valued connotations as the virtue of self-denial and of equally-allocated resources) and presence of surplus money (unsafe). Third, we find an opposition between the necessity to work hard (the safe norm, essential if one's to make a living in a hostile environment, to utilize limited resources to the maximum, and to provide for one's dependents) and no such necessity (if, say, one has to provide for oneself only). Fourth, there's the safe condition, in the domain of sexual behavior, of having a socially sanctioned partner--a wife, in short--as opposed to the dangerous condition of not having such a sanctioned relationship, which of course makes illicit sex more probable. And fifth, there's the safe quality of immobility--continuous presence, longevity of residence, and general dependability--versus the unsafe potential to be here today, gone tomorrow, to be generally undependable.

Hypothetically, what sort of choices were initially open to Hall in addressing the problem of community uneasiness on his account? He could have stuck to his guns, I suppose, and either made a song celebrating and reveling in his various "unsafe" qualities--indeed, just have started singing publicly and frequently the traditional "Bachelor's Hall," which does just that--and vilifying the "safe" qualities community norms held dear.[18] Such a song would likely have manifested the "positive feedback" structure of relationships between the contrasting paradigms, though just what effect it might have had on Hall's day-to-day life in the community one's not too sanguine about. Or he could have made some homiletic piece, perhaps a narrative about a bachelor who saw the errors of his ways and eventually married, a song whose likely semantic structure would have exhibited "negative feedback" and which may, though I doubt it, have mollified his neighbors. Or he could have tried the even more highly rhetorical strategy of transformation, redefining the situation by depicting the Codroy Valley as, say, a Garden of Eden in which we are all God's children living in mutual innocence, understanding, and affection. Evidently of a practical turn of mind, however, Hall chose the more credible and strategically effective mediational method, like Joe Scott in his wordly province of meaning conceptually lessening the degree of difference between socially safe people and socially dangerous people by bringing in a third paradigm of socially benign people.

Let's see how "The Bachelor's Song" achieves this mediation in each of the five semantic domains. First, in the domain of having kin versus having no kin, the song points out that Hall's lack of wife and children is not his fault--in fact, that he's tried very hard and very seriously to marry, but despite his good intentions and efforts, has been unlucky in his quest ("I can't get a wife around here /You all know how hard I looked"). In good intentions if not results, he says, I'm normative. Second, the discretionary income/no discretionary income opposition is addressed by the song's implication that Hall uses his surplus money not for self-indulgence but for gifts to others. (This point is not clearly present in the song--at least to one who doesn't know the culture. Szwed does, and so we take his point that the song emphasizes "flexibility of resources. . . . In everyday affairs the point is evident in reciprocal 'treating' behavior in local beer shops, where bachelors are able to 'out-treat' their married friends.")[19] The third opposition, need to work hard versus no need to work hard, Hall mediates by asserting that, whether he may need to or not, he in fact does perform very hard and very productive work; indeed, he stresses that a bachelor's workload is twice that of the married man's, since bachelors must perform domestic tasks like cooking, cleaning, mending, washing, and milking in addition to the more masculine field work:

> Now some fine day in the June month
> When my last seed it's growed,
> And there's not one tree left standing
> On my farm, below the road.
>
> When all this work is ended
> That I have planned in my mind. . . .

The fourth problem area, the domain of sexual behavior, Hall addresses by proclaiming that to fulfill his sexual desires he will go outside the community--so far away, in fact, as to cohabit with the geographically and culturally remote Franco-Indians and Eskimos. Similarly, the fifth opposition between immobility and mobility he partially resolves by stressing not only that he'll stay put until the necessary farm work is done but also that when he does travel it will be for a purpose, and an approved one at that: to seek some suitable mate, whether for sex or for marriage, not to wander whenever he feels like it, aimlessly and self-indulgently.

These five domains of mediating signifiers carry the general connotation of someone who is neither dangerous nor, for that matter, safe but--relatively speaking--benign. In British cultures the objectified role of such a quality is usually called--not "husband," of course, and not "bachelor"--but "a character." In Paul E. Hall's case this character role, we might suppose, was locally identified even more specifically: poet, songmaker, perhaps even artist. Certainly not safe, as the well-documented social effects of local satirical songs make clear, but then not really dangerous either (see fig. 4).

When subjected to the same interpretive instrument, the compositions of Joe Scott and Paul E. Hall become even more interesting to us than they already were, I think. Obviously, their similarities are easier to spot than the differences: the two men share a mediational structure in their poetic world views when the frame of reference is a worldly province of meaning. Indeed, one might make a case that the structural similarity extends even further, that like Joe Scott's signifiers of both culture and nature, Hall's characteristics of the married man and the unmarried man each contain conflicting positive and negative values, indicating a bivalence of commingled attraction-cum-repulsion. I've not gone that far, however, not wishing to take too many liberties with Szwed's analysis. In any event,

OPPOSITION

MEDIATION

Domain	Paradigm	Paradigm	Paradigm
	Married Men, especially husbands-and-fathers: socially safe (+)	**Characters** -- e.g. songmakers: socially benign (+, −)	**Unmarried Men**, especially bachelors: soc. dangerous (−)
	Signifier	Signifier	Signifier
FAMILIAL CONNECTIONS	have wife and children (+)	no wife and children not own fault (+, −)	no wife and children (−)
FINANCIAL STATUS	no surplus money; used to satisfy basic needs (+)	surplus money used to treat others (+, −)	surplus money; used for self indulgence (−)
WORK ORIENTATION	have to work hard (+)	work extra hard by choice (+, −)	don't have to work hard (−)
SEXUAL BEHAVIOR	have socially sanctioned partner in the community (+)	seek partners outside community (+, −)	no socially sanctioned partner in community (−)
SPATIAL BEHAVIOR	immobile (+)	mobile only for approved purpose (+, −)	mobile at will (−)

HOMOLOGY

Figure 4

as matters stand the similarity is interesting enough. It is also plausible, for the mediational structure fits the eccentric-but-accepted, "marginal" nature of each man's real social position (at least, until Joe turned truly bizarre in his later years; but by then, quite appropriately, he had evidently abandoned songmaking). To a lesser extent, a similarity also appears between two domains. First, the two songmakers share a concern with man's locational stability or instability--generally, his "movability." Scott casts this feature in wider terms of general permanence/impermanence, even insofar as life and death are concerned, Hall in the more specific terms of one's physical presence or absence when and where everyday labor is to be performed, but the domains are certainly compatible. Second, both songmakers address the question of the self's network of relations with significant others and the general quantity and quality of those relations. Concern about these two domains is consistent with what we know of general folklore world views.

This last relative similarity also shows up the domain's relative difference, just one difference among many in the songs that are no less interesting and plausible than the similarities. Most obvious is that the world view informing "Bachelor's Song" is much more concrete and simple than that underlying Scott's four songs. This difference is clear not only in Scott's transforming of this world into a cosmological province of meaning but also in the basic signifiers: Scott's concrete images signify relatively abstract ideas--permanence/impermanence, appearance/essence --while Hall's signify more tangible states and behaviors. Once again, these properties of the songs match the respective contexts: Hall's purpose was more instrumental and social, Scott's more reflective and psychological. Concomitantly, the popularity of "Bachelor's Hall" over time and across space was almost surely far more limited than the popularity of Joe Scott's four songs. And finally, we might suggest that Scott was more of a romantic than Hall, for at the paradigmatic level Scott sees nature as positively valued vis-a-vis culture, while Hall--at least for his rhetorical purposes--adopts a more normative stance, accepting the "cultured" married state as positive, the "natural" unmarried state as negative.

Could structuralist interpretation help in answering questions not only about meaning and comparability, but also about what makes a song popular in tradition, of how long it may remain so, and of the extent to which it might diffuse? For now, any answer to that question would be idle speculation. More immediately, I hope that interpretive analysis of meaning in folk poetry will be more widely atempted through replicable and comparable techniques, relating meaning believably to reality in both the song and its environment, and revealing folk poetry to be both important and interesting.

NOTES

[1]John F. Szwed, "Paul E. Hall: A Newfoundland Songmaker and His Community of Song," in Folksongs and Their Makers, ed. Henry Glassie, Edward D. Ives, and John F. Szwed (Bowling Green, Ohio: Bowling Green University Popular Press, /1970/), p. 149.

[2]I've borrowed this phrase from Gregory Bateson, Steps to an Ecology of Mind (New York: Ballantine Books, 1972), p. 315, where its use denotes a not incompatible referent.

[3]Not to mention, of course, the additional matter of how much and what sort of meaning a folksong's musical "text" carries.

[4]The one I use I've described as best I can in my English Folk Poetry: Structure and Meaning (Philadelphia: University of Pennsylvania Press, 1980), pp. 15-19.

[5]The best I've seen is the one designed by Jay D. Edwards; see his The Afro-American Trickster Tale: A Structural Analysis. Monograph Series Vol. 4. (Bloomington, Ind.: Folklore Publications Group, 1978).

[6]Edward D. Ives, Joe Scott: The Woodsman-Songmaker (Urbana: University of Illinois Press, 1978).

[7]Ives, p. 114.

[8]Ives, pp. 110-14.

[9]Ives, pp. 233-38.

[10]Ives, pp. 196-97.

[11]Ives, pp. 143-47.

[12]Ives, p. 152.

[13]Cf. Ives in Joe Scott: "the descriptions . . . give us less a picture of Saint John than they do a picture of what a seaside home should be if we are going to feel about Benjamin Deane the way Joe wants us to feel" (p. 231).

[14]Ives, p. 404.

[15]Ives, p. 133.

[16]Ives, pp. 132-34.

[17]Ives, pp. 120-21, 133, 431-33.

[18]For a traditional text of "Bachelor's Hall" see Kenneth Peacock, Songs of the Newfoundland Outports, National Museum of Canada, Bulletin no. 197, Anthropological Series no. 65. (Ottawa: National Museum of Canada, 1965), I, 237-238.

[19]Szwed, p. 163.

University of Texas
Austin

REDEFINING NARRATIVE FOLKSONG

TEN BROECK

1. The ladies and gentlemen from Baltimore come,
    Baltimore come, Baltimore come,
    To see that great Mollie and old Ten Broeck run.

2. In California where Mollie was bo'n,
    'Twas told in the records she's bo'n in a sto'm,
    Bo'n in a sto'm, bo'n in a sto'm,
    'Twas told in the records she's bo'n in a sto'm.

3. In old Kentucky old Ten Broeck was foaled.
    Ten Broeck bust records whereever he goes,
    Whereever he goes, whereever he goes,
    Ten Broeck bust records whereever he goes.

4. Old Mollie eats cabbage and bacon and beans,
    And Ten Broeck eats honey and sugar and cream,
    Sugar and cream, sugar and cream,
    Ten Broeck eats honey and sugar and cream.

5. Old Jay Gould bet silver and Vanderbilt gold
    That Ten Broeck run four miles the day he was foaled,
    Day he was foaled, day he was foaled,
    Ten Broeck run four miles the day he was foaled.

6. How the ladies did scream and the babies did squall
   When old Ten Broeck came through that hole in the wall,
   Hole in the wall, hole in the wall,
   When old Ten Broeck came through that hole in the wall.

7. The riders was mounted, the starter says, "Go!"
   Mollie she darted, but Ten Broeck he flew,
   Ten Broeck he flew, Ten Broeck he flew,
   Mollie she darted, but Ten Broeck he flew.

8. As Mollie and Ten Broeck was turnin' the bend,
   You couldn't see Mollie for the dust in the wind,
   Dust in the wind, dust in the wind,
   You couldn't see Mollie for the dust in the wind.

9. "Oh Johnnie, Oh Walker, Oh Johnnie, my son,
   Turn loose that bridle and let Ten Broeck run,
   Let Ten Broeck run, let Ten Broeck run,
   Turn loose that bridle and let Ten Broeck run."

10. Old Mollie was a fine mare and put on a style,
    But Ten Broeck beat Mollie one squa' half a mile,
    Squa' half a mile, squa' half a mile,
    Ten Broeck beat Mollie one squa' half a mile.

11. Well, rap on the counter an' hear glasses ring.
    God knows the whiskey old Ten Broeck did bring,
    Ten Broeck did bring, Ten Broeck did bring,
    God knows the whiskey old Ten Broeck did bring.

--A folksong of the turf. . . . On July fourth, 1878 Ten Broeck, great Kentucky stallion, and Mollie McCarty, pride of California, ran their famous four-mile race at Churchill Downs /then called the Louisville Race Track7, writing an enduring chapter in American turf history. Within an hour after Ten Broeck won, the Negro jockeys, swipes, and exercise boys were making up a song commemorative of the race. Music and words were never set on paper. I learned them while playing in the stables as a boy in my old Kentucky home. --Tom Akers, on a custom recording S.D.R. 105, C R A C O Transcriptions, San Diego Recording Studio, Crystal Palace Bldg., San Diego, California. Dated in pencil: 4/17/1928.

D.K. WILGUS AND ELEANOR R. LONG

THE BLUES BALLAD AND THE GENESIS OF STYLE IN
TRADITIONAL NARRATIVE SONG

Folklore as an object of study can be described as
"traditional ideas, manifested in such artifacts as tunes,
texts, cures, games, pots, or house-types from which
traditional ideas can be extrapolated." As a more narrowly
focused object of study, the ballad could then be described
as "traditional narrative song"--an "idea" that fits, that
seems at first neither to include too much nor to exclude
improperly. But does it, should it, include epic song?
Metrical romances? Versified Märchen? Consideration of these
questions forces one to realize that the "ballad idea" is,
after all, different from the "epic idea" or the "Märchen
idea," that it entails not only the elements of traditionality, narrative, and melody, but a specific way of
singing a story. And when one seeks more closely to examine
that way, one makes a further discovery: that the ballad
"idea" itself contains more than one way of singing a story,
and must be more rigorously articulated if justice is to be
done to each of those ways.

Formally, the "ballad idea" can be handily summarized:
it is a story sung in identifiable strophes or stanzas
corresponding to an identifiable rounded or recurrent
melody, and focused upon a single event or strongly unified
series of events. Particular "ballad ideas" (i.e.,
particular stories accompanied with a high degree of
consistency by particular melodies) can be, and have been,
extrapolated from their numerous manifestations in variant
text-tune combinations and influences.[1] They are not, as
Ketner has argued, mere "pseudo-Platonic" abstractions or
"ideal entities," but the very real substance without which
none of those manifestations and influences could exist--
even though the substantive "idea" is unlikely to be
precisely realized in any single one of its manifestations.[2]

Between these two kinds of "ballad ideas" (formal and
inclusive, conceptual and exclusive), however, there lie
intermediate "ballad ideas": story types, verbal structures,
modes of narration. This is the ballad as supposedly
exemplified by Child and defined by Gerould, the kind we
have come to call traditional. Its formal structure is the
couplet or quatrain, rhyming aa, abcb, or aabb with or
without refrain (melody frequently playing a major role in
this respect). Its meter (in English balladry) is Germanic,
based upon a pattern of stressed syllables (4-3-4-3) and

relatively indifferent to the number of unaccented syllables between. It characteristically tells its story in the mode Gummere called "leaping and lingering," with gaps in a narrative which is nevertheless linear, proceeding chronologically from beginning to end. And the story is told objectively and impersonally, eschewing comment upon the event. This constitutes one kind of "ballad idea."

A second typological idea is that of the "vulgar" (minstrel, broadside) ballad. Its stanzaic pattern is also the quatrain, varied like that of the traditional ballad according to refrain or melodic patterns. But its rhyme scheme is more likely to be in couplet form and/or to incorporate internal rhyme, and its meter is markedly regular, with stereotypical relationships between stressed and unstressed syllables (e.g., iambic, anapestic). Unlike that of the traditional ballad, its style is circumstantial, with no dramatic gaps and with an attention to detail that matches its more restrictive rhythm. It differs, too, in that it frequently indulges in subjective commentary.

It is important to emphasize that both of these "types" are ideas, no more mutually exclusive than the "ideas" represented in various text-tune manifestations ("Young Beichan" /Child 53/, for example, has a vulgar narrative pattern, while other stylistic traits are traditional.) Pure forms are rare, even in the case of identifiable and datable compositions. To be emphasized, too, is that both "type-ideas" draw for their subject matter, their stories, upon the same admixture of traditional (i.e., demonstrably long-lived and widely-known) and historical (i.e., demonstrably based on recent actual events and persons) materials. ("Mary Hamilton" /Child 173/ may serve as a convenient example, manifesting the influence upon this particular ballad-idea of not one but two traditional themes--"The Cruel Mother," or Child 20, and "The Criminal's Last Goodnight," or "MacPherson's Farewell"--and not one but two historical events.) Most importantly, perhaps, a theoretical if not a practical distinction can be made between the type in which the ballad was composed and the type in which it is manifested in any particular text-tune performance: traditional ballads may be vulgarized (especially, but not necessarily, in the form of broadsides or phonograph recordings), and vulgar ballads may become unmistakably traditional in style according to the tastes and speech patterns of their singers.

We have, then, been able to define "ballad ideas" on three levels: the "idea" of the ballads qua ballads (although particular ballads may, in form or subject-matter or both, resemble romance or Märchen far more than they correspond to the "idea"); the "idea" of ballads as particular text-tune traditions (although particular text-tune manifestations may expand or contract the material proper to the "idea," or amalgamate it with material from one or more other "ideas"); and the "idea" of ballads existing in more than a single form or type (although these types overlap in substance and may be interchanged in performance). It is with the third kind of "ballad idea" that this study is concerned; specifically we shall discuss our findings concerning a kind of ballad-making--a way of singing a story--which, while it is clearly related to the first two (and to a possible fourth, the "sentimental" ballad) in many of the same ways in which they are related to each other, differs from them so profoundly in at least one respect that its identity was unsuspected by ballad scholars until twenty years ago. Yet that characteristic is one that in Western Europe antedates the traditional type by at least five hundred years.

Stanzaically, the form we have identified is far more fluid in structure than the first two types, but the couplet (frequently extended to an aab triad) and the quatrain remain its most frequently resorted-to pattern. Refrains are slightly more common and tend to be shorter. Its metrical patterns are precisely those of the traditional ballad, with unaccented syllables falling at random between the four or three beats which govern the line. On the other hand, it shares with the vulgar ballad-idea the unabashed expression of attitude and emotion in subjective commentary upon the event with which it is concerned--to the extent that the leaping and lingering of the traditional ballad-idea becomes, as a manifestation of this ballad-idea, the near-total suppression of narrative sequence in favor of a series of comments upon a story which must in large part be inferred from these comments. In a word, the "ballad idea" in this case boldly departs from the linear narration, gapped or circumstantial, of its congeners: to sing a story not by directly relating that story but by celebrating it; not by following a chronological sequence, but by creating a sequence of concepts and feelings about it. The story is there, but not explicitly delineated; the units by which it is defined (stanzas, commonplace formulae) are ordered, but not in any normative sequence. This way of singing a story-- elliptical, allusive, organic--we call the "blues ballad."

The term "blues ballad" has been credited to D. K. Wilgus after his first use of it in 1961 in liner notes to Obray Ramsey Sings Folksongs from the Three Laurels.3 However, the term was apparently first used by W. C. Handy, who, in an interview with Dorothy Scarborough sometime before 1925, referred to his copyrighted song "Loveless

Love," saying that it was a "blues ballad" and "was based on
an old song called <u>Careless Love</u>, which narrated the death
of the son of a governor of Kentucky." Later Handy stated
that "Loveless Love"

> was based on the <u>Careless Love</u> melody that I had
> played first in Bessemer /Alabama/ in 1892 and that
> since has become popular all over the South. In
> Henderson /Kentucky/ I was told that the words of
> <u>Careless Love</u> were based on a tragedy in a local
> family, and one night a gentleman of that city's
> tobacco-planter aristocracy requested our band to
> play and sing this folk melody, using the following
> words:

> You see what Careless Love has done (3)
> It killed the Governor's only son
>
> Poor Archie didn't mean no harm (3)

At this point the police stepped in and stopped the
performance, saying the song was "a reflection on two
prominent families."[4]

> Two longer forms of the song have been recorded, one
from the late Mrs. Will Cline of McClean Co., Ky., in 1956:

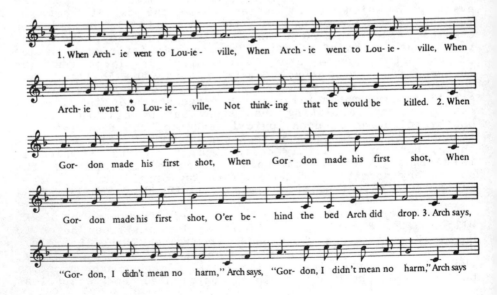

1. When Arch-ie went to Lou-ie-ville, When Arch-ie went to Lou-ie-ville, When
Arch-ie went to Lou-ie-ville, Not think-ing that he would be killed. 2. When
Gor-don made his first shot, When Gor-don made his first shot, When
Gor-don made his first shot, O'er be-hind the bed Arch did drop. 3. Arch says,
"Gor-don, I didn't mean no harm," Arch says, "Gor-don, I didn't mean no harm," Arch says

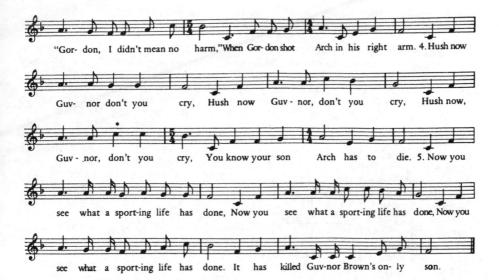

"Gor-don, I didn't mean no harm," When Gor-don shot Arch in his right arm. 4. Hush now

Guv-nor don't you cry, Hush now Guv-nor, don't you cry, Hush now,

Guv-nor, don't you cry, You know your son Arch has to die. 5. Now you

see what a sport-ing life has done, Now you see what a sport-ing life has done, Now you

see what a sport-ing life has done. It has killed Guv-nor Brown's on-ly son.

A text without tune was secured from Mrs. Lewis Good, Hopkins Co., Ky., 1950.

> When Archie went to Louisville
> He had no idea he'd be killed.
>
> When that telegram was read,
> Poor Archie was lying dead.
>
> They carried Gordon up to jail,
> A hundred men was ready to go his bail.
>
> "Oh, my boy, I told you so,
> Before you left your father's door."[5]

The song concerns the slaying of Archibald Dixon Brown, son of Governor John Young Brown, and Arch's paramour by the latter's husband, Fulton Gordon, who surprised them in a Louisville bawdy house 30 April 1895. It is a ballad, and a blues ballad at that. Our texts were not titled "Careless Love," though that would be apt; but "Careless Love" is the generally accepted title of the tune. (If we interpret Handy correctly, the title existed before the events of "Arch and Gordon.") Does Handy's comment mean that we deal not with an analytical but with a native category? Perhaps that depends on the extent to which we consider W. C. Handy a member of a folk group. We have never otherwise encountered the term "blues ballad" in traditional usage.

Before we discuss what we feel to be the characteristics of the American blues ballad, we should point out that there has been prior recognition and significant discussion of this ballad type, but largely in relation to Negro folksong. For example, in his generally perceptive chapter on "The Negro's Contribution to American Balladry,"[6] dealing largely with style and attitude rather than narrative technique, G. Malcolm Laws, Jr. singles out for analysis ballads he perceives to be of Negro origin apparently without realizing that some ballads he has placed in the White categories share the characteristics: e.g., "The _Titanic_ V" (Laws dD40), "Wild Bill Jones" (Laws E10), "Harvey Logan" (Laws E21), "The Gambler" (Laws dE43), "The Burning of the _Bayou Sara_" (Laws dG 39), "I Wonder Where's the Gambler" (Laws H22), "Ten Broeck and Molly" (Laws H27), and variants of "Logan County Jail" (Laws E17), "Ellen Smith" (Laws F11), "The Roving Gambler" (Laws H4)--not to mention songs which are rejected even from his category of "ballad-like pieces," e.g., "Hustling Gamblers/Darling Cory/Little Maggie" and "Reuben's Train/Train 45/900 Miles."

We would admit that Negro ballads are almost exclusively blues ballads, but maintain that Negro balladry is but one branch of the American blues ballad, albeit a branch which provides some of the finest flowering. But to refer to blues ballads as simply Negro ballads is erroneous and dangerous. It assumes an origin and history that have yet to be determined. It has caused the White blues ballad to be overlooked as a type. It confuses the origin of the type, the origin of an individual ballad, and the circulation of the ballads. We try to distinguish Negro blues ballads from White blues ballads even when they have crossed the "color line" in repertoire (which is more often than not). But, for example, after years of research, D. K. Wilgus and Lynwood Montell could not determine whether "Clure and Joe Williams" was of White or Negro origin. Finally, reference to the blues ballad as "Negro" has led to racial judgments, in that those whose aesthetic sensibilities have been offended by certain qualities of the blues ballads have judged them to be the products of a race incapable of coherent thought. As the blues ballad in general shares elements of tune, textual form, and formulae with traditional, vulgar, and even sentimental ballads, so the White and Negro blues ballads are mutually related.

As we have indicated, the blues ballad does not so much narrate the events of a story as it celebrates them. The amount of explicit narrative varies, as sometimes does the chronology of the events referred to. Perhaps "referred to" is the operative term in that the blues ballad text depends on a narrative referent, that is, an actual event occurring in a community or a traditional pattern such as "the murdered sweetheart" or "the criminal brought to justice." (It should be pointed out that the actual events tend to be perceived in terms of traditional models, as Anne B. Cohen has shown.)[7] In other words, the total story is a given, and the ballad performer, secure in his knowledge that his audience is familiar with the referent, whether actual or patterned, selects a scene or a number of scenes for presentation and, freed from the necessity of presenting circumstantial detail, concentrates on conventionalized dramatic scenes, oblique delineation of character through action and speech, and lyrical comment by characters or the narrator. The technique causes problems for the outsider, the investigator for whom the ballad was not intended. Consider the following example:

Sugar Babe

It's oh, law, boys, don't you know you done wrong,
    Sugar Babe,
It's oh, law, boys don't you know you done wrong,
Rocked my hack as I drove along,
    Sugar Babe.

Shorty jumped out an' he give a little yell
Sent old Junkins on to Hell.

Shorty shot Shavie with a Navy ball,
Pistol had a-fired he would killed us all.

Shorty killed two and he liked to killed three,
Gun had a-fired he would a-killed me.

Sent for the doctor and the doctor did come,
He come in a walk and he come in a run.

He looked at Burgie and he looked through his specks,
He said, "Old gentleman, 'tis your checks."

Took old Burgie back to jail,
No one there to go his bail.

"Burgie, old Burgie, what have you done?"
"Shot two men and the third one run."[8]

The text is enigmatic enough, but represents more than D. K. Wilgus and Lynwood Montell had when they began a ten-year investigation of the "Clure and Joe Williams" ballad:

Joe threw his pistol in the captain's face,
    Poor boy,
Joe threw his pistol in the captain's face,
Saying, "Back up your boat to the landing place,"
    Poor boy.

Clure Williams is dead and that ain't all,
He was shot with a slug instead of a ball.

Patterson, Patterson is turning gray,
While old Sam Franklin's fading away.[9]

A similar investigation of the "Shorty and Shavie" ballad might show its relation to the community events which inspired it. When a ballad deals with a national event such as the assassination of President William McKinley, as in "White House Blues," one can see more readily the elements the ballad composer (or composers) selected for celebration and the blues ballad conventions used in the process.[10]

    The difficulty of distinguishing Negro from White American blues ballads is clear. For example, "The Coon-Can Game" (Laws I4) was assigned to the Negro category apparently on the basis of "style." Yet Marina Bokelman's evidence indicated that it is of White origin and largely White circulation.[11] "John Hardy" (Laws I2) deals with a Black protagonist, has characteristics and commonplaces of both "traditional" ballads and those which we conceive as Negro ballads, and has been recovered largely from White informants. There is at least a traditional claim that "Delia" (Laws I5) was composed by a White musician.[12] "The Titanic I" (Laws D24), as usually recorded, has many vulgar characteristics and is known mostly by White singers. But its closest analogue is "The Hamlet Wreck," a Negro ballad of a North Carolina railroad disaster of 1911.[13]

    The apparent or at least possible development of "The Titanic I" suggests, though in reverse, another kind of distinction, that between ballads which seem to have originated as a product of the blues ballad idea and those which seem to have developed or been recomposed into that category. Certainly the strength of the American blues ballad as a traditional force is illustrated by the conversion of ballads seen as vulgar into blues ballad forms. A comparison of early and thoroughly vulgar forms of the "The Cruel Ship's Carpenter" (Laws P36) with a number of performances from the American South illustrates the conversion of the circumstantially detailed English broadside into the allusive, lyrical blues ballad. Imported ballads in which Laws says "the narrative element is weak," such as "The Rambling Boy" (Laws L12) and "The Roving

Journeyman"--known in the United States as "The Roving Gambler" (Laws H4)--easily assimilated further blues ballad characteristics.[14]

In selecting songs which originated as blues ballads, however, we have to depend on the absence of any known earlier forms in another style. To illustrate relatively pure blues ballads we are forced to choose either local ballads about which we have grass-roots information or ballads about which background information is non-existent. Furthermore, in our examples we cannot comment in detail on many attendant characteristics of blues ballads, such as commonplace systems or refrain patterns. But the examples do illustrate the narrative technique we feel to be central to the blues ballad idea.

A ballad which we can securely date and attribute to Negro provenance is a local song with titles too various to list. We shall call it simply "Molly and Nan." It concerns the attempt in 1889 of two Black men of the Coe Ridge community of Cumberland County, Kentucky, and two White women to travel across the Kentucky-Indiana border to be married. They were apprehended in Glasgow and the relationships were broken up. Details of the event based on official documents and oral history are provided by Lynwood Montell.[15] All evidence points to the generation of the ballad by one or both of the Black protagonists, Cal and John Coe (though one White informant said his brother added one stanza /WKFA T7-417). Montell has published a number of texts,[16] and there are further texts and tunes in WKFA. As Montell accurately points out:

> By knowing the story to a fair degree of accuracy, one can see that the song gives the full story. It would be virtually impossible, however, to take the song fragments and figure out the sequence of events without knowing the oral narrative traditions which accompany this ballad.[17]

We have chosen to present transcriptions of two performances by the same singer, illustrating the fluidity of the ballad.

A

Railroad, railroad, troublin' po' man,
Ye oughta seed ol' Cal and John gittin' back in the lan'.

Give up yo' gun, boys, give up yo' gun.
Ye oughta seed ol' Cal an' John givin' up their gun.

Walk up in jail, boys, walk up in jail,
Ye oughta see ol' Cal and John walking up in jail.

All on the stage, girls, all on the stage.
Ye oughta see Miss Molly and Nan gettin' back in the lan'.

Walk out of jail, boys, walk out of jail.
Ye oughta see ol' Cal and John walkin' out of jail.

Get on the stage, boys, get on the stage.
Ye oughta see ol' Cal and John gettin' back in the lan'.

George Allred, Meshack, Ky., 18 July 1959.[18]

B

Get off the train, boys, get off the train.
Don't you see old Cal and John crawlin' off the train?

Walk up in jail, boys, walk up in jail.
Don't you see Cal and John gettin' up that jail?

All on the stage, girls, all on the stage.
Don't you see them blue-eyed girls gettin' on the stage?

Back in the land, girls, back in the land.
Don't you see Miss Molly and Nan gettin' back in the land?

Walk out of jail, boys, walk out of jail.
Don't you see Old Cal and John walkin' out of jail?

Pick up your guns, boys, pick up your guns.
You ought to see Cal and John pickin' up their guns.[19]

These texts, as well as other recorded performances, lack the cliches associated with Negro blues ballads. The pattern is related to frolic songs such as "Big Ball in Town" and "Long Journey Home,"[20] which in turn are related to the spiritual song tradition.[21] But the ballad clearly celebrates an event significant to the community and communicates the essence and meaning of the event by depiction of selected scenes, selected in the first instance by the composer(s?), but also by those others who accepted the song. The narrative coherence of the song is provided by community knowledge of the events.

More difficult to assess is an example of what seems to be a White blues ballad: "Wild Bill Jones" (Laws E10). Since the tradition of "Molly and Nan" remained local, the investigators could determine the referent of the ballad. "Wild Bill Jones," however, has a relatively wide circulation in Appalachia and provides few, if any, leads to an actual referent. The patterned referents are generally related to Anglo-American criminal ballads, but the central action of disposing of an opponent in summary fashion seems that of Negro blues ballads, e.g., "Bad Lee Brown" (Laws I8) and "Brady" (Laws I9). The two examples we have chosen seem to exemplify what is central to the ballad, but illustrate considerable variance.

A

(originally B sharp)

Once while I was ramblin' around
I met with Wild Bill Jones;
He was a-walkin' and a-talking by Lulu gal's side
And I bade him fer to leave her along.

He says, "I am past twenty-two,
Too old fer to be controlled."
I drew my revolver from my side
And destroyed that poor boy's soul.

He reeled and he staggered and he fell to the ground,
And he made one dying moan;
He threw his arms around my Lulu gal's neck
Sayin', "My darling, you are left alone."

They took me down to Beattyville,
And they locked me up in jail;
But the saddest thing that ever I know,
Little Lulu wouldn't go my bail.

O bring me a hammer fer to beat out my brains,
And a piller fer to lay under my head;
If whiskey'll ruin a poor boy's mind,
Purty women'll kill him dead.

Five dollars in my pocketbook
And a fourty-four in my hand;
If you want to be a rounding boy,
Just follow the rounding man.

Come all my friends and relatives
While I have a dollar fer to spend;
For by this time tomorrow night
I'll have neither dollar nor friend.

O pass around the bottle, boys,
Let's all go on a spree;
Today was the last of Wild Bill Jones,
Tomorrow'll be the last of me.

(From the singing of Phoebe Jane Parker, Caines Creek,
Lawrence Co., Ky.)22

B

Last Sunday morning while rambling
I met with that Bumblebee Joe.
While walking along with Mattie, my love,
I asked him to leave her alone,
    I asked him to leave her alone.

He says, "Young man, I'm twenty,
By you I'll not be controlled."
I drew a razor out of my coat
And I cut that poor man's throat, etc.

And don't you see, Mattie, my love,
What you caused me to do?
I murdered a man this morning, my love.
It was all for the sake of you, etc.

Last Sunday (Monday) morning quite early,
Just at the break of day,
I heard those jail keys rattling, my love,
They are coming to take me away, etc.

"You say the state prison can't hold you,
Nor neither the county jail.
If neither of these will hold you, poor boy,
You'll be taken to the gallows and hung, etc."

The five o'clock train is coming fast;
My Mattie is standing around.
"I'd rather be dead and buried, my love,
Than to see you leave this town," etc.

Oh, what an awful pity,
Oh what a story to tell.
The whiskey surrounded this counsel of mine;
My Mattie has sent me to Hell, etc.

Oh, hand me a pillow to lay my head on,
A pistol to blow out my brains.
The whiskey surrounded this counsel of mine;
My Mattie has run me derange, etc.

(Sung by Mrs. Vera Martin, Tompkinsville, Ky., 26 August 1959).[23]

The ballad is chronological in its depiction of events, but we are given only type scenes and lyrical comment.

Judith McCulloh has raised problems regarding "terminology and concept in which the referent is 'lost'":

> What happens once the referent to a song like the Williams ballad is lost, say, when the folk community no longer remembers the incidents and the folklorists can no longer find out? Is the song still a blues ballad? In the variants Wilgus and Montell give I do not see any familiar underlying framework (such as the criminal pattern which Marina Bokelman found useful in tracing "The Coon Can Game") which could hold the variants together enough to call a ballad even in the blues ballad sense. To draw a parallel, the "Reuben" songs in the "Reuben 900/Miles" cluster are just as

"narrative," just as dramatic. Take this ballet
from Sarah Gunning[24] (letter, May 31, 1969):

Old Ruben he got drunk and he climbed upon a stump
And he shot in the river, bam, bam.

Old Ruben he got drunk and he pawned his watch and trunk
And I never saw Old Ruben do so bad.

   Chorus:

      Is that you, Ruben? Is that you, Ruben?
      Is that you, Ruben? Is that you, Ruben?

Old Ruben had a wreck and broke old Ruben neck
But it didn't hurt a hair on my head.

Old Ruben had a wife to mourn old Ruben life
But she better off with old Ruben dead.

Old Ruben engine fell apart and it broke old Ruben heart,
And me and old Ruben had to part.

If you don't believe Old Ruben dead look what a
      hole in Ruben head,

That the last word Old Ruben ever said.

The suggestion is strong, at any rate, that there
might have been a person (named Ruben or not) who
provoked a song which celebrated and commented on
his accidents or escapades. To my knowledge, no
information has come to light from either folk or
folklorist about such originating incidents.[25] Nor
have I deciphered any narrative pattern which
stands behind the "Reuben" songs.

    "Reuben," then, is a lyric complex which may
once have fit the definition of blues ballad. If
someone should discover the historical basis for
the "Reuben" songs, would they then (again)
constitute a blues ballad? At what point in their
investigation did Wilgus and Montell decide they
were dealing with a blues ballad?[26] (Can one text
be a blues ballad, or is the term properly reserved
for the Gestalt seen by the folklorist?) The crux
of the definition of this folksong type seems to
lie outside the material itself, a curious mutation
of defining by origin.[27]

The problems McCulloh raises are certainly real. Perhaps the "crux" of her questioning is that "the definition of this folksong type seems to lie outside of the material itself. . . ." Of course it does. The material does not define itself. Nor do performers, in our experience, provide distinctions or "definitions" of the type the folklorist fashions. And folklorists have been obsessed with the distinction between narrative and lyric songs. They have extracted material from lyric songs and attributed them to narrative songs in which they also occur. When faced with a genre that does not conform to their established standards they become understandably confused. That is why we prefer to speak of ballad "ideas" rather than of canons of ballad types. The example which McCulloh quotes is one of the "Reuben" texts which would seem to fit our rubric of "blues ballad." But what we take to be "Reuben" elements occur in a cluster with what we conceive to be other songs. To cite a brief example:

The Saw-Mill Man

If I die a saw-mill man,
Go bury me in the sand
Till I can hear the whistle blow a thousand miles.

You ort a-been down town
When that even' train come down
And a-catched old No. 4 as she rolled by.

The train is on the track
And I can't bring her back--
Can't get a letter from my home.

Reuben must a-been drunk
When he pawned his watch and trunk
To get his old doney out of jail.

If that won't do,
He'll pawn his wagon too
To get his baby girl out on bail.

(From Curtis Williams, Caines Creek, Lawrence Co., Ky.)[28]

The brief text contains three, possibly four, elements from the song clusters Norm Cohen delineates in his discussion of the "Reuben's Train/Train 45/900 Miles" complex.[29]

What disturbs us is not so much the borrowing or occurrences of lyric stanzas in blues ballads, but the way in which apparent blues ballads are buried in the midst of lyric stanzas. Two examples from the "Hustling

Gamblers/Darling Cory/Little Maggie" cluster will illustrate the point. The first example (from the Josiah H. Combs Collection, WFKA) contains a number of lyric stanzas found elsewhere, but which could be considered as a part of an original blues ballad.

Hustling Gamblers

Come all you hustling gamblers,
While I have one dollar to spend;
Tomorrow my pocket may be empty,
I'll neither have dollars nor friends.

Drink whisky, you hustling gamblers,
Drink whisky and pass it around;
I'm sure you'll drink plenty whisky
When I'm cold in the ground.

When I am dead and buried,
My pale face to the sun,
Just move the lid off of my coffin,
And think about the way you've done.

Give me your hand, little Cora,
I'll leave you with a broken heart;
This world is full of trouble,
And you have to stand your part.

The last time I saw little Cora,
She had a wine glass in her hand;
She was drinking off her trouble,
And thinking of another man.

When I am dead and buried,
And my friends all standing around,
Just pass around your bottle,
Say, "Here lays a gambler gone."

Wake up, wake up, little Cora!
What makes you sleep so sound.
The highway robbers are coming,
To tear your building down.

I received a letter from Cora,
And this is the way it read:
"O darling, I know you see trouble,
But never hang down your head."

Yonder stands little Cora,
A-drinking of sweet wine;
She's drinking off her trouble,
Just like I drink off mine.

Don't want no bawling and squalling
Around my grave carried on;
Just throw the sod all over me,
And leave me all alone.

The lyrical intrusions are mild compared with the following:

Dark Road's a Hard Road to Travel

How would you like to be a prisoner
With no place to lay your head,
With the cold iron bars around you
And the cold cold floor for a bed?

Oh, they say that my darling don't love me,
Oh, they say that I am too poor,
If I knew that was true my darling,
I would never come to see you any more.

Oh, the first time you saw me, darling,
I was on the East bound train,
But the next time you see me, darling
I'll be wearing the ball and chain.

Oh, my darling, I must meet you
But I hope to meet you above,
But remember, Darling Cora,
You are the only girl I love.

When I am dead and in my coffin
And my face you no more see,
While you are thinking of some other,
Darling, will you ever thing /sic/ of me?

If I had the wings of an angel
Or wings so I could fly
I would fly to the arms of my darling
And there I'd be willing to die.

Don't you hear those banjos playing
Don't you hear their mournful sound,
Don't you hear those pretty girls crying
Down in that lonely town?

Oh, my darling, I must leave you
And you must do the best you can,
You can hunt you another woman
And I'll hunt me another man.[30]

When I'm dead and in my coffin
And my words have all come true,
Oh, remember, dearest darling,
That I died forever loving you.

Oh, goodby, my love, God bless you.
You are mine wherever you may be
You may hunt this wide world over
But you'll never find a friend like me.

The last time I saw my darling
She was standing by the sea, on the sand,
A-drinking down her troubles
With another gambling man.

I am going to take a train tomorrow,
A train that is bound for the West
And if you should see my darling
Tell her I lover /sic/ her the best.

The dark road is a hard road to travel,
The light road is always the best,
The dark road will lead you to trouble
And the light road will lead you to rest.

If I had a-minded Mamma
I would not a been here today
With the cold iron bars around me
And my head on a pillow of clay.

Go dig me a hole in the meadow,
Go dig me a hole in the ground,
Go dig me a hole in the meadow
To lay this poor body down.

I am going to a new jail tomorrow
But I'm not going there to stay,
With the cold iron bars around me
And my head on a pillow of clay.

So remember, dearest Darling,
I am thinking and think of you.
You are the only girl I love
And I give my love to you.

It seems hard to part with my darling,
The only girl I love,
You may roam this wide world over
And you are the only one I love.

> I am going for a train tomorrow,
> A train for the West,
> So I'll remember you, darling,
> And may you be blessed.

(Sung by Mrs. Pauline Cable.)[31]

Is the folklorist justified in attempting to "dig out" a blues ballad from such a text? We are not sure, yet we are sure that the blues ballad "idea" is there.

The manifestation of the blues ballad idea in the United States is not simple; on the other hand, based on the evidence one might, with some assurance, outline its temporal and geographical occurrence. The tradition seems to begin sometime in the 1860's, reach its height about 1898, and end--so far as new creations are concerned--in 1922. There are indeed some bench marks. We have sought in vain for a clear example of a blues ballad from Black tradition before the Civil War. (There are satirical "corn husking songs" and some suggestive items.) In a Sut Lovingood story published in 1868 George Washington Harris quotes a ballad of a race between the mare Kate and the grey Ariel.[32] John Mason Brown in an article on "Songs of the Slave" in 1868 printed portions of a ballad called "The Noble Skewball."[33] Harris sets his ballad in 1833; Brown refers to his as a "negro ballad" which originated "many years ago." But we take Harris's 1833 date to be an anachronism, and are always sceptical of a "many years ago" ascription. Furthermore, an otherwise unreported Alabama blues ballad, "Luke and Mullen," was dated by its performer: ". . . that was the third year after Surrender. They started that song."[34] Thus we know that by 1868 the blues ballad tradition was flowering, especially in that it could absorb and was at least beginning to recast a ballad from another tradition, for the blues ballad "Skewball" quoted by Harris and Brown is a form of an Irish ballad telling of the defeat of a grey mare, Miss Portly, by Skewball on the plains of Kildare (Laws Q12). "Stewball" seems to have been the model for "Ten Broeck and Molly," dealing with an 1878 race in Louisville, Kentucky, and "Ten Broeck and Molly" in turn influenced performances of "Stewball."[35]

On the "White" side of the ledger, we can note what we might want to consider as blues ballads beginning to emerge in local songs during the Civil War: for example, one on the sinking of the Cumberland by the Merrimac in 1862:

> The Merrimac she went out;
> The Yankees wa'n't a-thinking,
> The fust thing the Yankees knew
> The Cumberland was a-sinking.[36]

For a more local song, consider the following from south central Kentucky:

Kidd and the Bacon[37]

Preacher Kidd is a preachin' man,
I know I'm not mistaken;
He'd preach all day and half the night
For a pound and a half of bacon.

It was a/t̄?7 Pink Ridge Church,
I know I'm not mistaken,
John E. Clark liked mutton so well
He gave Kidd all the bacon.

I went to Pink Ridge Church,
I know I'm not mistaken,
I saw wrote on the gable end,
All Kidd wants is the bacon.

The sheep shelled corn
By the rattle of the horn;
Hurry, shave, Brother Kidd,
While the water is warm.

I went to Oceola,
'Twas a dedication;
Sam Hardy ate the pound cake up,
Gave Kidd all the bacon.

I lost my horse the other day,
Where do you reckon I found him?
Way down in Jordon's Hollow,
And the Rebels all around him.

> Preacher Kidd is a preachin' man,
> I know I'm not mistaken;
> He's preach all day and half the night
> For a pound and a half of bacon.[38]

(Another text has the refrain: "All Kidd wants is bacon.")

The text has the allusiveness, the lack of developed narrative, even the lyric commonplace ("The sheep shelled corn") we associate with the blues ballad. And the referent of the song is still known in the community--at least it was in 1965.

The Reverend W. Mixon Kidd came from Virginia to Kentucky in 1832 and founded a number of Baptist churches in Metcalfe, Hart, and Green Counties. During the Civil War, in which he was apparently active in the pursuit of deserters, he got into trouble over some bacon. (One informant said Kidd stole bacon from someone's smoke house.) He was also in trouble with the Wallace family, who disliked him and supposedly killed his horse. ("Rebels," in stanza six, is sometimes rendered "ten thousand buzzards.") At any rate, William Wallace is said to have composed the satirical ballad centered around the bacon episode. If one questions the "White blues ballad" status of such a song, we can point to the ballad (or cycle of ballads) growing out of the execution of Tom Dooley in (mirable dictu) 1868.[39]

From 1868 we can spot datable ballads, e.g., "John Henry (Laws I1, circa 1873); "Ten Broeck and Molly" (Laws H 27, 1878); "Burning of the Bayou Sara" (Laws dG39,[40] 1885); "Molly and Nan" (1889); "Arch and Gordon" (1895); "Clure and Joe Williams" and "Railroad Bill" (Laws I13) (1896-1897). Undatable blues ballads from the Southern Appalachians seem to point to the 1870's because of their connection with moonshining and railroading. The year 1898 is a convenient bench mark as the center of the period in which Black underworld songs surfaced in the public consciousness. In 1891, "Ta-Ra-Ra-Boom-Der-E" (Henry J. Sayers); 1895-1986, "Bully of the Town"[41] (Laws I14); "Hot Time in the Old Town Tonight" (Theodore Metz)--all supposedly emenating from Babe Connor's celebrated St. Louis brothel. "Hot Time in the Old Town Tonight" is almost the Black blues ballad tune in terms of its employment--for "Railroad Bill," "White House Blues," "Louis Collins," and so on, including the satirical account of a soldier's experience in the Spanish-American War, known variously as "The Battleship of Maine," "McKinley Called for Volunteers," "Bloody War," and updated to fit later wars, including that of Viet Nam.[42] Blues ballads continue with "Frankie and Albert" (Laws I3; 1899), "Casey Jones" (Laws G1; 1900-

1901),[43] "White House Blues" (1901), and a number of songs on the sinking of the <u>Titanic</u> (1912). The end date might be seen as 1922 with the hanging of Frank Dupree in Atlanta and the subsequent blues ballad (Laws I11). However, the remodeling of "White House Blues" or "McKinley" to fit the death of Huey Long in 1936[44] perhaps indicates a continuing creativity in the form. And, indeed, blues ballads remained in Black and White repertoires, "Dupree" itself having continued life as a rhythm-and-blues item. But in Black tradition there was a marked shift in narrative form from the blues ballad to the "toast,"[45] emphasized by the conversion to toasts of such blues ballads as "The <u>Titanic</u>," "Stack-a-Lee," and "Bad Lee Brown." Nor have we noted any new composition in White tradition.

The geographical history of the American blues ballad is somewhat similar to its traditional history in that it parallels the post-Civil War expansion of American industry in river traffic, railroading, coal mining, and mass labor no longer confined to the plantations. The ballads came out of river towns, construction camps, "frolic houses," hobo jungles--situations for the cross-fertilization of Black and White traditions in relatively uninhibited fashion. The American blues ballad is clearly a product of the rural South in the throes of industrialization.

The pre-history of the American blues ballad-at least the immediate prehistory--is undoubtedly complex, particularly as it involves traditions themselves complex and--in their turn--controversial. Stanza patterns, tunes, and commonplaces from Anglo-Celtic tradition are a part of the blues ballad tradition. The "Ten Broeck and Molly" tune is a member of the British "Todlen Hame" family, which carries the "Cuckoo Bird" text, stanzas of which turn up in the "Stewball-Tenbrooks" complex. Similarly the "Captain Kidd" tune family is well-nigh ubiquitous in blues ballad and related lyric tradition: "Clure and Joe Williams," "Sugar Babe," "Crawdad Song," "Old Bill," "How Many Biscuits Can you Eat?" et al.[46]

It should be pointed out that, despite the connotations of the term, the American blues ballad predates the blues form in American culture. David Evans has argued, rightly we think, that the vocal blues stemmed from Black field hollers, which had African prototypes, and developed through a period of instrumental response to a vocal line. They then were shaped according to the strophic and harmonic structure of the blues ballad, derived from Old World balladry, resulting formally in eight-bar and twelve-bar structures. Blues ballad variants do occur in AAB text structures, but they seem late in the traditions of the ballads concerned:

Oh, Ten Brook was a bay horse as slick as a mole,
With a white spot on his fo'head like diamonds in gold.[47]

Old Tenbrook was a black horse, black as any crow, (2)
Had a ring 'round his forepaw, white as any crow
/snow?/.[48]

The patterns of repetition in the American blues ballad occur in Black and White spirituals and in Black work songs. While we might look to them for origins, we can also view the formal structures as parallel developments. Certainly we can postulate an interaction between Black work and social songs and the White lyrics and fiddle songs (instrumentals interspersed with sung verses). The evidence suggests various origins for individual ballads. For example, some seem to have arisen as roustabout songs by Ohio, Mississippi, and Cumberland laborers. Others may have developed in the "banjo song" tradition as narrative verses with instrumental accompaniment and alternating with instrumental solos. (Many recent performances are by unaccompanied singers. That may simply indicate a development from a frolic tradition which the folklorist was never able to record. Norm Cohen has suggested that the alternation of instrumental performance and sung verses has at least contributed to the non-sequential nature of blues ballads.)

The interaction among the traditions produced songs with a texture of formulae that are effective and memorable in their concrete imagery, especially their use of objects and colors to stand for ideas. The formulae of both White and Negro blues ballads (insofar as we can separate them), whether inherited from traditional and vulgar ballads or independently created, are alike in tone. It is commonplace to note that Negro balladry--for cultural reasons--is largely concerned with crime, violence, and sex. Its formulae of .38, .41, .44, and .45 guns, its commonplaces of rubber-tired carriages and rubber-tired hacks are parallel to and as effective as the traditional ballad formulae of little pen knives, lily white hands, and burial processions. But it must be pointed out that White blues ballads have a similar concern with crime, violence, and sex, which makes it difficult to distinguish White and Black productions, especially since the songs developed in the same or similar environments.

Because of the oral nature of the productions, techniques among types of ballads are bound to be similar.

The traditional ballad will make a significant point by a contrast of social attitudes expressed in concrete terms:

> There was dule in the kitchen and mirth in the ha'
> But the Baron of Brackley is dead and awa'.

And the blues ballad will say:

> Roosevelt's in the White House drinking out of a
>   silver cup,
> McKinley's in the graveyard, he'll never wake up.

Or:

> White man in the parlor reading latest news,
> Negro in the kitchen blacking Roosevelt's shoes.

So the White blues ballad will make effective use of contrast:

> Don't you hear them bluebirds a-singin',
> Don't you hear their mournful sound?
> They are preachin' Cory's funeral
> In some lonesome graveyard ground.

This recalls the traditional

> The baby was christened with joy and much mirth,
> Whilst poor Queen Jane's body lay cold under earth.

There is effective personification in the (what we take to be) White formula:

> See that train a-comin', comin' 'round the curve,
> A-blowin' of its whistle and strainin' every nerve.

The tough, defiant quality of

> Hang me, oh, hang me, and I'll be dead and gone, (2)
> Well, I don't mind your hanging, it's laying in the
>   ground so long.
> God knows, I been all around the world.

is balanced by the tenderness of

> Mz Collins weeped, Mz Collins moaned,
> To see her son Louis leavin' home.
> The angels laid him away.

The interaction of Afro-American and Anglo-American traditions in terms of melody, structure, and text suggests the model we have adumbrated for the American blues ballad: a narrative song form that has emerged through contact of White and Black performers and makers in the post-Civil War period. We believe the model is viable insofar as the emergence and development of the _American_ blues ballad is concerned. But there are factors in the pre-history of the American tradition which must be considered, both on the White and Black sides. It is the former that we wish to address.

First, there is a long tradition (unfortunately under-reported by folklorists) of local satirical songs in White communities apparently uninfluenced by the White-Black interactions we have noted. For example:

> Mun turned over and begin to snore
> And said, "Lord God! Garland, open the door."
>
> They opened the door and Luther gave a leap
> And hollered, "Come on boys, let's go to the creek."
>
> Mr. G--- got up and looked over the farm
> And said, "He shit on the bed as sure as you're born."

In about 1904, Luther H----, who lived on Little Reedy (in western Kentucky) was courting a girl close to the G---'s (Mun and Garland) and had been staying at their house for convenience. They decided he had overstayed his welcome, so they gave him some croton oil in milk. A short time later someone wrote this song about the event.[49] Such songs have the couplet form and allusiveness we associate with the blues ballad. Some local songs also have similar patterns of repetition, such as the song dealing with an 1847 execution in Cumberland County, Kentucky:

> Old Joe Coleman killed his wife (3)
>
> With a great big butcher, great big butcher knife.[50]

Satirical songs, sometimes called "quatrain ballads" because they recount a series of distinct events in successive stanzas, are not necessarily local (though often localized) and short-lived. "Tom Bo-Linn" or "Bryan O'Lynn" was cited by title in 1549 and is still popular in Anglo-Irish-American tradition.[51] Apparently originally a satire on "back country" Scots, it was adapted to fit the Irish and then Americans, as was this version which, in part, has more direct narrative (Merle Travis, _Back Home_, Capitol T 891, 12" LP):

I wouldn't want to make a enemy out of none of
you good folks from Todd County, Kentucky, but as
far as I know, this is where the feller I'm gonna
sing about come from. His name was John Bolin.

Way up in Todd County John Bolin was born.
His shoes was worn out and his britches was torn.
This end of his nose was a-tetchin' his chin.
"Now ain't I /a-foolin?7," said John Bolin.

John Bolin he had him no shoes fer to wear.
He took him a sheepskin and made him a pair,
With the woolly side out and the smooth side in.
"They're cool in the summer," said John Bolin.

John Bolin owned nothing except an old hoss.
He said, "What I need is a woman to boss,
To love and obey me through thick and through thin.
I'm goin' a-courtin'," said John Bolin.

He rode to a house at the east of Provo,
Hitched the old mare and he hollered, "Hello!"
"Come in, John Bolin, I bid you come in."
He said, "I've come here a-courtin'," said John Bolin.

"Come in, John Bolin, you're a most welcome guest,
Take which of my daughters you're a-likin' the best."
"I'll take one for love and take one for kin,
And marry them both," said John Bolin.
. . . .

We are then led to what we have sometimes referred to
as "The Irish connection." There certainly is a strong
"connection" between imported Irish ballads (or Irish forms
of ballads) and the American blues ballad. As noted above,
such ballads as "The Rambling Boy" (Laws L12) and "The
Roving Journeyman" have become more "bluesy" in American
tradition. And there is an uncanny resemblance in theme and
narrative method between the Irish "The True Paddy's Song"
(Laws J8) and the American "Battleship of Maine" in the
pseudo-comic account of the experiences of a recruit in the
unfamiliar military environment. (One is also, however,
reminded of a parallel with "Yankee Doodle.") These resem-
blances have encouraged us to look more deeply and widely
into the pre-history of the compositional style of the blues
ballad.

Through the diligent efforts of the Irish Folklore
Commission and its present host institution, University
College, Dublin, to say nothing of the Irish Folk Song
Society and its Journal, a remarkable corpus of Irish

463

traditional narrative song has been recovered, including ballads in the native language as well as those in English. And what emerges from even a cursory examination of these variant texts is a curious phenomenon: while many English-language songs in Ireland evidence the characteristics we are identifying as those of the "blues ballad idea" to a greater or lesser degree, those composed in Irish manifest them almost invariably.

For illustrative purposes we have selected four such Irish texts because of their obvious thematic affiliations with well-known traditional and vulgar ballads catalogued by Child and Laws. First a variant of "Barbara Allen" (Child 84) in which the enigmatic reproach of the heroine[52] is preserved in an otherwise lyrical exchange:

"I love you wholly, and welcome you are to me!
I love your eyes, and your bright open forehead;
I love your heart, that never thought of anyone but me,
My beloved young man, 'tis my grief we are parted!"

"Your love is no more than a handful of snow,
Or the foam cast by a stream on a March day,
Or a puff of wind on the surface of the sea,
Or a mountain torrent after a day of rain!"

"And when you have seen me show love and affection
        for anyone but you?
Or sit drinking with them affectionately at table?
For my heart never wished and my mind never fancied
Their company, though I was not bound to you."

"Truly, my darling, I did not mean to insult you.
Or to carry you off without your mother's leave,
Although in truth I would rather possess you
Than the twelve apostles or the guardian of the soul."

"Pray to God earnestly for your soul.
And to the blessed Virgin, she is the best spouse
        for you.
She is the one who will save you on the day when
        souls are judged.
Renounce my love and affection as long as you live"

"I will never renounce your affection as long as
        I live,
Nor for seven years after I am laid in the earth;
For your husband has never lain in bed with you,
And truly, when he does, I will lie between you."

"What hateful wickedness, after all my fondness
    for you,
To set my husband at enmity for me forever,
Quarreling and scolding me, being angry and
    cross with me
When I shall not have you alive to tell my
    troubles to!"[53]

An accompanying <u>fable</u> tells of their simultaneous deaths and the emergence of twining branches from their graves.

Another familiar Child ballad, "Mary Hamilton" (173), enters Irish-language tradition in the following form:

Pretty Molly, you have been brought to shame!
The doctors tell me you have had a baby,
You left the child in Patrick's graveyard,
With a street flag as a headstone.

You went in a coach, though you were barefoot,
Though you were drinking with him night and day.
The modest-spoken young man kept saying,
"Oh, God! Where have they taken Molly Bawn?"

Beautiful Molly of the thick, glossy hair,
Whose little honeyed mouth is the colour of the rose,
When you walk the roadway 'tis you are the moon,
And you would illumine the whole world.

She is the blossom of the branches, the blossom of
    life,
Though now she is lying in her last distress.
A letter has been received from the King of France
To say that Molly Bawn is the sister of the Emperor.[54]

Turning to the vulgar tradition, we find a story represented in America by "Joe Bowers" (Laws B14) in a form more fully dramatized but also more elliptical:

They are saying
That you are the dainty little heel in shoe.
They are saying
That you are the slender little mouth of kisses.
They are saying, O thousand loves,
That you have turned your back on me,
And, though a man is to be had,
The red-haired man's wife has gone off with
    the tailor.

I spent nine months
In prison, tightly bound,

Gyves on my ankles,
And a thousand fetters from that up.
I would give a leap
Like that of a swan beside an inlet
With desire to be lying
Down with the red-haired man's wife.

I thought, O first love,
That there would be one house between you and me.
I thought after that
That you would be dandling my child upon your knee.
The curse of the King of Heaven
Be on him took away my character,
That, and on all of them,
The lying crowd that came between you and me.

There is a tree in the garden
On which grow foliage and golden blossoms.
When I lay my hand on it
My heart almost breaks
It is my solace till death
To get this granted from heaven above,
One single little kiss
From the red-haired man's wife.

When the Day of Judgment shall come
On which hills and harbors shall be rent,
Mist will cover the sun,
And the clouds will be black as coal.
The sea will be dry,
And trials and tribulations will come,
And the tailor will be shrieking
On that day because of the red-haired man's wife.55

Finally, the too-young spouse whose death is the theme
of "A-Growing" (Laws 035) is lamented as follows in the
Irish language:

Ah, pity me, Mary, poor tramp in lonely places,
Weeping and sorrowing and making moan;
And rocking my babe, my arms for a cradle,
But no milk for his mouth can my body afford.

I am fainting with weakness, no use to conceal it,
My strength is dissolving like mists that fly.
From my heart in it beating blood trickles like
    teardrops,
What wonder, my God! for my Sally who died.

Sweet mouth had my maiden, no lies ever shaping,
And a manner unmatched among women for grace;

And breasts white and shapely for her child's
    sweet allaying,
But my love could not save her from death and the
    grave.

Had I been the suitor of a hag without beauty
Small wonder they'd blame me for paying her court.
But fresh as the dewdrops was Sally, my true love,
Who came in her youth, a bride to my home.

Oh, was it too soon, then, at sixteen to woo her?
Who lit in my young heart love's secret flame?
Dear heart of my bosom, 'twas fate I should lose you,
Who slipped from me soon to your home in the clay.

I'd rather go roving with you on the roadways,
Or have you at home with me milking my cows,
Than the king's store of gold for the dower of an
    old one,
But alas! 'neath the sod lies my love in her
    shroud.[56]

    In these variations upon familiar narrative traditions
we can see quite clearly the difference between the
traditional/vulgar mode of telling a story in song and the
"blues ballad" mode, which is distinguishable in Irish as in
American exemplars by its elliptical treatment of the
narrative, its emphasis upon feeling and response to events
rather than to the events themselves, and the looseness of
its stanzaic sequence. Nevertheless, these songs are not
lyrical in any categorical sense: the narrative is
unmistakably present as that which informs the manifest
content.

    We have said that the American blues ballad appears to
have sprung into existence almost full-blown shortly after
the Civil War, and disappeared (at least as a compositional
technique) in the 1920s. With Irish-language balladry,
however, the case is quite otherwise. Not only do such songs
continue to be produced in Ireland, but their antecedents in
Irish poetic tradition can be traced to the early Middle
Ages, as a matter of record pre-dating the traditional
ballad-idea by some four to six centuries.[57] Concerning
those antecedents, one Celtic scholar, Joseph P. Clancy, has
addressed the problem of extrapolating the narrative content
from their texts in language almost identical to that of
contemporary American students of the blues ballad:

    I believe that this poetry is based on a structural
    concept that is unfamiliar to us but that has its
    own validity, that at least deserves to be

> approached without prejudice and judged by its
> results. . . . /The poet_7 composes a lyric,
> assuming that his audience knows the basic story
> and concentrating on celebration or lamentation
> combined with compressed allusions to characters
> and actions. . . . Second, and most important,
> while some of these lyrics will "progress" in an
> expected fashion from a beginning through a middle
> to an end, the normal lyric employs what I have
> elsewhere called "radial" structure, circling
> around, repeating, and elaborating the central
> theme. It is all "middle," we might say, with
> apparently interchangeable structural units.[58]

Professor Clancy's remarks happened to be confined to Welsh
bardic poety, but they apply equally well to such Early
Irish texts as "Liadan's Lament," the Old English "Wife's
Lament" and "Husband's Message," and the Norse lays of
Gudrun among others. All four language-groups are well-
represented in poetry that is unequivocally lyrical, with no
such tantalizing hints at a narrative structure; with the
exception of the Old English, they also manifest a strong
tradition of prose narrative, often, but not necessarily,
embellished with lyric verses resembling that under
discussion.[59] What is significant, however, is that no
substantive evidence has yet been found for the existence of
narrative _in verse_ in Northern Europe prior to the
appearance of these "radial" poems[60]--and that, even
subsequent to the recording of narratives in versified form,
the "radial" style, quasi-lyrical, quasi-narrative,
continued to flourish in Irish popular poetry (e.g., the
Reicne of Fathaid Canainne and "The Bathing of Oisin's
Head"), side by side with more recognizably "modern" verse
narrative and with conventional lyric poetry.[61]

The poetry in question was at the outset, at least,
anything but popular. Rather, it was the product of the
highly-skilled, rigorously trained professional artists
whose function seems not to have varied greatly from one
Northern European culture to another; as distinct from the
historians, the law-givers, and the mistrels (although not,
by virtue of their training, incapable of carrying out one
or another of these tasks as well),[62] such artists were
retained by the aristocratic and powerful elements of their
societies for the purpose of composing eulogies and
lamentations appropriate to the status of their patrons.

They composed their poems, according to a famous
eighteenth-century account, lying alone in darkness, working
out from memory not only the images and metaphors, the
historical figures and events most suitable for allusion and

illustration, but also the classical metrics of the genre: non-stanzaic sequences of rhythmical lines, linked together by patterns of stressed syllables, initial rhyme, and formulary phrases.[63] Kenneth Jackson has pointed out that this process was by no means an improvisatory one: hours, even days, might be spent on such an effort.[64] But the resulting encomium, it must be emphasized, was lyrical, not narrative. It told no story, recited no king-list, chronicled no event. As poetry, it celebrated its subject; it was not required to inform or instruct its audience, and it did not.

Beginning in the sixth century, however, the literacy introduced by monastic settlements in Ireland, Wales, Scotland, and England revolutionized traditional concepts in verse-making.[65] For one thing, the Latin hymn, with its syllabic meter and end-rhyme, so affected native prosody that new terms had to be invented for the poetry modeled upon it: dan direach in Ireland, mesurau caethion in Wales, and (later) drottkvaet in Scandinavian.[66] For another, verse narrative in Latin became accessible[67]--and this, centuries before the hymn-stanza quatrain and the popular tale merged in what we now recognize as the traditional European ballad.[68]

We would hypothesize, therefore, that the "radial" style of story-telling was one consequence of this convergence of traditional native skills and aesthetic standards with the classical materials and techniques made accessible to native professionals by the monastic schools of Northern Europe.[69] End-rhyme and stanzaic structure were added to an already fairly complex system of prosody; more importantly, narrative was perceived, apparently for the first time in that part of the world, as a legitimate vehicle for the display of the new, enhanced craftsmanship. Poems in the "radial" style, therefore, differed sharply from their native predecessors in incorporating narrative as the central focus of their elegant rhetoric. But they differed even more sharply from their narrative models in native prose and Latin verse in treating the narrative not as an end in itself but simply as a different kind of subject, to be discussed, mused upon, and celebrated or lamented just as any other subject might be.

Except for the continuing Irish tradition, the "radial style"--the medieval version of the "blues ballad idea"-- failed to survive the decline of the bardic/skaldic institution and the simultaneous proliferation of the romance, the chanson de geste and the popular ballad during the High Middle Ages. Nevertheless, poetry in that style is just as identifiable in the period 600-1200 A.D. as is balladry in the "blues style" in the period 1868-1922. And it is just as baffling to medievalists as are American "blues ballads" to folklorists, and for precisely the same reasons.[70]

We think that we have found abundant evidence (of which we have presented only a sampling) for the antiquity of the "blues ballad idea"; for its persistence in Irish-language narrative song; and for its flowering in the post-Civil War American South. We may even make bold to say that its influence has extended not only to variants of traditional ballads (see above, pp. 463-64, 465-66), but to the Child corpus itself. What are we to make of "The Bonny Earl of Murray" (Child 181) if we do not recognize its affiliations with the elliptical, allusive panegyric most fully represented in the sixth-century Gododdin as well as with the American "Louis Collins"?[71] And while it seems that little remains to be said about the much-discussed "Mary Hamilton,"[72] the ballad seems to us noteworthy as a textual tradition. It is noteworthy not merely because that tradition comprises a fusion of two ancient narrative themes ("The Cruel Mother" and "The Criminal's Last Goodnight") with two historical events (the infanticides of 1563/4 and 1719 respectively),[73] but because a search of extant variants reveals the same absence of a canonical text, the same haphazard re-arrangement of stanzas and narrative sequence, the same fluidity of detail (with casual inclusion and exclusion of such matters as the manner of the babe's death, the physical examination of the mother, the identity of the father, the attempted abortion, the garments worn to the execution, and so forth) that we have found to be characteristic of the American "blues ballad idea" and the Irish-language ballad.

The book is far from closed on the "blues ballad." Indeed we have barely opened it. In particular, we do not know nearly enough about African poetic tradition and narrative technique, which, it seems reasonable to believe, must have played a part in the development of the genre equal to that of the Celtic tradition briefly outlined here.[74] We might compare, for example, the occurrence in the African Sunjata epic of a "Don't you know that . . . is dead" formula:

Don't you know that Darama Jollo's Fili is gone.

Don't you know that Tulli Mbaalo's Cherrio is dead.[75]

With the near-ubiquitous Afro-American:

If you don't believe John Dabney's dead,
Look at whatta hole in Dabney's head.

If you don't believe Jumbagot's dead,
Jus' look at crepe on 'Liza's head.[76]

But, as has been suggested in a somewhat different connection, "the object should not be simply to search out 'Africanisms' as survivals of African traditions, but to use Africa as a base line, as a starting point . . . parallel processes and functions must be searched out. . . ."[77] Nor do we know as yet why this particular "ballad idea" maintained such a tenacious hold on the Irish folk imagination, or precisely how it was translated, if indeed it was, into the American idiom. What we do hope to have done here is simply to establish the existence, the authenticity, and (possibly) the ancestry of a genre hitherto largely unrecognized and little understood.

NOTES

In addition to cited references, we are indebted to a number of contributors to the concept of the blues ballad and to the history and analysis of the genre and of individual items of the genre. Most recently members of a session on The Blues Ballad at the American Folklore Society Meeting in Minneapolis 16 October 1982--Marina Bokelman, Norm Cohen, Cecilia Conway, David Evans, Eleanor R. Long, D. K. Wilgus--helped to focus and clarify many of this essay's points. Over the years many members of blues ballad and other ballad seminars at UCLA have contributed immensely to our knowledge of the blues ballad tradition, including Marina Bokelman, David Evans, John Fahey, Roger deV. Renwick, Thomas Sauber, Walter Sereth, David Stern, and Peter Tommerup. We shall include some of their insights without referring to their specific contributions to the blues ballad material at UCLA.

[1]Thus it is possible for us to speak with confidence of a Child 42, a Laws L19, a Gruntvig 78, and to expect ourselves to be able to identify the text-tune affiliations of newly-encountered materials. That what is meant by a Child 42, a Laws L19, a Gruntvig 78 can best be defined as "a ballad idea," and that "the ballad" in sum is an idea, has been proposed before. See, for example, W. P. Ker, "On the History of the Ballads: 1100-1500," Proceedings of the British Academy, 4 (1910), 179-205; Phillips Barry, "Irish Folksong," Journal of American Folklore, 24 (1911), 332, and "An American Homiletic Ballad," Modern Language Notes, 28 (1913), 4-5; Bertrand B. Bronson, The Ballad as Song (Berkeley: University of California Press, 1969), pp. 72, 106 (and elsewhere in his writings); W. Edson Richmond, "The American Lyric Tradition," in Our Living Traditions, ed. Tristram P. Coffin (New York: Basic Books, 1968), p. 107. (This does not imply that we endorse the conception that Anglo-American ballad singers have at any time retained only the "idea" of a ballad story in their minds and created a "new" text in each performance.)

[2]Kenneth Lane Kenter, "The Role of Hypotheses in Folkloristics," Journal of American Folklore, 86 (1973), 121-26. Admittedly, this concept is a difficult one from a logical or theoretical point of view (that is to say, the concept of the "ballad idea" as both real and literally non-existent, as the substance but not the model or entelechy of its manifestations); however, it should present no difficulties to the habitual explorer of large quantities of archival materials, whose necessary and compelling (though

maddeningly complex) relationships to each other are manageable only on those terms.

[3]Obray Ramsey Sings Folksongs from the Three Laurels, Liner Notes by D. K. Wilgus, Prestige/International LP 1320, 12" LP, 1961. For W. C. Handy's use of "blues ballad," see Dorothy Scarborough, On the Trail of Negro Folk-Songs (1925; rpt. Hatboro, Penn.: Folklore Associates, 1963), p. 266.

[4]W. C. Handy, Father of the Blues, ed. Arna Bontempts (1941; rpt. New York: Collier, 1970), pp. 153-55. For examples of the "Careless Love" lyric see John A. and Alan Lomax, Folk Song: USA (New York: Duell, Sloan, and Pearce, 1947), pp. 64-65, and Vance Randolph, Ozark Folksongs IV (1950; rpt. Champaign: University of Illinois Press, 1982), 306-08. (Throughout, rather than citing full references to songs, we give only what is necessary for identification. For example, we could cite many commercial recordings of "Careless Love.")

[5]Reprinted from D. K. Wilgus, "Arch and Gordon," Kentucky Folklore Record, 6 (1960), 51-56, which includes a summary account of the events on which the ballad is based. Mrs. Cline's performance is preserved on Tape T7-1 in the Western Kentucky Folklore Archive at University of California, Los Angeles; a copy is in the "Wilgus Collection" in the Western Kentucky University Library. (Hereafter referred to as WKFA. Material subsequently cited from WKFA is preserved in both institutions.)

[6]G. Malcolm Laws, Jr., Native American Balladry (Philadelphia: American Folklore Society, 1964), pp. 83-94.

[7]Anne B. Cohen, Poor Pearl, Poor Girl (Austin: University of Texas Press, 1973).

[8]Henry Wacaster Perry, "A Sampling of the Folklore of Carter County, Tennessee," Master's thesis, George Peabody College for Teachers, 1938, p. 199.

[9]D. K. Wilgus and Lynwood Montell, "Clure and Joe Williams: Legend and Blues Ballad," Journal of American Folklore, 81 (1968), 299.

[10]Norm Cohen, Long Steel Rail (Urbana: University of Illinois Press, 1981), pp. 413-25.

[11]Marina Bokelman, "The Coon Can Game': A Blues Ballad Tradition," Master's thesis, University of California, Los Angeles, 1968.

[12]Chapman J. Milling, "Delia Holmes: A Neglected Negro Ballad," Southern Folklore Quarterly, 1, No. 4 (1937), 3.

[13]Frank C. Brown, The Frank C. Brown Collection of North Carolina Folklore, 7 vols., ed. Newman Ivey White, et al., (Durham: Duke University Press, 1952-62), IV, 674-76.

[14]Laws, American Balladry from British Broadsides, (Philadelphia: American Folklore Society, 1957), p. 172.

[15]Lynwood Montell, The Saga of Coe Ridge (Knoxville: University of Tennessee Press, 1970), pp. 122-32.

[16]Montell, pp. 127-31.

[17]Montell, p. 124.

[18]WKFA T7-29.

[19]Montell, pp. 130-31.

[20]See, for example, "Roll on the Ground," Library of Congress Archive of American Folk 2594 A2; 3113A (issued on LC/AAFS 8b; reissued on AFS LC2, 12" LP); Al Hopkins and His Buckle Busters, Brunswick 186; "Big Ball in Town," Gid Tanner and His Skillet Lickers with Riley Puckett and Clayton McMichen, Columbia 15204-D (reissued on County 506, 12" LP); "Big Ball Uptown," Taylor-Griggs Louisiana Melody Makers, Victor 21768; "Big Ball in Memphis," Georgia Yellow Hammers, Victor V-40138 (reissued on County 504, 12" LP); "Big Ball's in Town," J. E. Mainer's Mountaineers, King 662 (reissued on King 666, 12" LP); "Big Ball in Cowtown," Bob Wills and His Texas Playboys, Kapp 3506, 12" LP; "Big Ball in Texas," Mac and Lee's Collection of Famous Songs (New York, 1937, here copyrighted by Bob Miller and Vasca Suede, 1934); "My Long Journey Home," The Monroe Brothers (Charles and Bill), Bluebird B-6422 (reissued on Bluebird AMX 2-5510, 12" LP).

[21]See, for example, "Pisgah" and "Do Lord Remember Me," George Pullen Jackson, White and Negro Sprituals (New York:

J. J. Augustin, 1943), pp. 164-65; "Climbing up Zion's Hill," L. L. McDowell, <u>Songs of the Old Camp Ground</u> (Ann Arbor, MI.: Edwards Brothers, 1937), p. 40; "Heaven Bells Are Ringing," Wade Mainer and Sons of the Mountaineers, Bluebird B-8203; "Lights in the Valley," J. E. Mainer's Mountaineers, Victor 20-3241.

[22]Cratis D. Williams, "Ballads and Songs," Master's thesis, University of Kentucky, 1937, pp. 405-06.

[23]WKFA T7-33. Vera Martin sang with the help of a text dated 7 November 1925 from her ballet collection.

[24]Sarah Ogan Gunning, a half sister of Aunt Molly Jackson, was originally from eastern Kentucky.

[25]The statement is still accurate at this writing. Norm Cohen's discussion of the "Reuben's Train/Train 45/900 Miles" complex, pp. 503-17, provides no clue to a referent.

[26]Wilgus and Montell believed that they were dealing with a ballad or narrative song from the outset, on the basis of the first collected variant (p. 444 above). The characterization of "Clure and Joe Williams" as a blues ballad occurred after Wilgus had developed the concept on the basis of many similar songs.

[27]Letter 15 December 1967. McCulloh's comments grew out of her dissertation work on the related "In the Pines" complex. (See Judith McCulloh, "In the Pines': The Melodic-Textual Tradition of an American Lyric Folksong Cluster," Diss. Indiana University, 1970.)

[28]Cratis Williams, p. 338.

[29]Norm Cohen, pp. 505-07.

[30]The sentiments of the last two lines should be, it seems, reversed.

[31]Perry, pp. 168-70.

[32]"Bill Ainsworth's Quarter Race. A Story of the Old Times (1833) in East Tennessee," <u>Knoxville Press and Messenger</u>, 3 (4 June 1868); reprinted by M. Thomas Inge in

his edition of George Washington Harris' <u>High Times and Hard Times</u> (Nashville: Vanderbilt University Press, 1967), pp. 198-206. Also quoted in this context is "Bet your money on the bob tail-hoss / I bets mine on the gray." While Stephen Foster's "Camptown Races" was not published until 1850, it has folk roots, so it <u>could</u> have been sung in an earlier form in 1833. "Skewball" was in print in the United States by 1829.

[33]/John Mason Brown7, "Songs of the Slave," <u>Lippincott's Magazine</u>, 2 (1868), 622-23. Reprinted in Scarborough, pp. 61-63. See Bruce Jackson, <u>The Negro and His Folklore in Nineteenth-Century Periodicals</u> (Austin: University of Texas Press, 1967), pp. 117-19.

[34]<u>Music from the South</u>, Vol. 2: Horace Sprott, 1. Collected and edited by Frederic Ramsey, Jr., Folkways FP 651. 12" LP, 1955.

[35]D. K. Wilgus, "Ten Broeck and Mollie: A Race and a Record," <u>Kentucky Folklore Record</u>, 2 (1956), 77-89.

[36]F. C. Brown, II, 533.

[37]Fiddled by "Gustie" Wallace, Sulphur, Ky., 26 August 1965. Recorded by D. K. Wilgus and Lynwood Montell. WKFA 17-147. "Gustie" was the great-nephew of the reputed composer of the song. We could suggest a number of reasons for the difficulty of setting Gustie's fiddle tune to any known text of the song. However, there is no trustworthy text-tune combination with which to compare it.

[38]From Leon G. Kidd, Crailhope, Ky. Published in the "Greetings" column of the Louisville <u>Courier Journal</u> 22 May 1957. A number of other performances, some considerably shorter, are in the WKFA. A text from Indiana was published by Paul G. Brewster, "Some Folksongs from Indiana," <u>Journal of American Folklore</u>, 57 (1944), 282-87.

[39]F. C. Brown II, 703-14, IV, 325. The songs illustrated in Brown and elsewhere range from "vulgar" to "blues" to lyric lament.

[40]See also Mary Wheeler, <u>Steamboatin' Days</u> (Baton Rouge: Louisiana State University Press, 1944), pp. 40-41. While it is possible that these are distinct songs, both are blues ballads.

[41]The 1896 version by Charles E. Trevathan is the best known, but there were at least five other sheet music versions 1895-1896. See notes to <u>Mistrels and Tunesmiths</u>, Notes by Norm Cohen, JEMF LP-109, 12" LP, 1981.

[42]"The Battleship of Maine," Red Patterson's Piedmont Log Rollers, Victor 20936, transcribed in John Cohen and Mike Seeger, <u>New Lost City Ramblers Songbook</u> (New York: Oak, 1964), pp. 116-17; "McKinley Called for Volunteers," WKFA; "This Great War," United States Naval Academy, <u>The Book of Navy Songs</u>, Collected and Arranged by the Trident Society (Garden City, N. J.: Doubleday, Doran, 1943), pp. 130-31. "German War," WKFA; "Bloody War," Joseph Able Trivett, Folk Legacy FSA-2, 12" LP: "Bloody War," Jimmie Yates' Boll Weevils, Victor V-40065; "That Crazy War," Lulubelle and Scotty /Wiseman/, Okeh 06103 (transcribed in Cohen and Seeger, p. 118); <u>String Bean's Song, Joke and Picture Book</u>, n.p.; "That Crazy War," Dick Unteed, Rural Rhythm RRDU 212, 12" LP; "Sinking of the Maine," Bill Clifton, Starday SLP 213, 12" LP; "It's a Bloody War," Homer and Jethro, King 721; "If I Lose, I Don't Care," Charlie Poole and the North Carolina Ramblers, Columbia 15215-D; "Bloody War," Rutherford and Foster, Gennett 6807; "Fightin' in the War with Spain," Wilmer Watts and the Lonely Eagles, Paramount 3254A (transcribed by Malcolm V. Blackard, "Wilmer Watts and the Lonely Eagles," <u>JEMF Quarterly</u>, 5 /1969/, 137-38).

[43]Norm Cohen (pp. 134-57) argues that both a blues ballad tradition and a vulgar ballad tradition contributed to the popular song tradition of "Casey Jones."

[44]In MacEdward Leach and Horace P. Beck, "Songs from Rappahannock County, Virginia," <u>Journal of American Folklore</u>, 63 (1950), 276-78; reprinted in Tristram P. Coffin and Hennig Cohen, eds., <u>Folklore in America</u> (Garden City, N. Y.: Doubleday, 1966), pp. 90-91.

[45]See Roger D. Abrahams, <u>Deep Down in the Jungle</u>, 2nd. ed. (Chicago: Aldine, 1970); Bruce Jackson, <u>Get your Ass in the Water and Swim Like Me</u> (Cambridge: Harvard University Press, 1974); Dennis Wepman, Ronald B. Newman, and Murray B. Binderman, <u>The Life</u> (Philadelphia: University of Pennsylvania Press, 1976).

[46]Wilgus and Montell, p. 308, nn. 11, 12, 13.

[47]Mabel Thompson Rauch, "Biggest Little Horse in Egypt," Saturday Evening Post, 25 August 1945, pp. 21, 68, 75. Mrs. Rauch said her father learned the song in Louisville in 1879.

[48]John Byrd, "Old Timbrook Blues," Paramount 12997 (L-291-1), recorded in Grafton, Wisconsin, April 1930.

[49]WKFA. From Mrs. Kate Childress, Round Hill, Butler Co., Kentucky, June 1959. Reported by John F. Newport.

[50]D. K. Wilgus, "The Hanged Fiddler Legend in Anglo-American Tradition," in Folklore on Two Continents: Essays in Honor of Linda Dégh, ed. Nikolai Burlakoff and Carl Lindahl (Bloomington, Indiana: Trickster Press, 1980), pp. 128-30.

[51]F. C. Brown, II, 459-60.

[52]The relationship of Barbara's taunt to the "sympathetic death-twining branches" syndrome in Western-European oral tradition is explored by Eleanor R. Long, "'Young Man, I Think You're Dyin':' The 'Twining Branches' Theme in the Tristan Legend and in English Tradition," Fabula, 21 (1980), 183-99.

[53]Donal O'Sullivan, Songs of the Irish (New York: Bonanza Books, 1960), pp. 58-60. Translated by the collector.

[54]Donal O'Sullivan, ed., Journal of the Irish Folk Song Society, 29 (1932), 97-98. Translated by the collector.

[55]O'Sullivan, pp. 47-48.

[56]Evelyn Costello, ed., "Little Red Sally," Journal of the Irish Folk Song Society, 16 (1919), 30-31. Translated by the collector.

[57]See Kuno Meyer, ed. Selections from Ancient Irish Poetry, (London: Constable, 1911); Robin Flower, The Irish Tradition (Oxford: Clarendon Press, 1947); A. O. H. Jarman, "Aneirin: The Gododdin," in A Guide to Welsh Literature, ed. A. O. H. Jarman and Guilym Rees Hughes, I (Swansea: Christopher Davies, 1976) 68-80; Ceri W. Lewis, "The Court Poets: Their

Function, Status, and Craft," in Jarman and Hughes, 123-56; D. P. Kirby, "Welsh Bards and the Border," in Mercian Studies, ed. Ann Dornier (Leicester: Leicester University Press, 1977), pp. 31-41; Ifor Williams, The Beginnings of Welsh Poetry, 2nd. ed. (Cardiff: University of Wales Press, 1980).

[58]Joseph P. Clancy, The Earliest Welsh Poetry (London: Macmillan, 1970), pp. 4-5.

[59]It has been argued that "radial" poetry takes its origin from this form, commonly referred to as the cante-fable, occurring in Irish, Welsh, and Norse literature, and thought to be normative in those narrative traditions (Gerard Murphy, "The Ossianic Lore and Romantic Tales of Medieval Ireland," in Eleanor Knott and Gerard Murphy, Early Irish Literature /New York: Barnes and Noble, 1966/, p. 158; Clancy, p. 6; Ifor Williams, Beginnings, pp. 126-27; Daniel F. Melia, "'Empty Figures' in Irish Symbolic Poetry," Philological Quarterly, 56 /1977/, 295). While it is true that poetry in the "radial" style frequently is cast in first-person monologue or in dialogue, as is characteristic of cante-fable lyrics, and that the prose narrative in which those lyrics are imbedded satisfactorily accounts for the absence of detailed "story" in the lyrics themselves, study of manuscript traditions has largely discredited the theory. Ifor Williams found two distinct forms of the Welsh "Trystan," one entirely in elliptical englynion, the other in cante-fable style (Beginnings 130 ff.; see also Tom Peete Cross, "A Welsh Tristan Episode," Studies in Philology, 17 /1920/, 93-110.). Knott notes that "verse, significantly, is not characteristic of the earlier portions of the Ulster cycle" ("Irish Classical Poetry," in Knott and Murphy, p. 37.), adding that metrical passages in the Tain bo Cuailnge are for the most part "certainly later interpolations." And, discussing the "radial" Irish "Liadan's Lament," James Carney warns that "one must exercise great care in using the prose to interpret such a poem. It would be easy to show that in such sagas . . . the poetry and prose are not a single unit. The poetry survived alone, probably in manuscript; the writer of the saga used the older verse and sometimes misunderstood and misplaced it" (Knott and Murphy, pp. 3-4, n. 1).

[60]E. C. Quiggen, Prolegomena to the Study of the Later Irish Bards: 1200-1500 (Oxford: Oxford University Press, 1911), pp. 10-11. Ifor Williams, Lectures on Early Welsh Poetry (Dublin: Institute for Advanced Studies, 1944), p. 281. Peter H. Salus and Paul B. Taylor, "Introduction" to

The Elder Edda: A Selection, trans. Paul B. Taylor and W. H. Auden (New York: Vintage, 1967), pp. 15-16.

[61]Both the "Reicne" (Kuno Meyer, ed., Fianaigecht /Dublin: Hodges, Figgis, 1910/, pp. 10-17) and "Oisin's Head" (Eoin MacNeill and Gerald Murphy, eds. Duanaire Finn /London: D. Nutt, 1908/, pp. 11-14.) use the narrative theme of "Sweet Williams' Ghost" (Child 77), in which a dead lover returns to request a favor and/or impose a taboo, as the vehicle for "radial" narration. As Murphy observes, "some of /the pieces in the Duanaire Finn collection/ are almost wholly narrative; some pass freely from a lyric to a narrative mood; while others are almost pure lyrics with a slight narrative flavor" ("Ossianic Lore," pp. 188-89); see also Quiggin.

[62]See Nora Chadwick, The Druids (Cardiff: University of Wales Press, 1966); Clancy, pp. 3-4; Myles Dillon, Early Irish Literature (Chicago: University of Chicago Press, 1948), pp. 171-75, and The Archaism of Irish Tradition (London: G. Cumberlege, 1949); James Carney, The Irish Bardic Poet (Dublin: Dolmen Press, 1967), pp. 10-11; Kenneth Jackson, The Oldest Irish Tradition: A Window on the Iron Age (Cambridge: Cambridge University Press, 1964), pp. 26-27, 39-40; Knott, "Irish Classical Poetry," p. 61; Lewis, pp. 14-18, 36; P. W. Joyce, A Social History of Ancient Ireland, 2 vols. (New York and London: Benjamin Blom, 1913), p. 1.

[63]Knott, "Irish Classical Poetry," p. 63; Melia, pp. 285-300.

[64]Jackson, Oldest Irish Tradition, p. 26.

[65]Nora Chadwick, The Age of the Saints in the Early Celtic Church (London: Oxford University Press, 1961), and Nora Chadwick, ed., Celt and Saxon: Studies in the Early British Border (Cambridge: Cambridge University Press, 1964). See also E. G. Bowen, The Settlements of the Celtic Saints in Wales (Cardiff: University of Wales Press, 1956).

[66]See Eleanor Knott, Irish Syllabic Poetry: 1200-1600, 2nd. ed. (Dublin: Institute for Advanced Studies, 1966); Sir John Rhys, The Englyn: The Origin of Welsh Englyn and Kindred Meters (London: the Honorable Society of Cymmrodion, 1905); Gabriel Turville-Petre, "On the Poetry of the Scalds and of the Finns," Eriu, 22 (1971), 10, respectively.

[67]It cannot be without significance that the single extended narrative in verse surviving in the vernacular, the Old English Beowulf, is not only of uncertain date but bears evidence of having been based on Latin models. (Tom Burns Haber, A Comparative Study of the Beowulf and the Aeneid /1931; rpt. New York: Phaeton, 1968/). This is not to deny the antiquity of the narratives and narrative themes in question, or even their use as materials for allusion and reference in lyrical poetry as well as for circumstantial prose sagas; it is merely to say that the "oral epic" conceived to be characteristic of pre-literate societies cannot be demonstrated to have formed any part of the repertoires of traditional poets in this region so far as we know anything about them.

[68]Although James Travis has attempted to challenge the Kurt Thurneysen thesis regarding the Latin origin of Irish syllabic, end-rhyming verse, his effort cannot be described as successful. (James Travis, Early Celtic Versecraft: Origins, Development, Diffusion /Ithaca: Cornell University Press, 1973/; Kurt Thurneysen, "Zur Irischen Akzent-und Verslehre," Revue Celtique, 6 /1884-85/, 309-47.) Similarly, Lee Hollander's assertion that the art of the skalds defies "all attempts to derive it from any art practice in the Western World," has been sharply disputed by Gabriel Turville-Petre (Lee M. Hollander, The Skalds /Ann Arbor: University of Michigan Press, 1968/; Turville-Petre, p. 20). Even the Welsh Englyn was shown by Sir John Rhŷs to be a development based on Latin prosodic models (The Englyn). On the Latin origin of the ballad stanza, and its use in popular narrative song, see Eleanor R. Long, "On the Origin and Age of the Western European Ballad," Second International Conference on Nordic and Anglo-American Balladry, Biskops-Arno, Sweden, 30 August 1980.

[69]It is a matter of historical record that many Irish filid chose to take holy orders (Knott, "Classical Poetry," p. 22); others, however, were able to acquire the new learning without relinquishing their secular status (Chadwick, Age of the Saints, p. 157).

[70]Consider the following comments on the early, non-narrative panegyric: "In none of them do we get an elaborate or sustained description of any scene. . . . The half-said thing to them is dearest" (Meyer, Ancient Irish Poetry, p. xiii). "The style is always strict and concise, . . . tending always to treat /its subject/ as an abstract compendium of elements" (Flower, p. 28). And consider these comments on the nearest equivalent to oral epic poetry that

has survived from the sixth century A.D., the Welsh <u>Gododdin</u>
(Kenneth Jackson, <u>The Gododdin: The Oldest Scottish Poem</u>
/Edinburgh: University of Edinburgh Press, 196<u>9</u>/):
"Although . . . not a narrative poem, a certain kind of
time-sequence can be discerned in many of the references it
conta<u>i</u>ns. While there is little attempt to describe /the
event/ itself, there is some delineation of its background
and setting (Jarman "Aneirin," p. 70). "A certain number of
stanzas can be linked together, . . . but I also think that
stray pieces of early stuff have . . . been added to the
original kernel, simply because they happened to be in the
same kind of metre and diction generally" (Ifor Williams,
<u>Beginnings of Welsh Poetry</u>, pp. 62-63). On bardic narrative
in general: "These poems only allude incidentally and
cryptically to events and persons, so that what is
recoverable is by no means easily integrated into a known
and precise pattern of events" (Kirby, p. 31).

[71]Frederick E. Danker, "Towards an Intrinsic Study of
the Blues Ballad: 'Casey Jones' and 'Louis Collins,'"
<u>Southern Folklore Quarterly</u>, 34 (1970), 99-102.

[72]Tristram P. Coffin, <u>The British Traditional Ballad in
North America</u>, rev. ed., supplement by Roger deV. Renwick
(Austin: University of Texas Press, 1977), pp. 115, 164-72,
251-52; Eleanor R. Long, "Ballad Singers, Ballad Makers, and
Ballad Etiology," <u>Western Folklore</u>, 32 (1973), 225-36.

[73]Frances James Child, <u>The English and Scottish Popular
Ballads</u> III (Boston: Houghton Mifflin, 1888-89), 379-84;
Bertrand B. Bronson, <u>The Traditional Tunes of the Child
Ballads</u> III (Princeton: Princeton University Press, 1966),
150.

[74]"Africanisms" cited by Paul Oliver suggest strong
intrinsic similarities between African and Irish folk music,
among them a fondness for the flatted seventh (14), rhythmic
variations on a metric theme (15), the role and function of
the <u>griot</u> (45), a nasal, undulating, and ornamental vocal
style (66), and song content consisting largely of praise
and ridicule (Paul Oliver, <u>Savannah Syncopators: African
Retentions in the Blues</u> /London: November Books, 197<u>0</u>/,
p. 98). Although Oliver focuses upon the compatibility of
the music of the Sudanic savannah with that of the English
and Scots settlers, the "Irish connection"--the
opportunities for fruitful contacts between Irish immigrants
and African slaves and ex-slaves--seems to us eminently
worth exploring further (see William H. Tallmadge, "Anglo-

Saxon /v̄ersus7 Scotch-Irish," <u>Mountain Life and Work</u>, 45, No. 2 /19697, 10-12).

[75]Isadore Okpewho, <u>The Epic in Africa</u> (New York: Columbia University Press, 1979), pp. 139-41.

[76]Wilgus and Montell, pp. 297, 308-09.

[77]John F. Szwed and Roger D. Abrahams, "After the Myth: Studying Afro-American Patterns in Plantation Literature," in <u>African Folklore in the New World</u>, ed. Daniel J. Crowley (Austin: University of Texas Press), p. 82.

<u>University of California</u>
<u>Los Angeles</u>